A BRIEF HISTORY of ECONOMICS

Artful Approaches To The Dismal Science

A Brief History of Economics

Artful Approaches To The Dismal Science

E Ray Canterbery
Florida State University

World Scientific
Singapore • New Jersey • London • Hong Kong

Published by

World Scientific Publishing Co. Pte. Ltd.
5 Toh Tuck Link, Singapore 596224
USA office: 27 Warren Street, Suite 401-402, Hackensack, NJ 07601
UK office: 57 Shelton Street, Covent Garden, London WC2H 9HE

British Library Cataloguing-in-Publication Data
A catalogue record for this book is available from the British Library.

First Indian Edition 2022

A BRIEF HISTORY OF ECONOMICS
Artful Approaches to the Dismal Science

ISBN 978-0-00-099102-7 (pbk)

Printed in India

Brief Contents

Detailed Contents

Preface

This book is not simply an annotated roster of the Society of Dead Economists. As living economists grapple with modern economic problems and begin to alter their views, more and more readers are discovering a need for transitional books, books that bridge the gap between what economics has been and what it is becoming. *A Brief History of Economics: Artful Approaches to the Dismal Science* reflects this desire for a bridge over sometimes troubled waters.

Because the old masters of economics imagined with a broad social brush and used lively real-world examples, they are easier to understand than many modern writers, so I believe that this book is fully accessible to beginning readers in economics. At the other extreme, readers who approach this volume with a sophisticated understanding of economic theory but little, if any, exposure to the history of thought can now become acquainted with some of the most fascinating personalities of the ages. An inquiring mind is the only prerequisite.

Many concerns impinged on the decision to do *A Brief History of Economics*. First, I continue to perceive the need for a short introduction to economics that would be completely accessible to beginners but interesting to a lay audience. For the former, only aerobically fit students can cart in the fullness of space the standard, beginning text to class. In the end, the beginner has mastered little more than a few unrelated basics (though perhaps enjoying somewhat better muscle tone). For the latter, I believe that a need exists for a completely up-to-date treatment of contemporary issues such as globalization, financial market bubbles, and economic inequalities missing from today's textbooks.

Second, the beginner's interest in economics has been waning roughly in proportion to the growth in the number and magnitude of society's economic problems. Beginners, I have found, can be seduced by a subject wrapped in the soft cloak of biographies of figures (Adam Smith, David Ricardo, Thomas Malthus, Jeremy Bentham, Karl Marx, Alfred Marshall, John Maynard Keynes, Joseph Schumpeter, Thorstein Veblen, Milton Freidman, John Kenneth Galbraith, and Robert Heilbroner) and the warm familiarity of history—of the Jazz Age, of the Great Depression, of Reaganomics, and so on.

Third, I would like to extend the good luck of past generations to those of the present. The great economists—yesterday's and today's—not only convey ideas lucidly, they do so with great force, elan, and more often than not, wonderful humor. The current generation of readers should not miss the masters.

As a beginning, I return to the founder, Adam Smith. A popular but misguided understanding of what Adam Smith wrote and meant has been diminished to the wearing of the Adam Smith necktie (filled with little cameos of Smith's profile) out of devotion only to free markets and to remarkably limited government. This tie that binds is a symbol devoid of true Smithian meaning, serving mostly to constrict blood vessels and guaranteeing insufficient circulation of blood to the brain. The purchase of an Adam Smith necktie is at once a rational commercial act and a revelation of dogma overwhelming reason. Adam Smith, a lecturer on Moral Philosophy at Glasgow, would have rejected both out of four-in-hand.

I would urge, even implore, not just the beginner, but the seasoned reader, to read Smith's *The Wealth of Nations*. It is brimming with ideas, such as those to spill over from his colorful description of the pin factory to his famous passage: "It is not from the benevolence of the butcher, the brewer, or the baker, that we expect our dinner, but from their regard to their own interest." The latter is not only a great insight, but also great rhetoric, initially cast out of an alliteration of b's, continuing with the homely appeal to getting our dinner (rather than "optimizing consumer behavior"), and concluding with a mutually self-regarding sting.

To focus on pin factories and Adam Smith is to concern oneself with getting production started, igniting economic growth. It is the kind of concern faced today by Eastern Europe, the states of the former Soviet Union, and the developing nations. The mature industrialized nations generally are called "capitalistic," even though their ways of organizing production and distribution are contrary to the conventional caricature. The central problem of these nations, including even Japan, appears to be *too much* production and an *excess* of labor. The people in these nations, it would appear, are consuming as much as they desire, and yet their consumption is insufficient to fully employ themselves. This vulnerability of capitalism was noted many years ago by the great British economist, businessman and statesman—John Maynard Keynes.

He wrote:

> Ancient Egypt was doubly fortunate and doubtless owed to this its fabled wealth, in that it possessed *two* activities, namely pyramid-building and the search for the precious metals, the fruits of which, since they could not serve the needs of man by being consumed, did not stale with abundance. The Middle Ages built cathedrals and sang dirges. Two pyramids, two masses for the dead are twice as good as one; but not so two railways from London to York.

In this brief paragraph, drawing upon his knowledge of history, Keynes is able to summarize in the last *half* sentence what has been lost to the modern economic world, and what had become a central defect of raw, uncivilized capitalism during the 1930s. Today, instead of railways, he might have written about the superfluity of 900-lane parallel information superhighways carrying banal entertainment to netherlands.

Even with an information superhighway, it would be impossible to thank adequately all of those reviewers, readers, and friends who have contributed to this book. Over the years, John Kenneth Galbraith has faithfully read my manuscripts and, on this as well as many others, has been a source of inspiration and encouragement. His influence in these pages will be obvious. My dearly missed friend, the late Sidney Weintraub, provided thoughtful and meticulous comments on an early draft. Over time, another departed friend, Hyman Minsky, devoted considerable thought to and many suggestions for my discussions of finance and investment.

Inspirational friends and associates such as John Q. Adams and H. Peter Gray have served as wise and witty critics. Still another friend, the late Mancur Olson, provided valued reactions to my reading of his *Rise and Decline of Nations.* Not only did a book by Gerhard Mensch provide inspiration, but Gerhard provided insightful comments on manuscript material related to innovations and their effect on the economies of highly industrialized economies. For a few precious years at Florida State University, I had the pleasure of engaging in some remarkable dialogue with my friend Abba P. Lerner, one of the leading economists of the twentieth century. In a lucky and remarkable coincidence, Joan Robinson, another luminary, was reading some of my manuscripts at the time, parts of which now comprise my discussions on Keynesian economics. Abba proceeded to strike though many of Joan's comments with his abrupt, "She's wrong!," leaving me the awkward task of deciding, in those instances, what Keynes "really meant."

Such is the delicate responsibility of the historian—of anything. Just when we think we have made the final judgment, someone with great intelligence and authority creates doubt and raises questions. Being not quite sure about the past, we surely make forecasts with great temerity.

To reach its audience, a book must be published. For this, I am grateful to the uncommon support of David Sharp at World Scientific, not only for this volume but also for my *Wall Street Capitalism*. I also am grateful for the careful and helpful reviews by Richard Ballman, Augustana College; Frances Bedell, Westark Community College; Joseph Cairo, La Salle University; Michael Carroll, Colorado State University; and Richard N. Langlois, University of Connecticut. Joy Quek at World Scientific worked magic with her meticulous editing.

Finally, Carolyn, my partner in life, provided more good cheer than any author deserves and despite the magnitude of my exaggerated perception of what is merited.

E. Ray Canterbery

Introduction

Like airplane pilots, economists have used various approaches. Not surprisingly, some approaches to the history of their field have been less successful than others. Whether it be aeronautics or economics, we encounter boundaries or limits. Not knowing the limits of economics is like a pilot not knowing the constraints of gravity.

We want to know more than simply how narrowly an Adam Smith missed some ethereal runway. After all, the ideas of the great economists have enormous influence on societies and at the same time are molded by the cultural milieu that nurtured them. This interdependence comprises my central theme. Such is the true nature of economic literacy, something for which all citizens should aspire. If we are to place an Adam Smith or a John Maynard Keynes within his historical and intellectual context, we need to know what questions were important to him.

What led Karl Marx to think the contradictions of capitalism would lead to a fatal crash? Why was Thorstein Veblen so disturbed by the behavior of business managers as to want to restructure industry around engineers? As important as pure analytics, mathematics, and statistics are, if we know *only* the tools of the trade, we will be unable to know the place of economics within the broader community of ideas, much less be able to explain it to the uninitiated. We will be unable to engage in the rhetoric of the intellect.

We want to soar out of the narrow valley of rational reconstruction[1] to survey a wider horizon. A broader approach invites readers to range across the neighboring fields of history, philosophy, mathematics, politics, natural science, and literature. It allows us to place the great economists right where we want them, in their times.

We can then recognize what Adam Smith owed to Isaac Newton and Locke, and what Charles Darwin owed to Thomas Malthus. We can see the dilemmas of the Great Depression of the 1930s reflected in the writings not only of J.M. Keynes but of John Steinbeck and John Dos Passos. In F. Scott Fitzgerald's *The Great Gatsby*, we can find reflections of Veblen's influence and comprehend conspicuous consumption.

Making such connections does more than satisfy one's intellectual curiosity (though that is a very good reason, of itself). Historical perspective puts the lie to any claim that economics always is a progressive science—operating, like nuclear physics, outside time and in pursuit of eternal verities. Eternity is a very long time; yet, in the briefness of social history, communities have experienced many different economic systems. Even capitalism has bloomed as many species, its most elemental taking six millennium of recorded history to bud. Through the history of economics we can see economic ideas unfold, forcing us to broaden our vision—be more reflective, more thoughtful.

One way of being sure to hit the runway is to make it wider. *History* is basic to the study of ideas. We cannot recognize truly new ideas unless we are familiar with the ideas that economists have already explored. And we cannot understand the ideas of the great economists unless we understand the times of their lives. Times change, and so do economic systems; and so, we want to describe the development of economic organization from feudalism, to the market economy, to the complex mixed economy, to the present-day global economy.

Among economists history has not gone unrecognized. In 1993, the prestigious Royal Swedish Academy of Sciences awarded the

Nobel Memorial Prize in Economic Science jointly to Douglas C. North of Washington University and Robert Fogel of the University of Chicago, two important innovators in economic history. At the core of North's work is the query, "Why are some nations rich and others poor?" For North, as for Adam Smith, the answer lies in how institutions evolve and affect the performance of economies through time. (**Institutions** include formal systems, such as constitutions, laws, taxation, insurance, and market regulations, as well as informal norms of behavior, such as habits, morals, ethics, ideologies, and belief systems.) North has impelled many economists to appreciate the limitations of our "economic laws" and to acknowledge the sizable effect that outside forces or chance events are likely to have. Outcomes depend on circumstances. In effect, North brings history back into economic theory.

Besides, when economic ideas are woven out of the fabric of economic history, any subject, even a mathematical natural science, cannot avoid humanity; it thereby becomes humane. *Mathematics* brings miraculous rigor to economics but history prevents it from succumbing to rigor mortis.[2]

Literature has sometimes played a major role in our establishing society's attitude about economic matters. Literary figures sometimes describe contemporary economic conditions with greater accuracy than the economists. During the English Industrial Revolution, classical economists who provided industrialists with a defense of 12-hour workdays and children in factories were no match for Charles Dickens.

Some of the great economists were themselves literary figures, Keynes among them (save when he turned to writing economic treatises). Veblen, John Kenneth Galbraith, and Robert Heilbroner can be read as literature as well as economics.

Early economists often had to work with inadequate data, and what could not be shown with numbers had to be "sold" through felicitous expression. It is thus important to study the language in relation to the available documentation. The pessimism of Thomas Malthus (population will outrun the food supply) becomes understandable in light of the rate of urban population growth at the time.

Recently, the envelope of literature has been pushed even further. In **economic rhetoric** the successful economists are the persuasive ones.[3] We can study the pamphlets, letters, and notes of the great economists. David Ricardo prevailed over Malthus on behalf of the industrialists in part because he was more persuasive and could argue from a seat in Parliament.

Today many published "conversations with economists," come to us live from our contemporaries.[4] Although it is important to distinguish the "loose talk" of economists from their writings for posterity (a destination reached by the few), we can draw to some extent on this new form of literature.

For all its concern with form, the new rhetoric about rhetoric nonetheless relies on argumentation *within context.* Without the villainous mercantilists, Adam Smith's free trade arguments would have been as dull as the proverbial Scottish coastal town to which the tide, having gone out, refused to return. If David Ricardo had been championing industrialization during the Middle Ages, the more pious Malthus would have won their debate. Besides, there always was more than rhetoric. The great economists gave us entire systems for observing economic behavior.

It is imperative, then, to examine the *social and intellectual* currents that both shaped the thinking of the great economists and were shaped by them. A continual charge leveled against economics is that it lacks relevance. If true, it may be because some economists are out of touch with their intellectual forebears. They sometimes describe economic principles as if they were immutable laws of nature, operating on physical phenomena. There are intellectual reasons why this has happened, but there are social reasons to be concerned about it.

After probing the variety of social and intellectual trends, we can find no universal principle that unambiguously justifies one way of looking at the world as "best." Ambiguity, however, does not prevent us from generalizing about what communities value. One way of doing so is to consider the particular society's world view, what it believes to be truly important. A **world view** is a widely shared set of beliefs about the individual's relationship to the natural world, to his fellows, and to the Divine. More than anything, a world view is a vision. Obviously, not every individual or group will assent to the dominant world view, and not all elements of the world view will be equally shared. But if a particular world view is generally shared, it provides a framework for the predominant moral values of the society and can be used to account for common patterns of behavior.

Some world views are built around a natural order, others around a social order. The distinction between the two are important. The **natural order** comes more from human imagination than from human experience. When we speak of law and justice, for example, we are usually referring to a human social order, such as the one we live in. But most of the early economists believed that the economic laws they talked about resided in nature and were discoverable by human reason.

Social rules and laws are also important as means of reconciling the private passions and interests of individuals to the interests of the whole group or nation. A broader vision of society necessarily includes social rules as well.

Whereas the great English scientist and mathematician Isaac Newton made people aware of the natural order, the dalliance of economics with it and physical science began with Adam Smith. He, too, was under the influence. Newton's universe operated with the precision of a giant clock; Smith hoped to show the social order as part of the gearing. This seventeenth century *imagery* used to describe planetary motion has captivated many a scientific thinker. For the toilers in many scholarly fields (not, ironically, including modern astronomy and physics) Newtonian mechanics is still what science supposedly looks like. In the middle of the twentieth century, Paul Samuelson, destined to be America's first Nobel Prize winner in economics, was portraying economics as a science as unified and factually hardnosed as physics, and most of his lessor colleagues were nodding.

Some of the most interesting personalities were not nodding, of course; a few were awake and protesting. They are the iconoclasts or unorthodox thinkers, providing penetrating critiques of the world view of their day. Generally, they have opposed the natural order view and its reliance on immutable natural laws. They see even social orders subject to change. In truth, Adam Smith was a radical in his own time, though he subscribed to the natural order in one great book but gave the nod to social order in another. All the great thinkers were considered radical in their time and so, Marx, Veblen, Galbraith, Heilbroner, Friedrich von Hayek, Joseph A. Schumpeter, and others—should not be ignored.

The world view—even when enunciated by economists—helps to justify a particular social organization, but there are general ways that economic activity can be organized and specific forms that such organization has taken. The market exchange system characterizes Western economies that is now aspired to around the world, not only in East Asia but in the former communist states of Eastern Europe and the Soviet Union. Still, other systems have existed and not all market systems are alike. And aspiration is not realization.

The arrangement of society is critical. A society must continue to produce goods and services or it will die: Today's Russians are painfully aware of that. It must also find a way to distribute the benefits of production, or production will cease; all societies are aware of this quest. This second objective is closely allied with the world view, because production can be either coerced or voluntary, depending on what the society's members are conditioned to tolerate or demand. Generally, the possible arrangements of society can be summarized by a quartet—by custom (or tradition), by command, by competition, and through cooperation.

In the *customary economy,* each economic function is prescribed by tradition. People do what they do because that is what they and their ancestors have always done. In ancient Egypt, for example, every man was required by the principles of the Egyptian religion to follow the occupation of his father. In Western society, until the fifteenth or sixteenth century, the allocation of tasks was also very often hereditary, and a person's economic role was decided at birth. Even among some ethnic groups (such as the Amish) today, individuals will almost always choose their parents' occupation.

In a *command economy*, those who produce goods and services are told what to do, like an army that takes orders from a commanding officer. The area of command may be only economic and may coexist with political democracy. However, slave labor is also a kind of command economy. Though the city of Athens in ancient Greece is celebrated as the birthplace of democracy, even at its most "democratic," at least one-third of its population were slaves. The Roman Empire, too, relied on slave labor.

While custom and command can overlap, pure competition, can stand alone, but only if it *is* pure. Uniquely, in a *competitive market economy*, the system itself, rather than tradition or authority, decides what is to be produced and to whom the outputs are to be passed. Always in theory and often enough in practice, all power is exerted by the market for goods and services. People select occupations according to their own initiative and skills. Families select from marketplaces whatever goods and services they want or need, and producers produce what consumers demand at competitive prices. Because there are opportunities for choice built into it, Adam Smith called the competitive market a "system of liberty."

The economy of the United States is often pointed to as an example of a competitive market system, but Americans know that this is a fuzzy characterization. There are few ingredients of a customary economy in the United States today, but a large part of the economy is "public," which means there is a considerable amount of centralized command from the federal, state, and even local governments. Moreover, certain large sectors of the economy have only a few producers of a product and are involved in entanglements with labor unions in such a way that prices do not always materialize from an atmosphere of unfettered competition.

Cooperation can lead to a compromise version of the competitive market economy. Specific quantities of products and prices are determined by a free market system; however, the extremes of the distributions of incomes and wealth are influenced by a democratic government. In other words, the free market system is valued for its efficiency in production, but some degree of social judgment influences the distribution of incomes. The cooperative economy requires consensus politics and goal-sharing as an integral part of an interaction between the producers in the private sector and government agents in the public sector. These efforts may be coordinated through study commissions and administrative boards that involve the joint participation of workers, management, financiers, and government representatives. Social goals are based on an extensive dialogue and debate among business leaders, government officials, and the news media. The role of the media evokes a kind of town hall version of *Larry King Live*. The cooperative economy requires widespread ideological flexibility and an appreciation of social cohesiveness.

The Scandinavian economies, particularly the Swedish system, come closest to fitting the cooperative economy criteria. Although more than 90 percent of Swedish industry is privately owned, the central government is given the authority to modify market forces to encourage conformity with social objectives. Sweden is often cited as an example of the "welfare state," in which the system relies on very high tax revenues (about twice the GDP share of the United States), over half of which is redistributed in the form of welfare benefits. Moreover, the Swedish national income tax is highly progressive (the percentage of taxes being higher on higher incomes), yielding a marginal tax rate on worker earnings about twice that in the United States. One consequence is a much less unequal income distribution in Sweden compared with the United States. Most individuals belong to several of the widespread Swedish pressure groups that promote common interests and perform most of the coordinating function with the government.

The term *organization* often intimates a sense of neatness, but these four general, abstract types of economic organization seldom exist in a pure form. Mary Wollstonecraft (1759–1797), an early feminist and wife of political philosopher William Godwin (1756–1836), once wrote: "The same energy of character which renders a man a daring villain would have rendered him useful to society, had that society been well organized."[5] Organization may not be destiny, but it is truly important. Individuals, nonetheless, have played roles in getting society organized, even as society has helped in scripting these roles.

Not surprisingly, then, many variations of a customary, command, competitive market, or cooperative economy are possible, and when we turn to the particular kinds of economic systems in the modern world, we find that these systems, too, exist only in untidy mixtures. We often find elements of all four types of economic organization in socialist, communist, and even capitalist countries. Nazi Germany, for example, was able to brutally blend national socialism and state capitalism with slave labor.

In the interests of politics or ideology, we sometimes draw caricatures of socialism, communism and free market capitalism. The editorial cartoonist exaggerates in this way, sketching a swollen shadow of reality. Socialism, it is said, is characterized by ownership of all the means of production by the state. In reality, **Socialism** need not require public or common ownership of *all* the means of production, only those branches of the economy decisive for its functioning. The biblical Garden of Eden, it has been said, was Communism at its peak because goods were so abundant that they had zero prices. Adam and Eve could consume according to their needs. Real world **Communism**, however, cannot supply an endless amount of goods and services as free as air, consumed by everyone according to individual need. Dissatisfaction and temptation prevailed even in biblical Eden and east of it.

Capitalism is an economy based on private property and a two-way exchange system in which one good is traded for another or for equal value in money. In reality, this system has many permutations and has never depended on absolutely free competitive markets and the complete dedication of each person to economic self-interest. In a **cooperative economy**, the distribution of income and wealth is not decided entirely by a democratic political process. On the other hand, political democracy is virtually impossible to sustain in a society—even one otherwise organized around free enterprise capitalism—with giant, embarrassing gaps between the rich and the poor. In short, human judgments are involved, and an evolving world view is present.

Because of a world view agreed to by enough individuals to matter, economic organization is in great part a matter of human choice. A set of beliefs, a world view, nonetheless seems to be a necessary source of authority. Throughout modern history, socialist, communist, and capitalist economies have been defended by appeals to different world views. Western economic thought, dominated by defenses of market capitalism, has been traditionally linked to the ethic of individual rights. As early as Adam Smith (1723–1790), the market exchange system was presumed to depend on the free expression of individual rights: the freedom to buy whatever one wishes, to hire whomever one wants, to work in whatever occupation one desires, to work for whatever employer one chooses, to decide freely to keep whatever share of one's earnings one wishes—that is, complete freedom to exchange and accumulate.

We will not be giving away a "Hollywood ending" to our brief history by acknowledging that contemporary economists have written mostly about capitalism. Since that is so, understanding capitalism's essential characteristics is important. Today, most economists do not think of mutuality of interests as a part of economics. Initially, I defer to Robert Heilbroner, a longtime student of the system, to illuminate capitalism.

Heilbroner gives capitalism three identifying elements, the first of which is the presence of a thing or a process called capital.[6] The word capital has, according to Heilbroner, two distinctive meanings. Physical capital, something we can reach out and touch, is found in machines, factories, and infrastructure such as highways. To Karl Marx, however, capital is *a process*, a compounding link in a chain of transactions. Money is made into commodities and, then, commodities are made into money, the purpose of which is to end with more money than we began with. From this process comes the drive to accumulate capital.

The second identifying element of capitalism is the market mechanism, colorfully portrayed by Adam Smith, established and protected by law and custom, so that capital accumulation, amplified by Marx, in fact, can take place. Therefore, the economics of capitalism is the economics of markets (and pricing) and capital accumulation. No other system uses the market mechanism as a network.

The third element of capitalism, according to Heilbroner, is "political." As a social system, capitalism requires an architecture of horizontal and vertical order. The horizontal maintains stable relations *within* social classes; the vertical maintains widely accepted distinctions among classes. Unlike any other system, class distinctions are made by the possession or not of capital (dividing society between capitalists and non-capitalists) and by political power.

Other systems too have a hierarchy of classes, most notably, feudalism. Unlike feudalism, however, capitalism enjoys two realms of power—private and public. The institutions of the public realm often, but not always, further the interests of the capitalist class. Power in the private realm stems from capital accumulation. Power flows from capital ownership because, according to Heilbroner, of "the right accorded to *withhold* their property from the use of society if they wish."[7] This power is not absolute only because the social order often deploys customs and laws to bridle it.

Heilbroner's stylized rendition of the capitalist system is a valuable framework. By expanding his definition of capitalism, we can go on to identify many different "capitalisms." For example, in various eras of American history—the Gilded Age, the Jazz Age, and the 1980s and 1990s spring to mind—people have focused on making money with money, skipping altogether the difficult stage of producing commodities. For the recent era, I have used the term "Wall Street capitalism," an era in which many social rules have been broken.[8]

Which visions, which ideas capture the truth? It is not easy to know. My message is less ambiguous than any quick and ready answers: Economics is not frozen in time but in continual evolution. Those attracted to the fixity of natural science metaphors likely will feel uneasy with the ebb and flow of history and the shifting tides of doctrine. But there are compensations. In striving for a progressive science of economics, the unease of the economist with the way things are can provoke the imagination, as it so often did for the great economists. "The world owes its onward impulses," suggested Nathaniel Hawthorne, "to men ill at ease."

We begin with the custom and command of feudalism because of the clarity of its world view and because for many centuries it stood in the way of the evolution of free markets and of economic science. The classical economists still had to contend with some of its last remnants.

NOTES

1. Economist Mark Blaug once used the term "absolutist history of thought," and later, following Richard Rorty, used the term "rational reconstruction." See Mark Blaug, *Economic Theory in Retrospect*, 3rd ed. (Cambridge: Cambridge University Press, 1978), p. 2 and Mark Blaug, "On the Historiography of Economics," *Journal of the History of Economic Thought* 12 (Spring 1990): 27–37. Nobelist Paul Samuelson used the more evocative "Whig history of thought" in "Out of the Closet: A Program for the Whig History of Economic Science," *History of Economic Society Bulletin* 9, no. 1 (Fall 1987): 51–60. To Samuelson, Whig history presents the ideas of dead economists in modern theoretical dress, finds their errors by modern standards, thus offering evidence of progress in economic science. This, too, would be the meaning of rational reconstruction.

   Rational reconstruction is useful as far as it goes, but it does not extend beyond the limits arbitrarily defined by the present-day economist. For a well-reasoned and detailed argument for historical reconstruction, the approach used in this book, see Karen I. Vaughn's Presidential Address at the Twentieth Annual Meeting of the History of Economics Society, Philadelphia, June 28, 1993, printed as "Why Teach the History of Economics," *Journal of the History of Economic Thought* 15, no. 2 (Fall 1993): 174–183.

2. A longer, more detailed defense for the study of the history of doctrines is presented by Karen I. Vaughn, *op. cit.* An earlier defense was mounted by the late Nobelist George J. Stigler, "Does Economics Have a Useful Past?" *History of Political Economy* 1, no. 2 (1969): 217–230.

3. Economics as rhetoric got its start with Deirdre McCloskey, *The Rhetoric of Economics* (Madison: University of Wisconsin Press, 1985). McCloskey is among the most lucid and witty of present-day economists.

4. The pioneer book is Arjo Klamer's aptly titled *Conversations with Economists* (Rowman & Allanheld: Totoway, N.J., 1983).

5. Mary Wollstonecraft, in *Letters Written During a Short Residence in Sweden, Norway, and Denmark*, (Wilmington, Del: J. Wilson & J. Johnson, booksellers, 1796), Letter 19.

6. I am following the discussion in Robert Heilbroner, "Economics in the Twenty-First Century," in Charles J. Whalen, editor, *Political Economy for the 21st Century* (Armonk, New York, London, England: M.E. Sharpe, 1996), pp. 266–269. A still more extended discussion of the species appears in Robert Heilbroner, *Nature and Logic of Capitalism* (New York: W.W. Norton, 1985). Any book by Heilbroner is worth the read; his style is uniquely nice and easy.

7. Robert Heilbroner, *Behind the Veil of Economics* (New York: W.W. Norton, 1988), p. 38.

8. See E. Ray Canterbery, *Wall Street Capitalism: The Theory of the Bondholding Class* (River Edge, N.J./London/Singapore: World Scientific, 2000).

1

FEUDALISM AND THE EVOLUTION OF ECONOMIC SOCIETY

Seeing why the study of capitalism and free markets did not entrance the clergy of the Middle Ages is easy. Markets, as they were to reappear, did not then exist. Among what economists today would call "factors of production," land dominated to the virtual exclusion of all else. Those who sought wealth and power sought land. Usually, however, unlike most modern economies, land normally was not for sale. In this way feudalism, a land-centered way to organize production, commanded medieval times.

European feudalism was not only an economic system, but an extremely complex social and political system as well, taking different forms in different parts of Europe during the Middle Ages. Its general outlines nonetheless remained stable, a stability that gave order where anarchy otherwise would have prevailed. Since the system was noticeably kinder and gentler to the landholding aristocracy than to others, feudalism did not give way easily to the marketplace.

Still, Europe always has had a great variety of resources and climates and different types of crops and livestock so that the potential for exchanging dissimilar commodities was always there once travel was made relatively safe. Merchants must be able to travel safely so they can sell their goods in different towns. And society must be peaceful enough so there can be towns. Thus, law and order became the central virtue contributing to the decline of feudalism and the rebirth of markets.

Travel on the road to market economies took place over several centuries. Although it is impossible to specify the moment in history when the transformation from feudalism to a market system was complete, we can identify the major forces that brought about the change. As we shall see, even as the winds of change carried the seeds of the market, its full flowering was slowed by a force called mercantilism. Finally, only the surprising duo of Isaac Newton and Adam Smith could put society back on the road to harmony.

THOMAS AQUINAS AND THE WORLD VIEW

During the Middle Ages, the world view was dominated by the idea of the Cosmos, an all-encompassing harmony, a unified whole in which God's presence and spirit were embodied in all living things. Moreover, each part of the Cosmos had its own immutable place in the Great Chain of Being. God had ranked his creatures from the most inferior ascending upward. Trees outranked herbs. Every herb, tree, bird, beast, and fish had a particular place and use given to it by God, the Creator.

This medieval world view fit very neatly with feudalism, a highly structured economic system in which everyone had a specific place. In this world view there was no conflict between "rational knowledge" and faith. In the *Summa Theologica* of Thomas Aquinas (1225–1274), a complete and authoritative statement of medieval economic thought, the proper life required that each class perform its obligations according to the laws of God and nature.

This world view, however, did not mean that no "economic thinking" took place. Aquinas deplored lending money for interest and trading for profit, but he expressed no preference for the equal distribution of private property. In fact, the main test for the propriety of any exchange of goods and services was whether or not the exchange threatened the class hierarchy. A just price, in Aquinas's view, was a price that suitably supported the seller in his social rank. Since Aquinas's economic views are complexly intertwined with his religious faith, a science claiming to separate itself from religion was not born until the Renaissance.

We now begin, then, the long journey on the road to today's capitalism and to modern economics. Our first major stop—after a short detour through the Ancient World—will be real-world Feudalism, the dominant economic system of precapitalistic Europe. It characterized the almost 1,000 years between the collapse of the Western Roman Empire (A.D. 476) and the fall of the Eastern (Byzantine) Roman Empire (A.D. 1453), the Middle Ages.

Historians are more or less forced to lump together huge spans of time and give them titles, such as the Ancient World or the **Middle Ages**, in order to give the past a coherent order; but obviously the transition from one period to another is not that simple. The Roman Empire, for example, did not die giving birth to the Middle Ages. A great deal of Roman civilization survived in one form or another, changing as medieval civilization began to develop. Some of Rome's economic legacies contributed to the growth of feudalism.

UP FROM ANTIQUITY

Feudalism in Western Europe grew out of the slave economy of the Western Roman Empire. Slaves, of course, are of no economic use unless they produce enough of the necessities of life—food, clothing, and housing—to enable them to do their daily work, plus a little more. During antiquity, slaves were the main producers of the "little more," or a surplus. The city of Athens in ancient Greece is celebrated as the birthplace of democracy, but even at its most "democratic," at least one-third of its population were slaves. Athenian women had few property rights, were married without consent, and lived under the guardianship of male relatives.

The Roman Empire was a centralized political bureaucracy that relied on slave labor both in the major cities and towns and on the huge agricultural estates (villas). (There were also large groups of free artisans and laborers.) During the **Dark Ages**, from the end of the Greco-Roman civilizations through about the 900s, those villas that had not been destroyed by barbarian raiders from the north and east became landed estates.[1] The Roman cities—some in ruins—shrank to towns and villages. The slaves tended to remain slaves until a decline in population made labor scarce and expensive. Although slavery did not end with the Roman Empire, it continued in Western Europe on a greatly diminished scale.[2]

Because of the major social and political disruptions at the end of the fifth century, law and order began to crumble. Citizens of the empire could no longer rely on Roman centralized control and legal authority for protection. Furthermore, much of Greco-Roman knowledge was lost with the collapse of the political order.

A BRIEF HISTORY OF THE DEVELOPMENT OF FEUDALISM

By the end of the sixth century, Europe was profoundly uncivilized. To be "free," one had to be a warrior and have weapons. War was a common form of economic activity. Pillaging (then a form of economics and politics) included the acquisition of cattle, ornaments, and slaves, as well as weapons for the next assault.

But successful aggressors were themselves obvious targets for plunder, and pillage was therefore a poor "solution" to the question of how goods and services could be produced and distributed. People had to be able to hold on to what they had; as a result, mutual self-protection societies began to evolve within the framework of the existing agricultural economy.

Feudalism was based upon mutual duties and obligations. One human being was no longer supposed to own another outright (though exceptions were made), but the chains were not completely broken, the bondage being of a different kind. The serf, the lowest person on the feudal economic scale, was bound to the land, retained for himself subsistence, and exchanged service for protection by *his* master, who, in turn, was given control of both the serf and the all-important land in exchange for service to *his* master, the king or duke. The nobility provided mutual protection services through those who became knights or warriors. The king atop the social pyramid—be he King Phillip Augustus or King John—was in control of both the land and the serf. The king then could transfer control from one master to another.

Among the nobility, marriage, land, and politics were hopelessly intertwined, a condition best explained by noble thirteenth century example. As part of a peace treaty to seal the victory in Normandy of French King Philip Augustus over King John of England in January 1200, a marriage was arranged. John's sister Eleanor had two eligible daughters, 13-year-old Urraca and 12-year-old Blanche (girls were legally mature at age 12 and available for sealing political alliances or gaining property). As royal luck would have it, Louis, the 13-year-old heir to the French crown, was desperately in need of a bride. John's mother and the princesses' grandmother, Eleanor of Aquitaine, selected Blanche.

John promised estates from his French lands plus 20,000 silver marks as Blanche's dowry. The dower was comprised of royal French lands in Artois, in northeastern France. These transfers of property were also part of the peace treaty. Thus, the story of this Blanche, in contrast to the Blanche of Tennessee Williams's *A Streetcar Named Desire,* is of both custom and command, not of passion. Louis's Blanche would never have had to say, "I have always depended on the kindness of strangers."[3]

As with Blanche and Louis, family had little effect on the obligations of a man to his lord or king, whereas the king and other lords had control over the families of their vassals so that women and children had even fewer social rights than did men. In England no woman could marry without the assent of her lord, and the lord could even transfer his ward's marriage, for a fee. For example, in 1214, the aforementioned King John of England conceded his first wife, Isabella of Gloucester, whose marriage had been annulled in 1200, to Geoffrey de Mandeville, Earl of Essex, for 20,000 marks.

King John, like other noble owners of a large plots of land, being unable to personally control all he owned, decentralized his land, assigning parts of it to less powerful men, whom his own decree made lesser nobles. King John further extended the delegation of responsibility, in turn, by these tenants-in-chief to subtenants, who actually did most of the work on the land. The right to farm the land obligated these subtenants (called serfs, or "free" peasants) to render military and other services to the noble in the name of the king.

In the work they did, the serfs were like the slaves in the Roman economy, but the property rights system had changed: A "contractual" set of obligations had been substituted for slavery. The sparseness of the population and the joint defense needs of the serfs and the nobles were forces making serfdom mutually irresistible in the early Middle Ages. We cannot be sure about population trends preceding and during the Dark Ages; but the general impression is that the population of the Roman Empire tended to decline, and the decline was speeded by a bubonic plague epidemic in the sixth century. The epidemic continued for over 50 years, and this contributed to making labor a scarce resource.

Thus, we can see that the feudal ties that bound the serf to the land had obvious advantages over slavery. The tenant-in-chief did not have to worry that his slaves would be stolen or taken from him as long as he remained loyal to his lord. And the serf enjoyed at least some of the benefits of his own labor as well as a degree of protection from the pillaging barbarians.

Even if the land changed lordships, the serf was tied to the land by his unwritten contract and fulfilled his obligations to the next lord. The manor often was passed to the next lord by inheritance. Thus, an individual's relationship to his fellows was decided mostly by custom, which evolved into common law, rather than by economic efficiency.

The right to use land was generally inherited by the eldest son, and unmarried daughters and the younger males were then sometimes left to beg at the gates of the manors. Women could acquire a property share only by marriage. The intent of the feudal system was the survival of the fief, not necessarily the survival of the family or its members.

Land occasionally was "sold," its sales financed by a king. An abbey chronicler in England (monks in abbeys have supplied much of the data on feudalism) recorded the sale of the village of Elton for 50 golden marks to a king in 1017, but such transactions were rare.[4] No one seems to know whether Elton was worth it because no market for land, as we know it today, existed. As with the arranged pubescent marriage between Louis and Blanche, more often they could *transfer* land to others. Though not an invention of feudalism, the close tie of marriage to landed property failed to unravel with feudalism, as fans of Jane Austen know.

Sometimes literature came with the land. The aforementioned Eleanor of Aquitaine, once married to Louis VII, King of France, ensured that the art of the troubadours (the knight-poets of southern France) flourished in the courts of her husband, his nobles, and her children. When she left Louis to marry Henry of Anjou, soon to be Henry II and King of England, she thoughtfully brought both Aquitaine and her southern poets, including Marie, a court woman poet, as a dowry. In the *Lais of Marie de France,* a king takes the wife of one of his loyal knights as a lover. Faithful to feudal values, however, the lovers are punished; they come to a scalding end (and vice versa) in a bath of boiling water.

The Manorial System

Economic activity in feudal society was generally organized around the life of a manor, a largely self-sufficient agricultural plantation controlled by a lord and tilled by the peasants and serfs. The manor was little different from that of Scarlet O'Hara's Tara; it provided most of life's material essentials in one place. By the **High Middle Ages** small villages had grown around the manor, or vice versa, and sometimes the villages encompassed more than one manor. These small, often isolated settlements were havens of civilization in an otherwise anarchic world.

Manorial organization had two basic aims: To produce enough to keep the manor going, and to provide authority and agricultural surplus for its lord. *What* was produced? Food, shelter, and clothing to keep the peasants and serfs in working order, the lord contented, and some surplus. *How* was it produced? In the custom of the manor. *For Whom* was it produced? Beyond the workers' subsistence, products were distributed mostly to the lord and king by custom. Although the manor strove for self-sufficiency, the uncertainties of agricultural production made necessary some exchange of products between manors, often on a "loan" basis.

On an English manor, the agricultural peasant or serf would have about 30 acres to farm, with the cultivated areas fenced. Each year, one field out of two or three was left fallow and unenclosed for animal grazing. Mixed in among the peasants' land were the strips of land kept by the lord for his own use (his demesne). Each serf household owed week-work (one laborer) of about three days a week on the demesne farm. The serf had to supply his share of the needed oxen, heavy plows, and other implements. Thus, in addition to providing for their own subsistence, the serfs provided surpluses for the lord and king while supporting the knights. In return, the knights, the lords, and the Church provided what little safety, peace, and justice there was.

Keeping law and order was not cheap. The outfitting of one knight required an outlay equivalent to about 20 oxen or the farm equipment for about ten peasant landholders.[5] To take care of his military needs, the king exacted military duty and other services from his lords, who in turn reminded their knights of their military obligations. Involuntary military service was a part of the feudal contract.

Today, feudalism seems an undesirable, even grotesque, economic system, especially for the serfs. There were some peasant uprisings such as the Peasants' Revolt of 1381 that threatened the English ruling class, but by and large the serfs and peasants were merely living in the "manor" to which they were accustomed and did not imagine anything better. There was little they could have done to bring about change even when they desired it. Besides, they generally saw serfdom as an improvement over slavery. And they were right.

The Social Theory of Feudalism

In feudal society the serfs worked, the warriors fought, the clergy prayed, the lords managed, and the king ruled. Kings generally managed quite well. In 1170 to 1171 Henry II received an estimated 23,500 pounds in revenue, of which he and his entourage spent about 5,000 pounds on themselves. At the time, an average parish income was about ten pounds yearly.

We might have expected class conflict, but more conflicts erupted between families and states than among these classes because social organization was rigidly hierarchical. A person born into serfdom gave little thought to the possibility of upward mobility into the noble class. Either tradition or contract decided almost every kind of social bond. Nevertheless, some ruling idea is also needed to hold society together, and the feudal world view is made whole by the individual's relationship to the divine. Even kings generally ruled divinely.

At the time of the great Crusades of the twelfth century, chivalry flowered as a moral system fusing religion and the martial arts. Drawing inspiration from a pre-Christian past—the Trojans, Alexander the Great, and the ancient Romans—chivalry originally prized ancient pagan virtues, including pride, a sin in Christian theology. When Europe had to defend itself against Norsemen, Moslems, and other "pagans," the pacifist ideas of the Gospels were set aside, and the Church blessed the knight's arms and prayed for him.

Chivalry justified the knight's daily activities in a way that the much maligned merchant could only envy. As a "middleman," the merchant seemed to serve no useful purpose in an agricultural economy except to line his own pockets. The knight was equally suspect initially because his most effective tool was the death blow. Thus, the knight's sword had to be put to the service of widows, orphans, the oppressed, and the Church so that "God and Chivalry are in accord."

Ultimately, however, neither chivalry nor business enterprise could be contained. Though chivalry thereafter governed the life of the nobility, it was—like all moral codes—as much illusion as reality.

That did not make it any less powerful as a social force, however. The Church provided the additional glue that was needed for holding medieval society together.

The Church itself held a large number of manors and was accumulating wealth in the form of land, contributions from nobles, and tithes, a strict tenth of the gross produce of the peasants down to the potherbs in their gardens and two shillings in the pound from the personal earnings of the expanding class of shopkeepers and poor artisans. The Church's traditionally great resistance to worldly goods was directed toward the accumulation of wealth through trade rather than the accumulation of wealth itself.[6]

Original sin, so deeply embedded in medieval thought, made reform or change hardly worth considering: If humans are fundamentally corrupted, neither they nor society has changed. A woman was either a virgin and a saint or a harlot on the way to hell, a place whose mean temperature had been carefully calibrated, though few seemed to know it, except it to be *very* hot. Until the late Middle Ages, a woman could choose the ambiguity and guilt of marriage or the virginal protection of the convent. Thus, in a way, religion was used to rationalize existing social and economic conditions.

Margery Kempe's memoirs, the first autobiography in English, illuminate the power of religion.[7] Born about 1373 in Bishop's Lynn, in Norfolk, she dictated her memoirs as an old woman in 1439. By the end she thought that Christ was her coauthor. Little ruled her life—like so many others—else save religion. In her youth, Margery had committed a sin (doubtless a sexual one) and felt condemned to hell with its well-known torments.

Margery chose marriage over the convent. Though she broached the subject of her sin with the local priest, he admonished her so severely, she never finished the confession and was, she thought, doomed to die without forgiveness. Afterwards, she began to see visions of devils, breathing fire, attempting to swallow her. She attempted suicide, and was scarred for life.

Her self-described recovery was equally dramatic. Christ appeared, radiant in beauty and love, clad in purple silk, and asked why she had forsaken him, though he had never forsaken her. Then, he ascended to heaven on a beam of light. Peace returned to Margery — at least for several years. For John, her neglected husband, the worst was yet to come: Margery saw sex as an evil act and she now believed sainthood to be just around the corner.

Some people today might claim Margery to be simply mentally ill. If so, however, it was a widespread affliction during the Middle Ages. Religion dominated not only the day's thoughts, but dreams as well. Always, the visions were important.

The Church, like the chivalrous knight, was nonetheless supposed to be charitable. From its massive resources, gifts or one-way economic transfers were given to the poor, but the required tithing and fees were often sufficient burdens on the lower classes to create the poverty that the Church's charity was intended to relieve. Because many landowners were clerics, the landowners' exhortation to be diligent to the lords and generous to the Church served virtually a double (they would have said noble) purpose.

Even prior to the twelfth century, the law and the power of authority were frequently thought to be God's punishment of humanity for its sins. The residue of this belief made the nastier work of the armored men on horseback—forcible suppression of heretics, the excommunicated, and enemies of the Holy See—easier, if less chivalrous, than romantics would have us believe. Neither medieval thinkers nor tenants-in-chief tried to disguise the reality and advantages of a stratified society. A hierarchical social theory prevailed.

As late as the time of the great English poet Geoffrey Chaucer (c.1342–1400), the knight was still a romantic ideal:

> There was a *Knight*, a most distinguished man,
> Who from the day on which he first began
> To ride abroad had followed chivalry,
> Truth, honour, generousness and courtesy.
> He had done nobly in his sovereign's war
> And ridden into battle, no man more,
> As well in Christian as in heathen places,
> And ever honoured for his noble graces.[8]

But another traveler on Chaucer's pilgrimage, the Merchant, is sketched with ambiguity, reflecting his still uneasy social position:

> He was expert at dabbling in exchanges.
> This estimable Merchant so had set
> His wits to work, none knew he was in debt,
> He was so stately in administration,
> In loans and bargains and negotiation.
> To tell the truth I do not know his name.[9]

Even so, markets and merchants could no longer be denied.

THE REBIRTH OF MARKETS

By as early as A.D. 1050, conditions in Europe had stabilized sufficiently to allow a slow revival of commerce to begin. The terror of foreign marauders had declined. Warfare was still a way of life among local lords, but that, too, had declined somewhat. The security provided by feudal institutions contributed to population increases, and the number of manors and villages grew. Indeed, by the thirteenth century, the best agricultural land had probably been occupied.[10]

Towns began to form in the densely populated areas. Crafts began to flourish, and crude manufactured goods such as armor and harnesses were traded for raw materials and food from the countryside. This increase in trade and the specialization of labor skills became the source of mutual reinforcement for commerce: For example, carpenters or blacksmiths could not be wholly self-sufficient and had to rely on trade.

Importantly, many of the new towns became independent of the feudal lords and developed their own governments and their own defense. This was not an easy process; more than one town was looted by an angry lord because it refused to give in to his demands, but over the centuries the independence of walled towns became an established part of the European economy.

Beginning in the late eleventh century, a substantial increase in international trade accompanied the Crusades. In the twelfth century, the towns of northern Italy, central Germany, and Flanders became important commercial centers as trade and population continued to expand. By the thirteenth century, French champagne, Flemish wool, and the raw materials of German mines became part of a growing commerce that incited the development of banking and other new commercial institutions.

But we are getting a little bit ahead of ourselves. Let's go back to a medium-sized medieval town and try to reconstruct how it might develop from a community mostly dependent on **barter,** or the exchange of one good for another, into a true marketplace, and how the townspeople evolved from artisans to merchants.

It might begin with the exchange of gifts, perhaps at a religious festival. Goods may have been brought originally for personal consumption during the festival, and people who have brought a variety of commodities may have been tempted into bartering. Eventually, such a religious festival might turn into a village fair, the original religious motive almost forgotten.

Barter nonetheless is very inefficient. It requires many double coincidences. Say you are an artisan and agree to build a clock for a peasant who offers ten dead ducks in exchange for the clock. Your family can eat two ducks that night, but eight of the ducks are sure to spoil. For a balanced meal, you must quickly find a peasant who harvests vegetables and also likes ducks. If your roof leaks, you have to find the same double coincidence with a carpenter. If all this is not enough, you have to remember that one duck exchanges for five loaves of bread or for ten candlesticks.

Money is the great simplifier. It can be used as a common denominator or unit of account for every good and service. So as the exchange of goods and services began to expand, the merchants had to rediscover money (coinage had been commonplace during ancient times). We can imagine a weaver who has managed to accumulate a small amount of cash and decides to use his money to buy goods at the fair and resell or barter them some days later after the fair is over and they cannot be so easily acquired. Succeeding in this, the weaver may find that he has made a tidy profit, and he may decide to specialize in buying and reselling goods and let his wife do the weaving. He becomes a middleman. However, he dislikes the inconvenience and risk of carrying goods around the countryside (travel still isn't all that safe), so he picks out a spot in the town and opens a shop where he will sell his goods. Soon his friend the carpenter opens a shop across the muddy street, also selling bartered goods.

As early as 1160, the records of the aforementioned village of Elton, England, contain occupations and offices such as miller, blacksmith, shoemaker, carpenter, weaver, merchant, tanner, baker, tailor, and painter. By the time of *The Canterbury Tales* we can add a haberdasher, a dyer, and a carpet-maker, all members of guilds. Moreover, in addition to five husbands, the woman from Bath could display material finery:

> Her kerchiefs were of finely woven ground;
> I dared have sworn they weighed a good ten pound,
> The ones she wore on Sunday, on her head.
> Her hose were of the finest scarlet red
> And gartered tight; her shoes were soft and
> new.[11]

Life in the medieval town had changed forever.

This was the start of a commercial, or mercantile, economy that greatly diverged from feudalism. In particular, the rise of the independent merchant led to a new attitude—the assertion of individualism—and potentially to a new economic system—the market economy. The property rights system of feudalism was doomed. The maverick merchant, operating at the frontiers of the customary or command economy, had transformed communities.

Although European feudalism managed to survive for almost 1,000 years, it first ended in England, for reasons later important to us. Until then, religion dominated the day's activities and the night's dreams. Until the rebirth of markets, an economist would have had little about which to write. Put differently, an economist's need for markets for self-expression reveals much about what is to come.

THE WINDS OF CHANGE ALONG THE ROAD TO HARMONY

The period from around 1000 to 1300 is called the **High Middle Ages** for many reasons, including a commercial revolution that occurred during those centuries. The rebirth of markets is an important element in this revolution, but other changes were taking place as well.

Various innovations generated *agricultural surpluses* sufficient to feed both the peasant and the wandering merchant. Crop rotation helped to provide food for seasons when the weather was unreliable; windmills and heavy plows (now pulled by newly shoed and harnessed horses instead of the slower oxen) began to replace labor. The marketing of these surpluses not only released some labor from agriculture, it made the manor more reliant on purchasing and less self-sufficient. In time, although the feudal class distinctions largely remained, the manorial system itself began to break up.

Trade began to expand. As early as the First Crusade, beginning in 1095, adventuresome people broke loose from their feudal ties and became traveling merchants. Venice was a thriving commercial center; even tourists and pilgrims began to crowd St. Mark's square in Venice, much as they do today. Growth in commerce and trade was not smooth. Wars were almost continuous, and famines and plagues occurred now and then, due at least in part to rapid population growth, lack of sanitation, and inadequate medical knowledge. The most devastating of the plagues was the Black Death of 1348 to 1351 during which, it is estimated, the population of Europe declined from 73 million in 1300 to 45 million in 1400.[12]

Another major factor that changed the European landscape, particularly in England, was the *enclosure movement*.[13] With trade came a growing market for wool to make clothing. Thus, much of the land that had once been open was fenced in (enclosed). The landowners now could profit from either farming or raising sheep because the revival of trade made specialization, compared with the self-sufficient manor, efficient again.

The greatest loss to the smaller farmers was the common land on which they had, by custom, fed their poultry, pastured their cows, and chopped wood for fuel. Many peasants were therefore compelled by dwindling economic prospects to abandon their independent farming and become day laborers in agriculture. Others were forced from farming altogether and into industries in the countryside in the form of the putting-out system or cottage industries, which prospered because of the labor made available by the enclosure. Still fewer found work in shops in town.

A land-owning noble did not have to be very clever to figure out that a lone shepherd could watch over sheep in a pasture, whereas ten or 12 laborers might be needed to grow food on the same land. Thus, we have reached the point where people could sell their labor—to a woolen manufacturer, say, or to a wealthy landowner. And, with a burgeoning population, labor was cheap.

Land was also for sale by the Church, which needed more cash for bigger cathedrals, and by the king, who needed bigger armies to defeat his rivals. (The great cathedrals, often taking a century or longer to build, may still be richly enjoyed in Durham and Canterbury in England and Amiens and Chartres in France.) Land was not cheap at all; only the nobles and the richest merchants could afford it.

An *abundance of money* is essential to grease the palms of merchants. Gold and silver were flowing into Europe via Spanish and Portuguese explorations, and there was abundant coinage to make the market economies float. Not much more is needed for a market system. It was a slow revolution, but the traditional duties, values, and obligations of feudalism were gradually eroded by the use of money in an exchange economy. The old feudal order struggled in vain against this emerging cash economy. The pleasures of money and new economic and political organizations that emerged were worth certain sacrifices of privilege and security—at least for all those except the shrinking feudal aristocracy.

New weaponry, a part of improving technology, transformed the killing fields during the Middle Ages and in time would promote the nation state. With the new weapons, kings were able to extend protection over *all* their subjects without the help of knights, who now faced technological unemployment. Early, in the Battle of Courtrai in 1302, the flower of French knighthood, heavily armored, was laid waste by foot soldiers, Flemish burgers armed with pikes. Later, in 1359, on one of those intermittent forays by the English into France that made up much of the Hundred Years' War, page and soldier Geoffrey Chaucer was captured. He was ransomed to a grateful king the following year. During *that* war, it was the English longbow—not Chaucer (who turned to poetry)—that undid the French. Then, with a finality that marked the end of the Middle Ages, the successful breach of the walls of Constantinople in 1453 brought gunpowder to the attention of warriors and made the old-style walled city a questionable defense.

By 1453, nation-states (integrated counties and kingdoms) in the modern sense had begun to emerge. By the end of the fifteenth century, civilization was blessed with both the handgun and the cannon. Feudalism had been characterized by relatively small political units. A tenth-century map of the area today known as France would show many separate counties and dukedoms, all owing feudal allegiance to the king in Paris, but the largest and most powerful of them were like independent states and could more or less do as they pleased. A map of "France" in the early fourteenth century would still show many counties and dukedoms, but a far greater number were controlled directly by the king.

As *nations and weapons* grew up together, the nation-state took over from the feudal lord and his manor the provision of protection for the citizens. The king needed revenue, and the citizens often were willing to pay for protection. In England and the Low Countries, for example, representative bodies began to set tax rates, and the king traded land and promises for additional revenue.

Meanwhile, markets, not only for goods, but as noted, for land and labor continued to flourish. Although the morality of profit-making continued to be suspect (despite earnest efforts by merchants to give it a good name), a gradual change in attitudes toward material accumulation from commerce was to come about, largely as a result of *the Reformation*. This change is important, because, as noted by Heilbroner, private material accumulation is a prerequisite for capitalism.

The Reformation began as a religious movement *within* the Church, aimed at correcting specific abuses of spiritual power, particularly the sale of indulgences (certificates for partial remission of the punishment for sins already confessed and repented). As early as the late fourteenth century, the evangelical Lollards and the otherwise devout Margery Kempe were reacting to the sale of pardons and indulgences with denunciations of the Pope's authority, especially after 1378, when there were rival popes, one at Avignon and one in Rome.[14] The Reformation culminated in a thorough modification of much of the Church's doctrine and the establishment of the various Protestant churches.

The emerging merchant class was very active in this movement. Protestantism offered a haven to the worldly religious spirit of the merchants because it taught them that hard work and the accumulation of wealth were virtues. The stern and autocratic French theologian John Calvin (1509–1564) developed an interpretation of Christian beliefs that was especially welcome. He taught that the Old Testament values of accumulation and exchange were not invalidated by Christ's teachings about the rich and the kingdom of Heaven (Matthew 19:24), because all books of the Bible were the word of God and the word of God was one. The faith of Calvinists was manifested in hard work and frugality. Because "Heaven helps those who help themselves," prosperity became a leading indicator of piety. In this way, the temporal and the spiritual were, if not married, happily living together in John Calvin's teachings.

Thus, over some six centuries the forces that would guarantee the establishment of and justification for competitive market economics in much of Western Europe were grinding away at the economic roots of the manor and the political organization of feudalism. The most powerful forces were increasing agricultural productivity and the resultant breakup of the manor, travel and exploration, the enclosure movement (especially in England), the buying and selling of land and labor, the rise of the nation-states, the expanding use of money in commercial transactions and as revenue for governments, and a broader acceptance of the idea that wealth accumulation and economic progress are good things.

MERCANTILISM AND BIG GOVERNMENT

We have not quite yet reached the full market economy itself. We first encounter a detour called mercantilism, which was the prevailing European economic system in the years between the decline of feudalism during the early fifteenth century and the start of the Industrial Revolution (1780). Just as free competitive markets were about to unleash themselves, the rulers of various European nation-states decided in their self-interest to put some controls on the mercantile economy. These rulers still conceived of power in feudal terms.

Mercantilism (the term derives from the Italian word for merchant) was an alliance between government and business. At first, the merchants were to be dominated by the government; later, the merchants would turn the tables as they became pamphleteers, extending mercantilist thought themselves in their special-interest pleading. Like feudalism, mercantilism worked in different ways in different countries, but the basic idea behind it was always the same—the government should manage the economy for the purpose of increasing national wealth and state power.

Because power and wealth were equated with gold and silver, the government should (1) stimulate the output of domestic goods, (2) limit domestic consumption, (3) put tariffs on imports, and (4) try to create a favorable balance of trade (more exports than imports). The exports were paid for with gold and silver, which in turn could be used to build a strong army. The limits on consumption were aimed not only at the masses. Since imports tended to be luxuries, the sumptuary laws designed to regulate extravagance and luxury hit the wealthy hard even as they improved the balance of trade.

Gold and mercantilism tended to go hand in hand because precious metals were used as internationally acceptable money. Just at a time when trade was rapidly expanding in Europe, an acute shortage of gold and silver bullion developed. This monetary threat to trade was arrested by the influx of Spanish bullion, gold, and silver mined by the Spanish in their American colonies. But the increased supply of gold caused product prices to triple in Europe between 1500 and 1650, and because the prices of simple manufactured goods rose much more rapidly than either wages or rents, the merchant class ascended along with prices.

The accumulation of financial capital by the merchant class enabled it to extend the simple factory system (producing guns and ammunition) during the sixteenth and seventeenth centuries. Such production did not constitute the modern factory (the first genuine factories in England probably being the Lombes silk mills in the early 1700s), but it did increase the degree of Smithian specialization and productivity. Production, trade, and commerce thrived. Sensing the advantages of a new source of revenue, the monarchs in the new nation-states provided military protection for these commercial ventures.

However, not every nation had the gold supply that mainly was in Spain. In other countries, the monarch had to use monopoly powers to build up a favorable balance of trade for the nation. Since these nation-states were determined never to run short of gold again, the merchants of France and England experienced the happy—though not entirely unplanned—coincidence of building their nations while earning profits. In England particularly, the merchants and the landed aristocrats formed a working alliance as smooth as the silk they imported. Thus, the English merchants and the nobility developed a mutual back-rubbing association in which it was not uncommon for the merchants' daughters to not only massage but marry nobility.

The mercantilists interest in gold and silver made them aware of a direct relation between the quantity of money and the price level. As one mercantilist quaintly expressed it, "Plenty of money in a Kingdom doth make the native commodities dearer." Thus, at first gush, it would appear contradictory to encourage the influx of gold through a favorable trade balance. Would not a gushing money supply push up prices and thus "make the native commodities dearer" or, as the Federal Reserve might say today, cause inflation? Higher domestic prices would then dampen exports, and there would go the mercantilists' prized trade surplus.

There was no contradiction. Gushing gold would "quicken trade," wrote the mercantilists, causing higher levels of production (including the manufacture of guns and gunpowder), which would more than offset any increase in the price level from the same source. Indeed, they saw an expansion of money and credit as essential to unimpeded trade growth.

The pursuit of national gain dominated the mercantilist era. The new association between money and wealth (in feudal society, we recall, land was wealth), plus the new nationalism, led the nation-state to use economic policy as the main instrument for procuring power. The mercantilists saw their nations in a struggle for supremacy and focused on conquest and the acquisition of colonies. National defense was the dominant organizing force of mercantilism, much as local defense had been for feudalism. From 1600 to 1667, the great powers of Europe were at peace during only one year.

As a prime example, the French mercantilist system developed by Jean Baptiste Colbert, minister of finance under Louis XIV from 1661 to 1683, brought virtually every aspect of economic production under government control. Companies owned by the Crown were established to trade with France's expanding colonial empire. Shippers and shipbuilders were subsidized by the state. Ports were improved and canals built. French industry and commerce, including luxury industries such as glassmaking and lacemaking, became matters of official concern. Even their production methods and standards of quality were set by the state.

When an industry appeared threatened by foreign competition, Colbert would spring to its defense. For example, he increased the tariffs on imported cloth and subsidized the immigration of Dutch and Flemish weavers and merchants into northern France, probably saving the French cloth industry from the competition of Dutch producers.

However, the costs of Colbert's policies ultimately proved greater than the benefits they created: The French economy did not flourish under his extreme mercantilist practices. Colbert simply got carried away with his regulatory bent. For example, in 1666, his harsh rules stifled initiative in the same weaving industry. The fabrics at Chatillon were to contain precisely 1,216 threads; at Auxerre, Avalon, and two other towns, 1,376; and at Dijon and Selangey, 1,408. Any threads less or more would be confiscated, and after three violations, the merchant would be arrested.

A different approach was clearly needed, and the intellectual ferment of the times would soon supply one, the policy of laissez-faire as first articulated by the physiocrats, and later a basic tenet of Adam Smith's theory of the market mechanism. To understand this revolution in thought, however, we will need to consider its origins as thinkers began to dissect mercantilism.

NOTES

1. Even the Dark Ages were not quite as dim as some historians have written. And, though not within the scope of Western history, the Middle Ages were golden in Byzantium and the Arab world. Our generalizations apply to the dominant attitudes, conditions, and organizations of Western Europe, especially to much of England.

2. By the High Middle Ages (from about 1000 to 1300), the freeing of slaves was so common that the prayer books contained an appropriate ritual. Often the slave was freed posthumously, by will, by the master. For example, in 1049, Gemma, the widow of a functionary in southern Italy and the master of Maria, freed her slave. Maria inherited Gemma's bed and four measures of wheat from the coming harvest.

3. These were Blanche's final words in Williams' *A Streetcar Named Desire* (1947) scene 11.

4. This was a Dane deal, hence the use of "marks." The Danes were in England prior to the Norman Invasion.

   The Domesday Book, an inventory of the wealth of England executed at the orders of William the Conqueror 20 years after the Norman Conquest of 1066, is a floodlight of valuable data following the informational darkness of the "Dark Ages." The other main sources of information on the Middle Ages are clerical writings such as the referenced abbey chronicler.

5. Henry William Spiegel, *The Growth of Economic Thought* (Englewood Cliffs, NJ: Prentice-Hall, 1971), p. 49.

6. John T. Gilchrist, *The Church and Economic Activity in the Middle Ages* (New York: St. Martin's Press, 1969), pp. 50–58.

7. Margery Kempe, *The Book of Margery Kempe*, eds. H.E. Allen and S.B. Meech (Early English Text Society, 1940).

8. Geoffrey Chaucer, *The Canterbury Tales*, translated by Nevill Coghill (London: Penguin Books, 1977), p. 20.

9. Chaucer, *ibid.*, p. 27.

10. See Douglas C. North and Robert Paul Thomas, *The Rise of the Western World: A New Economic History* (Cambridge: Cambridge University Press, 1973), p. 12.

11. Chaucer, *op. cit.*, p. 31.

12. For original data and sources, see North and Thomas, *op. cit.*, pp. 71–74.

13. The pace of the enclosure movement was, of course, different in diverse places. It began in England in the twelfth century and was mostly completed there before 1700 (see J.R. Wordie, "The Chronology of English Enclosure, 1400–1914," *Economic History Review* 36, no. 4 (November 1983): 483–505, November 1983). Yet the enclosures made little progress in the rest of Europe until the nineteenth century.

14. See Louise Collis, *Memoirs of a Medieval Woman* (New York: Harper & Row, 1983), p. 23.

2

Adam Smith's Great Vision

Everyone who has played golf at St. Andrews knows about the Firth of Forth and most would know about Adam Smith (1723–1790), born in Kirkcaldy, a quiet Scottish seaport across the Firth of Forth from Edinburgh, where his father was controller of customs. Later, Smith was to suggest doing away with collectors of tariffs, advice luckily not taken, for he later was made commissioner of customs in Edinburgh.

Smith's life, like the economic world he imagined, was orderly and harmonious. Nothing very dramatic or very terrible ever seems to have happened to him. So far as we know, he had no burning passion for any woman, nor any flaming romance—perhaps because his eyes protruded and his lower lip came closer to his formidable nose than handsomeness ordinarily allows. His head shook from a nervous affliction.

And he was uniquely absentminded. Charles Townshend (1725-1767), an admirer of Smith, as Chancellor of the Exchequer had contributed mightily to the American Revolution by imposing a heavy tariff on American tea (among other goods) and inspiring the Boston Tea Party. One day while showing Townshend the sights of Glasgow (population c. 25,000), Smith took him on a tour of the great tannery and absentmindedly walked directly into the tanning pit. Apparently minimizing this stumble, Townshend paid Smith £500 a year for life to take his young stepson, the Duke of Buccleuch, Smith's celebrated Grand Tour of the continent. Smith, the tutor, and the young Duke left for the south of France in 1764; to relieve the tedium, the tutor began to write a treatise on political economy.

As Townshend knew, Smith was also highly gifted. He studied Greek and Latin literature at Oxford (which he hated). It was on his return to Scotland and to the University of Glasgow that he studied moral philosophy. In the eighteenth century, moral philosophy included natural theology, ethics, jurisprudence, and political economy. The science of economics as Smith conceived it was thus far more broadly based in his day than it is in ours. Smith's lectures on ethics, given when he was a professor of moral philosophy at Glasgow, became his first acclaimed book, *The Theory of Moral Sentiments* (1759).

Philosophers once were thinkers who knew most of whatever scholarship was known. Not surprisingly, then, Adam Smith was informed by the intellectual giants preceding him, not the least of whom was Isaac Newton and the idea of natural law. Before moving on to Smith's economics classic, we tarry a bit to understand the influence of Newton and the Physiocrats, who took natural order very seriously.

NEWTON, SMITH, AND NATURAL LAW

When people hear the name Isaac Newton, most probably think of an apple and the law of gravity. Some may be reminded of celestial mechanics. A few may recall the differential calculus. It is for contributions to physics and mathematics that Newton is ordinarily remembered.

But Newtonian principles, formulated toward the end of the seventeenth century, have had a powerful influence on all branches of science. Newton's description of a clock-like universe, which capped the Scientific Revolution, became the basis for generally accepted notions about the nature of physical reality and thus shaped Western thought for more than 300 years.

Newton's law of universal gravitation states that forces of attraction and repulsion among bodies in space keep them in motion and balance. Gravity, a force like the mainspring of a giant clock, causes the universe to run predictably forever, without breakdowns. The Newtonian system made concrete the idea that all phenomena and all experiences consist of the arrangement of atoms following mechanical, mathematically regular laws.

Newton's mechanics thus brought with it the doctrine of scientific determinism, the principle that all events are the inescapable results of preceding causes. For example, once a planet is found in the scheme of celestial mechanics, its position thereafter is completely and unambiguously disclosed for all time by the knowledge of its position at a single instant in time. Henceforth—until the work of Planck and Einstein in the twentieth century began to have influence—scientists conceived of nature as a giant mechanical contrivance whose behavior could be revealed by observation, experimentation, measurement, and calculation.

The notion of the Cosmos as mechanical, as a finely tuned, clock-like piece of machinery, would quickly become crucial for the world view of people in the early eighteenth century. With Newtonian science, a God emerged who was derived from natural law and in harmony with the order of the universe He made. God, like His universe, was rational and dependable. This optimistic conception of reliability, intensified by the conviction that the Creator was kind and charitable, produced a profound sense of relief. The American clergyman Cotton Mather (1663–1728) could breathe easily for "Gravity leads us to God and brings us very near to Him." To understand the forces of gravity was to better comprehend God's wondrous ways.

Newton's own ways nonetheless were "wondrous" in a non-charitable and unkind way. A president of the Royal Society and the first scientist ever knighted, Newton spent most of his later life embroiled in petty disputes, including one with the German philosopher Gottfried Leibniz, regarding who had first invented calculus. Newton's subsequent behavior casts darkness across his character. Utterly lacking in knightly chivalry, Newton found his harmony in a mechanistic solar system.

Chivalry aside, Newton's genius could not be denied. By the beginning of the eighteenth century, Newton's great scientific synthesis had bred a new world view. Although Newton's principles moved humans from their sure-footing at the center of the Cosmos and toward the insecurity of a sun-centered universe, they were reassured by the orderliness and predictability of a universe governed by natural law with God as the unseen ruler. The idea of a natural order governed by natural law dominated the new world view.

THE PHYSIOCRATS

Because cause and effect were as certain as they were clear in physics and astronomy, many scholars presumed history, human behavior, and economics to be governed by natural laws. If laws are divinely predetermined, scholars reasoned, then people should discover what these laws are so that they can cooperate with the "preestablished" natural order controlling them. After Newton's time, any other world view would be measured and challenged by it.

This concept of order was the basis of the political philosophy of the French physiocrats who preceded and influenced Adam Smith and the English classical economists. The physiocrats, who were led by François Quesnay (1694–1774), the court physician to Louis XV and Madame de Pompadour, were named for **physiocracy**, the law of natural order. The ideas of these philosophers, taken from the natural sciences, were representative of those radiating through the literate classes in France and England by the middle of the eighteenth century.

Science or not, these scribes were rising to the defense of the interests of the peasant farm workers of France and opposing the interests of the French landowners and the mercantilists. Although Paris had become a city of merchants and coffee houses, agriculture remained dominant in France as it was eroded in England. Then as now, French agriculture was more than an occupation, it was a "higher calling," even an artful way of life, at least in the instances of French cheeses and wines.

The physiocratic school proceeded to attack the mercantilists where it hurt most—in their wealth. The physiocrats claimed that land—a gift of nature—was the only real wealth because it enabled agriculture to produce a positive net product in excess of its production costs. Since farming was the only truly productive enterprise, gold was not wealth. Worse, unlike agriculture, manufacturing produced only as much as it received and, therefore, generated no surpluses.

For the agrarian peasants, the picture was even more dispiriting. They received cash payments for their crops but had to pass these monies on as rent to those who had bought or retained the Church's and the king's land, the dreadful landed nobility. The unproductive class of manufacturers was also paid for the goods it produced. All received payment for what they produced except the landowners, who collected rent but produced nothing. With his famous **economic table**, Quesnay went on to illustrate how the surplus from agriculture flowed—like the blood coursing through the veins of Madame de Pompadour—through the entire economy as rents, wages, and purchases, supporting the lowest and the highest social classes.

The physiocrats' attack on mercantilism was intended to eliminate the feudal landholders' tax exemption, the intolerable tax burden placed on the farming peasants, and the protected status of manufacturers. All land should be taxed, concluded the physiocrats, a view that furrowed the brows of only the nobility and the clergy. Free trade, especially in the export of agricultural products, should replace mercantilistic tariffs.

The French landed aristocracy, which conceded far less prestige to the merchants than did their English counterparts, surrounded Louis XV at Versailles. Despite in-palace support from his patients, the king and the madame, Quesnay and the physiocrats could not overpower the nobility. What has survived is the physician's metaphor of the circulation of Madame de Pompadour's blood, the ***tableau économique***.

Adam Smith liked the laissez-faire bent of the physiocrats' thought, but he rejected their attitude regarding the sterility of manufacturing. His ideas would prove to be more durable than those of the physiocrats, partly because he had positive things to say about industry and, more important, because he said them on the eve of the Industrial Revolution in England.

ADAM SMITH'S APPROACH

During his grand tour (1764–1767) Adam Smith visited the leading members of the physiocrats' school in Paris and Versailles in 1765. The physiocrats' motto, *Laissez faire, laissez passer* ("Let things be the way they will!"), was to become his commercial battle cry. The slogan neatly summarizes the shared view of the physiocrats and Smith that the natural advantages of free market competition should not be spoiled by government interference.

Smith feared that commerce would be smothered by the blanket of mercantilist regulations. He noted firsthand that French peasants (those farm workers) still wore wooden shoes or went barefoot, in contrast to even the poor Scottish peasants shod in leather. Like the physiocrats, Smith did not believe trade restrictions to be beneficial or gold to be wealth. Gold was simply money, a wheel of circulation, whereas product was real wealth.

Adam Smith saw an unimpeded expansion of markets as a liberating force, fresh air sweeping across all England and perhaps sweetening even foul France in its rush. Expanded commerce brought new products that would be purchased with the surpluses of the landed aristocracy. The expansion of markets would enable the economy to grow, and workers and merchants would be free at last, dependent on neither lord nor bureaucracy. Smith believed that commerce was a civilizing influence and that only mercantilism stood in its way.

Smith, too, could embrace the physiocrats' image of natural law ruling economic and social behavior, but hopefully in the interests of the merchants and the factory owners. For this, however, Smith could turn to Newton. The Scottish universities were highly active in spreading the ideas of Newton at a time when Smith was one of the great Scots at Glasgow University. In an essay on the history of astronomy, he described Newton's system as "the greatest discovery that ever was made by man." Smith believed in a universe whose harmonious and beneficial organization is proof of the wisdom and goodness of its maker.

He prophetically expected Newton's system to become the model for all scientific systems, and he witnessed his faith in Newton by successfully applying to social and economic phenomena the idea of the universe as a perfectly ordered mechanism operating according to natural laws. The harmony and balance that Smith saw as a natural and desirable consequence of commercial expansion and progress was the source of much of the social optimism of later centuries. And for this social order, mercantilism was unnecessary.

Once the economy had been set in motion by the hand of God, Smith believed, there was no need for any improvements. Attempts to repair it would only upset the mechanism and disturb its ability to function in an orderly way. In his founding of classical economics, Smith was driven by a desire to emulate the most widely respected scientific system of his time. Thus the impact of Newton on social science and society continues to this day.

INDUSTRY AND THE WEALTH OF NATIONS

Adam Smith's *An Inquiry into the Nature and Causes of the Wealth of Nations*, published in 1776, began a revolution in economic thinking. This remarkable book became the basis for the new academic field of political economy and the centerpiece for the first school in economics, the classical school. It also became an important political force, helping to change English economic policy during the next century.

A new perception of economics was required by a rapidly expanding commercial world in which the familiar tradition and command systems were retreating. The rise of the science of economics as a separate discipline thus paralleled the flowering of the market system, the accumulation of capital in private hands, and a dizzying upward spiral in the growth of the industrial factory system.

Spinning like a tornado around virtually every great book is paradox. Today, Adam Smith is widely hailed as "the spokesman of manufacturing interests" and "the prophet of the Industrial Revolution." Yet the thrust of *The Wealth of Nations* is against "the mean rapacity, the monopolizing spirit of merchants and manufacturers, who neither are, nor ought to be, the rulers of mankind." Why? Because the merchants and master-manufacturers are the builders of the despicable mercantilism he attacks. Oddly, too, there is little in the book to suggest the coming of the Industrial Revolution, and for good reason.

True, in 1613, John Browne's armament factory in Brenchley was employing 200 people in the casting of guns, which made it a sizable factory. By the time *The Wealth of Nations* appeared, the typical water-driven factory held 300 to 400 workers. Adam Smith, however, was aware that only 20 or 30 of such factories could be found in the British Isles.

A century of successful exploration, slave trading, merchandising, piracy, and territorial conquest had made Great Britain one of the world's wealthiest, most powerful nations by 1750. Although much of this wealth had gone to the Crown and the nobility, a good deal of it was filtering down to an expanding commercial middle class. This change in the distribution of income created an expanding market for food, utensils, ale, wine, clothes, and so on. Rising consumer demand, in turn, confirmed the need for improvements in industrial procedures.

In a way, Britain was ready for the Industrial Revolution in the seventeenth century. Yet the industrial explosion did not occur until almost two centuries later. A look at British industry in the early 1700s will help us understand why.

Efficient, large-scale manufacturing is next to impossible using wooden machines; iron and steel are essential for their durability. Iron was first cast with the heat of firewood and charcoal. By 1527, coal was being mined in the lordship of Bromfield, where a 21-year mining lease was granted to one Lancelot Lother.[1] Around 1620, John Rochier, a Frenchman living in England, applied for a patent to produce steel by using hard coal. By 1635, steel of sufficient quality to meet the needs of the cutlery industry was being produced in Sheffield and Rotherham. Sheffield was said to be "a cut above the rest." Later, James Watt's rotary-motion steam engine (designed in the basement beneath Adam Smith's office at Glasgow) supplied a more efficient and reliable energy source for the blast required for coke-smelting and steel-making.

Despite all this activity, British iron and steel production was actually declining in the late seventeenth and early eighteenth centuries. To a great extent, the social attitudes of the landed gentry, who owned the land where the coal seams were discovered and were prominent in both the coal and iron industries, were responsible. They were more interested in quick profits than in the investment of capital amounts too great for quick paybacks. Moreover, the highest purpose of the ambitious trader or small manufacturer continued to be the purchase of a landed estate, wealth still being associated by tradition with land, not with the profits of the rabble running manufacturing. Much of the capital flowing into Britain from slaves, tobacco, and other trade also went into conspicuous consumption—elegant estates and fine gowns. It took a new kind of attitude to accumulate finance capital for building industry.

The farmers who worked in the Lancashire cotton industry in its early stages had that special attitude. For example, the expansion of Matthew Boulton's cotton mill was made possible by his father's lifetime savings in the hardware industry. The brewing industry was dominated by the Quakers, whose commercial instincts were quietly parsimonious. In good times and bad, the Quakers seemed good for what "aled" the Englishman.

Even so, Adam Smith never saw most of the features that came to be called the Industrial Revolution. Indeed, in France, where Smith had begun to write *The Wealth of Nations*, even agriculture was backward. By 1776, the shops and mines of the emerging industrial age could be seen in the English countryside, but giant factories, factory towns, and armies of workers had yet to appear. Though

Napoleon I (1769–1821) said it later, with intent to insult, Smith also called Britain a "nation of shopkeepers."

In the bustling world of commerce at the edge of the early Industrial Revolution, Smith was the right scholar for the time. It was too much to expect religion to cover all the alleged sins of the rapidly expanding merchant class, and the merchants needed a new economic philosophy. The merchants and the rising manufacturing class seized on those ideas from Smith that provided justification for a growing economy in which money facilitates the efficient market exchange of goods and services.[2] Adam Smith is remembered not for his intent, but rather for the social uses to which a distillation of his ideas was put. Ever since, Smith's ideas have been put into service by commercial interests.

SMITH'S THEORY OF ECONOMIC DEVELOPMENT AND GROWTH

The Role of Self-Interest

Historically, self-interest has been as unpopular as money lenders. In Smith's *The Theory of Moral Sentiments*, selfishness is transformed. We are able to put ourselves in the position of a third person, an enlightened impartial observer, and in this way have empathy for someone in trouble, thus softening the sharper edges of our self-interest.

In Smith's *Wealth of Nations*, the individual pursuit of self-interest in a two-way exchange economy guarantees social harmony. In his economic behavior, an individual neither intends to promote the public interest nor know that he is promoting it. He intends only to provide for his own security. Smith wrote, "It is not from the benevolence of the butcher, the brewer, or the baker, that we expect our dinner, but from their regard to their own interest." Such self-interest and economic self-reliance were perfectly natural, grounded in "the desire of bettering our condition," which "comes with us from the womb, and never leaves us till we go into the grave."[3]

Economic self-interest is morally beneficial, too: "I have never known much good done," says Smith, "by those who affected to trade for the public good." But the self-interested action of one person is "good" only if it is limited by the self-interested actions of others.

The Division of Labor

Smith shifts the focus of economics away from the mercantilist's fixation on precious metals as wealth and toward the production of goods and services as wealth. Growth in the production and sales of goods and services increased the wealth of nations. By "wealth," Adam Smith meant the annual flow of what we now call gross domestic product (GDP). The starter key to the growth of wealth in a nation was the division of labor—the breaking down of a particular task into a number of separate tasks, each performed by a different person. Different specialist-occupations would develop, and the skill of each laborer would increase as the worker concentrated on doing only one thing well.

In a famous example, Smith calculated that ten men dividing labor in a pin factory—one draws out the wire, another straightens it, a third cuts it, a fourth points it, a fifth grinds the top for receiving the head (which requires two or three distinct operations), and so on—could make 48,000 pins a day, or 4,800 each. One man doing all the steps could make perhaps 1, perhaps 20!

People are willing to specialize because, by working in a job in which they are most productive, the workers can earn sufficient income to purchase commodities they produce less efficiently. For example, the excellent baker does not necessarily have to be a good candlestick maker; rather, by being able to produce two loaves of bread for every candlestick produced by someone else, the baker can exchange two loaves of bread, which he makes quite easily, for every candlestick he needs, which he cannot make as well as the candlestick maker. Such exchanges were not done directly by barter but with money as the go-between.

The expansion of markets facilitates the specialization of labor because greater numbers of people consuming greater quantities give rise to the organization of more and more production in longer production runs in a factory system. One way to enlarge the market is to pursue free trade in those goods in which nations enjoyed **absolute advantage**. Tea could be produced in India and Ceylon using less labor than would be needed for its production in the American colonies. Likewise, the colonies could produce tobacco with less labor than could India and Ceylon. India and Ceylon, Smith would say, have an absolute advantage in tea, and the American colonies have an absolute advantage in tobacco.

Capital Accumulation

If the division of labor starts up the growth process, capital accumulation keeps it humming. According to Smith, the capital stock of the factory owner consists of fixed capital (machines, tools, plant) and circulating capital, a fund used for buying raw materials and for paying labor. The latter, a **wages fund**, grows as production and profits expand. Wages are paid to labor in advance of production and sales because of the time elapsing while production takes place.

Careful savings by the manufacturer (as the sole owner of an enterprise) lead to capital accumulation. The national output grows from such accumulation, and thus payments to workers can increase as manufacturers use savings from expanding profits to hire more workers. The workers require as a minimum, food, clothes, and lodging. Then as workers spend more on necessities, total demand increases, and even more is produced in the next period. And economic growth is good!

NATURAL LAW AND PRIVATE PROPERTY

By the mid-eighteenth century, most educated people believed that God did not control people and events personally but only indirectly, by means of laws at work in nature. Isaac Newton's story of God creating the universe as a self-propelled machine gave a more lasting spin to the virtue of self-interested individualism. After all, what harm can one worker or one manufacturer do to the rest of society as long as the outcomes will always be determined by natural law? This view was bolstered in politics by John Locke (1632–1704), who claimed that natural laws and natural rights existed prior to governments. Never mind empathy; persons need be responsible only to themselves.

Besides justifying ungoverned individualism, this Newtonian-Lockean world view also vindicated private property. Private thrift and prudence by individuals were now rewarded on earth, and sufficient savings would lead to the ownership of private property. And if one had accumulated a great amount of private property, it must have been the machine's will. Once property was accumulated, its protection was a natural right because it belonged to the one who produced it. Accumulation became virtuous.

Smith distilled Locke's natural rights argument in favor of private property and its protection until it was 86 percent proof. Government was to be feared because it alone could strip persons of their private property and hence also deprive individuals of their liberty. The sanctity of private property became another justification for a laissez-faire economic policy.

Smith transformed the virtues of natural law into the requisites of what later would be called capitalism. Profits are "good" because they provide the incentive for master manufacturer's savings. Inside every manufacturer beats the heart of a Scotsman. Capital accumulation is "good" because its technological results create a division of labor, which in turn enhances productivity and the expansion of international trade. Without privately owned property, the master could not assemble the means to build and equip factories and provide employment for themselves and a wages fund for others. All this was best for society and therefore should proceed naturally, without any governmental restrictions.

SMITH'S THEORY OF VALUE

One of the most difficult problems in economic theory is what determines the value of a product and the distribution of the income from its sale among all those who have a hand in producing it. Economists call the solution to the problem "the theory of value." Adam Smith did not give a complete solution; he did, however, provide *his* explanation.

The Labor Theory of Value

A **labor theory of value** gives the value of a product as being equivalent to the labor time required to produce it. Adam Smith introduced the idea only as a historian looking for value in a nonmonetized economy. In the "early and rude state of society" preceding the accumulation of capital and the ownership of land, Smith said, commodities exchange in proportion to the amounts of labor required to produce them. In a nation of hunters, he suggested in a famous example, if it takes twice the labor to kill a beaver as to kill a deer, one beaver will exchange for two deer. In a nation of hunters, money would not to be involved in such transactions. Hunters' incomes can be counted in terms of the numbers of beavers and deer they kill.

Even in the primitive economy of hunters, however, specialization is important. Hunters who are also runners will probably shoot more deer than beaver. Hunters who are good at sitting and waiting will be successful with beaver. Total "production" increases—more deer and more beaver—if hunters specialize in their best pursuit. Also, exchange or trade in animals will mean that all hunters ultimately gain more if they each stick to hunting only one kind of animal.

In this primitive hunting economy, we cannot make a distinction between the value of the commodity itself and the value of the amount of time required to produce it, the two values being essentially the same. In a modern economy, however, goods will be exchanged for money. Profits will be paid to those who own capital and rent to those who own land. In other words, there is a manufacturer and a landlord with whom the value of a product (the income from its sale) must be shared. Either (1) the income going to the manufacturer and landlord is an earned reward or (2) workers are being deprived of an income share from the product that is rightfully theirs.

Which of these alternatives did Smith believe to be true? Even though he writes that the worker must always "lay down the same portion of his ease, liberty and his happiness," Smith has the employer paying labor a wage differing from the value labor places on itself. Smith ends up making little use of a labor theory of value.

The Market Mechanism and Its Magical Returns

Smith does not deny the right of the capital owner to receive profits or the landlord to receive rent. Indeed, he depicts the presence of these income shares as "natural" in an economy growing and accumulating capital. The wages fund consists of advances to workers for which the fund's owner, the manufacturer, is entitled to a return. Argues Smith, an average rate of wages, profits, and rents natural with respect to its time and place exists in every society. The interests of workers and landlords are harmonized by the progress embodied in capital accumulation.

The money price of a commodity is also a part of this natural economic balance. When a product sells for a price just sufficient to compensate the worker, the manufacturer, and the landlord at the prevailing, average rates of compensation, it is being sold at its natural price, or for exactly what it is "worth." In Smith's words, "The natural price, therefore, is, as it were, the central price to which the prices of all commodities are continually gravitating." Changes in supply and demand will cause the price of a commodity to rise and fall around the natural price, but the effects of these fluctuations on price are temporary because, according to Smith, the long-run natural price is set by the unit costs of production.[4]

In the long run, then, the price of every commodity resolves itself into the sum of the "natural rates of wages, profit and rent." All industries have constant costs in production, and any change in demand alters only output, not price. In the short run (a period when the manufacturer's productivity cannot be changed), prices are determined by the interplay of supply and demand under competitive conditions.[5]

This whole process—the ebbing and flowing of prices—is part of the market mechanism, the natural laws at work in the world of commerce. Individual self-interest is the motivating force in this free market system. The built-in regulator keeping the economy from flying apart is competition.

If a town's blacksmith charges an exorbitant price for horseshoing, competitors will soon build blacksmith shops in town. Unless the blacksmith then lowers the price, he will be driven out of business by competition. Buyers, who are aware of all the outlets for horseshoing, will avoid the higher-priced shop and shod their horses elsewhere. A large number of sellers, the consumers' knowledge of prices and shops, and the mobility of economic resources limit the ability of any single supplier to influence prices. The self-interest of one is held sway by the self-interest of others. An individual is "led by an invisible hand to promote an end which was no part of his intention."

The laws of the market mechanism also determine the quantity of goods produced. An increased demand for horse whips will increase their price at the current level of production, motivating manufacturers to make more of them, thus limiting the rise in price. However, resources used in the production of a commodity, say bread, already will have been shifted into the horse whip industry. More horse whips is precisely what society "wanted" in the first place. Smith emphasizes the ascent of liberty under such competition. The consumer has become king, shoving aside the feudal noble, mercantilist planners and monopolists.[6]

The awe-inspiring laws of the market mechanism also regulate the income of the workers and manufacturers. When prices begin to rise in the horse whip business, horse whip profits will rise, too, until competition steps in and limits each manufacturer's profits. If a worker demands "too high" a wage, the manufacturer will simply hire another, "competing" worker. Of if wages rise in one occupation, such as furniture making, workers will move into that occupation for the higher income until a "natural" adjustment occurs: The increased supply of labor in furniture making limits the rate of wage (and income) increases.

The market is its own guardian; it is completely self-regulating. Even with its ups and downs, price will only temporarily vary away from the actual average cost of producing a good, that is, the natural price. The producers of commodities and services will be producing what individuals in society really want. Workers will be paid in accordance with what they can contribute to the production of those goods society desires.

The popularity of *The Wealth of Nations* is primarily attributable to three specific forces.

(1) Smith's antifeudalist, antimercantilist, antimonopolistic, even antigovernment views struck a responsive chord in many of his readers. Expanding commerce had brought a measure of liberty and security to individuals. People whose forebears had lived in servile dependency upon royal masters and suffered continual warfare saw feudalism breaking down with the rise of a money exchange economy. They saw the pro-war policies of the mercantilists diminishing as heated trade with neighboring states melted political disagreement. Smith spoke of the beneficence of the Newtonian universe, of new liberties through natural law, and of the necessity for release from the arbitrariness of government, all of which found an eager, receptive audience in England, France, and elsewhere.

(2) Eighteenth-century England was not outrageously different from Adam Smith's vision. England really was a nation of shopkeepers engaged in lively, rivalrous competition, and the average factory was quite small. Price changes often did evoke changes in the volume of production. Wage changes did sometimes eventually lead to shifts in occupation.

(3) The book was optimistic and democratic. No longer was the potential for sharing in the growing wealth of England limited to the wealthy landowners. In truth, from the point of view of the ruling

classes, Adam Smith was a radical. The rulers saw no advantage in a decentralized economic system in which the government's role was replaced by the "natural order." The French Revolution followed *The Wealth of Nations* by 13 years, and many English people found in Smith's doctrines of freedom and his criticism of public policies a subversive spirit like that which lit the fires of the French revolt.

Smith's view that the market mechanism and individual rights are linked has proved to be enduring. In Smith's view, human welfare is at its highest when unrestrained markets serve the needs and desires of the consumer. These requirements and wishes are met by the natural tendency of producers to manufacture and sell what the consumer really wants.

Smith eliminated the old painful moral dilemma between individual selfishness and social order. As long as competition reigned as the great equalizer and persons were otherwise civilized, there was no conflict between self-servers in the economy and maximum social welfare. Smith's economics then is aligned with his sentiments.

Smith provided a vision for economic science, and many economists today still accept it. The natural market system of balances, they say, follows a path of increasing national wealth. The natural tendency to trade and exchange at costs and prices held low by competitive bidding leads to the increased efficiency garnered through specialization. Specialization combined with saving results in capital accumulation. Growth automatically follows. Smith's views were interpreted in such a way that they had a strong influence on the most enduring general policy conclusion in economic history: The marketplace would work properly only if let alone—the policy of laissez-faire.

SMITH, REALITY, AND THE VISIONS TO COME

Smith's vision of commerce was influential and widely acclaimed in the Western world. Later economists would develop Smith's theories and make them more precise, but none would match the richness of his explanation of life under a competitive market system.

There are, however, significant differences between Adam Smith's view and later defenders of free-market capitalism as a system necessarily driven by selfishness and greed at any cost. The self-interest in Smith's economics is acceptable to him only because societal harmony is its consequence. There is no contradiction with his earlier observation that, no matter how selfish a person may be, "There are evidently some principles in his nature which interest him in the fortune of others and render their happiness necessary to him though he derives nothing from it except the pleasure of seeing it."[7] A person's empathy with others will deter undesirable social behavior; the pursuit of wealth is only one aspect of a person's desire for self-betterment.

We nonetheless cannot lose sight of those who seized upon those Smithian ideas most serviceable to their cause. Smith may have been absent-minded but he was not oblivious to weaknesses in his own system and the special interests around him.

Although the division of labor gives rise to the wealth of nations, the monotonous life of the detail worker "corrupts the courage of his mind, and makes him regard with abhorrence the irregular, uncertain, and adventurous life of a soldier," increasing the cost of national defense to fellow citizens, because he may become "incapable of defending his country in war," thus requiring government actions. The ease and security of the still mighty landowners would also leave them "indolent and ignorant."

His doubts about natural liberty were quickly and too conveniently forgotten. Smith found employers everywhere conspiring to keep wages below the level required to keep the worker "tolerably well-fed, clothed and lodged." Smith also found merchants and manufacturers quick to attack high wages but slow to see the "pernicious effects of their own gains." He was concerned about manufacturers becoming so powerful as to have an unfair advantage over workers. The business master, he argues, can always hold out much longer in a labor dispute: "A landlord, a farmer, a master manufacturer, or merchant, though they did not employ a single workman, could generally live a year or two upon [their] stock....

Many workmen could not subsist a week, few could subsist a month, and scarcely any a year without employment." And so, in the long-run "the workman may be as necessary to his master as his master is to him, but the necessity is not so immediate."

By the time the disciplined reader lays down *The Wealth of Nations*, he will have found some sour notes in the purported harmony of Newton's natural order. Smith writes in a famous passage: "People of the same trade seldom meet together, even for merriment and diversion, but the conversation ends in a conspiracy against the public, or in some contrivance to raise prices." Such giants as the East India Company, a mercantilistic monopoly chartered by the British Crown, went beyond the propriety of small private businesses, and Smith loathed it. "Artificial" prices above natural prices were an undesirable consequence of legal regulations, exclusive corporate privileges, statutes of apprenticeship, and monopolies.

Though he was strongly opposed to intervention in the market mechanism, Smith certainly was not opposed to all governmental activity. In general, he favored government provision of military security, the administration of justice, and privately unprofitable public works and institutions. When we turn to specifics, the list runs to 15 items, among which are the government's right to impose tariffs to counter tariffs, to punish business fraud, to regulate banking, to provide post offices, highways, harbors, bridges and canals, and so on. Even so, only if private domestic markets were unfettered would the consumer continue to reign as king. For the same reason, Smith also opposed monopolization of the production of a commodity by one producer. Yet, on balance, Smith considered the civilizing effects of commerce to be a blessing worth defending against the medieval and mercantilist forms of social organization.

The Wealth of Nations remains one of the great books of Western civilization. Like all great books, it is important at a number of different levels: (1) as an inspirational polemic rejecting mercantilism in England (though it takes 200 pages for an already sick mercantilism to die); (2) as a philosophy imposing order on social chaos; and (3) as a scientific economics system focusing on the market system.

The themes of polemic, philosophy, and science are intertwined; one strand cannot be followed without the other two.

The idea of economic growth did not even exist during the Roman Empire or the Middle Ages. We therefore move on to complete the setting in which the struggles of the other classical economists took place—the English Industrial Revolution and its political environment—and to better understand their motivations and ideas. These thinkers were inspired by life in their times.

NOTES

1. William Rees, *Industry Before the Industrial Revolution* (Cardiff: University of Wales Press, 1968), Vol. 1, p. 72.
2. Smith wrote at a time when "manufacturers" were primarily identified with the half-entrepreneur, half-merchant of the domestic handicraft system. He used the terms *master, manufacturer,* and *master manufacturer* interchangeably. *Master* denoted both the craft skills of the manufacturer and the master-worker managerial relation. Later, Karl Marx (1818–1883) befittingly named the manufacturers *capitalists.*
3. The quotes in this chapter from *The Wealth of Nations* are known to most economists. They have been repeated often and reside in the public domain. In order to reduce unnecessary clutter, I do not footnote and cite the quotations by page numbers. The diligent scholar nonetheless can find all the words in the expected places of the definitive edition of *The Wealth of Nations* edited by Edwin Cannan in 1904, reprinted as Adam Smith, *An Inquiry into the Nature and Causes of the Wealth of Nations,* ed. Edwin Cannan (New York: Random House, 1937).
4. In a classic example, Smith refers to the effect of a public mourning on the price of black cloth. A temporary shortage of black cloth raises the price of mourning cloth and the wages of tailors but has no effect on the wages of weavers because the scarcity is transitory. However, with the shift to black, the price of silk of color slumps, and the wages of workers producing it falls.
5. In the course of his Book I, Chapter 7, of *The Wealth of Nations,* Adam Smith leaves out only homogeneity of the product as a condition of competition in a discussion modern textbook authors can only envy.
6. Indeed Adam Smith had one of the first of good words in economic thought for the consumer. "Consumption," he wrote, "is the sole end and purpose of

all production; and the interest of the producer ought to be attended to, only so far as it may be necessary for promoting that of the consumer."

7. Adam Smith, *The Theory of Moral Sentiments*, ed. Ernest Rhys (London: Everyman's Library, 1910), p. 162.

3

Bentham and Malthus: The Hedonist and the "Pastor"

Adam Smith's vision became the basis for a school of thought. The classical economists, the first of whom was Adam Smith and the last, John Stuart Mill (1806–1873), dominated political economy for at least a century in England. Following the paths pioneered by Adam Smith, the classical economists lobbied for the freedom to own and move private capital such as those high-speed pin-making machines. Their objective was political and revolutionary: They wanted the control of the government taken forever from the hands of the landlords and placed in the hands of the merchants and manufacturers. The classical economists were often significant voices in the political conflicts of their day, including debates over free markets, the abolition of tariffs, welfare legislation, and free competition among manufacturers. Indeed, two were members of Parliament.

What Adam Smith could only imagine, the other classical economists could observe first hand. They were able to see the Industrial Revolution in full flower, and British classical economics emerged from the political struggles of that revolution. What captivated Smith about the small pin factory was the division of labor, not the machines, and his ideas were kept alive mainly by his attack on the old order of the landed aristocracy and on mercantilism. Smith nonetheless had a vision of an industrial revolution, and, had he lived to see it, he would no doubt have been impressed by pin machinery.

A SKETCH OF THE CLASSICAL ECONOMISTS

Though the classical economists differed sharply on details, they agreed in their condemnation of governmental provision of all but military security, criminal justice, and privately unprofitable public works and institutions. Any regulations beyond those termed "rightful acts of government" were considered ruinous to commerce and industry. This prevailing attitude was shared and succinctly expressed by essayist Thomas Babington Macaulay:

> Our rulers will best promote the improvement of the nation by confining themselves strictly to their legitimate duties, by leaving capital to find its most lucrative course, commodities their fair price, industry and intelligence their natural reward, idleness and folly their natural punishment, by maintaining peace, by defending property, by diminishing the price of law and by observing strict economy in every department of the state. Let the Government do this, the people will assuredly do the rest.[1]

The most prominent classical economists following Smith were Thomas Malthus, David Ricardo, James Mill and John Stuart Mill, but the ideas of two others—J.B. Say and Jeremy Bentham—also influenced economic thought.

They were nineteenth century, middle-class liberals, sharing a belief in the liberal tradition of laissez-faire and private property protection as described by Macaulay. Nineteenth century British liberalism would emancipate the middle class from domination by the government, a liberalism a world apart from the contemporary American variety, in which government activism on social issues figures so prominently.

Still, they preferred disputation to complete agreement. All were in search of economic laws or a consistent and dependable truth.

The writings of Smith, Bentham, Ricardo, and the Mills, in the great tradition of Scotch and English thought beginning in the eighteenth century, were characterized by a love of truth combined with clarity of expression and freedom from extreme sentimentality. The continuity in this thought or feeling extends to others—Locke, Hume, and Charles Darwin. All had a great influence on the way people thought.

David Ricardo (with the help and encouragement of Bentham and James Mill) developed the most influential refinement of Smith's vision in his three editions of *Principles of Political Economy and Taxation* (1817, 1819 and 1921). James Mill provided a well-written summary of classical economics, *Elements of Political Economy* (1821); his son, the economist and social philosopher John Stuart Mill, later wrote *Principles of Political Economy* (1848), which went through many editions and was still in use as a textbook in the United States as late as the 1920s. As for Malthus, he was both a follower of Bentham and a disbeliever. He engaged in two historic but friendly debates, first with Bentham and James Mill and then against his friend David Ricardo.

J.B. Say was a leading French advocate of laissez-faire with radical views. Although Say had incurred the imperial displeasure of Napoleon Bonaparte, the classical economists, Malthus excepted, embraced his law of markets, which denied the possibility of a "general glut," or oversupply of goods, and had been developed in Say's *Traite d'economie politique* (1803) and by James Mill in 1808.

According to **Say's law**, production under free market competition will always generate an equivalent amount of demand for the goods produced. If a particular commodity is overproduced, a partial glut might result, but it would automatically self-correct under conditions of competition. If one commodity is in excess supply and is selling at a loss, another will be produced in insufficient quantity and be selling at a sufficiently high price to attract the unemployed resources. As Say put it, "The creation of one product immediately opened a vent for other products." Total demand would always be sufficient.

Like Smith, Say empowered money only as a medium of exchange for goods, not as an asset that people might want to hold for other reasons. Hoarding of money therefore was thought to be irrational, and no one hesitated to spend money on something of value—namely, other goods. Savings would immediately be spent for investment goods and labor, which meant an income receipt by the resource suppliers. Again, total demand would always equal total supply. As a result of this wondrous belief in the impossibility of general gluts, where goods in great quantities go unbought, the classical economists did not focus on the possibility of economic stagnation. And so like Smith before them, they saw no need for government assistance and embraced laissez-faire.

It is difficult to avoid brief mention here of Karl Marx, sometimes viewed as a second branch or rotten branch of the classical tree. In the first volume of *Das Kapital: A Critique of Political Economy* (1867), Marx adopted some of the ideas of Smith and Ricardo—such as mistrust of monopolies and the labor theory of value. But much of what Marx had to say conflicted with Smith's idea that social harmony would arise from the pursuit of self-interest and with Ricardo's and Malthus's defense of laissez-faire. Since Marx viewed capitalism as only one stage of development in an economy, it is appropriate to treat him apart from the classical school (look for Marx in Chapter 6).

The classicals were diverse in other ways: Malthus and J.S. Mill were, for different reasons, near the "radical" fringe of the new political economy. Malthus did not share Smith's optimism, believing instead that unbridled population growth would rob people of the benefits of capitalism. Mill (and Bentham before him) challenged the classical school's faith in the universality and permanence of natural law. Most of all, Mill's humanitarianism, warmth, and empathy for the poor and the downtrodden were not shared by many of the other classical economists, especially not by Malthus.

I pause, for repetition often serves a useful purpose. For the classical economists, the chase of the truth always was afoot. Overarching the optimism or pessimism, glut or equilibrium, moralism or reason, and the invisible or visible hand is a search for economic laws.

CLASSICAL MOMENTS AND THE INDUSTRIAL REVOLUTION

If Adam Smith was able to observe factories, some thriving industry, and markets before 1750, then what constituted the Industrial Revolution? It was the explosion in industrial output, a boom compared with anything before. After 1780, about every measure of production sharply speeded up in a race to end the century. Between 1780 and 1850, the growth of the British national product per person averaged from 1.0 to 1.5 percent per year, a rate that doubled real output per person every half century. By 1826 Benjamin Disraeli (1804–1881), later the Prime Minister of England, could write: "Man is not the creature of circumstances. Circumstances are creatures of men."[2]

Despite Abraham Darby's 1709 use of coke in steel-making, no other entrepreneur followed Darby's example until mid-century. Then, the number of blast furnaces quadrupled between 1760 and 1790 to over 80. By 1830, there were 372 and in 1852, 655. The production of pig iron was some 30,000 tons in 1770, one-quarter million tons by 1805, nearly three-quarter million tons by 1830, and two million tons by 1850.

The spectacular growth of the cotton textile industry is reflected by raw cotton imports used in cloth production. In 1850, raw cotton imports were 620 million pounds compared to only eight million pounds at the start of the American Revolution. There were fewer than two million cotton spindles in 1780, but 21 million by 1850. Power looms were introduced in 1820; there were 50,000 looms by 1830, and 250,000 by 1850.[3]

Like most revolutions, the Industrial Revolution, no matter how explosive, was conceived in the sands of time. Only later could historians begin to see, retrospectively, the forces behind the Revolution, perhaps the most dramatic being the great acceleration in new inventions. The Royal Society of London for the Promotion of Natural Knowledge, the society of which Isaac Newton was an early president, was granted royal patronage in 1662, thus stimulating a general interest in science and enhancing its prestige. A substantial and important minority of manufacturers in the late eighteenth century were members of such scientific societies and therefore aware of scientific developments. Manufacturing being improved by scientific progress was an accepted fact. Moreover, the inventions came in convenient clusters. Before 1734 came the coke smelting of iron, the Newcomen steam engine, and John Kay's flying shuttle (for weaving). But, predictably, the greatest concentration came in the last third of the century.

Richard Arkwright, a barber who clipped hair near the weaving districts of Manchester, saw the need for a machine that would enable the spinners of the in-home (cottage) textile industry to keep up with the more technically advanced weavers. James Hargreaves met this need with his famous spinning jenny (patented in 1770), which increased each spinner's output eight-fold. With two rich hosiers, Jedediah Strutt and Samuel Need, Arkwright also produced the water frame (1769), which enabled weavers for the first time to use cotton instead of linen thread in the vertical threads of cotton cloth and thus to spin cloth of much finer quality. A decade later, Crompton's "mule," so-called because it combined the functions of the spinning jenny and the water frame, pulled spinners' productivity up from eight-fold to ten-fold. The British cotton industry was transformed.

Thomas Newcomen's early eighteenth century invention, the steam engine, had been used mainly to pump water out of the coal mines, where fuel was cheap and abundant. But after James Watt, Adam Smith's friend, discovered how to lower fuel consumption, the steam engine became more widely useful. By 1800, there were perhaps 1,000 of the machines puffing away in Britain, with about 250 of those in the cotton industry.

Steam power was a liberating force for large-scale capitalism. Steam, unlike water power, could be deployed anywhere, closer to markets where raw materials could be bought and finished products sold, and closer to population centers. Soon, cities were surrounded by factories and enveloped in black smoke.

A later development in steel-making was puddling (1784), by which iron was converted to steel by frequent stirring in the presence of oxidizing substances. Then, with improved steel, the first useful threshing machine was built for agriculture (1786), and the lathe was improved for industry (1794). The lathe and other machine tools could be used to make other machines; thus began a new era in which machines were used to produce other machines. Financial capital accumulation was merely important; the technology of the machines purchased with such funds was crucial.[4]

Luckily, foreign markets for British goods grew much faster between 1700 and 1750 than did England's home markets. While domestic industries were increasing production by only seven percent, the export industries output soared nearly 80 percent. Thus, foreign markets sponged up the spillover of these new, improved products being produced at falling production costs. This trade, as Adam Smith had promised, was facilitated by the rapid breakdown of mercantilist restrictions in England, in sharp contrast to the absolutism, the Colbertism, and the stagnation of the French economy during the same period.

But, of course, people cannot eat cotton, steel, or machines. We cannot ignore the favorable influences from agricultural improvements. Increased food supplies from rising agriculture productivity led not only to population growth, but more demand for new products. By 1730, the precarious balance between harvests and population had tipped in favor of feeding the people, though not all of them all the time. This increased productivity released cheap labor from food production.

Even so, only a special social environment would allow James Watt to come together with Matthew Boulton, already a wealthy manufacturer of simply made buttons and buckles, to form a company for manufacturing steam engines. The British were greatly concerned with property rights so that patents protected the works of the British inventors like Watt, and, for the Boulton's, property was made relatively secure by laws favoring its accumulation. This environment allowed Richard Arkwright (who employed 150 to 600 workers in many factories) and other industrialists of modest beginnings to retire as landed millionaires. This capital accumulation so highly prized in Adam Smith's vision of economic growth, was sustained in Britain by the feudal institution of inheritance. Likewise, Arkwright, the once lowly barber, was knighted Sir Richard.

THE EVAPORATION OF SMITHIAN HARMONY

It is perhaps impossible to overstate the effects of the Industrial Revolution on Britain and, in time, on the whole world. Many of the traditional modes of life were destroyed or changed beyond recognition. For some, life became better; for others, it became worse; but for everyone, life was transformed.

The rapidly growing population was being pushed out of (by rising productivity) or pulled from (by relatively rising wages) the country and the towns' cottage industries and poured into the cities' factories. The inevitable urban growth brought with it crowded conditions, pollution, disease, crime, and a host of other ills. The prevalence of these and other social problems is universally recognized by historians.

During this period of rapid industrial growth, the landed nobility was benefitting from the rising price of food. And the rising, hardworking industrialist class was expressing self-righteous indignation both at the landowners who could profit while sitting on their lands, and at the factory workers who wanted more jobs and better wages from a factory system built by risk-taking industrialists. Was this what Adam Smith meant by the all-encompassing harmony of interests? Not only did these conditions encourage pessimism, but they also invited explanation. The other classical economists would provide plenty of both.

For these economists, "harmony" was mostly something to be enjoyed in a musical performance; elsewhere, and particularly in economics, it had vanished with the eighteenth century. The other classical economists heard dissonance as the various social classes—usually defined by their ownership of capital, land, or their own labor—began to clash. Some saw a danger that the conservative landed gentry would get in the way of industrial progress. Others worried that industrialization was not progress. The discordant times stimulated some cacophonous economic debates.

THE PHILOSOPHICAL RADICALS, ESPECIALLY JEREMY BENTHAM

Most of post-Smithian economics is influenced one way or another by the Philosophical Radicals. These thinkers attempted to introduce a principle, analogous to Newton's in the natural sciences, on which a science of moral and social life could be founded. Beyond this, they hoped to provide the basis for a reform movement known as **Philosophical Radicalism**.

The movement is primarily associated with Jeremy Bentham (1748–1832), who had a major influence on his dear friend James Mill (1773–1836). Bentham (more than Smith) was influenced by the eighteenth century Scottish historian and philosopher David Hume, who taught that all our ideas are derived from impressions, and therefore human behavior is ultimately the result of sense experience rather than reason. Bentham's social ethics had pleasure associated with moral goodness and pain with evil.

Of the two voices, Bentham's became the more respected later for its originality, despite the paucity of his writings. Bentham has had a strong influence on economics as a thinker and practical reformer. A rather strange person whose eccentricities grew with age, Bentham (an Oxford graduate) founded the University of London and left to it his entire estate. But his will required his remains to be present once a year at meetings of the university board. And so it is to this day. Stuffed and dressed, his skeleton sits in a chair, holding a cane in a gloved hand. To add to the macabre effect, a wax head surveys the room from atop the body, while Bentham's actual head (preserved) lies between his feet. Since his death, Bentham has not missed a meeting!

Bentham, somber and methodical in youth but whimsical and youthful as an old man, developed a congenial philosophy, the central doctrine of which was **hedonism**: Whatever is good is also necessarily pleasant. The sole aim of life should be to seek one's own greatest happiness.

This doctrine is rescued from infantile selfishness, however, by being combined with **utilitarianism**, the belief that an individual's conduct as well as government policies should be directed toward promoting the greatest happiness for the greatest number of persons. Legal, moral, and social sanctions act as constraints on acts of individualistic self-interest that might impede the greater good. Bentham thus departed from a strict laissez-faire position; he even advocated socializing the life insurance business.

Bentham applied these concepts to society as a whole, using a kind of social arithmetic to add up pleasures and subtract pains from them. Because all individuals in society count equally, he argued, any action will result in identical experiences of pleasure and pain for each one. The total welfare of society is equal to the total welfare of all individuals in it. Thus, if one person *gained* more welfare from a change in the government's policy on, say, rent control than a second person *lost*, the total welfare of society would increase.[5]

However, Bentham went on to say, people do not necessarily associate their own interests with the general interest, and therefore the kind of social behavior required for social harmony has to be learned. (He is rebutting Smith's claim in *The Wealth of Nations* that the "natural" or unlearned pursuit of self-interest contributes to the greatest happiness of the greatest number.) Bentham saw education legislation contributing to the greatest happiness of the greatest number. College students should be blissfully happy—if for no other reason, for hearing this.

At first blush, Benthamite utility appears to be a way to make objective and quantifiable the demand side of the market, the side barely addressed by Adam Smith and the other classical economists. Supply was based on the costs of production and therefore had an objective reality. Utility and demand, however, appear to be subjective: They are in the mind of the beholder. Bentham nonetheless captured economists' imagination and their preference for being objective by using money as a measure of pleasure and pain. This insight anticipated the marginalist schools of the 1870s that continue to instruct young economists.

This innovation, however, was virtually rebutted by another anticipation: Money meant different things to different people, according to how much they held. An amount of £15 might mean nothing to a rich man but might elevate a poor man to modest comfort. This notion—that each extra unit of money provided less pleasure than the last—was to become the principle of the diminishing marginal utility of money. Bentham's two economics strings ended in a knot: How can we assign values to pleasure purchased by British pounds if the pounds themselves measured different satisfactions?

This little puzzle made it still more difficult to build a theory of demand. As we shall see, this particular difficulty was overcome as soon as economists stopped asking the question! The problem was not solved by the classical economists, but the ideas of subjective utility and the marginal utility of money became central later, to the marginalists.

Bentham certainly gave the classicals—especially James Mill—plenty to ponder. The elder Mill helped to make Bentham important, but there was reciprocity. Bentham was 60 years old, known then, if at all, for the invention of a prison constructed so that a single warden could observe each and every cell. Mill introduced Bentham to the group later known as the "Philosophical Radicals," and gave Bentham a school and a reputation, until then the two main deficiencies Bentham suffered. James Mill was 35 years old, a Scot come to London to improve his lot. So, in return, Bentham gave Mill, then an East India official and hack journalist, a badly needed doctrine.

The book eventually to be called "the first textbook in Philosophical Radicalism," *An Enquiry Concerning the Principles of Political Justice*, was published in 1793 by William Godwin (1756–1836), a political writer, novelist, and philosopher who was close to the lunatic fringe of the Philosophical Radicals. Godwin was at the stormy center of a distinguished intellectual circle. His wife, Mary Wollstonecraft, was an author and an early champion of the rights of women; his daughter,

Mary Shelley, wrote *Frankenstein*; and his son-in-law, whom he greatly influenced and outlived, was the famous philosophical poet and radical, Percy Bysshe Shelley (1792–1822). Godwin also was to influence the early leaders of English Romanticism, especially Samuel Taylor Coleridge (1772–1834), whose friend William Wordsworth (1770–1850) had sympathy (in his youth) with democratic liberalism and the common speech of common people.

The English Romantic poets feared that the unity of reason, imagination, will, and intuition within man would be destroyed by science as reason alone. Or, as Coleridge put it,

> The Good consists in the congruity of a thing with the laws of the reason and the nature of the will, and its fitness to determine the latter to actualize the former.... The Beautiful arises from the perceived harmony of an object, ... with the inborn and constitutive rules of the judgment and imagination: And it is always intuitive.[6]

Godwin proposed a simple form of society without government in which human perfection would ultimately be attained. The institutions of society affecting the distribution of wealth, he contended, prevent the achievement of human perfection and ultimate happiness. Godwin called for an equal division of wealth, providing for necessities and leaving sufficient leisure time for the intellectual and moral improvements leading to earthly perfection.

Both Godwin and Shelley were greatly influenced by the doctrines of the **Enlightenment,** in which human reason would triumph over inequality and harsh government policies. When Shelley came to know of the Peterloo Massacre, which was the result of a government-ordered cavalry charge on a working-class rally at Manchester, his outrage and pity inspired his *Mask of Anarchy* [1819] wherein,

> I met Murder on the way—
> He had a mask like Castlereagh.

Utopian ideas have an obvious appeal, and many people in Godwin's day seemed to want to believe them, but to others they seemed naive and crudely optimistic, even more crudely optimistic than Bentham's utilitarianism. For these cynics, realists, and foretellers of gloom and doom, Thomas Malthus was an anti-Godwin godsend.

THOMAS MALTHUS AND THE POPULATION BOMB: A FLASH FOR THE UNENLIGHTENED

The fame of Thomas Malthus (1766–1834) rests on his dark theory of population growth. What Malthus was attacking was not the modest cheer of Adam Smith. Rather, it was the *excessive* optimism characteristic of the lunatic fringe of the utilitarians. Malthus's position shows his total disagreement with Godwin.

Originally the family name was Malthouse, as in brewer's malt. No doubt because of the religious roots in the family tree, the name was modified. Robert Thomas Malthus, whose theory would probably drive many to drink, was enrolled at Cambridge in 1785, where he instead indulged in cricket and skating and won prizes for Latin and English declamations. He became an ordained minister of the Church of England but rarely acted in that capacity. After his fame as an economist was ensured, Malthus became professor of history and political economy at Haileybury College, run by that gigantic mercantilistic monopoly, the East India Company in London.

Malthus was cheerful, benevolent of sentiments, mild of temper, loyal, and affectionate. He is described as tall and elegant in appearance and in conduct a perfect gentleman. The irony in this demeanor soon will be apparent. A portrait painted by John Linnell in 1833 shows Malthus to have a ruddy complexion with curling reddish or auburn hair and a strikingly handsome and distinguished frame. Because his speech was impaired by a cleft palate and a hare-lip, Malthus spoke slowly and gently. Yet his unwavering confidence and sonorous voice put people at ease.

Malthus directed others to a great obstacle to the future age of perfect equality and happiness as envisioned by Godwin: The tendency of the population to increase faster than the means of subsistence. In 1798, in the culmination of a dispute with his father (who sided with Godwin), the 32-year-old Malthus published anonymously "An Essay on the Principle of Population, as It Affects the Future Improvement of Society: With Remarks on the Speculations of Mr. Godwin, M. Condorcet, and Other Writers."

Malthus believed the economic system to be dictated by supreme order, but he could not agree with Adam Smith that all of the consequences of that order were necessarily beneficent; some of the problems appearing in nature, he said, could be downright unpleasant. Malthus did see some room for small motions by the "visible hand" of humanity—in this respect, he was influenced by Bentham's utilitarian ethics, the idea of "the greatest good for the greatest number." But he tended to be much more conservative than the other utilitarians, even reactionary.

While rejecting the utilitarian optimism about human progress, Malthus defended the traditional English class structure (with the landed aristocracy at the top), which the utilitarians believed stood in the way of full democracy. Thus, whether it was welfare legislation, tariffs to aid landowners, or the problem of preventing depressions, Malthus always came down hard on the side of preserving the existing class structure while relying on the principle of utility for evaluating improvements.

Malthus was such a cautious utilitarian that he virtually redefined the term. Among the utilitarians, he was a conservative among radicals and a pessimist among optimists. Still, the gulf was not so great as to preclude amicable discussions regarding differences of intellectual judgments. For one thing, Malthus saw much more of social utility for the general welfare in the traditional institutions, which he defended and the radicals attacked. He also saw less utility of that kind in their reform proposals than they claimed in their more optimistic moments.

All of which brings us to another excess, Malthusian pessimism. Malthus devised an illustration for his argument that people tend to increase in number beyond their means of subsistence. This illustration involves two numerical progressions. If there were no limit to the food supply, the population of a country would easily double every 25 years, at a geometric rate of increase. But the increase in food production under ideal conditions would be, as Malthus put it, "evidently arithmetical." Thus we see the humans in the cities increasing in the ratio of 1, 2, 4, 8, 16, 32, 64, 128, 256, 512, and so on, and subsistence increasing as 1, 2, 3, 4, 5, 6, 7, 8, 9, 10, and so on. As Malthus put it, "In two centuries and a quarter, the population would be to the means of subsistence as 512 to 10: In three centuries as 4,096 to 13, and in 2,000 years the difference would be almost incalculable."[7]

But people had lived in cities for centuries already. Why had the population explosion never come? Malthus had a grisly answer: The tendency of the population to exceed food production was restrained by the "positive" checks to population—those events raising the death rate—in the form of famine, misery, plague, and war. Poverty and regret, he concluded, are the natural punishments for the "lower classes." Relief for the "unworthy" poor, such as provided by the English poor laws, only made matters worse, as more children would survive. Only the "class of proprietors" could be trusted with fecundity. The conclusion is as obvious as it is gloomy: Poverty is inevitable.

Malthus had some second thoughts as early as 1803, when he published a revision of his essay. He acknowledged the possibility of morally acceptable "preventative" checks on population—fewer marriages, postponed marriages, sexual continence, and strict adherence to sexual morality. Such changes in behavior could reduce the size of families, although it was somewhat unrealistic to expect them. Two other possible reducers of the birth rate, prostitution and birth control, were ruled out on moral grounds.

Malthus himself married late, thus practicing part of what he preached, and eventually fathered only three children. In his day, Malthus was Great Britain's foremost political economist. His dark presentiments moved the historian Thomas Carlyle to call economists "Respectable Professors of the Dismal Science," an epithet that is still widely quoted and that, some would say, is still quite apt.

Malthus's ideas about the moral inferiority of the poor were adopted in the Poor Law Amendment of 1834. All relief outside the prison-like workhouses was abolished for able-bodied people. Relief applicants had to pawn all their possessions and enter the workhouse.

Women and children usually were sent to work in the cotton mills, away from the temptations of the nuptial bed. The intent of the law was to make quiet starvation more dignified than public assistance. This system remained the basis of British poor-law policy until the eve of World War I. Vindicated by human laws, Malthus was still subject to those of Nature, which subtracted him from the population four months after the passage of the Poor Law Amendment.

Data can be adduced both to substantiate and to refute the Malthusian population doctrine. The British data for 1750 to 1800 appear to fit the Malthusian model. The population of Great Britain increased only eight percent between 1700 and 1750; between 1750 and 1800, it was 60 percent (an enormous leap by the standards of the time). Declines in mortality and increases in productivity raised population growth; the swollen labor supply then lowered real wage rates. Then, population increased an incredible 100 percent between 1800 and 1850. By 1860, however, rising population and falling living standards no longer went hand in hand because productivity was rising so rapidly.[8] Eventually, the Industrial Revolution broke the old cycle. Recent statistics on per capita food consumption in Western Europe, North America, and Japan show the theory to be incorrect.

Even so, certain poor areas of the world resemble the more agrarian society of Malthus's day and tend to support the theory. Humanity is threatened by its own replication in Africa, parts of Latin America, and India. Although these conditions support Malthus's views, he failed to anticipate some important connections. First, humans can reduce their fertility through modern birth control methods. Second, advances in agricultural technology, such as the development of new grain varieties (the Green Revolution) has resulted in increased yields in food production. Granted, we cannot ignore the various neo-Malthusian theories predicting that the world's energy resources, which in part support agriculture, may someday become exhausted. But these theories may also underestimate our ability to create new technologies to meet such threats. Godwin had argued that technological inventions were susceptible to perpetual improvement. Third, and perhaps most important, the shift from an agrarian society to an urbanized one reduces the needs for the family to reproduce its own labor.

Remarkably, nonetheless, Malthus had an important influence on theories of evolution. Charles Darwin (1809–1882), the British naturalist, knew the possibility of producing hardier varieties of plants and animals by selective breeding. He was searching for a theory of evolution that would account for natural selection. He had reached a dead end when, in 1838, he read Malthus's *Essay on Population* (for amusement, according to one account, as strange as that may seem).

Darwin was struck by the light shed by the struggle for food and the geometric progression of population on the evolution of plants and animals through natural selection. He borrowed those ideas Malthus had applied to humans and generalized them to cover the plant and animal kingdoms.[9] As we shall see in Chapter 8, these Malthusian (adopted as Darwinian) ideas were perpetuated in economic thought through Social Darwinism, which ironically shifted the idea of selection by nature back to the competitive struggles of humans in their social and economic lives.

Before plumbing other depths of classical despair, we need to mention briefly another contribution of Malthus, his **theory of gluts**. Malthus strongly dissented from the position of Smith and Say with regard to the possibility of unsold goods. He saw an unlimited human desire for goods (perhaps not as intense as that for sex). However, he suggested that, if the individual who wished to buy had nothing to sell that others wanted, goods would remain unsold. A manufacturer will not hire a worker unless the laborer produces a value greater than the laborer's wage—a surplus equaling the employer's profit. Obviously, the worker is not in a position to buy back the surplus, so others must. Full employment is ensured only if all output is bought.

Malthus worried about who would buy the surplus. He saw the capitalists as misers interested primarily in amassing fortunes and thereby not to be counted on. In this respect, the landlords constituted the preeminent class because, given the returns from nature, the landholders generated income in excess of their production costs. The genteel landlords also had a will to spend (for servants, if for nothing else), and such spending was the best way to overcome economic stagnation. For this as well as for other reasons, Malthus was soft on landlords, and his position was to lead to a rhetorical confrontation with the formidable David Ricardo.

NOTES

1. In "Southey's Colloquies on Society," *Edinburgh Review*, December 1830.
2. *Vivian Grey*, Book I, Chapter 2 (London: Longmans, Green, 1892) [1826].
3. These data are derived from the discussion in R.M. Hartwell, *The Industrial Revolution and Economic Growth* (London: Methuen & Co., 1971), pp. 120–126.
4. For additional names and details, see A.E. Musson and Eric Robinson, *Science and Technology in the Industrial Revolution* (Manchester: Manchester University Press, 1969).
5. Bentham's classification scheme was more elaborate than the words "pleasure" and "pain" might ordinarily mean. He divided a whole range of conscious human experience into "pro-attitudes" and "con-attitudes." All drives and aversions, from the slightest to the greatest, from the sudden whim to the deepest desire, were included. Perhaps synonymous with pleasure is volition. That is, what pleases a person is simply what that person wills to do. But even this has its problems. By old custom, the native of Japan who was offended stabbed himself out of volition. It is difficult to consider such an act to be "pleasurable."
6. Samuel Taylor Coleridge, *On the Principles of Genial Criticism* (1814), quoted in John Bartlett, *Familiar Quotations* (Boston: Little, Brown & Co., 1991), p. 436.
7. Thomas R. Malthus, *On Population*, ed. Gertrude Himmelfarb (New York: Random House, Modern Library, 1960), p. 13.
8. Peter Lindert, "The Malthusian Case," unpublished note, 1984.
9. For the full story, see Lamar B. Jones, "The Institutionalists and *On the Origin of Species*: A Case of Mistaken Identity," *Southern Economic Journal* 52 (April 1968): 1043–1055, 1986.

4

The Distribution of Income: Ricardo versus Malthus

Adam Smith wrote how civil government, to make the ownership of property secure, is "in reality instituted for the defence of the rich against the poor, or of those who have some property against those who have none at all." Smith focused on income and wealth distributions because they were powerful political and social concerns. So did Malthus. And so did two other great economic thinkers of the early nineteenth century, David Ricardo and John Stuart Mill.

Ricardo was a sometime member of the House of Commons, a place of debate over international trade issues as well as over the distribution of income. Whereas Malthus was the academic divine turned practical, Ricardo was a businessman-politician turned great theoretician. Their political debates nonetheless defined what Ricardo would theorize about. J.S. Mill wrote the great economics textbook for his generation, was also elected to Parliament, and, near the end, was to call himself a socialist. These were times of great intellectual excitement.

DAVID RICARDO, THE STOCKBROKER-ECONOMIST

David Ricardo (1772–1823) was Malthus's close personal friend *and* intellectual adversary. Between them, they developed an economics that has been described by Robert Heilbroner as a tragedy in two acts. In Act I, Thomas Malthus set forth the dire human consequences of overpopulation. In Act II, Ricardo showed that the lazy, leisure-loving landlords would be the only beneficiaries of the economic system, while the industrialists, to whom the nation looked for national growth, would become frustrated and powerless.

Ricardo was the third of 17 children in a family of well-to-do Dutch Jewish immigrants; that is, his family was part of the population problem. Ricardo's formal schooling ended when he was 14 years old and he entered his father's stockbrokerage business. At age 21, he married a Quaker woman and joined the Unitarian Church, causing his father to disown him.

Ricardo thereupon set up his own brokerage firm with borrowed funds and was soon richer than his father. He retired from business at age 43 to devote himself to economic studies and to dabble in politics (buying himself a seat in Parliament). When he died of an ear infection at the age of 51, he was worth about £725,000, a kingly sum in those days. The bulk of his estate was in land and mortgages, an irony that will soon become apparent.[1]

Though Ricardo would have conceded that amassing wealth was worthwhile, he was a man of firm convictions and high principles who often advocated policies in conflict with his own interests. After acquiring much land, he advocated economic policies inimical to landowner interests. In Parliament, he represented a constituency in Ireland, where he had never lived, and argued for reforms that would have deprived him of his seat. He was one of the richest men in England, yet he advocated a tax on wealth.

When at the age of 27 Ricardo read *The Wealth of Nations*, he acquired a taste for the study of political economy. His first published work was a letter to a newspaper on currency problems, a promise of things to come. He became a national figure in economic analysis during the Bullion controversy on the causes of the rise of prices during the Napoleonic War years, arguing that an overissue of bank notes had raised the value of gold.

Ricardo soon met James Mill, who introduced him to Jeremy Bentham, who drew him into the small, tight circle of Philosophical Radicals. In 1811, he was approached by Thomas Malthus, beginning a deep and lasting friendship. Despite their personal closeness, when Malthus published his intended rebuttal of Ricardo, *Principles of Political Economy* (1820), Ricardo used some 220 pages of notes as surrebuttal. Their heated arguments delved into every nook and cranny of theory and policy.

To understand the economic conditions of the times is to better understand Ricardo's contributions. As Adam Smith had seen, the establishment of a free, middle-class state required the freeing of business from mercantilist regulations, and to a great extent a regime of real industrial competition had emerged in Britain. The governments of Britain and post-Napoleonic France denounced interference with the organization of production and with relations between masters and workers, and trade unions were prohibited. And, that was that!

THE SOCIAL SCENE: LIBERTY, FRATERNITY, AND UNEQUAL ECONOMIC CLASSES

At the edge of the Industrial Revolution, the American Revolution of 1776 and the French Revolution of 1789 struck at the hearts of the European landed aristocracy and the old notions of the divine rights of monarchs. Many British people sympathized with the spirit of the age. Adam Smith had met Benjamin Franklin on his Grand Tour and had been greatly impressed with the prospects for his newly emerging nation, only partly because Franklin had coined the wise saying, "a penny saved is a penny earned."

Although the French Revolution destroyed all that remained of the superstructure of feudalism in France, its original purposes were sidetracked by the imperial Napoleon. Britain, in an ultimately successful attempt to resist Napoleon's conquest of Europe, was involved in a series of wars with France from 1793 to 1815, wars that put a great strain on the type of British liberalism represented by Smith and his followers.

In 1794, the Habeas Corpus Act was suspended for five years, all secret associations were banned, all meetings attended by more than 50 persons had to be supervised, printing presses had to be registered with the government, and the export of British newspapers was banned. In the most dastardly blow of all, lecture rooms charging admission (as most did) were legally classified as brothels!

In 1799 and 1800, the Combination Laws prohibited any kind of combination of either employers or workers for the purpose of regulating conditions of employment. If there was hope for the British libertarians amid this sea of oppressive legislation, it was the selective enforcement of the Combination Laws against workers and embryonic labor unions but not against employers. The merchant class at least could breathe easily.

When the smoke cleared from the battlefields of the Napoleonic Wars, the monarchies and the aristocracies still held control, but the economic power required for sustained political dominance was now starting to shift to the expanding middle class. In the larger cities of Britain (London contained about a million souls), France, and the Low Countries, the leaders of the old mercantilists' government-by-the-wealthy were reluctantly beginning to share their leadership with a small number of factory owners, the new "captains of industry."

To many of those in the middle class, the accumulation of money had not yet become an end in itself (as late as 1815, most families' lives were untouched by money). The sons of the old patrician families at the top of the class, whose fortunes had been made in colonial enterprises and earlier long-distance trade, tended to become bankers and merchants rather than manufacturers. They considered wealth to be only a means to secure the leisure of the landed gentry. The ideas of Adam Smith and other classical economists, which gave Calvinism a rational base, were to contribute to a revision of this attitude.

As the old world of mercantilism faded, a new society was forming in Britain, France, and the Low Countries. A new "economic man" was emerging—hard-working, energetic, self-made. His virtues were self-denial, self-discipline, initiative, and a willingness to take risks for personal gain. He could not permit laxity in workers or see any value in welfare.

Franklinian thrift was his watchword, and every penny saved was for reinvestment in his business. High wages and government regulations were bad for business. Factory management required long hours and diligent supervision, and so he spent days over his machines and his ledgers, perhaps contentedly. One ambition dominated his life: To increase the output of his machines to their very limits. He was not the kind of man you would want to drink ale with.

Factory chimneys crowded the horizon in cities like Manchester and Lille, but there were still hundreds of towns where economic life had not greatly changed since the time of Dante and the Middle Ages. The overwhelming majority of the population of every European nation-state except Great Britain still lived from the land.

Moreover, the landowners on the Continent still had substantial political power and were able to continue to enclose common lands and drive the farmers onto smaller tracts. (This process had left only one-fifth of British land *un*enclosed by 1810, about the time enclosures were getting going in the rest of Europe.) The peasants and the small freeholders and renters were somewhat better off—freer to buy, sell, work for themselves, perhaps change their occupation. Yet life was still very hard for all the working classes.

Although Adam Smith had second thoughts about merchants and contempt for the landed aristocracy, his great vision had disparate elements of the economy combining in a harmony of interests for a steady upward progression for society. Contrary to Smith's expectations, however, as mechanization increased, clashes of economic interest also grew. Worse, Smith's lengthy funeral incantation for mercantilism was premature. David Ricardo and Parson Malthus were at the center of these conflicts, as the wars spurred on the industrial expansion.

RICARDO TAKES ON THE MERCANTALISTS

Still, to the classical economists, the further extension of freedom, at least in the economies of England and France, required ending mercantilism, as they knew it. Thus Jean Baptiste Say felt compelled to attack trade restrictions in France by proclaiming Smith's gospel in a series of lucid articles, and Ricardo stepped forward in that role in Britain, modifying the ideas of Smith and Say to suit the developing economic conditions there.

These, then, were the conditions confronted by Ricardo: The last vestiges of mercantilism, the still powerful landed gentry, a rapidly growing population, and widespread urban poverty. Ricardo opposed tariffs and excessive profits from land. Consistent with laissez-faire tradition, however, he also opposed interfering with the malignancy of poverty; he chose only to explain the disease.

In his writings, Ricardo was able to explain the distribution of income shares among workers, capitalists, and landowners with more precision than Smith. And he saw clearly, as the optimistic Smith did not, that in cutting up the economic pie, the contestants might be moved to turn their knives on one another.

The Debate over the Corn Laws

Ricardo's main, spare abstractions concerning the English economy were sparked by parliamentary debate in 1814 to 1815 over the proposed Corn Laws, which would prohibit the import of grain until the price of domestic grain increased a specific amount. The central conflict pitted the rising industrialists against the landowners, who had expanded cultivated acreage when produce from the Continent was cut off by the war and now wished to avoid being ruined, on the outbreak of peace, by a sudden flood of imported cereal grains. The industrialists believed the Corn Laws to be special treatment for a favored few at the expense of their own capital accumulation: Higher food prices from the more intensive cultivation of English lands would mean the industrialists had to pay higher wages.

Since the landowners controlled Parliament, the Corn Laws passed easily, but the debate the laws stimulated did much to define economic interest groups. As usual, Malthus lavished praise on the landlords; Ricardo attacked the consequences of what they were doing. A legislative issue thus became a contest in economic analysis and a revelation of class conflict. How was the national income to be distributed among the landlords, the manufacturers, and the workers?

Lurking behind the debate was an idea later dubbed the **law of diminishing returns**: The more one input of *equal quality* is increased in production while the quantities of all other inputs of *equal quality* remain unchanged, the smaller will be the resulting addition to output, because the added input has smaller and smaller shares of the other inputs to work with. That is, more and more farm workers tilling the same hectare of land will yield fewer and fewer extra bushels of grain. In agriculture, then, the larger the population, with the amount of land fixed, the higher the price of food must go, even though total food production is greater. Furthermore, not only did the more intensive tilling of land of the same fertility have differential effects on economic classes, but so did the use of land of varying quality. Malthus, however, had at best a very crude version of the above modern statement of this "law," whereas Ricardo formulated diminishing returns across soil of diminishing quality.

Disagreement over "Rent"

Malthus was the one who had started the argument. He identified the subsistence wage with foodstuffs. The worker's wage is what the worker eats. Since a rapid increase of food crops is not possible because the supply of fertile land is limited and technical improvements do not come fast enough, food production cannot stay apace of population growth and workers pay will begin to fall beneath the subsistence wage. Famine becomes one of Malthus's lamentably "positive" checks on population growth.

Ricardo agreed with Malthus regarding the pressures of population on natural resources. From this agreement tempered by a protracted debate, Ricardo brought forth his **differential theory of rent**, which John Stuart Mill would later describe as one of the cardinal doctrines of political economy. Ricardo's argument was characteristically more precise than that of Malthus. For both, however, the crux was the landowners' profits, or "rent."

The most fertile land, said Ricardo, yields the greatest harvest for the least labor and capital. But as the population multiplies and the demand for grain swells, land of poorer and poorer quality must be brought under the plow. The same number of workers and tools will yield fewer bushels of grain on the poor land. The price per bushel of grain will be decided by the higher cost of cultivation on the poorest land parcel.

How so? Consider the landowners who have only poor soil. Suppose on the poorest plot of their poorest land they produce 500 bushels and their cost of labor and tools is £1,000. Then their grain is raised at a cost of £2 per bushel. As it turns out, price is set by the least favorable circumstance under which production is carried out. If people demand grain until the poorest of the poor land is used, they must pay the cost of production on the last piece of inferior soil tilled. In this case, then, the market price of grain is £2. Next, consider the landowners of the most fertile land. Suppose that the owners of more fertile land produce 1,000 bushels—twice as much—for the same £1,000 total cost. Their cost per bushel is only £1, but they can sell at double that, and they are better off by £1 per bushel.

To Ricardo, **economic rent** is paid to the owners of the land for "the use of the original and indestructible powers of the soil." This rent is not the same as returns derived from *improvements* made on the land, which give rise to *profits* rather than *rent*. Malthus considered higher rents for landowners a salutary thing, but Ricardo did not, for a reason that takes a bit of explaining.

Simply put, Ricardo believed rent to be *unearned* income. Landowners who have to work longer hours for their bushel of wheat (or, perhaps more exactly, work their laborers longer hours) sell it at the same price as farmers who own the richest delta land in the country. Unlike the role played by labor costs, rent does not determine the price of grain. Rather, the price of grain decides the amount of rent.

Sadly, it is a poor land, rich land story. For the landowners of poor land, the price represents only a return on their labor and capital. The price also represents a return for the labor and capital on the highly fertile land. Because laborers are required to work fewer hours per bushel of grain on the rich land, however, the price also provides a gratuitous income, or what Ricardo calls **economic rent**. The owners of the poor land receive only wages and earned profits; the owners of the fertile land also receive rent. Therefore, Ricardo reasoned, the landowners' "rent" from Nature alone was unjustified because it was created apart from the amount of labor and capital necessary for the production of grain.

If we stopped here, we would have only Ricardo's Sahara-like, terse, mundane piece of economic abstraction. But Ricardo ingeniously showed how rent reaches out and touches all of society. As population expands at a Malthusian rate, less productive land comes into cultivation, the poorest land is tilled, the cost of producing an extra bushel rises, and food prices go up. With higher food prices, the money wage rate just sufficient to keep the worker alive must be higher than before. However, real wages tend to remain at the subsistence level, a principle often called the **iron law of wages.**

Worse, the higher money wage has to be paid in manufacturing as well as in agriculture. Like Adam Smith, Ricardo had the worker being paid from the capitalist's **wages fund**. Higher wages meant a lower profit rate for the industrialists, who then would have a smaller fund to be invested in new plants, equipment, and tools, or for hiring more workers.

As Ricardo's new but gloomy picture of society comes into focus, we begin to understand why, as he put it, the interest of the landowner "is always opposed to the interests of every other class in the community." Manufacturing growth slows because the declining profit rate accompanying the higher money wage rates slows the pace of capital accumulation. The workers struggle along on a subsistence real wage as food prices continue to rise. Meanwhile, the owners of fertile farmland are better off than ever. The landowners will not use their rent to invest in manufacturing, because the businesses are not making a profit rate as high as their rental rate, an unearned return to leisure.

Free trade too comes to the fore. The "olde tyme" protectionism—the Corn Laws—would perpetuate the landowners' privileges and weaken the other social classes. Ricardo saw the *industrialists* as the true source of productive social growth. Moreover, he saw the economy as self-adjusting in the absence of government barriers, so that Say's law would preclude industrial crises.

Malthus vigorously disagreed. As usual, his dissent mixed economic analysis with a conservative preference for the staid, landed aristocracy. Progress was with the landlords whose higher rents would empower them to make permanent improvements in the productivity of their land, while their spending on luxuries would prevent general gluts. More generally, Malthus was concerned with what a rapid expansion of manufacturing would bring with it: A concentration of population in the cities, where conditions, as all could see, were unhealthy. He preferred the bucolic landed estates.

Malthus believed employment in manufacturing was essentially unstable because consumers' tastes were fickle. This potential instability, he feared, would lead to worker unrest. Perhaps most important, Malthus expected that the evils of industrialization would undermine the cultural blessings of a society built on a genteel landed class. Malthus was perplexed that Ricardo, a landowner himself, did not appreciate the virtues of people of his own kind.

Ricardo, like Smith, saw mostly good in the expansion of industry. He envisioned unwise policies like the Corn Laws leading the economy into a **stationary state**—a decline in the industrialists' rate of profit and its dampening of accumulation would lead to this stagnation. Population growth would cease, net investment would be zero, and per capita income would also stagnate. Free trade—the absence of tariffs—could delay the coming of this dreaded stationary state.

Again like Smith, Ricardo underscored the importance and value of capital accumulation and of orderly growth and market equilibrium.

He wanted business freed of restrictions that might reduce its ability to maximize profits, so that saving and capital accumulation would continue.

A Theory of International Trade

Ricardo was also an internationalist: National rivalries—tariffs, trade restrictions, and wars—he believed, would slow the development of capitalism. He used a remarkable analytical device to prove why trade had mutual benefits. He probably was the first economist to suggest a separate theory of international trade.

In his law of comparative cost, Ricardo showed why it benefits nations to export those commodities in which they have a relative cost advantage. Since he expressed the unit cost of production in labor hours required to produce (in his famous example) wine and cloth, the theory illustrates a labor theory of value. In the example, Ricardo, a *gentleman* of Parliament, gave the absolute cost advantage to Portugal, England's trading partner. Portugal produced both wine and cloth with less labor than did England. The example is shown in Table 4.1.

Table 4.1

LABOR HOURS REQUIRED TO PRODUCE A BOLT OF CLOTH OR A KEG OF WINE

	Cloth	Wine	Relative Price of Wine in Cloth Terms (P_w/P_c)
England	100	120	1.2
Portugal	90	80	0.89

Portugal has a **comparative advantage** in wine, since its cost advantage for wine is relatively greater than England; that is, the ratio of labor costs of 120/100 for England is greater than the 80/90 for Portugal. These ratios in turn give the barter price of a keg of wine in bolts of cloth—1.2 bolts of English cloth will buy a keg of English wine. Trade is worthwhile because the English can buy a keg of Portugal's wine for much less than 1.2 bolts of cloth, though no less than 0.89 bolts of cloth!

Trade ends up being mutually beneficial at barter exchanges between 1.2 and 0.89 bolts of cloth per keg of wine. It is Portugal's advantage to ship wine to England, where a keg of it commands 1.2 bolts of cloth, as long as 1 keg of wine can be traded with England for more than 0.89 bolts of cloth. It is to England's advantage to specialize in cloth if less than 1.2 bolts of cloth is given for a keg of wine.

With deceptively simple intellectual force, Ricardo justified trade even for nations that had higher production costs all the way around and extended Adam Smith's idea of the advantages of the specialization of labor to the world economy. Most important for that moment in history, Ricardo forged yet another telling argument against the Corn Laws.

RICARDO'S CONTRIBUTIONS

Ricardo's most lasting contributions are (1) the nature of his own economic methods, (2) the importance he attached to income distribution, and (3) his theory of international trade. With Ricardo, economics detaches from philosophy and becomes an independent discipline, freed from any principles except those generated by its own unadorned inner logic.

True, abstract economic class conflict occurs, but there are really no people in Ricardo's thought, only idealizations. In Adam Smith's festive writing, there are diligent, flesh-and-blood workers busily specializing, and clever, calculating businessmen maximizing profits. Ricardo reduces these fully clothed, colorful economic portraits to gray outlines.

Ricardo's rhetoric responded to the economic issues of his day, but his scribbling derived from his imagination, not from research. The orthodox economists of the 1960s to 1970s called him "the Newton of economics," their highest accolade, and even his pure abstraction can suddenly take on real-world implications. For example, Ricardo tried to generalize his simple corn model by finding an "invariable standard of value" for expressing relative prices. The labor theory of value in which all value derives from labor time and a composite commodity he called "gold" proved inadequate. However, in Chapter 11, we shall see how Piero Sraffa solved the problem while clarifying some real-world issues concerning income distribution.

There is, to be sure, an implicit human concern, even Heilbronian tragedy, in Ricardo's view of income distribution. His main theoretical concern was the division of the nation's income among the three main social classes in the form of wages, profits, and rent. Flat subsistence real *wages* would keep the worker alive but not necessarily well. Naturally rising *rents* would take more and more of the national income. A declining *profit rate* would fail to keep the industrial economy expanding.

And, tragically, the *only* beneficiaries of the system during Ricardo's time are the landowners, whose monopoly of the natural properties of the soil allow them to gain at everyone else's expense. Wages are payment for work effort, and either profit or interest is the price of capital, but rent is greater than just the price paid for the use of the soil. Ricardo loathed seeing the industrialist, the one responsible for progress, in such a pinch.

The two-act tragedy was never played out. The Corn Laws proved to be ineffective legislation and were repealed in 1846, some two decades after Ricardo's death. To this day, Britain does not have to depend on homegrown foodstuffs. Moreover, the population in Western Europe never exerted the pressures on land resources that Malthus and Ricardo had foreseen. Ricardo's comparative cost theory of international trade nonetheless has retained its vitality.

The great debates and the fabulous friendship of Malthus and Ricardo were halted only by death. The final sentence in Ricardo's last letter to Malthus illuminates their great mutual respect:

> And now, my dear Malthus, I have done. Like other disputants, after much discussion, we each retain our own opinions. These discussions, however, never influence our friendship; I should not like you more than I do if you agreed in opinion with me.[2]

A decade later, Malthus too was gone.

THE CLASSICAL LEGACY

The policies of the classical economists were ultimately to benefit society by encouraging capital accumulation and economic growth, but the gains were not equally distributed. The wage earners suffered especially heavy costs during the Industrial Revolution. Although Adam Smith was sympathetic to the working class, the effect of his main principles and of those of Ricardo was to give business people (especially industrialists) respectability in a society last seen extending its greatest honors to the landowning nobility and the gentry. Industrialists achieved new status as promoters of the nation's wealth. Malthus's beloved landed gentry gradually receded. Still, as we will find, unearned incomes never really vanished; only the names engraved on the trophies were changed. It remained for the "last of the classicals" to rally the workers' interests and to raise troubling issues regarding the distribution of income. So, we now turn to John Stuart Mill.

NOTES

1. Ricardo lived and wrote his economic tracts at his Gatcombe Park estate. In the 1970s, the estate was sufficient to attract Queen Elizabeth II, who purchased it for Princess Anne and her husband. It still stands.

2. Quoted by John Maynard Keynes, in *Essays and Sketches in Biography* (New York: Meridian Books, 1956), p. 38. The essays were first published in 1951 by Horizon Press Inc.

5

The Cold Water of Poverty and the Heat of John Stuart Mill's Passions

Special interests looking out for themselves are nothing new; during the Middle Ages, kings, queens, and clerics did well while not always doing good. As just noted, in Ricardo and Malthus's time, the landed gentry pursued their own interests even as the rising industrialist class challenged them for a bigger piece of the pie. Luckily for the industrialists, the ideas of the classical economists, the new orthodoxy, could be exploited not only in defense of capital against land but capital against labor.

Worse for the underdog, a stern interpretation of the political economists could be turned to the defense of some barbaric working conditions as an inevitable part of a free system. Poverty was represented as nature's own medicine, and its pervasiveness meant only that society greatly needed a purgative. Since workers could not look to Ricardo, Malthus, and their dismal science for support, they began to look elsewhere for attention.

WORKERS IN THE REAL INDUSTRIAL WORLD

One of the worst abuses of the early factory system was the exploitation of women and children, who were prized as valuable and obedient workers, especially in the spinning and printing factories. Indeed, the number of adult males working in such factories was relatively small. Women and children had the fewest civil liberties and were least able to make effective protests against brutal working conditions. Disciplined easily, they worked for little compensation.

In Britain, thousands of male and female children from seven to 14 years of age were compelled to work every day from dawn to dusk. (We know the names of some, such as Elizabeth Bentley, a millhand working for a Mr. Burk in Leeds in 1815.) Supervisors sometimes beat them to keep them awake and at work. There were rare "model" employers, such as the utopian socialist Robert Owen (1771–1858), owner of the Lanark mills, but even his famous benevolence must be seen in context. He was praised in his own day because only 14 of the nearly 3,000 children that he employed over a 12-year period died and not one became a criminal.[1]

As noted, the expansion of the British cotton industry was exceptional during this era, a good place to try to discover if the working class became better off during the Industrial Revolution. Statistics show that the change from cottage industry to the factory improved living standards in some respects, while in other respects it worsened them. After all, it was higher money wages and regular employment that brought many of the workers out of the cottage industry and agriculture and into the Lancashire factories. Reportedly, male unskilled operatives in 1806 to 1846 could earn 15 to 18 sixpence, and skilled operatives could earn 33 to 42 sixpence a day, compared with some 13 1/2 sixpence earned by agricultural workers in Lancashire.[2] Women and children were paid a fraction as much. The higher-paid Lancashire laborers could afford meat, whereas agricultural peasants were living mostly on bread and water.

Those coming from the farm might have found the factory punitive; the workers lost the freedom to schedule their own work as their will was bent to steady working hours. Still, the deplorable conditions in the new factories largely mirrored a venerable tradition of harsh supervision in farms and workshops, and in the latter places it continued long after remedial legislation was enforced in industrial settings. Sometimes the children found the factory more tolerable than their home environment.

Though industrialization was eventually to improve everyone's income level (not equally), the real wages of labor and workers' quality of life either declined or failed to increase noticeably during the Industrial Revolution. Drawn like moths to the flames of the factory, the surplus agricultural and cottage industry labor moved into the factory towns and cities at a rate exceeding the growth in demand for it. The new technologies in agriculture, the cottages, and the factories were labor-saving. The inventions of Arkwright and Hargreaves greatly reduced the labor requirements of cotton spinning, eliminating hand cotton spinning almost as fast as the machines could be built.[3] Urban growth brought with it crowded conditions, pollution, disease, crime, and a host of other ills. The prevalence of these social problems is universally recognized by historians of the period.

We are left, then, with a melancholy conclusion: In its time the Industrial Revolution was no great boon to the workers, although urbanization and rapid population growth probably contributed more to the urban slums than did the factory system itself. At times when factory employment was high, workers enjoyed higher incomes, but the expansion of industry did not in itself increase by much their share of the wealth of the nation. Not until about the 1860s did the standard of living of the British working class significantly improve.

CHARLES DICKENS TAKES ON POVERTY, FACTORY CONDITIONS, AND THE CLASSICAL ECONOMISTS

But no matter how imposing the architectural splendor of the orthodox argument, the economic conditions of this new industrial era were not met with universal enthusiasm. Although the general public may have agreed with Smith, Ricardo, and the industrialists on the importance of liberty, poverty and frequently horrendous working conditions failed to gain many champions other than the factory owners. That "radical" poet Percy Bysshe Shelley attacked both business commerce ("the venal interchange") and the Calvinist ethic in his *Queen Mab* (1813):

> Commerce has set the mark of selfishness,
> The signet of its all-enslaving power,
> Upon a shining ore, and called it gold....[4]

Coleridge and Wordsworth and other writers of English Romanticism (1789–1832) who outlived Shelley, shared these sympathies, though not with his fervor. Still, the definitive attack on the abuses of the factory system and the disease of poverty was left to a great Victorian novelist.

The works of Charles Dickens (1812–1870) offered memorable descriptions of life among the working classes and industrialists. Dickens himself was yanked from school at age 12 and put to work with other boys pasting labels on blacking bottles, an experience bitterly recounted in the autobiographical *David Copperfield* (1849–1850). *This* David Copperfield is not a magician, but his writing is magical.

In *Oliver Twist* (1837–1838), Dickens presents an attack on workhouse and slum conditions as seen through the nightmarish experiences of an innocent young boy. In *Dombey and Son* (1846–1848) one can see the growing power of industry as opposed to the waning power of mercantile interests. Dickens's most vivid picture of industrial society comes later in *Hard Times* (1854), combining a moral fable with realistic social analysis in the depiction of Coketown, Dickens's prototypical industrial town. Dickens sets his story

> ...in the innermost fortifications of that ugly citadel, where Nature was as strongly bricked out as killing airs and gases were bricked in; at the heart of the labyrinth of narrow courts upon courts, and close streets upon streets, which had come into existence piecemeal, every piece in a violent hurry for some one man's purpose and the whole an unnatural family, shouldering, trampling, and pressing one another to death; in the last close nook of this great exhausted receiver, where the chimneys, for want of air to make a draught, were built in an immense variety

> of stunted and crooked shapes, as though every house put out a sign of the kind of people who might be expected to be born in it;....[5]

Dickens breathes life into Ricardo's starkly abstract income classes: Thomas Gradgrind, a retired merchant; Stephen Blackpool, a worker; and Josiah Bounderby, the factory owner. Gradgrid is a caricature—but not too broad—of the calculating Benthamite, to whom everything is cut and dried:

> A man who proceeds upon the principle that two and two are four, and nothing over, and who is not to be talked into allowing for anything over.... With a rule and a pair of scales, and the multiplication tables always in his pocket, sir, ready to weigh and measure any parcel of human nature, and tell you exactly what it comes to.[6]

Dickens's contempt for classical economics is shown by his naming two Gradgrind children Adam Smith and Malthus.

Blackpool is a power-loom weaver who looks older than his 40 years because of his hard life. (In the plot of the novel, he is unjustly accused of a crime committed by one of Gradgrind's older sons.) To Dickens, the paternalism of feudalism has been replaced by the paternalism of the factory owner. The contrast between Blackpool's status and that of his employer, Mr. Bounderby, shows the harmonious private enterprise of Adam Smith in an unflattering light:

> Stephen came out of the hot mill into the damp wind and cold wet streets, haggard and worn. He turned from his own class and his own quarter, taking nothing but a little bread as he walked along, towards the hill on which his principal employer lived, in a red house with black outside shutters, green inside blinds, a black street door, up two white steps, BOUNDERBY (in letters very like himself to upon a brazen plate, and a round brazen door-handle underneath it,....[7]

Rather than a piece of bread for lunch, Mr. Bounderby was having a "chop and sherry." Taking some sherry but offering none to his employee, Bounderby says condescendingly,

> We have never had any difficulty with you, and you have never been one of the unreasonable ones. You don't expect to be set up in a coach and six, and to be fed on turtle soup and venison, with a gold spoon, as a good many of 'em do! ...and therefore I know already that you have not come here to make a complaint.[8]

Mr. Bounderby knows what Stephen wants better than he does.

Dickens was neither an economist nor a philosopher, and some commentators on *Hard Times* have complained that he did not understand Bentham and utilitarianism. It could as well be argued that Shelley didn't understand commerce, and it would be equally beside the point. Their function as artists was to report and comment on what they saw, which was that, although industrialism was perhaps not evil in itself (Gradgrind and Bounderby are not "villains"), it led to abuses desperately in need of correction.

Some reforms did come out of these creative forces and from a Parliament sufficiently outraged to hold hearings on factory and urban conditions. The factory inspector was a notable achievement. From the point of view of reform, one advantage of the factory system is that, because production is organized in one place, abuses of the system can easily be monitored and ultimately controlled. Contrary to the industrialists' interpretation of classical economics, government was beginning to get into the act.

JOHN STUART MILL: SOMEWHERE BETWEEN CAPITALISM AND SOCIALISM

The lives of Charles Dickens and of John Stuart Mill (1806–1873), the last great economist of the classical school, overlapped. The coincidence, if that is what it is, is filled with an irony that does not end at Dickens' edge. Initially devoted to the ideas of Smith, Ricardo, Bentham, and his father, J.S. Mill parted company with their ideas on the relation of production and the income distribution. To the great distress of the orthodoxy, J.S. attempted to separate the science of production from the distribution of its rewards. To this day, he is given low marks by the economics orthodoxy for this "fuzzy thinking." Still, he restored much of Smith's optimism to what had become a quite dismal science.

The Young Disciple

John Stuart Mill's father, James, although he helped found the Philosophical Radicals, is most famous—or notorious—for the extraordinary education that he imposed on his young son. The senior Mill had nine children, and he wanted one to be properly educated to be a disciple of his and Bentham's ideas.

Willy nilly, John was chosen to receive a Benthamite education. He began to learn Greek at the age of three years and Latin at eight years. He mastered algebra and elementary geometry by age 12 while studying differential calculus. Also by this time, he had written a history of Roman government.

Apparently a late bloomer in economics, John Stuart Mill did not begin the study of political economy until the age of 13. Between the ages of 15 and 18 years, Mill edited and published five volumes of Bentham's manuscripts. At age 19, he was publishing original scholarly articles. At age 20, he had a well-earned nervous breakdown.

Poetry and Love for a Recovering Classical

Much of J.S. Mill's subsequent life was marked by an attempt to overcome a childhood devoid of affection and tenderness—his father had been harsh and sarcastic, his mother almost invisible. Mill overcame his intense, analytical training enough to appreciate poetry, particularly William Wordsworth's. Doubtless Mill had read, of other stanzas, from Wordsworth's *Ode on Immortality* (1807),

> The Rainbow comes and goes,
> and lovely is the Rose.

Mill credited Wordsworth's poetry with aiding his recovery from his mental crisis (Bentham had ridiculed poetry as a childish game). He learned to be moved by many of the romantic, revolutionary impulses of his age. Unlike Wordsworth and Coleridge, Mill did not abandon his youthful radicalism as he grew older.

Even so, the greatest emotional influence on Mill was his long relationship with Harriet Taylor. Although at their first meeting in 1830, Harriet was the bluestocking wife of a well-to-do businessman, love managed to bloom, and following one of the less publicized Victorian conventions, John and Harriet traveled together on the Continent and spent holidays together in the English countryside. When Mr. Taylor finally died in 1851, they married.

Harriet was described by objective observers as graceful and pretty, though her portrait belies it. Mill credited her as well with great intellect, including virtual co-authorship of his influential philosophical tract, *Essay on Liberty* (1859). Perhaps, in Harriet's case, Mill had been inspired by a stanza in Coleridge's *Love* (1799):

> All thoughts, all passions, all delights,
> Whatever stirs this mortal frame,
> All are but ministers of Love,
> And feed his sacred flame.

No doubt it was her inspiration and insights that led Mill to modify his view of socialism in successive editions of his *Principles* and to devote much thought and writing to feminist issues in his later life. His *The Subjection of Women* (1869) surely reflects Harriet's influence. In his *Autobiography* (posthumously published), he called himself and Harriet, socialists. We could hardly imagine a more ironic end for the last of the classical economists.

Mill's Ideas on the Income Distribution

Mill's great summary of classical economics, *Principles of Political Economy* (1848), was the leading textbook in its field for more than 40 years. The book is a survey of all the ideas of Smith, Malthus and Ricardo, but it arrives at a happier ending because of Mill's own discoveries. His most important and controversial discovery was the separation of distribution from production. Its popularity is related in part to the apparent improvements in the economic conditions that began to be real for workers in the 1860s, which justify the book's optimistic tone. The book's success, making him the dominant economist of his age, altered the classical economic school during Mill's lifetime.

Like Smith and Ricardo, Mill thought the industrialist's rate of profit would continue to fall and even agreed with Ricardo's explanation—inevitably rising food costs in the face of a growing population. Although he also envisioned a stationary state for the economy, at this point Mill began to part company with his famous predecessors. Smith and Ricardo saw the stationary state as undesirable; Mill saw it as the crowning achievement of economic progress. And, unlike his predecessors, Mill emphasized the importance of a more equal distribution of income, a concept not unrelated to the stationary state.

Though Mill valued material accumulation, he also directed humans toward striving for higher goals. In Britain, he thought, the *desire* for wealth need not be taught, but rather the *use* of wealth and an appreciation of the objects and desire that wealth could not purchase. As he put it, "Every real improvement in the character of the English, whether it consists in giving them aspirations, or only a juster estimate of the value of their present objects of desire, must necessarily moderate the ardour of their devotion in the pursuit of wealth."[9] Beside the "economic man" walked a "noneconomic man."

Once Britain had achieved a sufficiently high level of wealth, Mill saw no reason for a continued growth in production, as long as population growth were limited. And proper education of the masses, according to Mill, would check the birth rate. He did not want the laws of production repealed; he simply wanted the division of labor and capital accumulation to take the economy to a high plateau, the rarified air of the stationary state in which production ceased to grow. To Mill, the stationary state was a blissful, pastoral existence in which justice in the distribution of income and wealth ranked above relentless accumulation.

Mill's separation of the science of production from the rules governing distribution rests on a distinction between natural law and mere custom—a distinction we dealt with in Chapter 1. In Mill's view, the laws of scarcity and diminishing returns derive from nature just as much as the laws of gravity and of the expansion of gases. But although the factors of production must be combined according to scientific principles, the *distribution* of that production is a social issue and its rules, customary.

To Mill, the distribution of income obeys the laws and customs of society. Even what a person has produced by his individual toil, unaided by anyone, he cannot keep, unless society allows him to. Where Ricardo saw the necessity of allowing natural price changes to keep the landlord from garnering all income, Mill could envision a law that would evict the landlord from his "own" land.

Mill's Ideas for Reform

Whatever the relation of rich to poor, then, if society did not like what it saw, it had only to alter those conditions. Society could—if it had the will—expropriate, redistribute, tax, subsidize, and generally raise havoc with the distribution of income initially decided by the economic machine.

Still, it was Robert Owen, the Utopian Socialist, not J.S. Mill, who launched the English working-class movement in 1833. Owen drew together the leaders of the working-class movement into the Grand National, the first trade union. Mill saw the stationary state, which, he thought, was within a "hand's breadth" in England, as the first stage of a benevolent socialism. Within the stationary state, reforms would take place. The state would tax away the inheritances of the rich and prevent the landed gentry from gaining Ricardian rents. The associations of workers such as the Grand National would end factory control by the master manufacturers. Through modest reforms, benign evolution would preempt the need for revolution.

Mill remained a reformer within the system, a modest socialist quite unaware of the writings of his contemporary, Karl Marx. He favored free public education, regulation of child labor, government ownership of natural monopolies such as gas and water companies, public assistance for the poor, and, if labor wanted it, government enforcement of shorter working days.

Remarkably, the revolutionary *Communist Manifesto* (1848) of Karl Marx and Friedrich Engels was published the same year as Mill's *Principles,* but the relatively improving economic conditions in the 1860s and 1870s, bad as absolute worker poverty had been, kept the "radical" ideas of Marx underground, gave succor to the emerging optimism of mainstream English economics, and fed J.S. Mill's positive thinking. In Mill's many opportunities for the revision of the *Principles,* he remained a reformer. We next will delve deeper into the ideas of Marx and Engels and contemplate further their collective fates.

Despite his timid deviations from classical orthodoxy, many economists have complained that John Stuart Mill was confused. If so, the confusion is between heart and mind. It has been the luck of economists since his day to watch society treading the path blazed by Mill, while they, as scientists, have been content to work with the more predictable laws of nature. In any case, Mill's warmth, humanitarianism, and sympathy for the poor and disadvantaged took some of the chill off Ricardian political economy. As we shall see, however, later economists were to come in from the warm.

NOTES

1. Richard L. Tames (ed.), *Documents of the Industrial Revolution, 1750–1850* (London: Hutchinson Educational, 1971), p. 96.

   Interviews of factory workers by parliamentary commissioners provide a considerable body of evidence on the treatment of women and children. One such interview is with Elizabeth Bentley, a millhand, in 1815. Among the excerpts:

   What age are you? Twenty-three. *What time did you begin work at the factory?* When I was six years old. *What were your hours of labour in that mill?* From 5 in the morning till 9 at night when they were thronged. *What were the usual hours of labour when you were not so thronged?* From six in the morning till 7 at night. *What time was allowed for meals?* Forty minutes at noon. *Suppose you flagged a little, or were late, what would they do?* Strap us. *Constantly?* Yes. *Girls as well as boys*? Yes *Is the strap used so as to hurt you excessively*? Yes it is.... I have seen the overlooker go to the top end of the room, where the little girls hug the can to the backminders; he has taken a strap, and a whistle in his mouth, and sometimes he has got a chain and chained them, and strapped them all down the room. *You are considerable deformed in person as a consequence of this labour*? Yes I am. *And what time did it come on*? I was about 13 years old when it began coming....

The more complete transcript appears in John Carey, ed., *Eyewitness to History* (Cambridge: Harvard University Press, 1987), pp. 295–298.

2. Rodes Boyson, "Industrialization and the Life of the Lancashire Factory Worker," in *The Long Debate on Poverty* (Surrey: Unwin Brothers, for the Institute of Economic Affairs, 1972), pp. 69–70.

3. Hand-loom operators had been employed in large-scale industry prior to the Industrial Revolution. As early as 1736, two brothers employed 600 looms and 3,000 persons in the Blackburn district.

4. Percy Bysshe Shelley, "Queen Mab," in *The Complete Poetical Works of Shelley*, ed. George Edward Woodberry (Boston: Houghton Mifflin & Co., Cambridge edition, 1901). [1813]

5. Charles Dickens, *Hard Times*, introduction by G.K. Chesterton (New York: E.P. Dutton, 1966), p. 61. [1854]

6. *Ibid.*, p. 3.

7. *Ibid.*, p. 68.

8. *Ibid.*, pp. 68–69.

9. John Stuart Mill, *Principles of Political Economy*, ed. J.M. Robson (Toronto: University of Toronto Press, 1965), Vol. 2, p. 105. [1848]

6

KARL MARX

The classical school had become the orthodoxy. Like governments, or even economic systems, for that matter, orthodoxies are sometimes overthrown. Revolution is, however, a daunting undertaking; by definition, orthodoxy has society generally on its side. Still, every science has its radical fringe, made up of those who are discontented with the orthodoxy or with society. By now, it had long been forgotten that Adam Smith was a radical in this own time. Although John Stuart Mill helped to gain recognition for the trade union movement in England and bring about tax reforms, his *Principles* served only to strengthen the classical orthodoxy, which after Ricardo and Malthus already was a powerful thing.

We must look elsewhere for radical ideas, where better than for the most renowned radical of all, Karl Marx (1818–1883). Mill's contemporary built an alternative and more complete system on classical foundations. Though Marxian economics has been repulsed in England and the United States, his ideas were to become enormously influential, ultimately dividing the global system between capitalist and socialist nations.

MARX AND HIS SOULMATE, ENGELS

Marx, the enigma, was perhaps designed to be misunderstood from the beginning. Although his first career was as a libertarian journalist inveighing against the ruling Prussian Kaiser, Marx is notorious in the United States and England because Joseph Stalin, a brutal dictator, claimed "Marxist philosophy" as the cover for Stalinism. Predictably, some of today's most orthodox economists contended that with the breakup of the Soviet Union, a capitalist utopia would rise from the ashes of communism.

Marx was born in Trier, in the German Rhineland of the Prussian kingdom, where his father was a lawyer, a member of the bourgeoisie or the capitalistic middle class so detested later by "Marxists." He grew up in a more or less liberal, intellectual atmosphere and intended to have an academic career, but political events made that impossible. He turned to journalism and became increasingly outspoken in his denunciation of political oppression in Europe, for which he was eventually exiled to England, the home of the orthodoxy.

Marx's name is always linked with Friedrich Engels (1820–1895), a fellow German, a lifelong associate, and an unlikely collaborator. Their backgrounds and personalities contrast sharply. Engels is the better writer whereas Marx is the more profound thinker, a meticulous, somewhat ponderous scholar with less gift for the rhetoric.

Engels was an upper middle-class capitalist, rather handsome and athletic, tall and thin with bright blue eyes—the figure of a man who liked to fence and to ride with the hounds—and with a taste for wine and working-class women, especially an Irish lass named Mary Burns. Engels had a natural gaiety and an enthusiasm for literature and music. He especially liked the poetry of Percy Bysshe Shelley (1792–1822) for its attack on orthodox Christianity and secular tyranny. Whereas David Ricardo was *un*sympathetic with Shelley's attack on commerce as "the venal interchange," Engels could embrace still more from Shelley's *Queen Mab* (1813), such as

> Power, like a desolating pestilence,
> Pollutes whate'er it touches; and obedience,
> Bane of all genius, virtue, freedom, truth,
> Makes slaves of men, and, of the human frame,
> A mechanized automation.[1]

As Bentham might have put it, Engels read Shelley for both pleasure and pain.

The contrast between Engels and Marx could not have been greater. Marx had a head too large for his short, stocky frame, a flowing beard, and a stern look. He was gruff, slovenly, and given to brooding. His domestic life was a scene of almost continuous squalor, disorder, and poverty. Engels supported the Marx household financially from 1848 on.

Yet the two shared one thing: a detestation of the status quo and a fierce conviction that it must change. Engels's father sent Friedrich to Manchester, England, to work in the family textile business, Ermen and Engels. Engels was already a convert to socialist theory, and what he saw in Manchester confirmed his beliefs. He wrote what is still perhaps the strongest indictment of industrial slums ever written, a staggering description of hopeless filth, despair, and brutality.

In Engels's account of 1844, the reader can visualize the burial ground for the paupers, the Liverpool and Leeds railway station, and, high on a hilltop, the workhouse, or the "Poor-Law Bastille" of Manchester, looking down on the working quarters below. Here, as in most of the workingmen's quarters of Manchester,

> the pork-raisers rent the courts and build pig-pens in them ... into which the inhabitants of the courts throw all refuse and offal, whence the swine grow fat; and the atmosphere, confined on all four sides, is utterly corrupted by putrefying animal and vegetable substances.[2]

Engels and Charles Dickens shared the same sources—the actual social conditions in and out of the factory. Like Dickens, Engels detected class distinctions whereby the paternalism of feudalism had been replaced by the paternalism of the factory owner. We recall how Dickens has Stephen Blackpool, the worker, coming out of the hot mill and turning from his own class towards the hill on which Mr. Bounderby lived. Bounderby, lunching on "chop and sherry," is very condescending.[3]

Engels witnessed pregnant working women, many ultimately becoming prostitutes, and children who went into the factories at the age of 5 or 6 (even Dickens was not put to work in a factory until the ripe old age of 12), receiving little care from mothers who were themselves at the factory all day and no education from a community looking only for the performance of simple, repetitive mechanical operations. Marx read Engels's work and admired it, and their collaboration began, most infamously, with the *Communist Manifesto* of 1848.

Because of this work and his own dramatic actions, Marx is better known as a revolutionary than as a classical economist. In 1848, after all, it took courage to say, "Let the ruling classes tremble at a Communist revolution. The proletarians [workers] have nothing to lose but their chains. They have a world to win." Prussia still believed in the divine right of kings and had no parliament, no freedom of speech, no right of assembly, no liberty of the press, and no trial by jury. Such despotism dominated most of the seats of power in Europe.

The *Manifesto* was part of the European revolutionary fervor of 1848. The work has had a long history, but its first and most immediate effect was on Marx's own fortunes: He was exiled from Belgium, where he had been living. On the next day, a long-awaited revolution broke out in Paris. The new French government invited Marx to come to Paris. Other great cities, Naples, Milan, Rome, Venice, Berlin, Vienna, Budapest, revolted. Europe was, for the moment, ablaze.

But only for the moment. By June 1848, the Paris revolt had nearly spent itself as the National Guard gained the upper hand. The cold water of the old order was thrown on the revolutionary fires throughout Europe, and they were put out. In July 1849, Marx was expelled from the Rhineland by the Prussian government. He then went to London, where he lived until his death in 1883. Despite his notoriety, the revolutionary actions of Marx filled only a short span of his life.

THE INFLUENCE OF HEGEL

Marx's revolutionary dissent began with his first encounter with the philosopher Georg Wilhelm Friedrich Hegel (1770–1831). Hegel's philosophy is almost absurdly difficult to understand, but its relevance to Marxism is at least fairly clear.

To Hegel and contrary to Descartes and the rationalists, matter and mind are intertwined. Economic, social, and political life is in a process of continual growth. After any one social institution gains power, it is challenged by another. Hegel explains this process by the dialectic: One fact (thesis) works against another fact (antithesis) to produce a wholly new fact (synthesis). For example, feudalism (thesis) encountered a new force, the market economy (antithesis), and the result of this encounter was an entirely new system, capitalism (synthesis). Properly understood, history is a dialectical progression.

However, humanity's progress toward self-realization is not smooth, for self-alienation can happen. In a sense, Marx turned Hegel inside out. Instead of seeing man as self-alienated, Marx saw organized religion as a reflection of self-alienated man. As Robert C. Tucker explains Marx's view, "Religion is a phenomenon of human self-estrangement,"[4] a position failing to endear Marx in Christendom. Marx himself probably had little affection for the masses of people his system is supposed to free, unlike Charles Dickens, who practiced benevolence as well as writing about it. But Marx did see humans overcoming alienation by recognizing themselves as the proper objects of love, care, and worship.

Marx, devoted to reason, believed the course of history to be evolutions of entire social systems from lower (slavish) to higher (democratic and socialistic) forms. Instead of describing the struggle of individuals under natural laws, Marx describes a class struggle: One group overthrows another and thereby decides which economic system is to prevail. The landlords win under feudalism (as Ricardo understood quite well), the merchants under mercantilism, the capitalists under capitalism, and *everybody* under communism or socialism (these last two terms are used by Marx and Engels more or less interchangeably). Institutions such as organized religion slow the progress from lower to higher social orders, and the historical process could be speeded up by destroying them.

THE STING OF ECONOMIC ALIENATION

Marx saw in the relationship of human beings to their government a process of alienation similar to the one he perceived in religion. Humans hurl social power into a separate orbit, the state, which dominates them. Political alienation, however, is an institutional reality, and its resolution requires an actual social revolution, that is, a collective act in which the citizens reclaim the social power once tossed to the state.

The state is intertwined with, and at times indistinguishable from, the economic life of society, which is yet another sphere of human self-alienation. People, according to Marx, fail to develop their full human potential because of their slavish devotion to producing more and more goods for the marketplace. Eventually the "animal spirits" that drove people to the accumulation of profit would be exposed as simply a lower stage in human development.

Because of the intensity of alienation, of obscured self-realization, caused by the capitalist stage of economic development, when the middle-income class, or bourgeoisie (the Bounderbys) got the upper hand, it put an end to all feudal patriarchal, idyllic relations.

> It has pitilessly torn asunder the motley feudal ties that bound man to his "natural superiors," and has left remaining no other access between man and man than naked self-interest, than callous "cash payment." It has drowned the most heavenly ecstasies of religious fervor, of chivalrous enthusiasm, of philistine sentimentalism, in the icy water of egotistical calculation. It has resolved personal worth into exchange value....[5]

Marx and Engels painted a definitive contemporary portrait of nineteenth century capitalism, an extension of man's self-interest that he would grow to dislike, a stage of history alien to man and not the peak of civilization. The process of the self-development of humans will, according to Marx and Engels, culminate in communism.

THE MARXIAN ECONOMICS SYSTEM

Whereas Adam Smith was euphoric about an enduring industrialism and David Ricardo was fearful of its premature death because of the political strength of the landowners, Marx saw capitalism as only a necessary evil, to be superseded by a higher state where private property would not exist.

Although agreeing with Ricardo about the value of a commodity being decided by the amount of labor time necessary for its production, Marx's devotion to a labor theory of value was complete. Moreover, for Marx, there is a difference between the labor value of a commodity and its exchange value.

The labor value of any commodity is equal to the amount of average labor time required for its production. The capitalist pays a price for labor—treating labor power as just another commodity—a subsistence wage just sufficient to keep the worker alive, at work, and able to reproduce the commodity. This wage rate, therefore, is the equivalent of one day's labor power as a commodity. (Marx defines subsistence wage in various ways, sometimes culturally.)

But the capitalist defines himself by using capital (machinery) to produce goods, and therefore current labor will produce some amount of commodity value above its own value, an exchange value in excess of its labor value. Marx called the difference between the two **surplus value**, which is the source of the owner's profits. In today's economics terms, this surplus would be the sum of rent, interest, and profit.

The Surplus Value of Labor: Absolute and Relative

Most of the other classical economists had the penny-pinching capitalists diligently accumulating the financial capital to buy the plant and its machinery through hard work and thrift. Marx discounts the implied high ethical nature of the factory owner and sees labor value itself producing the machinery and the plant.

He makes a distinction between **absolute surplus value** and **relative surplus value**. The former is the excess of new value created in a day over the value of the labor power, enlarged merely by lengthening the working day (evocative of those 12-hour workdays). The latter arises out of improvements in technology reducing the labor time required to produce a product and leading to a higher degree of specialization for the worker.

Relative surplus value corrupts absolutely, for it is the motive behind the accumulation of capital. It is something for the manufacturer to admire and claim. The larger the capital and the higher the state of technology, the greater the output from the labor force, and presumably, the greater the profits.

The greed for riches and the desperate pursuit of exchange value are boundless. A market system with the relative surplus value made possible by exchange ignites capital acquisitiveness. The original, postfeudal justification for private property came from this desire to accumulate capital and thereby relentlessly increase profits through market exchange.

Marx also rejects the romantic notion of capital as property being accumulated through the frugality of the few. He notes:

> This primitive accumulation plays in Political Economy about the same part as original sin in theology. Adam bit the apple, and thereupon sin fell on the human race. In times long gone by there were two sorts of people; one, the diligent, intelligent, and above all, frugal elite; the other, lazy rascals, spending their substance, and more, in riotous living.... Thus as it came to pass the former sort accumulated wealth, and the latter sort had nothing to sell except their own skins. And from this original sin dates the poverty of the great majority that, despite all its labour, has up to now

> nothing to sell but itself, and the wealth of a few that increases constantly although they have long ceased to work. Such insipid childishness is every day preached to us in the defense of property.[6]

Even Marx had his literary moments.[7]

The Beginning of Monopoly Capital

Marx envisioned changing technology as well as increasing competition creating fewer and fewer, larger and larger firms. A higher state of technology will require a larger plant and more capital for production. Competition allows the strong to dominate both the weak and the less strong, which ultimately leads to monopolistic practices. Monopoly capital means enormous wealth concentrated in the hands of a few, who can price commodities without much regard for the consumer. Thus, laborers as consumers fail to gain the benefits envisioned by Adam Smith.

The evolution of pin manufacturing in the United Kingdom, hardly known for industrial concentration, illustrates well what Marx was anticipating for much of the factory system. Pins, like iron, have changed little in the two centuries since Smith. However, technology and the degree of density in the industry have changed greatly.

In the mid-eighteenth century, pin-making was essentially a cottage industry, with a great deal of production taking place in workhouses. The replacement of labor by machine production recast the structure of the industry. Pin-making machines combined the many separate operations from which the Smithian benefits of the division of labor flowed (though Smith did acknowledge the positive effect of the invention of machines to replace labor). Over time the speed of these machines has increased—from about 45 pins per minute (ppm) in 1830 to 180 ppm in 1900 and to 500 ppm in 1980. Whereas Adam Smith had each person making 4,800 pins a day in 1776, two hundred years latter the daily output per worker in the United Kingdom was an estimated 800,000 pins—a productivity increase of 16,667 percent!

Should anyone care a pin about this story? Going to its point, it is simply this: During the Industrial Revolution machines increasingly replaced labor, and the cost of such machines built barriers to entry naturally leading to fewer firms in each industry—that is, to industrial concentration. As late as 1900 there were some 50 pin factories in Birmingham alone, but by 1939 the number in the entire United Kingdom had shrunk to about 12, and by 1980 there were only two, the Newey Group, with a pin factory in Birmingham, and Whitecroft Scovill, which has a factory in Gloucestershire. Today, specialization in the United Kingdom has nearly reached the single factory limit.[8]

Worker Alienation

In Marx's famous ***doctrine of increasing misery***, the conditions of labor worsen compared to the improved conditions of the capitalist. When the relative lot of the workers becomes intolerable, they will rise up against the capitalists in a social and economic revolution. Behind this doctrine is the theory of estranged labor, in which capitalism alienates and dehumanizes workers.

Why was labor estranged? First, laborers did not control the nature of the product, but rather it controlled them and dictated their labor. Second, factory workers did not work for themselves but for their employer. Any benefits accrued to the workers would have to be consumed in their leisure hours; there was no direct satisfaction from work. Moreover, in Manchester and elsewhere, refuse and filth greeted the workers at home.

Alienation develops in the market exchange system for a number of reasons. Marx and Smith both believed that a finer and finer division of labor would increase productivity, and also that, as Smith put it, "the man whose whole life is spent in performing a few simple operations...generally becomes as stupid and ignorant as it is possible for a human creature to become." Specialization from the division of labor is evil, Marx concluded, not only because of monotony but because it divorces workers from their fellow workers and from the end product. Capitalism is dehumanizing.

Even if the accumulation of capital results in higher wages, wages will not keep pace with profits. Incomes may be enough to stave off hunger, but as relative income differentials continue to widen, social discontent will begin to stir. Work does not enhance the satisfaction of a need, it is merely a means of satisfying needs external to it. In Marx's words:

> What, then, constitutes the alienation of labor? First, the fact that labor is external to the worker, i.e. it does not belong to its essential being; that in his work, he does not affirm himself but denies himself, does not develop freely his physical and mental energy but mortifies his body and ruins his mind. The worker therefore only feels himself outside his work, and in his work feels outside himself. He is at home when he is not working, and when he is working he is not at home.[9]

The worker was no longer the craftsman creating, but the servant of a new industrial process. Even the word *master*, which had meant the master of a craft, came to mean a person who was the master of other people.

And so, workers and employers are polarized. With monopolies, more and more of the wealth of the nation sifted through the hands of workers and piled up at the feet of the capitalists. What Adam Smith merely detested—monopoly—Marx saw as inevitable. Added to this potential for conflict is the workers' attitude toward work itself.

As the workers begin to see their labor as drudgery, they lose the recreation or delight coming from variety. During the Industrial Revolution an enormous change in labor took place from direct hand production—like that still done today in certain arts and crafts—to a production system requiring routine operations. Indeed, one reason that unions were unattractive to workers in the early days of the trade union movement in England is that many workers felt that membership in a union meant acquiescence in a hated factory system.

The Business Cycle

From the ashes of monopoly capital, Marx built the first sophisticated model of the business cycle—of boom and bust. Marx saw the successive depressions of capitalism becoming increasingly severe, so much so that the workers would finally revolt, overthrow capitalism, and build a socialist economy. As Marx put it, "the knell of capitalist private property sounds. The expropriators are expropriated."[10] His theory of the business cycle is technical, and we can do no more than summarize it here.

The Industrial Revolution began with a surplus of agricultural and cottage-industry workers seeking employment in factories. The surplus of workers enabled factory owners to keep the wage rate at a subsistence level (Ricardo's iron law of wages), but as industry expanded, the demand for labor grew until full employment. At these higher levels of labor demand and employment, the owners of capital had to pay higher and higher wages to get enough workers for their factories.

Labor-saving machinery turned out to be a godsend: with it, *fewer* workers could produce the same number of pins. The problem of high wages could be temporarily solved by replacing workers with machines—known today as technological unemployment. Marx thought the number unemployed this way sufficient to be termed an "industrial reserve army."

So far, so good—for the capitalist. But, beyond a certain point in this process, capitalists began to be self-defeating. The new labor-saving machinery and soaring productivity flooded the markets with extra goods just as the workers' incomes were being restricted by that very same machinery. Lower income meant lowered consumer demand.

As sales revenue fell, the producers stopped making plans to add to a capital stock, now producing goods in excess of what could be sold. Even today economists look to a decline in the capital-goods industry for a portent of economic downturns. The decline eventually causes unemployment, lower total wages, and falling national income.

Up to this stage, Marx had anticipated John Maynard Keynes's theory of insufficient total demand, about which more later.

Contrary to Keynes and in tune with the neoclassicals, Marx saw recovery from these cyclical slumps as automatic. However, the assurance of economic recoveries did not guarantee the survival of capitalism. Moreover, the causes of recovery were different from those espoused by the neoclassicals. The surviving large business firms swallowed the failing small firms and restored profits, but the cycle became increasingly fragile. Each time the business cycle turned downward, it plunged deeper. The Great Depression of the 1930s would have surprised Marx less than the failure of revolution to follow it.

FLAWS IN MARX'S VISION

Many people made premature predictions about the death of capitalism during the Great Depression of the 1930s, and the American Communist Party gained some adherents, including even some Hollywood stars, as Ronald Reagan was to confess, on their behalf. But by the end of World War II, the mixed enterprise system of the United States bore only a family resemblance to the kind of capitalism that Marx had attacked.

For one thing, national defense spending escalated during the cold and hot wars with the Soviet bloc and other communist nations. (Ironically, the Soviets may have been responsible for faster growth in the United States.) For another, the government often intervened on behalf of both the capitalists and the workers. Marx correctly saw the government as the enforcer of property rights and the protector of the entrepreneurs' economic power. For example, minimal capital gains taxation and low or avoidable inheritance taxes became measures protecting private property. Marx believed that governments would even go to war to expand the size of markets for products and provide roads, railroads, and canals in the interests of profitable commerce. Despite his affinity for libraries, Marx was not naive.

As noted, the *Communist Manifesto* was published in the same year as J.S. Mill's *Principles*, but the improving economic conditions in the 1860s and 1870s kept Marx's radical ideas underground, gave succor to the emerging optimism of mainstream English economics, and fed J.S. Mill's modest reform proposals. During 1862 to 1875, the real wage in England improved by 40 percent. Still, Marx anticipated, in some detail, the evolution of capitalism, but he underestimated the resiliency of reformed capitalism and the effectiveness of patriotic appeals to labor. He, too, did not anticipate the aspirations of the working class for a capitalistic lifestyle. The system that Marx wanted overthrown is now only vestigial, and the potential for revolution against industry has consequently diminished. If whatever the American economy is today were to be replaced by a Marxist one, it would not be pure capitalism that would be overthrown; you cannot overthrow what does not exist.

NOTES

1. Percy Bysshe Shelley, "Queen Mab," in *The Complete Poetical Works of Shelley*, ed. George Edward Woodberry (Boston: Houghton Mifflin, Cambridge edition, 1901).
2. Friedrich Engels, "Working-Class Manchester," extract from *The Condition of the Working Class in England in 1844*, in *The Marx-Engels Reader*, 2nd ed., ed. Robert C. Tucker (New York: W.W. Norton & Company, 1978), p. 583.
3. Charles Dickens, *Hard Times*, introduction by G.K. Chesterton (New York: E.P. Dutton, 1966), pp. 68–69.
4. Robert C. Tucker (ed.), *The Marx-Engels Reader* (New York: W.W. Norton & Co., 1972), p. xix.
5. Karl Marx and Friedrich Engels, "The Communist Manifesto," in *Capital, the Communist Manifesto, and Other Writings*, ed. Max Eastman (New York: Random House, 1932 [1848]), p. 315.
6. Karl Marx, *Capital* (Moscow: Foreign Language Publishing House, 1961), Vol. 1, pp. 713–714.
7. Or, perhaps, we are reading Engels's editing.

8. These data are gleaned from a neat little article by Clifford F. Pratten, "The Manufacture of Pins," *Journal of Economic Literature* (March 1980): 93–96.

9. Karl Marx, *Economic and Philosophic Manuscripts of 1844* (Moscow: Progress Publishers, 1959), p. 69.

10. Karl Marx, "Capital," *op. cit.*, p. 763.

7

Alfred Marshall: The Great Victorian

Karl Marx did not prevail in the Anglo-Saxon world. Adam Smith's vision, later sharpened by David Ricardo and then finally glossed by John Stuart Mill, remained intact for about a century. Then during the 1870s the **marginalist school** of economics came along, and marginalism began to dominate Western economic thought until at least the mid-1930s. Marginalism still maintains a sturdy grasp on **microeconomics**—the study of what determines the relative prices of all things, including labor and capital. It does not stop there; today, microeconomics has a stranglehold on several aggregate economic models under the rubric of **macroeconomics**.

The marginalist school evolved more or less independently in several countries. Its major envoys were Carl Menger in Austria, Hermann H. Gossen in Germany, Léon Walras in Switzerland, William Stanley Jevons and Alfred Marshall in England, and John Bates Clark in America.

Austrian and neo-Austrian economics began with the publication (in Austria) of Menger's *Principles of Economics* in 1871. Two years after its publication, Menger, a lucid lecturer, had sufficient stature to be appointed to the chair of economics at the University of Vienna and to serve as tutor to Crown Prince Rudolf. The refinement and spreading of Menger's views by students Friedrich von Wieser (1851–1926) and Eugen von Böhm-Bawerk (1851–1914) ignited the "Austrian tradition." When Böhm-Bawerk, von Wieser's brother-in-law, ascended to Menger's post at the University of Vienna, he gave marginalism its name.

Among these scholars, Alfred Marshall (1842–1924), whose name is virtually synonymous with **neoclassical economics**, ascended as the high priest of economic science after John Stuart Mill. Though marginalist to its core, neoclassical economics is many other things: It is a resurrection, reinterpretation, and extension of the doctrines of Adam Smith.

As noted earlier, finding the value of a product and the distribution of the income from its sales among all those helping hands producing it is a central problem in economics, the solution of which is called "the theory of value." Smith and the classicals had price as value being decided mostly by cost of production. Jeremy Bentham, as we have witnessed, not only laid claim to the importance of pleasure and pain but also to its measurability in money units. Before the end of the Victorian drama that unfolds in this chapter, Bentham returns in a supporting role, and a new "theory of value" will emerge in which demand plays the major role.

Capital also comes to center stage. In the manner followed by most of the neoclassicals, Walras defined **capital** as machines, instruments, tools, office buildings, factories, and warehouses. This classification, narrower than Smith's, made capital one of the *several* productive inputs on the same footing as labor and land. When capital becomes more important, as Marx noted, so do the capitalists.

The heavy velvet curtain opens to some scenes from the marginalist school.

PLEASURE AND PAIN AT THE MARGIN

The utilitarian moralist Jeremy Bentham, the great eccentric whom we first met in Chapter 3 and last saw as a mummy at the University of London, returns to center stage. Bentham's idea of human nature, which fit the ethic of self-interest and influenced Malthus, the Mills, and Ricardo, was based on the pleasure/pain dialectic. As noted, a thing promotes the interest of the individual *and* the community when it tends to add to the sum total of his pleasures or diminish the sum total of his pain. Bentham's hedonism (the doctrine that whatever is good is also necessarily pleasant) is the cornerstone for the marginalists' calculus of pain and pleasure in which competition maximizes pleasure while minimizing pain.

The point of change in pleasure or pain is called the **margin**, an idea the marginalists and Marshall used to explain economic behavior. *Marginal pleasure*, as we might suppose, would be a miserly increase in pleasure for a moment in time. Rational people will avoid any extra pain unless it is offset at the margin by an equal measure of pleasure. They are rational balancers (at the margin) of pleasure and pain, a balancing act describable with Newton's elegant calculus. In this way Bentham's hedonism, utilitarianism, and rationalism were blended in a scientific abstraction that came to be called the **economic man.**[1]

During the Industrial Revolution, as we have already seen, the idea of the economic man (or person; sex is not an issue, save for Malthus) had practical uses; for the marginalists, its incorporeality was its virtue. The marginalists imagined a world in which people act in response only to conscious and consistent motives, inclinations, or desires. Nothing is capricious or experimental; everything is deliberate.[2]

According to the marginalists, for example, a woman of the times would never impulsively buy a new, bright yellow smock-frock. People know what the consequences of their actions will be (banishment from the garden club) and act accordingly. The purpose of choice is to benefit the decision-maker, every person being the final and absolute judge of his or her own welfare. The medieval world of spirits, herbs, and magic is no match for these hedonistic, lightning-fast computers of pleasures and pains.

Abstract economic man resides in a society of intense competition, an idealized laissez-faire world. This competition usually is said to be based on the following conditions:

- The number of buyers and sellers is so great that no single one can noticeably influence the market price of either the material used in production or the final commodity.
- Products are generic and are substitutable for each other. A dress is a dress; a carriage is a carriage; a horse is a horse, of course.
- There is considerable freedom of entry into production in each market. There are few restrictions resulting from the high cost and risk of setting up business, nor is there any barrier due to such things as license regulations.[3]
- Every consumer and every producer has considerable knowledge about prices at all times. The woman looking for a new dress knows that all prices on dresses available in "her economy" are virtually identical, and the dress manufacturer knows all the alternative profit returns for producing products other than dresses.
- The distance to markets is not addressed as an issue; the woman buying a dress may do so in London, where she lives, or in San Francisco.

These conditions are implicit in Walras but otherwise were not strictly stated until the 1920s by economists such as Frank Knight and Arthur Pigou (about whom more later). When an economic man is the sole producer of a product, he is a pure monopolist.

THE MARGINALISTS' BRIDGE

The early marginalists (Jevons, Menger and Walras), following Bentham, valued a product as an object or service giving pleasure (massage) or preventing pain (aspirin). Jevons wrote to his brother Herbert on June 1, 1860:

> ...as the quantity of any commodity, for instance, plain food, which a man has to consume, increases, so the utility or benefit derived from the last portion used decreases in degree. The decrease of enjoyment between the beginning and end of a meal may be taken as an example.[4]

The value of the last morsel, the *least wanted,* sets the value for all. William Stanley Jevons, painfully shy, had few friends and was notoriously the worst of lecturers; he was hardly an efficient pleasure machine himself.

This subjective psychological valuation at the margin is illustrated in Table 7.1, which is patterned after an example used by the Austrian Karl Menger in 1871.

Table 7.1

DIMINISHING MARGINAL UTILITY AND THE HIERARCHY OF WANTS

Hierarchy of Wants	**I**	**II**	**III**	**IV**	**V**
Want	**To avoid starvation**	**To be clothed**	**To be housed**	**To be transported**	**To enjoy luxury**
Commodity or service to satisfy want	Food	Clothes	House	Horse	Ale
1-unit increase	5	4	3	2	1
Another-unit increase	4	3	2	1	0
Another-unit increase	3	2	1	0	
Another-unit increase	2	1	0		
Another-unit increase	1	0			
Another-unit increase	0				

Though Menger was not a Benthemite, the table nonetheless illustrates the **Law of Diminishing Marginal Utility**. The table shows five human wants to be satisfied by the purchase of commodities or services. First, a person will rank wants in descending order of their importance (I, II, III, etc.). Then, a person will accrue different levels of satisfaction from consuming more and more units of the object satisfying a particular want (to avoid starvation, to be clothed, etc.). Arabic numbers (5, 4, 3, 2, 1, 0) are used to indicate the amount of *extra satisfaction* associated with each unit increase (marginal increase) in the quantity of the good. Declining numerical values represent the diminishing want–satisfying power to an individual of additional units of the same commodity or service.

We can see how each increment of food consumed gives less additional satisfaction than the immediately preceding unit. Satisfaction in avoiding starvation tends to diminish as consumption grows. For example, the sixth increment of food yields no extra satisfaction. Even Josiah Bounderby, the factory owner in Dickens's *Hard Times*, could eat only so many lamb chops and drink so much sherry.

Since the marginalists were chasing a theory of value, they had to connect diminishing marginal satisfaction to price and amounts demanded. As they turned it out, the consumer willingly pays a price equal only to marginal satisfaction. As marginal utility declines with a greater amount demanded (consumed), the price the consumer is willing to pay must also decline. The consumer willingly pays the least for the last morsel. In this way, a downward-sloping demand schedule is constructed.

Like the classical economists, the early marginalists thought of economic laws as natural laws. They also shared with the classicals a strong faith in individualism, believing competition to be the great leveler that converted the brute self-interest of individuals into a collective virtue. But the fundamental agreements between the two schools should not obscure their differences.

The classical economists were primarily concerned with production over the long run. Much of *The Wealth of Nations* is about producers dividing up their labor in order to increase production to its limits. Thus, while David Ricardo emphasized long-run cost of production (supply) as the main determinant of the value of commodities, the early marginalists focused on short-run demand.

MARGINALISM AND THE THEORY OF DISTRIBUTION

Even the distribution of income did not escape the grasp of marginalism. John Bates Clark (1847–1938), America's foremost marginalist economist, was the outstanding writer in this area. Clark, a gentle man who failed to offend even his critics, succinctly summarized his views in the opening paragraph of his *Distribution of Wealth* (1899):

> It is the purpose of this work to show that the distribution of the income of society is controlled by a natural law, and that this law, if it worked without friction, would give to every agent of production the amount of wealth which that agent creates.

Clark's theory is partly derived from the **law of diminishing returns**: If the amounts of a producer's capital, land, and managerial skills remain constant while labor is added, then the output of each additional worker will decline because that worker has smaller and smaller shares of the other inputs in hand. Each worker ends up receiving a real wage equaling this marginal product of labor. Clark also gives capital (now meaning only factories, machines, etc.) a diminishing marginal product. However wages may be adjusted by bargains freely made between individuals, he also claims, the total wage payments to workers from such agreements tend to equal that part of the product of industry traceable to the labor itself.[5] The same evaluations hold for capital so that it also now has undisputed value at the margin. Clark thus enabled the neoclassicals to extend their "theory of value" to all the factors of production.

The rights to private property are absolute and should be protected by the state. The government should not interfere with the "natural laws" of income distribution. Insofar as private property rights go unobstructed, such rights assign to all people what they have specifically produced. In the private enterprise system, the division of the total income from production into wages, interest, and profits is completely equitable and ethical because every person is paid exactly what he or she is worth at the margin. "And nothing more!" Dickens's retired merchant, Thomas Gradgrind, might have cheered.

According to Clark, the distribution and accumulation of income and property are a reflection, over time, of the marginal worth of the person in the production process.

MARSHALL AND THE NEOCLASSICAL NICETIES OF VICTORIAN ENGLAND

As the play moves toward a climax or, perhaps more aptly, an anti-climax, the scene shifts to Victorian England where Alfred Marshall will command the stage for a very long run.

Those marginalists smoothed the path for the classical revival, a restoration substantially different from classical economics in details and less dreary than Malthusian fecundity. Yet, because the underlying classical superstructure revealed by John Bates Clark was still intact, the neoclassical "revolution" had all the excitement of a Victorian Age Sunday school picnic.

Queen Victoria reigned during more years of the century (1837–1901) than not. A complacent mood characterized the first half of her reign (until about 1870), fed by a pride in stable constitutional government, optimism from increasingly industrial prosperity, and an unshaken confidence in the inherent rightness of the liberal and evangelical virtues of industriousness, self-reliance, temperance, piety, charity, and moral earnestness.

During the Victorian Age the novel was the foremost literary genre—an increasingly popular form of entertainment—and poetry became less important. The early nineteenth century novels of Sir Walter Scott (1771–1832) and Jane Austen (1775–1817) showed little direct social concern. The novels of Austen, for example, imply a desirably ordered existence, in which the comfortable decorum of the English family is disturbed only by a not too serious shortage of money, by love affairs temporarily gone wrong, and by the intrusion of self-centered stupidity. The good, if not rewarded for their goodness, suffer no permanent injustice. Life is seen as fundamentally reasonable and decent; when wrong is done, it is punished. These cheerful outcomes, wherein the good characters end up happily and bad characters unhappily, meet Miss Prism's definition in Oscar Wilde's play *The Importance of Being Earnest* (1895): "That is why it is called fiction."

Even so, the tradition of the Romantics remained in the early poetry of Lord Alfred Tennyson (1809–1892) and Robert Browning (1812–1889). Browning might have been summing up those early years in *Pipa Passes* [pt. I, 1841]:

> The lark's on the wing;
> The snail's on the thorn:
> God's in his heaven—
> All's right with the world.

But such sonnets were not long for this world. The Victorian Age is defined more by those writers critical of their society. By mid-century, the problems following the Industrial Revolution were considered by the Bronte sisters, by W.M. Thackeray, and, as noted and most notably, by Charles Dickens. Even Tennyson and Browning were to find their own idiom in which to express doubts and anxieties similar to those of the novelists.

The orthodoxy, housed in Cambridge University in England—then the citadel of Victorian temperance, piety, and morality—shrugged off such Malthusian–Ricardian dismalness and set about to restore the good cheer and harmony of Adam Smith. The association there of first Alfred Marshall and Arthur Pigou and later Joan Robinson, Piero Sraffa, and John Maynard Keynes accounts for Cambridge's unique stature in the world of academic economics during the first half of the twentieth century.

At the head of this distinguished lineage towers Alfred Marshall (1842–1924), tall in stature and reputation. William Rothenstein's portrait of Marshall, which hangs in the hall of St. John's College at Cambridge, shows him to have been the stereotypical professor—fine white hair, white mustache, delicate features, kind but brilliant eyes. He *was* the Great Victorian.

Marshall was to preserve the legacy of the classical economists while refurbishing their thought with marginalism and some ideas of his own: Hence, the aptness of *neoclassical.* He differed somewhat from the classicals in allowing room for modest departures from laissez-faire in the direction of cautious reform. He shifted the focus of economics away from the struggles between the labor and capitalist classes and toward nameless individuals and small, "representative" business firms.

Marshall was a mixture of mathematician, physicist, economist, and moralizer. He came from a strict Victorian Evangelical Protestant background, his father intending the son to be ordained in the Evangelical ministry. At Cambridge, however, Marshall switched his studies from theology to mathematics and physics and eventually to economics. He rebelled not against orthodox theology but rather against the further study of the classics then required for the ministry.

Something of the atmosphere of Marshall's youth is suggested by the title of a tract that his father wrote in opposition to the feminist movement: *Man's Rights and Women's Duties.* There is little in Alfred's attitude toward women to suggest that the son was greatly different from the father. As for Mary Paley (later Alfred Marshall's wife), when a schoolgirl, her father would not permit her to read the works of Charles Dickens, the Victorian writer most cool toward the Victorian age.

At about the time Alfred Marshall took up the study of economics, English intellectuals began to feel the heat of Charles Darwin and Herbert Spencer. The ideas of Darwin enjoying the widest dissemination—usually through popularizers such as "Darwin's Bulldog," Thomas Huxley (1825–1895), whom Marshall knew from dinner parties—pertained to the physical and biological struggle for existence, natural selection as a result of individual differences, the survival of the fittest (Spencer's phrase, not Darwin's), and the evolution of the species. The conflict between the Biblical version of the Creation and that implied by Darwinian evolution raged during the Victorian Age.

Like so many at the time, Marshall saw no conflict between the two explanations. He was a disciple of Darwinian evolutionary progress, Christian morality, and the utilitarian ethic of Bentham. To Marshall, evolutionary progress meant that the entire society materially improved, not just the hardy few, as the Social Darwinists claimed (and further explicated in Chapter 8). His general philosophical bent can be illustrated by a passage in which he describes his feeling about economics when he first began to study the subject: "Its fascinating inquiries into the possibilities of the higher and more rapid development of human faculties brought me into touch with the question: How far do the conditions of life of the British (and other) working classes generally suffice for fullness of life?"[6]

Two other significant intellectual influences on Marshall were the renowned physicist James Clerk Maxwell and Marshall's personal friend, the mathematician W.K. Clifford. When Marshall's serious study of economics began, J.S. Mill's and David Ricardo's versions of the Smithian system were still unchallenged. Marshall focused on the theoretical rigor of Ricardo and began to involve himself with diagrams and algebra, founding the modern diagrammatics of economics. He would work out a problem first in mathematics, draw the diagrammatic, and then take down this scaffolding, relegating it to footnotes.

As a moralizer, he was a cautious optimist. He sided with his father regarding the "proper" role of women: Even Mary Paley Marshall said that in the classroom her husband "preached." In the first half of the eighteenth century, essayist Alexander Pope had epitomized a certain kind of Newtonian optimism by his claim that "Whatever is, is right." According to Joan Robinson, the moralizing of Marshall "...always came out that whatever is, is very nearly best."[7]

By the time he was 35, Marshall had privately worked out the foundations of his entire system. According to Marshall's one-time student and biographer John Maynard Keynes, Marshall kept "his wisdom at home until he could produce it fully clothed...," partly because, being thin-skinned, he feared being wrong.[8] Like Newton, he was slow to publish; Alfred Marshall's great book, *Principles of Economics*, did not appear in its first edition until 1890 and in its last not until 1920. Even in 1931, the professor for John Kenneth Galbraith's first course in economics at Berkeley taught from *Principles*. Once more, we return to its contents.

MARSHALL'S CONTRIBUTIONS

Though marginal utility lies somewhere behind Marshall's concept of demand, he wanted to reduce the unscientific subjectivity of utility by using money as a measuring device (as Bentham had suggested), much as kilowatt-hours meter electricity use of any type. To avoid Bentham's dilemma in which the marginal utility of money or income also was diminishing, Marshall imposed a constancy on the marginal utility of money.

The other marginalists would say that if a suit is three times as useful to you as a pair of trousers, then you will pay $30 for the suit and $10 for the trousers. Marshall shifted this around, saying that, *because* you are willing to pay three times as much for the suit as for the pants, the suit is three times as useful to you. Marshall's explanation best suits economists today because prices are quantifiable in money units, whereas psychic satisfaction is difficult, if not impossible to measure.

Marshallian Supply and Demand

A stream of equilibrium prices runs through Marshallian economics. In both the physical sciences and economics, **equilibrium** is a state of balance between opposing forces or actions. Equilibrium is either static or dynamic, depending on whether the object in a state of balance is stationary or in motion. In physics, an object in dynamic equilibrium is moving along a path over time that is predictable. A force—based on a mysterious X-factor Newton called gravity—is sufficient to keep a planet in a predictable path and thus in dynamic equilibrium.

Marshall's most important contribution to economics was to combine the production theory of the classical writers with the demand theory of the marginalists into the famous "Marshallian cross" that, in turn, became the basis for the neoclassical "theory of value." This now classic example of static equilibrium in economics is Alfred Marshall's explanation of **equilibrium price** maintained by the forces of supply and demand.

Farmers will supply a greater number of bushels of corn per month the higher the price per bushel paid to them. As each extra bushel of corn will cost more to produce than the immediately preceding bushel because of diminishing marginal returns, the farmer will supply only one more bushel if the price paid is raised to equal the marginal cost of production. Rising marginal costs ensure an upward-sloping supply curve for corn. The neoclassicals presumed diminishing marginal returns and rising marginal costs to apply equally to manufacturing.

Consumers will demand a greater number of bushels of corn per month if the price is lowered. The idea of quantity being demanded rising as price falls comes from the marginalist concept of diminishing marginal utility. As each extra bushel consumed gives less and less satisfaction, the price must be lower and lower to ensure its purchase. This is the normal **law of demand**, in which the quantity of corn demanded increases as the price of corn declines. All the forces reach a balance when the demand and supply curves cross, like the blades of a pair of scissors, providing an equilibrium price and the Marshallian revolution. This price will persist and forces will be in a state of rest. Other forces, such as income or cost changes, can shift the demand and supply curves themselves and a new equilibrium price will result.

Another important and useful concept attributed to Marshall is the idea of **elasticity**. Although Henry C.F. Jenkin (1833–1885), a professor of engineering who turned to economics in 1868, had alluded to the concept of elasticity in an 1870 publication on supply and demand, Marshall extended the idea until it was his own. As he put it, "The *elasticity* or *responsiveness* of demand in a market is great or small according as the amount demanded increases much or little for a given rise in price."[9] Very simply, economics teachers define price elasticity of demand for beginning students as the percentage change in quantity demanded divided by the percentage change in price. The flexibility of the elasticity idea enabled Marshall to extend it to supply and to factor markets as well as to income classes.

Out of all this, neoclassical marginalism was to claim a solution to the century old problem of value theory. Smith, Ricardo, and the other classicals had supply curves. The classical supply schedule was upward-sloping for agriculture, but it failed to defy gravity and was horizontal for manufacturing. Since the classical price in manufacturing was set by the cost of production and did not rise as output expanded, output could increase without limit or, as Marshall would have said, "be perfectly elastic with respect to price."

Once the average production cost or unit cost in manufacturing is set, so is classical price. As the manufacturer is producing at constant costs (each extra unit produced costs the same as the one before it), he is indifferent as to how much is produced at that unit cost and sold at that price. Thus, the amount supplied is limited only by what buyers demand.

This classical view is fine as far as it goes. The only role of demand is to set the level of output. But what if production costs are not constant? Suppose the cost of each extra unit of output *exceeds* the cost of the increment before it (as in Ricardian agriculture and as in Marshall). Then, we have an upward-sloping supply curve in which price is no longer decided by the average cost of production but rather by the *marginal* cost of production. Then, marginal cost is matched up with the marginal utility of the consumer by an equilibrium price. Price (value) is determined simultaneously with the amounts demanded *and* supplied. The neoclassicals had a formal way of representing subjective demand and increasing costs, and thus were able to solve a classical puzzle by providing the missing pieces.

Marshall extended his idea of price at the equilibrium point of supply and demand to create an entire Newtonian system in which all the elements of the economic universe are kept in place by mutual counterpoise and interaction. The equilibrium point became the basis for a new "theory of value," and eventually "value" became synonymous with "price" so that economists now use the term "price theory."

Despite Marshall's immersion in mathematics, he never lost sight of the role of institutions in the economy. They, he believed, assured the stability that he observed. In particular, Marshall disagreed with

J.B. Clark regarding his marginal productivity explanation for income distribution. Marshall wrote that "the doctrine that the earnings of a worker tend to be equal to the net product of his work has by itself no real meaning; since in order to estimate net product, we have to take for granted all the expenses of production of the commodity on which he works, other than his own wages."[10] Marshall considered it wrong to speak about marginal productivity independent of the effects of various institutions such as guilds and firms on wages and income distribution.

UP AGAINST WALRASIAN EQUILIBRIUM

In the mid-1870s, Léon Walras (1834–1910) published a complex mathematical general equilibrium theory that embraces all commodity and factor markets simultaneously.

Walras's inspiration (like Smith's) was Newtonian mechanics: He could demonstrate how the harmony of the spheres operated in his idealized market system as well as in the heavens. Walras's analogy of an economic universe—much like a machine, with prices moving up and down, functioning like levers and pulleys—is more direct and blunt than Smith's. Although he was held in relatively low esteem among economists in his own day, Walras is now regarded as perhaps the greatest of the pure theorists, a change that reflects a keen fascination with mathematics. Walras also actively pursued policies aimed at improving human welfare.

Walras's general equilibrium notion differs from Marshall's favorite vista of markets. Walras's system is very much in the tradition of Quesney and J.B. Say (see Chapters 2 and 3) because full employment is guaranteed by automatic market adjustments. Suppose that all markets except the wheat market and one non-wheat market are in equilibrium. An excess demand in the wheat market must find an excess supply counterpart in another market or markets. If, at its present price, the amount of wheat demanded is greater than the amount supplied, the price of wheat is the lever raised to pull down the excess in demand. Because all markets are intertwined, however, this price rise must disrupt equilibria in other markets because such equilibria were defined with reference to the initial price of wheat, which turned out to be the "wrong" price. Thus, further adjustments in all other markets must be made, and then again in the wheat market, and so forth. In this way, the whole system moves inexorably toward a wondrous multi-market equilibrium.

How could everyone know enough about all quantities and all prices so as to ensure such synchronic equilibria? Walras's answer lies in his theory of **groping** (*a tâtonnement process,* in Walras's language). (Groping probably has a different meaning for today's college students.) In Walras, buyers and sellers announce the amounts they wish to trade at prices "cried at random," as in a commodities trading pit. For example, buyers reduce their price offers when there is an excess supply and increase than when there is an excess demand.

They continue to cry out their uncommitted intentions to purchase until they hit on a price that just clears the particular market (the equilibrium price). Both buyers and sellers by trial and error discover the true equilibrium price before they ever undertake to exchange any goods. Ultimately, Walras resorted to the use of an auctioneer. In the groping process an auctioneer (the **Walrasian Auctioneer**) processes all the bids and offers, decides which prices will clear all markets, and *only then* allows trading.

The Walrasian system may seem extremely abstract, because it is. Descartes's rationalism seems to have pushed Walras into a narrow analogy of Newton's system. Actually, in a modern economy, individuals do not cry out prices or wage rates, and auctioneers are engaged only on special occasions. Moreover, the successful achievement of a simultaneous multi-market equilibrium would contain its own irony: In such a condition, the modern world would have no more need for Walras or economists than did feudalism. Walras, conveniently, favored a market socialism whereby the government would enforce competitive markets so that his theory would hold (see Box 7.1).

Box 7.1 Looking Ahead at the Nobel Prizes: The Extension of Walras's General Equilibrium Theory

In 1972, Kenneth J. Arrow and Sir John R. Hicks were jointly awarded the Nobel Prize in economics "for their pioneering contributions to general economic equilibrium theory and welfare theory." Hicks constructed a complete equilibrium model based on assumptions about the behavior of consumers and producers, giving Walras's equations greater concreteness, showing how changes in consumers' tastes had consequences for the whole economy. Kenneth Arrow, together with Gerhard Debreu, in 1954 re-formulated Walras's model with mathematical set theory, and established the conditions which must be fulfilled if a neoclassical general equilibrium system is to have a unique and economically meaningful solution.

Later, in 1982, Gerard Debreu was awarded the Nobel Prize in economics "for his rigorous reformulation of the theory of general equilibrium." From Adam Smith came the notion that the striving by individuals to maximize their own welfare led, as if by an invisible hand, the price mechanism to yield the greatest possible welfare for everyone. Debreu, independently of Arrow, established the mathematical conditions which guarantee that the price mechanism brings about an efficient utilization of resources in accordance with the desires of consumers. Whether this happens in a real-world economy, however, was left unanswered.

More details and biographies can be found in Assar Lindbeck (ed.), *Nobel Lectures in Economic Sciences, 1969–1980* (Singapore/New Jersey/London/Hong Kong: World Scientific, 1992), pp. 103–131 and in Karl-Göran Mäler (ed.), *Nobel Lectures in Economic Sciences, 1981–1990* (Singapore/New Jersey/London/Hong Kong: World Scientific, 1992), pp. 79–102.

Marshall's fancied approach contrasts with that of Walras. With prices and quantities in markets other than the one under consideration held constant or assumed to be small in their effects, Marshall introduced the idea of *partial equilibrium*. In constructing the demand curve for English wool, Marshall would define the demand for wool as related to the price of wool with the prices of other commodities such as cotton, money income, and consumer tastes held constant. Walras would consider the prices of *all* commodities, including cotton and the price of wool. (Money income and tastes still would be presumed constant.) Whereas Walrasian general equilibrium is exactly like the solution of any system of simultaneous equations, Marshall was willing to take one market at a time and isolate it from the rest of the economy.

It is easy to see which—partial or general equilibrium—would be easier to understand. To this day, undergraduates are taught microeconomics with Marshall's partial equilibrium approach; they do not have the mathematics background to solve simultaneous equations. Still, general equilibrium has been used for advanced economic research since the 1950s and dominated the research time of economists in the 1990s.

We are left with an interesting puzzle. Since Marshall had more training in mathematics than Walras, why did Marshall frown on general equilibrium? The answer is simple and direct: Marshall, the better mathematician, saw errors in Walras's approach and knew that the mathematics required for proper solution to the general system was then not known.

In Marshall's intuition, equilibria in sundry markets are subject to sudden disruptions. With equilibria amounts and prices oscillating, a much more complex mathematical system than the one devised by Walras would be required. Economists did not become sufficiently familiar with the mathematics of chaos, nonlinear dynamics, and complexity that describe such systems until the 1990s.

Marshall was correct to quibble: Walras left many questions unanswered or unanswerable, not the least of which was the absence of the auctioneer. Still, Walras, not Marshall, dominated economic scholarship at the end of the twentieth century. Later, in Chapter 17, we will revisit that issue and what it means for the future of economic science.

THE GREAT INFLUENCE OF ALFRED MARSHALL

The changes that Marshall brought about in economics were not described as revolutionary in his own time. For one thing, there is no sharp break between his values and those of the classical economists. Both defended capitalism for about the same reasons. Second, Marshall's ideas were known by and discussed with his students, colleagues, and others who met and talked with him long before he committed them to print. Third, Marshall's style and presentation are modest and understated. The *Principles* introduces many concepts for the first time without any suggestion that they are novel or remarkable. The style is simple, unadorned, and unemphatic—much as Marshall appears in portrait. The book seems to be an ingenuous attempt to disclaim any credit for discovering the economic truths it so earnestly pursues.

Yet, Marshall was acclaimed as the greatest economist of his time. He was adequately Victorian, the right professor for this season of economic history. Victorian England was at full sail in front of the steady breeze of late nineteenth century exhilaration and progress. With improvement in the wind came optimism about the course of industrial society and some basis for it. Average real wages began to rise after 1850, and fewer and fewer ordinary laborers were begging, stealing, sending their children off to work in the mills or simply starving to death. Because of technological changes, the work week began to decline: At the New Castle Chemical Works, the workweek gratefully had been reduced from over 60 to 54 hours.

Why did the English system perform, for the most part, so well during the first half of Queen Victoria's reign (1837–1870)? The British success was based on its near monopoly position in world industrial production until well past mid-century, its consequent development as the premier trading nation of the world, and its related role as banker to the world.

British prosperity depended on international trade for two reasons: (1) Britain's giant, productive industrial machine poured out goods and services well in excess of the purchasing means of the average British worker. (For much of the century, the British worker had sufficient income to buy only necessities.) (2) Because of the small size of Britain and its limited natural resources, it relied on less developed countries, such as India, for imports of food and raw materials.

The less developed countries and Britain had a complementary relationship. Great Britain's relationship with the industrializing advanced nations (such as the United States, France, and Germany) was potentially a competitive one as they became more like the English. In the meantime, however, England and the chief European nations united on a gold standard between 1863 and 1874, which greatly simplified the operations of financing world trade. Importantly for Britain, world trade financing centered on London because of Britain's large reserves of gold and its expertise in international finance.

Even when Britain appeared to be at the peak of its powers, however, events began moving against it. The second half of Victoria's reign (1870–1901) was marred by an increasingly jingoistic nationalism, by the specter of mass unemployment, by the undermining of religious convictions via Darwinism, and by a growing disillusionment with traditional moral values. Even then, the sun's movement with respect to the British Empire was short of proverbial. The earlier Victorian climate of economic expansion nonetheless had given rise to a group of clarifiers who examined the workings of the system in considerable detail but who expressed no fundamental doubts about its basic worth nor made unsettling forecasts about its future.

Despite what seems an innate predisposition to accept this Victorian status quo, Marshall had a greater flexibility toward laissez-faire economics than did many of his classical predecessors. He generally agreed about economic laws being natural laws, but he did not necessarily agree about their goodness. His compassion for human well-being was genuine. Those who today associate Marshall's name with the Euclidean geometry of microeconomics is probably unaware of what Marshall wrote in the preface to his *Principles*: "The study of the causes of poverty is the study of the causes of degradation of a large part of mankind."

Marshall's influence was enormous. An economist of the day said (in 1887) that half the economics chairs in the United Kingdom were occupied by Marshall's former students.[11] The neoclassical school, now extended into general equilibrium, holds center stage in Western countries, along with a modified Keynesian school, while both share the international field with Marxism and institutionalism. Neoclassical economics rules, even though by the 1880s—a decade before the first edition of the *Principles*—except for Marshall's discussion of monopoly, the underlying suppositions about competitive conditions were too unrealistic to warrant its use for policy guidance. Even Walras believed that competition would have to be imposed by government. Marginalism preserved the conditions of classical economics even as its relevance declined.

Marshall's *Principles* nonetheless is an impressive sociology of nineteenth century English capitalism, permeated with a broad historical sense of the evolution of economic institutions. His followers chose to develop only Marshall's analytic footnotes and not his idea of historical evolution. An overly simplified Marshallism that disregarded history pervaded the college teaching of economics until, according to an eminent economist, "Many of the more lively intellects got thoroughly sick of it."[12]

The Victorian world was one where manners, morals, and quietitude were more important than action. How fitting. Nothing ever happens in the abstract time of neoclassical economics. It resided within Balliol Croft, the Marshalls' home. Equilibrium is a wonderful state of rest, little different from the appointed afternoon time at which Sarah (the Marshalls' maid) would come to Alfred's study—after his *tête-a-têtes* with students—and serve a cup of tea and a slice of cake on an adjacent stool or shelf.

Outside the walls of Balliol Croft, however, historical time was ticking like a time bomb. In Marshall's own time, history was taking great leaps—the Russian Revolution, the Great War, and the rise of anticolonialism. And what lay down the road? Capitalism would decline in Europe, monarchies would fall, and the Great Depression would come. Marshall's warning in his *Principles* was *Natura non facit saltum*, or "Nature does not make a leap." Were all these changes marginal? Was reality a giant Walrasian general equilibrium condition?

When the Victorian curtains were finally drawn on this human drama at Balliol Croft, on Alfred Marshall's death in 1924, the greatest economists in England paid homage. The basics, the mathematics and diagrams from the footnotes of his *Principles,* would survive the Victorian Age. His richer institutional insights would not. Ironically, it remained for the nomadic, other-worldly Thorstein Veblen, one of John Bates Clark's students, to revive a role for institutional reality.

NOTES

1. In the calculus, *ds* represents infinitesimally small incremental changes so that the rate of change in pleasure can be written as dp/dt, where dp is the small increment of pleasure and dt is the time unit. Although the *ds* are infinitesimally small, the resultant ratio, such as dp/dt, is not necessarily small. One-zillionth divided by three-zillionths still is 1:3.

2. For a similar description of the economic man concept, see Frank Knight, *Risk, Uncertainty and Profit* (New York: Harper & Row, 1921), pp. 77–78.

3. Latter-day users of perfectly competitive assumptions do take risk into account but find that their basic conclusions are not changed, except for the explanation of profits. For more on this topic, see *Ibid.*

4. From Jevons's *Letters and Journal,* edited by his wife, p. 151. The excerpt is from a long passage quoted by John Maynard Keynes, *Essays and Sketches in Biography* (New York: Meridian Books, 1956), p. 142.

   Elsewhere, Jevons provides an example of both the calculus and the marginal concept. Jevons denotes a as the quantity of corn held by one person and b as a quantity of beef held by another. If the two persons exchange x of corn for y of beef and the market is purely competitive, there is only one ratio of exchange, $dy/dx = y/x$ (which is in differential notation). After exchange, one person has $(a - x)$ of corn and y of beef, while the second has x of corn and $(b - y)$ of beef. If $f_1(a - x)$ and $g_1(y)$, $h_2(x)$ and $j_2(b - y)$ are the *marginal utilities* of corn and beef to persons 1 and 2 respectively, then Jevons's conditions of maximum satisfaction for each of the two parties in a barter exchange is given by $f_1(a - x)/g_1(y) = y/x = h_2(x)/j_2(b - y)$. That is, the two persons are satisfied when the ratio of the marginal utilities is inversely proportional to the ratio of exchange.

5. Because wages are paid in money in a fully monetized economy, the extra products of labor in physical output units (marginal physical product) must be multiplied by the price of the product in order to obtain the *value* of labor's contribution (marginal value of product, under perfect competition) and hence the "appropriate" wage rate.

6. Alfred Marshall, *Money, Credit and Commerce* (London: Macmillan & Co., 1923), p. ii.

7. Joan Robinson, *Economic Philosophy* (Chicago: Aldine Publishing Co., 1962), p. 74.

8. John Maynard Keynes, *Essays in Biography* (London: Macmillan & Co., 1933), p. 212.

9. Alfred Marshall, *Principles of Economics*, 8th ed. (London: Macmillan & Co., 1920), p. 102.

10. Alfred Marshall, "Personal Letter to J.B. Clark in 1908," in *Memorials of Alfred Marshall*, ed. A.C. Pigou (New York: Kelley and Millman, 1956), p. 519.

11. H.S. Foxwell, "The Economic Movement in England," *Quarterly Journal of Economics* 2 (1887): 92.

12. Joseph A. Schumpeter, *Ten Great Economists* (New York: Oxford University Press, 1965), p. 95.

8

THORSTEIN VEBLEN TAKES ON THE AMERICAN CAPTAINS OF INDUSTRY

During the Victorian Age, not only did the English dominate economic thought, they held sway over much of the world's economy. In many ways, the United States was nonetheless exceptional; it was home to the "American Dream." Still, the dream has gained much of its optimism from the eighteenth century belief in a beneficent, finely tuned universe, an idea that, as we have seen, was given its most memorable scientific expression by Isaac Newton, its political rationale by John Locke, and its economic expression by Adam Smith and Alfred Marshall.

Moreover, English Puritans were among the earliest settlers of North America, a fertile ground for the Protestant ethic. The main economic thrust of Calvinism and Puritanism was to condone and encourage the accumulation of wealth as both moral and prudent, a way of doing Smith's and God's work at the same time. The Protestant ethic not only contributed to the rise of capitalism in Europe and America, but thrifty, industrious Protestants, making and saving money, were also ensuring their own salvation.

By the mid-nineteenth century, the Industrial Revolution had spread from Europe to the United States, where the marriage of the Protestant ethic and the American Dream begot some colorful offspring. From about 1870 through 1910—a period in American history usually known as the Gilded Age—the American Dream assumed an almost entirely materialistic form. In this chapter, we address the effects the Industrial Revolution in the United States had on the economic scene, and discuss the satirical reaction to the Gilded Age by the formidable and colorful Thorstein Veblen.

The orthodox view, of course, would support the evolving status quo. However, the Marshallian orthodoxy as well as something called Social Darwinism would have to share the field with Veblen and the institutionalists, the only uniquely American economics school. Indeed, some would say that during the 1920s the institutionalists were as influential as the neoclassicists in the United States, both in and out of the universities. They were among those "more lively intellects," as Joseph Schumpeter put it, who "got thoroughly sick" of neoclassical economics. First, however, let's note the unique American perspective from which the bankers and the industrialists could gather spiritual strength.

HORATIO ALGER AND THE BENIGN UNIVERSE

Horatio Alger, Jr. (1832–1899), a clergyman who wrote fiction for boys, has become synonymous with one version of the American Dream. Alger's novels were updated versions of the Old Testament stories of Noah, Abraham, Joseph, and David—stories of good men who gain wealth through their recognized virtues.

The Alger stories inject into the Protestant ethic an element from Newtonian science, the idea of a universe that rewards. If the good get rich, then it is fair (if not entirely logical) to presume the rich to be good. Material success in the Alger stories results from a curious mixture of design and chance. Inheritances come only to the "deserving," whose upward mobility is ensured by their ardent aspirations.

In a typical Alger novel, *Brave and Bold,* poor but honest Robert rescues a rich man and subsequently inherits a small fortune. Now in easy circumstances, he attends a famous school, where he makes rapid improvement. At novel's end Robert "promises in time to become a prominent and wealthy merchant," his good fortune coming from both his own good qualities and a benign providence ceaselessly steering him to the right place at the right time.

Alger's stories personify American optimism at its shallowest. Yet the basic *value* behind the stories—Nature knows best—runs deep, Robert's "luck" being the manifestation of some higher plan. This identification of Nature's God with good fortune for the deserving poor and with goodness among those of fortunes has never been entirely abandoned; indeed, it remains to this day a prominent element in much TV evangelism and political posturing.

As ever, if too few become extremely rich and powerful, stories for boys and religion alone cannot purge their sins. As the Old Testament itself cautions, virtue is not always rewarded: "...the race is not to the swift nor the battle to the strong, nor bread to the wise nor riches to men of understanding, nor fortune to men of skill; but time and chance happeneth to them all." And so the new American captains of industry uplifted their eyes to Isaac Newton and Nature, because Newton's scientific methods were adapted by three highly influential Victorians: The biologist Charles Darwin, the philosopher Herbert Spencer, and the sociologist-economist William Graham Sumner. But first came the revolution.

THE SECOND INDUSTRIAL REVOLUTION

Again, factories came before the revolution. Men such as Samuel Slater and Moses Brown had factories as early as the 1790s. Francis C. Lowell and textile manufacturing came somewhat later. Before the mid-1830s, only a small number of gunmaking enterprises enjoyed specialization as extensive as that of Adam Smith's pin factory. Specialization came once the production of all parts of a gun was integrated within a single factory—lock, stock and barrel. The prototypical early modern factory was the U.S. Army's Armory at Springfield, Massachusetts, with its workforce of 250 men. In a sense, then, the U.S. government introduced the modern factory to the nation.[1]

Although the United States enjoyed sustained industrialization from 1815 to 1860, economic development speeded up from 1840 to 1860. Then the Civil War (1861–1865) disrupted many growth industries, particularly in the South, which experienced negative growth in commodity output per capita for the decade of the 1860s.[2] When Scarlet returned to Tara after the war, nothing was the same, not even Rhett Butler.

The American Industrial Revolution probably was on its way by 1840 or surely before the war. During the half century thereafter, per capita gross national product grew at an average annual rate of about two percent. By the 1880s, nationally the average annual value of manufacturing finally exceeded that of agriculture. What had happened in England during the first half of the nineteenth century was happening in America during the second half. It has been called the Second Industrial Revolution.

Science and technology had a great affect on both revolutions. The Second was marked by technological advances in railway engines, chemistry, and electrical science, and by a new power source that would transform American lifestyles, the internal combustion engine. Because of labor shortages, U.S. industrial technology from the 1840s on generally proceeded along different lines than in England. Not only did the new energy sources from steam, electrical power, and internal combustion make machines more powerful and automatic, the U.S. technology, designed to replace labor, led to very large scale plants and firms compared with those in England. American industry could achieve lower unit costs with a heroic scale of production, which economists later called "economies of scale." In manufacturing then, one would expect to see increasing returns to scale rather than the diminishing returns to scale of Ricardian agriculture.

Steel was used in the engines and the rails for the railways now spanning the continent. The age of mass production was underway as industries fed on each other. Sir Henry Bessemer first produced steel in large quantities by direct conversion of pig iron into steel, lowering the cost of production by about seven-eighths. The uneven quality of Bessemer steel was overcome by William Siemens's open-hearth process in the 1860s. In the next decade Andrew Carnegie, a taciturn Scottish immigrant, converted to the open-hearth technology, surpassing every steel producer in the world by ruthless use of the market, increasing his scale of production and often selling below costs until competition had been driven from the market. Those steel rails, priced at $120 a ton in 1873, had fallen as low as $17 a ton in 1898. Total steel production, only 77 thousand short tons in 1870, reached 11,227 thousand short tons in 1900 and 34,087 by 1913.[3]

As production was transformed, so too was the nature of business organization. Early on, informal alliances of railway companies were used as a way of avoiding ruinous competition that would have driven rates below costs. The depression after 1873 ended the adequacy of these alliances. Formal federations came next, only to be undone by the most formidable of the late nineteenth century speculators, Jay Gould.

Entrepreneur Henry Ford and his Model T gave America the climactic moment of the Revolution. In 1909, Ford decided to make only one model car, paint it only one color, and sell it initially for $850 and up. "Any customer can have a car painted any color that he wants so long as it is black," he said. An incredibly practical design that would go even where there were no roads (and roads were few), Ford's Model T became a way of life even as his moving assembly line became a way of production. Sales hit 10,607 in 1908 to 1909, and the factory had to refuse orders. In 1912 to 1914, 248,307 Model Ts were produced; in 1920 to 1921, the number rose to 933,720. Because of Ford, the automobile was ubiquitous by the 1920s.[4]

This massive production brought with it mass consumption. Henry Ford believed that he had to pay his workers enough (the "$5 day") so that they could buy his car. He fully understood extent of market as well as economies of scale. "If production is increased 500 percent, costs may be cut 50 percent, and this decrease in cost, with its accompanying decrease in selling price, will probably multiply by ten the number of people who can conveniently buy the product."[5] Workers' incomes were, Ford understood, the artesian well for sales to the masses.

The United States had quietly become a great economic power by 1840; its GNP was perhaps just below those of Britain and of France. The estimated GNP growth rate was about 48 percent per decade in 1834–1843 to 1894–1903. Per capita growth was remarkable: About 16 percent per decade.[6] Rapid urbanization came with industrialization, just as it had in Britain. The percentage of the U.S. population residing in incorporated places of 100,000 or more was only 3.0 in 1840 but 18.7 in 1900. Soon thereafter, the automobile and road-building would combine to create urban sprawl.[7]

BRITISH INDUSTRY: THE SUN ALSO SETS

Meanwhile, undetected by the neoclassicals on their home turf, economic conditions in Great Britain also had greatly changed by 1870. In mid-century, Britain was producing perhaps two-thirds of the world's coal, perhaps half of its iron, five-sevenths of its small supply of steel, and about half of the cotton cloth produced on a commercial scale. Nonetheless, as the United States, France, and the German confederation continued to industrialize, Britain's relative advantage began to shrink, and not simply from its cotton cloth being washed and hung out to dry. By the last decade of the century, Britain remained a great industrialized power but no longer the leader. Worse, the industrialized world was experiencing a long depression that blemished the Victorian boom (1873–1896).

The new international business climate was creating storms on the British seas just at a time when Britain's resources were strained to their limits and existing British technology was fully exploited.[8] Britain faced new competition from two directions. First, the less developed nations now had alternative outlets for their raw materials and food—namely, other industrialized countries. Second, the United States, France, and Germany were competing with Britain for worldwide industrial sales.

There were also other less noticed tensions. Even though real wages had increased during the Victorian era, they had not advanced uniformly. As much as 40 percent of the working class lived in what was then gently called poverty; about two-thirds would, at some time or other in their lives, become paupers. Not more than 15 percent of the working class lived in what was then regarded as comfort.

It is no wonder that by the early 1870s, British trade unionism (like giant enterprises before it) became a fly in the soup of intense competition. The trade unions initially included only skilled and better-paid craft workers and therefore were not large. In the closing years of the century, however, unskilled workers began forming large organizations of their own. The turn of the century, in fact, marks the origins of the British Labour Party.

The labor movements in both Britain and America had very tough sledding indeed until the labor shortages accompanying the Great War. That the public at large was so strongly antipathetic to labor was due in no small part to the widespread acceptance of the principles of Social Darwinism, about which much more is to come.

THE RISE OF THE ROBBER BARONS

Whether in England or the United States, there is a sharp contrast between those entrepreneurs focused on the honest production of more and cheaper products and those fascinated with making money for unscrupulous ends by unscrupulous means. Men like Henry Ford and Thomas Edison were thought to characterize the former. We next turn attention to the most notorious of the latter, who bequeathed an age with their name. Andrew Carnegie was somewhere in-between.

The amount of financial capital needed for large-scale industry made it necessary for business to look to private banks and the capital markets for money. Gradually, a separation appeared between the financial control of business and industrial enterprises and the means by which production took place. Joint stock companies—so maligned by Adam Smith himself—enabled persons to own a company through common stock ownership without being involved in production or management.

Worse, competition became too intense for its own survival. For giant business enterprises, competition became obsolete because investments in plants and equipment were too high for success to be trusted to the workings of the market mechanism, where competition was a kind of genteel balancing act. Still, Amasa Leland Stanford, president of the Central Pacific Railroad from 1863 until his death in 1893, wrote in his 1878 annual report to stockholders: "There is no foundation in good reason for the attempts by the General Government and by the State to especially control your affairs. It is a question of might, and it is to your interest to have it determined where the power resides." The imaginary competition still entrenched in business ideology, however, led to few government regulations on business behavior, and the separation of ownership and production opened the door to irresponsible financial manipulation. Stanford's laissez-faire nonetheless was tainted with hypocracy; at the time of his statement, he was enjoying profits from the construction company that was using government funds to build his railroad.

It was that great speculator Jay Gould who forced the Pennsylvania Railroad line to abandon its cooperative strategy with other lines and to build the country's first interterritorial railroad empire. Gould, Daniel Drew and Jim Fisk deployed ingenious though illegal tactics early in 1868 to prevent Cornelius Vanderbilt, who had gained control of the New York Central a year earlier, from taking over the Erie line. Gould became Erie's president and largest stockholder. Despite his unscrupulousness, Gould failed to put together a national system. In his attempt to corner the gold market in October 1869, he lost the financial leverage to undo Vanderbilt.

But Gould was not finished. He embarked on an adventure in railway combination that made his earlier attempts appear meek. The 1873 depression had left Union Pacific (which, with the Central Pacific, was the first transcontinental railway) stock at a low price. Gould began to buy it and by spring of 1874 had control. He bought every railroad in sight; soon, Gould controlled 15,854 miles of roads, or 15 percent of the U.S. mileage.[9]

The rise of railroads and heavy industry and the phenomenal expansion of banking elevated the fortunes of families whose names have become synonymous with the density of money and power. Preeminent among them is the name of Morgan.

The firm that became J.P. Morgan was founded in London in 1838, and acquired by Junius Morgan in 1856. The House of Morgan presided over American finance at 23 Wall Street, fittingly flanked by the New York Stock Exchange and Federal Hall. Junius's son, J.P. Morgan, Sr. (a.k.a. Pierpont, 1837–1913), and grandson, J.P. Morgan, Jr. (a.k.a. Jack, 1867–1943), added to its wealth and influence. The two J.P. Morgans are often confused in the public mind, not only because of their similar appearances—bulbous nose, pear-shaped body, and bald head—but also because of their singular ruthlessness.

In 1861, the fledgling Pierpont saw the Civil War as just another profit opportunity. Arthur M. Eastman had purchased 5,000 smooth-bore Hall carbines from Abe Lincoln's government for $3.50 each. Pierpont lent $20,000 to Simon Stevens, who bought them from Eastman for $11.50 each and improved them by rifling their smooth bores. He then resold them to Major General John C. Fremont, the naive commander of the Union forces in Missouri, for $22 apiece. The creative financing of J. Pierpont Morgan enabled the government to buy back its own, albeit improved, rifles at *six times* their original price in the time a 90-day Treasury bill takes to mature.[10]

But Pierpont's rifling of the U.S. Treasury was small bore compared with his later actions. In 1900, he headed the second largest steel group in the country at a time when Carnegie Steel was the dominant player in the crude steel market. Carnegie was threatening to begin production of finished steel products such as wire and pipe. Fearing that price wars would erupt and the industry would be demoralized by dreaded competition, Pierpont issued bonds for Carnegie's steel company and for hundreds of others, bringing them under his control. With the formation of the United States Steel Corporation, the production of half the nation's steel then hung on the decisions of one man—a *banker*. Pierpont's competition was so cutthroat that by 1901, it appeared that U.S. Steel might become a monopoly.

The term robber baron should not be used lightly. During the Middle Ages, a **robber baron** was a feudal lord who preyed on and stole from people passing through his domain. The term was revived in the last quarter of the nineteenth century to describe those relatively few businessmen who controlled American industry. Besides Gould, Fisk, Carnegie and Morgan, they included Peter A.B. Widener, Charles Tyson Yerkes, James R. Keene, E.H. Harriman, James J. Hill, John D. Rockefeller, H.H. Rodgers, George F. Baker, William Rockefeller, William C. Whitney, and George F. Baer. All these men celebrated their twenty-fifth birthdays between 1860 and 1870, which means that their adult attitudes and behavior emerged during the years immediately before and after the Civil War. Meanwhile, they mastered at least one problem posed by the war: Mass production and the attendant necessity for large-scale production.

THE SOCIAL DARWINISTS

The conditions in Britain and the United States during the last half of the nineteenth century might have left two unsettled questions for economics. How does one justify the enormous wealth accumulated by the industrialists under "perfect competition," and how does one excuse the poverty of those failing to benefit from the system? The surprising answers came from the new discipline of sociology and its English founder, Herbert Spencer (1820–1903).

That Good, Olde Tyme Religion

Religion had a lot to do with it. Besides their mastery of mass production, the robber barons also had something else in common: At least seven were churchgoers, and six were actively engaged in church affairs. J.P. Morgan was probably the most prominent layman in the Protestant Episcopal church, whose communicants included about half of the 75 multimillionaires in 1900 in New York City.[11] The Rockefeller brothers were prominent Baptists.

Many of the barons believed that God was their ally. John D. Rockefeller said, "God gave me my money," and Baer attacked labor during the coal strike of 1902 by saying,

> The rights and interests of laboring man will be protected and cared for—not by the labor agitators, but by the Christian men to whom God in his infinite wisdom has given the control of the property interests of this country.[12]

Some of the robber barons such as J.P. Morgan had huge slush funds for buying votes in Washington and in state capitals. They fleeced the public on the stock exchanges by making exorbitant profits in stock-watering operations. Still, they all fully expected to be marked present when the roll was called up yonder.

These men were not pristine hypocrites. We saw in Chapter 1 how Calvinism and Puritanism accommodated the accumulation of material goods and a devout spiritual life with little difficulty. Likewise, Pierpont Morgan and E.H. Harriman, irresponsibly battling for control of a railway, brought on a financial panic; yet they worshipped devoutly. Rockefeller ruthlessly drove competitors out of business, but he sang hymns with the Sunday school children of the Euclid Avenue Baptist Church. Henry Ward Beecher, then the most renowned of American divines, and others taught the goodness of richness from their pulpits, but they were preaching to the choir of Morgan, Harriman, and Rockefeller.

It, too, was the politically correct stance of both major political parties. Samuel J. Tilden, the Democratic nominee for president in the 1876 election, gave secular substance to the credo the following year at a testimonial dinner for Junius Morgan:

> You are, doubtless in some degree, clinging to the illusion that you are working for yourselves, but it is my pleasure to claim that you are working for the public. [Applause.] While you are scheming for your own selfish ends, there is an overruling and wise Providence directing that the most of all you do should inure to the benefit of the people. Men of colossal fortunes are in effect, if not in fact, trustees for the public.[13]

Henry P. Davison, one of Morgan's partners, could tell a Senate committee investigating monopoly. "If in practice it were wrong it could not live.... Things correct themselves."[14]

If this be market equilibrium, surely it is remote from great competitive forces. Doubtless, the neoclassicals did not expect laissez-faire to bequeath the robber barons. If any forces could afford to be "at rest" or in equilibrium, it would be those of the Carnegies, Morgans, and Rockefellers, running the railways, the steel mills, and the banks. But those operations were based on monopolistic practices.

Herbert Spencer's Scientific Basis for Social Harmony

Faith can stretch only so far; just as the tobacco barons ultimately needed expert medical doctors to explain the health benefits from tobacco use, the robber barons increasingly needed science's blessing. Luckily, they got both.

Inspired in great part by Malthus's treatise on population, Charles Darwin had developed the theory of natural selection: Changes favorable to survival in a given species tend to be preserved in nature, and unfavorable changes tend to die out, eventually resulting in the evolution of a new species. Herbert Spencer took Darwin's ideas (which he misunderstood) and turned some physical science ideas on their heads and merged them into a "scientific sociology." It came to be known as Social Darwinism—the concept of the asphalt jungle.

In Spencer's view, the fact that the rich get richer and the poor get poorer was just nature's way of improving the species and the economy at the same time. This was a tableau agreeable to the robber barons and their attendants and retainers, as well as to the middle class (those who, while not rich yet, were reassured by the American Dream that it was just a matter of time).

Since the evolutionary process tends toward *increasing order,* wrote Spencer, his scientific sociology does not conflict with the most dismal laissez-faire doctrines. Because humanity's conditions are getting better and better and society is becoming more orderly through natural law, humans should not interfere with natural progress. To aid the poor, either by private or public aid, interfered irreparably with the progress of the race. The Darwinian law that the fittest, most adaptable members of a species survive was construed to mean that the existing order of things is "best" since it is arrived at by a natural, selective process.

Thus, while Horatio Alger's heroes could achieve in fiction the American Dream of rising to the top, the doctrines of the Social Darwinists would have preserved a social process that made sure such successes were in fact infrequent. Social programs improving the odds for success and allowing some of the "unfit" to move up would have been repugnant.

Spencer also resolved the genuine religious crisis that Darwinism had precipitated for many Christians, including the robber barons. Noah Porter (1811–1892), a Congregational clergyman and head of Yale University during Thorstein Veblen's attendance there, had surrendered to the evolutionary forces by 1877, when in an address he found "no inconsistency between the findings of this museum on the one corner [which contained evidences to prove evolution] and the teachings of the college chapel on the other."[15] Religion was therefore able to accommodate science, though many people were repelled by the idea that humans evolved from apes.

Henry Ward Beecher expressed his wish to meet Herbert Spencer in Heaven. Better, Spencer's books sold by the hundreds of thousands, and his reception in New York in 1882 would have been the envy of Madonna's press agent.

The Social Darwinism of William Graham Sumner

Although a generation of scholars wallowed in Spencer's wake, the most eminent of the Americans was William Graham Sumner (1840–1910). He brought together the three great traditions of western capitalist culture—the Protestant ethic, classical economics, and Darwinian natural selection—by ingeniously putting Newton, God, and the science of biology all on the side of classical economics, bridging the gap between the economic ethic set in motion during the High Middle Ages and the science of the nineteenth century. Sumner's sociology equated the hardworking, thrifty Protestant with the "fittest" in the struggle for survival, while reinforcing Ricardian inevitability and laissez-faire with a hard-bitten determinism that seemed both Calvinistic and scientific. Sumner was jolly direct, proclaiming that "the millionaires are a product of natural selection ... the naturally selected agents of society for certain work. They get high wages and live in luxury, but the bargain is a good one for society."[16]

Other interpreters of Darwin shrank from a direct analogy between animal struggle and human competition, but Sumner saw economic competition as an admirable reflection of animal existence. In the struggle, people went from natural selection to social selection of fitter persons and from "organic forms with superior adaptability to citizens with a greater store of economic virtues."[17] This selection process depended on unrestricted competition, which Sumner compared to a natural law, as inevitable and necessary as gravity. When liberty prevails, those people of courage, enterprise, good training, intelligence, and perseverance will come out on top in an automatically benevolent, free competitive order. John D. Rockefeller, the founder of Standard Oil, could thus explain competition to his Sunday school class:

> The growth of a large business is merely a survival of the fittest.... The American Beauty rose can be produced in the splendor and fragrance which bring cheer to its beholder only by sacrificing the early buds which grow up around it. This is not an evil tendency in business. It is merely the working-out of a law of nature and a law of God.[18]

John D., of course, had nipped quite a few oil companies in the bud before they could blossom into an American Beauty like Standard Oil. He was not offering anyone else a rose garden.

As to Sumner, he was worried that the distribution of income in a competitive process might be compromised by partial redistribution by vote, a fear used to support arguments against the graduated income tax. Since capital is accumulated through self-denial, its possession proves that the advantage has been secured by the superiority of the accumulator. The capitalist becomes virtuous, while the prodigal worker is a sinner. Taxing the rich at higher rates than the poor would be to burden the superior with the support of the inferior.

Thus, Sumner and Spencer championed the guardians of a process that made the rich richer and the powerful more powerful. Even Andrew Carnegie became a disciple, describing how his troubled mental state was miraculously relieved by his reading of Darwin and Spencer.

> I had found the truth of evolution. "All is well since all grows better," became my motto, my true source of comfort.... Nor is there any conceivable end to his [the human being's] march to perfection. His face is turned to the light; he stands in the sun and looks upward.[19]

The Social Darwinists came to the same conclusion as orthodox economists: Laissez-faire is desirable because to regulate business would be to defy natural law. The robber barons agreed that survival of the fittest, themselves, was a law of nature and human regulations were redundant. They came to see their competitive struggles as essentially no different from the struggles for survival observable in nature. The laws of nature distributed wealth, and people must not try to fool Mother Nature.

The doctrines of Spencer and Sumner may seem cold-blooded today, but they are not cold and dead. During the 1930s, when the general manager of the Atlas works of Pittsburgh was asked what might be done to raise the wages of workers from 75 cents a day, he could reply scientifically: "I don't think anything can be done.... The law of the 'survival of the fittest' governs that." Likewise, many of the arguments regarding "ending welfare as we know it" in the United States during the 1990s sounded like echoes ringing down through the ages.

DARWINISM REVISED: VEBLEN AND THE INSTITUTIONALISTS

Not everyone agreed with Spencer and Sumner, nor did they necessarily consider the robber barons benign. In particular, the orthodoxy was to be confronted by a satirical, serial icon-killer who taught economics but gained fame as a social critic. His name was Thorstein Veblen, and he was, ironically, one of J.B. Clark's undergraduate and Sumner's graduate students; to this day he also remains a distinguished literary figure.

Unlike Mill's or Marshall's *Principles*, Veblen's *The Theory of the Leisure Class* (1899) may well be the only book on economics published in the nineteenth century still read for amusement *and* relevance today. Even economists, in a notable display of self-irreverence, have turned its title on its head to "the leisure of the theory class."

Economics and literature are inseparable in Veblen. Unlike the divergent paths taken by literary figures and other notable economists, Veblen blends art and science by his masterful, inventive use of English prose. He, like F. Scott Fitzgerald, was influenced by the English novelist Joseph Conrad's precise but difficult prose style.[20]

In response to the excesses of the robber barons, Veblen (1857–1929) anatomized the neoclassicals while founding the only uniquely American branch of economic thought, the *institutionalist* or *evolutionist* school.[22] Veblen and his followers, incensed by the great wealth inequalities and the robber barons' obsession with money, helped to establish the democratic welfare state in the United States. (At the same time, labor organizer Eugene Debs was giving stirring speeches, and membership in labor unions was growing.) The socialist philosophy and Marxist ideology played that role in England and on the Continent. Veblen nonetheless turned, not to organized labor, but to the experienced technicians then in possession of the requisite technological knowhow to save capitalism before it fell victim to the "absentee owners" of factories.

The Veblenesque World

Veblen began his advanced studies at Yale in 1882, the year Social Darwinist Herbert Spencer began a grand tour of the United States, culminating in a "last supper" at Delmonico's, then a famed watering hole of the New York rich. Other economists read Marshall's *Principles*, enjoyed and apologized for the status quo, and saw little or no need for reform. Veblen, however, described a nation controlled by a few millionaires, robber barons who had accumulated vast wealth not through production, but largely through financial manipulation.

Personally, Veblen was a strange man. He had furtive eyes, a blunt nose, an unkempt mustache, and a short, scraggly beard. He was aloof and dressed simply, usually in tweed pants that were anchored to his socks by large safety pins. Of his few indulgences—smoking an expensive brand of Russian cigarettes, finding lost balls on golf courses, and women—only the latter led him into dangerous territory. In his golf walks, he had the air of being in a world apart from everyone else. He was.

Veblen was also out of step with the day's conventional economic thought. John Bates Clark, the dean of American economists at the time and, oddly enough, Veblen's mentor, as noted, envisioned the returns from capital coming from the marginal physical product of capital and perfectly competitive prices. Veblen's reading of capitalism is dramatically different. Those who accumulate wealth, Veblen writes, do so for reasons going beyond the simple satisfaction of physical wants: The rich accumulate and consume wealth in a grossly conspicuous way because the display is indicative of power, honor, and prestige in a materialistic culture. Through intricate phrases, Veblen's subtle logic gave society enough rope to hang itself.

Origins of the Leisure Class

Veblen's first and most popular book, *The Theory of the Leisure Class*, published the same year as Clark's book on distribution, introduced a number of terms, bitingly sarcastic at the time but destined to become a part of economic language, such as *leisure class; pecuniary emulation* (popularly known as "keeping up with the Joneses"); and, most famous of all, *conspicuous consumption*, the phrase he coined for ostentatious display of wealth.

For the leisure class, writes Veblen, "the incentive to diligence and thrift is not absent; it is action so greatly qualified by the secondary demands of pecuniary emulation, that any inclination in this direction is practically overborne and any incentive to diligence tends to be of no effect."[23] As Veblen could observe, around the turn of the century Commodore Vanderbilt, a skillful entrepreneur who also robbed the public with abandon, spent $3 million to build a house, the Breakers, providing his suitably corseted wife (for the sake of being a conspicuous "trophy") with something more than minimal shelter. Vanderbilt was able to buy Vanderbilt University for only a half million, a sum that causes his conspicuous household consumption to appear wasteful.

To Veblen, unlike to Marshall, waste plays an important social role. "Throughout the entire evolution of conspicuous expenditure, whether of goods or of services or human life, runs the obvious implication that in order to effectually mend the consumer's good fame it must be an expenditure of superfluities. In order to be reputable it must be wasteful," writes the iconoclast.[24]

Institutions Behind Their Times

Veblen's book also originates the evolutionist argument about economic institutions, using a Darwinian biological metaphor in a novel way. The Darwinians had said that in the evolutionary development of biological organisms, natural selection allows the fittest to survive. Veblen countered that institutions also evolve, but there is always a *cultural lag* between the ideas of today and today's institutions based on the ideas of yesteryear.

"Institutions," says Veblen, "are products of the past process, are adapted to past circumstances, and are therefore never in full accord with the requirements of the present."[25] Veblen hangs Social Darwinism upside down, whereby evolution is a suffocating force because "these institutions which have so been handed down, these habits of thought, points of view, mental attitudes and aptitudes, or what not, are ... themselves a conservative factor."[26] Right side up (i.e. being upside down), the surviving institutions are the *least fit* for the present.

This Veblenesque world, of course, is upside down from that of proper neoclassical society. With its wealth sheltered from the bitter winds of economic change, the leisure class naturally embraces the dictum that whatever *is*, is *right*. Contrariwise, Veblen says that whatever is—institutionally—is very likely to be *wrong* because it will have evolved at a slower pace than the social conditions institutions ought to reflect.

The person shaped by outdated institutions is more complicated than the neoclassical's "economic man." Veblen derides the hedonism of the neoclassical school and the basis for the Marshallian demand curve, which would have "a gang of Aleutian Islanders slushing about in the wrack and surf with rakes and magical incantations for the capture of shellfish ... to be engaged on a feat of hedonistic equilibration in rent, wages, and interest."[27]

Whereas Adam Smith and Alfred Marshall saw competition as an essentially beneficial impulse keeping business in check, Veblen saw it as predatory, despicable, a habit slowly overcome by the "Captains of Industry." "Gradually," writes Veblen, "as industrial activity further displaces predatory activity... , accumulated property more and more replaces trophies of predatory exploit as the conventional exponent of prepotence and success."[28] Veblen's "economic man" lives in a world where competition could cause serious clashes that would be resolved to favor the powerful.

The Vested Interest vs. The Engineers

Veblen sees people forming groups to protect their mutual self-interests, the "vested interest." Having different interests, conflicts are inevitable, but the basic *values* of the different groups are never in question. The unionists at the A.F. of L. do not want to overthrow the bankers, for example, because they are too busy emulating the conspicuous consumption of the vested (with gold watches on gold chains), earning interest. Competition is in the service of a holistic value—*the love of money*. If the distribution of wealth and income were equitable, such pernicious and pointless competition would not exist. Even sexual infidelity, an arena that Veblen knew intimately and once thought to be the poaching ground for only the wealthy male, was to be invaded by the masses. The workers don't want to eliminate the absentee owners; they want to join the leisure class.

Veblen ultimately broadened economics, bringing into play such "nonpure" economic forces as social institutions and psychological attitudes toward wealth. He has made many economists stop and think about their bloodless, skeletal models of economic behavior. Veblen was also a brilliantly witty writer; even if *The Theory of the Leisure Class* were bad economics—which it is not—it would still be a work of unique genius, one of the few influential books during the twentieth century.

In his academic posts, Veblen witnessed the dominant influence of the modern robber barons. Just as feudalism sustained a Christian paternalist ethic, the Christian barons of industry salved their consciences by giving large amounts of charity not only to hospitals and private colleges and universities but directly to the poor. They did so in most cases, however, only as a parent would care for a child.

Veblen understood a robber baron charity that began at the mansion. Businessmen had endowed universities—Veblen's universities—and greatly influenced university presidents who in turn urged their professors to respect property, privilege, and those who held them. For this reason and others, including women's inexplicable tendencies to aggressively pursue him, Veblen moved often.

He began at Cornell University and, then went with his wife Ellen to the University of Chicago (endowed by the Rockefellers). To the disgust of President Harper at Chicago, Veblen, though living with Ellen, went abroad with a prominent Chicago woman. It was time to get on the road again, first to Stanford University (endowed, ironically, by Leland Stanford), then to the state-supported University of Missouri (after divorcing Ellen), and during the early 1920s to the New School in New York (on a salary subsidized by contributions from his former students). Veblen was nominated to the presidency of the prestigious American Economic Association in 1924 but demurred with characteristic cynicism; the position came too late to be of professional use.

Nevertheless, Veblen's books continued to influence economics: He expanded on themes first played in *The Theory of the Leisure Class*, in *The Theory of Business Enterprise* (1904), *The Instinct of Workmanship and the State of the Industrial Arts* (1914), *The Engineers and the Price System* (1921), and *Absentee Ownership and Business Enterprise in Recent Times: The Case of America* (1923), and helped to direct attention away from perfect competition and toward monopoly. Veblen's argument that big business is primarily interested in maximizing profits rather than maximizing production is illustrated in skeletal form in the pure monopoly model. But Veblen went beyond this, arguing that the *instinct for workmanship* declines and the importance of salesmanship increases when money takes precedence over goods. Big business is also more interested in vending goods than in making them serviceable to meet people's needs. To Veblen, the salesman perfected his dubious art by promising everything but delivering nothing.

The institution of manufacturing and distribution determines production, employment, and pricing outcomes. This would explain why, as an economy moves to a higher plateau of production, the numbers of salespeople, advertisers, and accountants increase, displacing the production experts. As Veblen relates, it is the expert men, the technologists, engineers, or whatever name may best suit them that must take the leadership. It follows, writes Veblen, that

> the material welfare of all the advanced industrial peoples rests in the hands of these technicians, if they will only see it that way, take counsel together, constitute themselves the self-directing General Staff of the country's industry, and dispense with the interference of the lieutenants of the absentee owners.[29]

In a rare expression of optimism, Veblen envisioned the "engineers" overthrowing the "absentee" capitalists and reclaiming industry. As the economy develops, Veblen also noted, entrepreneurs are required to take fewer risks.

Veblen not only deviated from the orthodoxy, he savagely attacked it, dancing wildly on its remains.

THE NEOCLASSICAL ASCENDENCY AND PUBLIC POLICY

In intellectual circles, if not in society broadly, Social Darwinism began to wane before the end of the nineteenth century, but like protectionist sentiments when a domestic firm is threatened, it reawakens whenever welfare for the poor is on the agenda. Still, Social Darwinism had always held a view more radical than that held by many orthodox economists. The American Economic Association (AEA) was formed in great part to counter the classically liberal bias of economics favoring the industrialists to the exclusion of the masses. Richard T. Ely, the central figure founding the AEA in 1885, singled out Sumner as the kind of economist he hoped would not join the association.

Veblen nonetheless did not prevail. In Veblen's day the neoclassicals ultimately held on to majority opinion among economists and society at large. Economists, struggling to assume the cloak of science, would not be diverted from the unassailable Marshallian cross. Neoclassical theory could explain pure monopoly (one industry = one firm) and "free competition," but it generally steered clear of the prevailing, murky kinds of competition between these two extremes, the world of Veblen. Veblen also had to struggle against a tendency in the seminaries of higher learning that he observed and ascribed to all institutions—the dislike of innovation.

Still, there was something rather disturbing about the pervasiveness of equilibrium in science. Even while Alfred Marshall was enjoying his stature as the high priest of economics, reality seemed so far removed from the model as to challenge it. The giant trusts evaded competition on the road to ruin rather than to harmony, as U.S. Steel, Standard Oil, General Electric, AT&T, Ford Motor Company, and American Tobacco Company were staking out monopoly claims in American industry.

By 1886, the U.S. Supreme Court had extended the Fourteenth Amendment rights to the corporation. Although this amendment had been aimed at protecting the rights of freed slaves, its extension to corporations made their property a natural right. Thereafter, state legislation regulating hours of work, child labor, factory conditions, and monopolies was struck down. Dissenting against unrestricted laissez-faire as the law of the land, the great Justice Oliver Wendell Holmes was reduced to only a dissenting opinion—"the fourteenth amendment does not enact Mr. Herbert Spencer's *Social Statics*."

Veblen was not merely spinning theoretical yarns impoverished by lack of real-world data. In Veblen's drama, social recognition in the United States, and the power that went with it, could be bought by the Rockefellers, Vanderbilts, and Morgans. Even Congress, often considered the epitome of institutional lag, was investigating corporate chicanery by 1890, the year of Marshall's *Principles*. Its Industrial Commission provided Veblen with 19 volumes of data and evidence on holding companies and watered stock. Later, Teapot Dome, the notorious oil scandal of the Harding administration, illustrated Veblen's notion of "commercial sabotage," the conscientious withdrawal of efficiency by industry in order to maintain prices.

The excesses of the millionaires of the 1890s to 1920s were not entirely ignored by other economists. High on the approval list of most were the efforts to preserve competition in what came to be called "antitrust laws." Moreover, these economists argued the case for regulating the natural monopolies such as public utilities, although many argued that unsustained by government, monopoly profits would attract competition and be self-defeating. Others chose to look away from monopoly because of the advantages of falling costs in the path of large-scale production, thereby throwing the winds of regulation to caution.

The administrations of Presidents Harrison, Theodore Roosevelt, and Taft earnestly struggled to regulate the kinds of businesses, such as James Buchanan Duke's American Tobacco Company (that controlled about 80 percent of the nation's tobacco production), scorned by Veblen. In particular, Roosevelt brandished much blood and thunder but was a little stick against the strong undercurrent of pro-business sentiment in the Congress and the courts. Reform was often slow and ineffective. In a 1911 ruling concerning John

D. Rockefeller's Standard Oil Trust, the Supreme Court set forth its famous "rule of reason," which stated in effect that not the size and power of businesses but only the illegal or unfair use of them should be regulated. This ruling has more or less dominated the U.S. government's attitude toward giant business ever since.

A NOTABLE ABSENCE OF HARMONY

Laissez-faire was pursued more in theory than in practice. During the rise of the robber barons, when government *did* intervene, usually it was on the side of giant enterprise. The Civil War (1861–1865) brought the industrial interests of the northeast to political dominance, not to mention the Morrill Tariff (1861), which raised duties on imports and set the tone for high tariffs after the war. Federal subsidies to the transcontinental railways were provided in the Pacific Railway Acts (1862 and 1864).

Did control of key industries by one or a few firms really have adverse effects on consumers? Economies of scale have the wonderful effect of reducing unit costs and, potentially, prices of the products or services. These benefits end only when a single firm or a few dominant firms use their market power to raise prices above average costs and reasonable profit rates. Large-scale industry, falling production costs, lower prices in many industries, and huge profits seemed to go hand-in-hand during the final half of the nineteenth century. Standard Oil Trust's profit rate over its life has been estimated as twice what it would have been under competitive conditions.[30]

The economic problems of the era, however, often stemmed from the political power of the giant industrialists to have their way, and the effects of financial market clout of the great speculators. In September 1873, a stock market crash and a banking panic were triggered by the failure of Jay Cooke and Company, which had been the great marketeers of Union bonds during the Civil War. This too came at a time of financial manipulation in railroad securities, the main issues sold in the market at the time. The depression that followed did not end until 1878. Again, in May of 1884, a stock market and banking panic ensued, followed by a two-year depression. Once again, in February 1893, there was a stock market and banking panic and collapse, which lasted until 1897.

The crashes, the panics, and the depressions exacted their toll in unemployment, lost incomes, and working class agitation. In 1877, layoffs and wage cuts on the railroads triggered many local strikes, and the United States came close to political revolution that year. Violence led to the destruction of much railroad property, the Fourteenth Amendment notwithstanding. A riot at the McCormick Reaper Works left workers injured and an anarchist newspaper calling for "revenge." This led to the infamous Haymarket Square incident in which seven policemen were killed and 68 wounded.

The hard times of the 1890s also bred violence at Andrew Carnegie's Homestead steel plant near Pittsburgh. Wage cuts, the refusal to recognize a union, and the company's use of hundreds of strikebreakers led to a battle between workers and management forces. Twenty men were killed and an estimated 50 wounded.

"Darwinian competition" is an apt description in many respects, for this new sociology was to place the robber barons exactly where they wanted to be—in control. Even when the barons incurred self-inflicted wounds, these were often at the expense of a general public that was not fully compensated by the new Christian paternalism. And so it came to be, by 1920 that good and venerable name among American entrepreneurs, Ford, produced 45 percent of all automobiles sold. Thorstein Veblen saw though the self-interest that left economic conditions far short of harmonious. But, of course, by then there were distractions: We had won the war to end all wars, the Jazz Age was a time to feel good, and the hangover of the Great Depression was in our future. For the neoclassicals—as for ordinary people—the best of times would blend into the worst.

VEBLEN PASSES INTO LEGEND

If there is an academic legend in the United States equaling F. Scott Fitzgerald's in fiction, it is the legend of Thorstein Veblen. Yet, Horatio

Alger, Jr. could never have drawn inspiration from Veblen's career. Few with such immense talent have so relentlessly pursued failure with such great success. Because of his many dalliances, his unorthodox ideas, and his studiously ineffectual mumbling as a teacher, Veblen never rose high in the academic ranks and was paid little.

As the story is told, Veblen was invited to Harvard University to be considered for a position. At the farewell dinner, President A. Lawrence Lowell delicately brought up Veblen's most notorious academic blemish. "You know, Dr. Veblen, if you come here, some of our professors will be a little nervous about their wives." To which Veblen is said to have replied, "They need not worry; I have seen their wives." The story, true or not, is part of the legend, for women's attraction to Veblen was fatal for his academic career.

Near the end of his life, Veblen returned to California. He had always been almost helpless in his personal life, often nurtured through daily demands by his few devoted students, including Wesley Mitchell. Once Veblen understood the revolt of the engineers and technicians was not coming in his lifetime, he slowly turned toward death. He lived in a ramshackle shack among nature. At age 70 he stopped writing. A few months before the Great Crash of 1929, he died, alone and mostly ignored by other economists.

Yet the stock market debacle highlighted his claims: Financial speculation had superseded any interest in production. Veblen's books—now classics—enjoy the esteem that eluded the man in his own time. His lexicon, found today in economics, also is found in novels such as *Even Cowgirls Get the Blues,* in which the "all thumbs" Sissy is explaining the wisdom of "the Chink," a kind of mystical guru. "It was," says Sissy, "only among mobile cultures ... that surplus, a result of overachievement, led to potlatches and competitive feasts—orgies of conspicuous consumption and conspicuous waste—which attach to simple, healthy, effective economies the destructive elements of power and prestige."[31] The book later was to become a "major motion picture": Veblen would have been amused.

Veblen, too, was to influence that other legend, F. Scott Fitzgerald, who, with Zelda, defined the Jazz Age. Then, too, events during

Veblen's life—the Great War, the small peace at Versailles, and the Roaring Twenties—would provide a stage for another great economist, John Maynard Keynes.

NOTES

1. Alfred D. Chandler, Jr., *The Visible Hand: The Managerial Revolution in American Business* (Cambridge, Massachusetts and London: The Belknap Press of Harvard University Press, 1977), pp. 72–73. Also, see the discussion of the integrated textile mill as a less advanced, yet large-scale production unit on pp. 67–72.

2. See Stanley Engerman, "The Economic Impact of the Civil War," reprinted in *The Reinterpretation of American Economic History*, eds. Robert Fogel and Stanley Engerman (New York: Harper & Row, 1971), pp. 371–372.

3. *Historical Statistics*, series P 265–267. The data are cited in more detail in Jonathan Hughes and Louis P. Cain, *American Economic History*, 4th ed. (New York: HarperCollins, 1994), Table 17.3, p. 313.

4. The complete story of Ford and the Automobile Age is told by Jonathan Hughes, *The Vital Few: The Entrepreneur and American Economic Progress*, expanded edition (New York and Oxford: Oxford University Press, 1986), Chapter 7.

5. The original quote is from an article by Henry Ford on "Mass Production" appearing in the 13th edition of the *Encyclopedia Britannica*. It is reprinted in Clifton Fadiman, General Editor, *The Treasury of the Encyclopedia Britannica* (New York and London: Viking, 1992), p. 403.

6. These estimates appear in the path-breaking study by Robert E. Gallman, "Gross National Product in the United States 1834–1909," in *Studies in Income and Wealth*, ed. Dorothy S. Brady (New York: NBER, Columbia University Press, 1966), Vol. 30, Table A1.

7. The data on urbanization are from *Historical Statistics*, derived from Series A 57–69 and cited by Jonathan Hughes and Louis P. Cain, *op. cit.*, p. 317.

8. See Deirdre N. McCloskey, "Did Victorian Britain Fail?" *Economic History Review* 23 (December 1970): 446–459.

9. These activities as well as many others are told in great detail by Alfred D. Chandler, Jr., *op. cit.*, Chapter 5.

10. The story is related by Ron Chernow, *The House of Morgan: An American Banking Dynasty and the Rise of Modern Finance* (New York: Atlantic Monthly Press, 1990), pp. 21–22.

11. Frederick Lewis Allen, *The Lords of Creation* (New York and London: Harper & Brothers, 1935), p. 87.

12. *Ibid.*, p. 91.

13. *Tribune*, November 9, 1877. Also quoted in Lewis Cory, *The House of Morgan* (New York: Harper & Brothers, 1930), p. 80.

14. Quoted by Fritz Redlich, *Steeped in Two Cultures* (New York and Evanston, Ill.: Harper & Row, 1971), p. 44.

15. Charles Schuchert and Clara Mae LeVene, *O.C. Marsh, Pioneer in Paleontology* (New Haven: Yale University Press, 1940), p. 247.

16. William Graham Sumner, *The Challenge of Facts and Other Essays*, edited by Albert Galoway Keller (New Haven: Yale University Press, 1914), p. 90.

17. *Ibid.*, p. 57. See also Joseph Dorfman, *The Economic Mind in American Civilization, 1606–1865* (New York: Augustus M. Kelley, 1966), Vol. 2, pp. 695–767.

18. William J. Ghent, *Our Benevolent Feudalism* (New York: Macmillan Co., 1902), p. 29.

19. Andrew Carnegie, *Autobiography of Andrew Carnegie* (Boston: Houghton Mifflin, 1920), p. 327.

20. Joseph Conrad's best-known book is *Heart of Darkness,* a novel that has been made into several movies.

22. I prefer **institutionalist** and shall use it hereafter to describe the school.

23. Thorstein Veblen, *The Theory of the Leisure Class*, with an introduction by John Kenneth Galbraith (Boston: Houghton Mifflin, 1974), p. 41. [1899]

24. *Ibid.*, p. 77. For a treatment of how Veblen's demand theory has entered mainstream economics, see E. Ray Canterbery, "*The Theory of the Leisure Class* and the Theory of Demand," in *The Founding of Institutional Economics*, ed. Warren Samuels (London and New York: Routledge, 1998), pp. 139–156. This book chapter also suggests how different economics would be with a more Veblenian vision in which the presumption of surpluses superceded the idea of scarcities.

25. *Ibid.* p. 133.

26. *Ibid.*

27. Thorstein Veblen, *The Place of Science in Modern Civilization and Other Essays* (New York: B.W. Huebsch, 1919), p. 193.

28. *The Theory of the Leisure Class, op. cit.*, p. 37.

29. Thorstein Veblen, *The Engineers and the Price System* (New York: B.W. Huebsch, 1921), pp. 136–137.

30. The data on Standard Oil is from Stanley Lebergott, *The Americans: An Economic Record* (New York and London: W.W. Norton & Company, 1984) p. 333.

31. Tom Robbins, *Even Cowgirls Get the Blues* (New York: Bantam Books, 1976), p. 238.

9

THE JAZZ AGE: AFTERMATH OF WAR AND PRELUDE TO DEPRESSION

Perhaps the Victorian world had always been more popular imagination than reality. In economics, the harmony assured by the equilibrium of supply and demand bred excessive optimism. Excessive optimism bred complacency in attitudes and public policy. The John Bull market would never decline; it is the kind of euphoria sometimes experienced in financial markets wherein prices are expected never to recede. If we count in historical minutes, however, reckonings were just around the corner.

THE EDWARDIAN AGE AND THE EARLY BLOOMSBURY YEARS OF JOHN MAYNARD KEYNES

Meantime, England enjoyed a pleasant but brief interlude. The period between the death of Queen Victoria in 1901 and the start of the Great War is usually identified in England as the Edwardian Age, an era of more relaxed attitudes toward sex and manners. Even though King Edward VII was a symbol of self-indulgence, the Edwardians nonetheless preserved much of their Victorian heritage intact.

English society was still firmly dominated by class: English wealth was still in a few hands. But there had been notable changes. The Education Act of 1870 had made the poor literate or semiliterate, and the cheapness of newsprint was preparing them for full democracy. The Fabian Society—of reformist, not revolutionary, socialism—became an important intellectual force. At home and abroad the mood had moved a great distance from the puritan ethic.

Although no one knew it at the time, this new age would produce a great economist who would, in due course, push Marshall off center stage. Though coming of age during Edwardian times, the background of John Maynard Keynes (1883–1946) was eminently patrician—the name goes back to one of William the Conqueror's retainers, William de Cahagenes, at the Battle of Hastings in 1066. Keynes's father, John Neville Keynes, was himself the leading logician-philosopher among the neoclassicals. Keynes's mother, a graduate of Cambridge, was mayor of the city. Both lived to attend their son's funeral in Westminster Abbey.

Keynes's early education and childhood were what one would expect of Victorian and Edwardian England. He had a governess, a local kindergarten and prep school, and a scholarship to Eton. Later, he had a distinguished scholarship in classics and mathematics to King's College, Cambridge. Keynes was tall and distinguished, but thick lips and a thin chin, only partly disguised by a mustache, brought him up short of handsomeness. As a boy, he thought himself ugly, a judgment he never changed.

Keynes found the new Edwardian mores congenial to his own lifestyle, which contrasted starkly with the spartan regimen of his old Cambridge professor, Alfred Marshall. A bibliophile and supporter of the arts (organizer of the Camargo Ballet and builder of the Arts Theatre at Cambridge), Keynes seemed most at home in the lively company of artists and writers. Though he could be devastating in arguments with "fools," he was almost always outwardly cheerful—as effervescent as the champagne he frequently enjoyed.

Keynes was immensely influenced by his membership in the elite Bloomsbury group of London, composed of gifted English writers, artists, and intellectuals who frequently held informal discussions in Bloomsbury, a section of London near the British Museum, from around 1907 to the 1930s. The rise of the Bloomsbury group coincided with the beginnings of modernism in literature and art. In literature came the great novels of Joseph Conrad (1857–1924), D.H. Lawrence (1885–1930), E.M. Forster (1879–1970), and James Joyce (1882–1941). Gertrude Stein, destined to be the den mother to the postwar "lost generation" that included F. Scott Fitzgerald and Ernest Hemingway, was the American in Paris. In art came the postimpressionist movement and cubism.

Keynes was actually involved in Bloomsbury's prehistory toward the end of his first term as a student at Cambridge. Then and there he met two of Bloomsbury's "founder members," Leonard Woolf and Lytton Strachey (a friend, but Keynes's rival in male love affairs[1]). Later, the official London life of the Bloomsbury circle began in 1908 when Vanessa Stephen (later Vanessa Bell) and Virginia Stephen (later Virginia Woolf, the novelist) came on board. Elected a fellow of King's College the next year, Keynes moved to the center of the circle.[2] Forster celebrates the gaiety and candor at King's College associated with Bloomsbury in his *The Longest Journey* (1907).

Though it never numbered more than two dozen or so, this charmed circle set the contemporary artistic standards of England, and its members would have mixed well with F. Scott and Zelda Fitzgerald's chic set in Paris and America. Bloomsbury also included E.M. Forster and his *Howard's End*; art critics Clive Bell and Roger Fry; William Walton, the composer; Frederick Ashton, the choreographer; Duncan Grant, a portraitist and probably Keynes's greatest love interest among males; and other leading artists and intellectuals. Bloomsbury considered literature as anything worth reading; they drew no clear line between the style of fiction and that of nonfiction. A man of great skill and confidence, Keynes debated every issue with assurance.

Keynes was to draw his philosophy from Bloomsbury; it is stunningly individualistic, as summed theologically in his 1938 memoir,

> We were among the last of the Utopians..., who believe in a continuing moral progress by virtue of which the human race already consists of reliable, rational, decent people, influenced by truth and objective standards, who can be safely released from the outward restraints of convention and traditional standards and inflexible rules of conduct, and left, from now onwards, to their own sensible devices, pure motives and reliable intuitions of the good.[3]

Like Thomas Malthus before him, Keynes's early optimism and sunny disposition would be overtaken by the irrationality of others and by historic events, especially by war. Soon, however, it would be difficult to separate the destiny of Keynes from that of his country.

IMPERIALISM AND THE RUSSIAN REVOLUTION OF 1917

Britain had long had a thriving though informal colonial empire; it seemed almost essential to a small island needing to sell its manufacturers abroad. The British East India Company had traded in India for more than a century prior to the conquest of Bengal in 1757, after which The Company became the ruling power in much of India, and exploitation began to replace trade. Its informal empire changed dramatically when Britain had to vie with other industrialized nations for the attention of the less developed countries. European imperialism became truly serious during the last quarter of the nineteenth century.

From the 1880s, imperialism—the political division of the world into *formal* colonies of the great powers combined with the *deliberate* establishment of economic dependencies—became popular among *all* the industrialized nations. By 1900, one-fourth of the world's population was under European and American industrial domination. When its power had been mostly economic, the British Empire seemed sufficiently benign, but the political form of colonialism moved Britain toward strident imperialism. Sometimes the economic contests between the great powers became bloody.

Cecil Rhodes and John A. Hobson

Alfred Marshall shed no light on imperialism; the lamppost of supply and demand was focused on smaller matters. Besides, warfare seemed greatly removed from equilibrium and harmony. John A. Hobson, an Oxford grad turned public school teacher, was not so constrained. Even Cecil Rhodes, whose raid into the Transvaal had ignited the Boer War between the English and Dutch, justified the Empire as a way of acquiring new lands and providing new markets for the goods produced so efficiently by English capitalism. After having visited Africa and even having dined finely with Rhodes on the eve of the Transvaal raid, Hobson wrote in his *Imperialism* (1902) something remarkably close to what Rhodes had surmised.

Hobson noted a deep contradiction within capitalism whereby income and wealth distributions became too unequal to sustain it. Even the warm and fuzzy John Stuart Mill never went that far. Marx had found enough contradictions in capitalism to make it pretzel-like, but Hobson had no sympathy for Marxism, an irony soon to be evident. The Hobson paradox can be simply stated: Although the masses are great in number, their wages are spent entirely on necessities, limiting the goods they can buy. The rich have gigantic incomes, but they are small in number. Since producers fail if they cannot sell everything they make, oversaving or underconsumption must be avoided. Since wage-earners cannot buy all of those goods and services that gild Lily, only the consumption by the rich can save capitalism at home. And, well, there is the rub (even if it be an indulgent massage). As was well-known, John D. Rockefeller could not possibly spend all of his vast wealth. Even if the rich wanted desperately to avoid savings, sadly, they were left with no choice. Worse, the rich genuinely *wanted* to save.

Since wage-earners have the desire without the means and the rich have the means without the need or desire, purchasing power might be insufficient. Of course, as noted, J.B. Say, not to mention Smith, Ricardo, and Mill had those excess savings going directly into new investment, leaving no surplus of goods in the overall economy. But, Hobson saw a problem, if wage-earners were having trouble buying all those goods being produced by hyperproductive capitalism, why would entrepreneurs buy still more capital and generate still greater surpluses?

Hobson's solution is the same as Rhodes's. The excess savings of the rich would be used to build factories in Africa; the surfeit of goods going unsold in England could be sold to those poor Africans. The virtuous cycle does not even end there; cheap raw materials such as rubber could be sent back to England for the manufacture of tires. Colonization would save English capitalism.

It sounded too good to be true, for it was. As noted, many nations had by now industrialized—producing surpluses—and were competitors. These nations—Germany, Italy, Belgium, Japan, and the United States—wanted a piece of Africa, India, Latin America, or whatever region had poor people but abundant natural resources. Such imperialism, the aggressive pursuit by the industrial nations for pieces of other markets and resources, paves the way to warfare. The competition for markets ends up at the end of gun barrels. The English getting into the Dutch had started the Boer War. Not that everyone lost; just as the Boer War created a legendary Winston Churchill, the charge up San Juan Hill bequeathed the adventuresome Theodore Roosevelt.

Lenin Arrives on the Scene

While Hobson was ignoring Marx, Vladimir Il'yich Ulyanov (Lenin) was among those reading Marx in the early 1880s and 1890s. In the annals of violence, the Russian Revolution of October 1917 usually is linked to Marx, although at the time he had been dead for more than three decades. It is a tenuous linkage, at best. Marx and Engels had expected the Communist Revolution to occur first in an advanced industrial country, not in a backward, feudal society like Russia. Nonetheless, to Marx's great surprise *Das Kapital* had been translated into Russian in 1868 and enjoyed greater success there than elsewhere. At arm's length from Marx, the October Revolution was decisively influenced by two events: The outbreak of the Great War in the summer of 1914 and the April 1917 arrival of Lenin at the Finland Station in St. Petersburg.

Russia was ruled by the autocratic Nicholas II. Still poor and agrarian with a discontented peasantry, Russia was now at war with the formidable forces of Prussia's Bismark. The Great War had pushed Russia into the social and political disintegration so poignantly depicted in Boris Pasternak's *Dr. Zhivago*. The mixed blessing of the war is expressed in its epilogue:

> And when the war broke out, its real horrors, its real dangers, its menace of real death were a blessing compared with the inhuman reign of the lie, and they brought relief because they broke the spell of the dead letter.

Discontent with the management of the war and with economic conditions in St. Petersburg led to the fall of the Czar in March, 1917. (Ultimately, too, the outcome led to many movies about Anastasia.) The vicissitudes of war also brought down the short-lived Provisional Government of Aleksandr Kerensky, a caretaker government that took too little care. Lenin, the great revolutionary, did not bring down the Czar or Kerensky. They both fell by weight of their own incompetence.

Lenin nonetheless provided two things, a theory for "revolution" in countries still living off the land and political leadership during a period first of anarchy and then of civil war.

Lenin was born in 1870 in a small town on the storied Volga to parents who could provide him with a good education. In the tradition of the time, Lenin quickly moved into the ranks of the radical intelligentsia. He was a disciple of Marx with a difference. Although Marx looked like a revolutionary whereas Lenin looked more like a CPA, Lenin was much more the revolutionary. Both combined journalism with revolutionary actions, Lenin being a regular contributor to *Pravda*, or *Truth*.

Lenin came to Cracow, in what is now Poland, in 1912, after a three-year jail sentence in Siberia. Cracow was a part of the great Austro-Hungarian Empire (ruled from Vienna) and, in Lenin's favor, was only a short distance from the Russian Empire. When Lenin was not smuggling newspaper copy to *Pravda*, he was holding forth with other revolutionaries in a (still existing) pleasant coffee house, Jama Michalilkowa, the meeting place of choice for revolutionaries.

Lenin Arrives at the Finland Station

The Great War initially created a problem for Lenin. The Austrians, who had thought Lenin to be a useful foil for the Russian Czar, now incompetently presumed he might be a Russian spy. Again, Lenin faced arrest and a short stay in jail before he and his family were allowed to go to Switzerland, then a haven for revolutionaries of all stripes.

In Switzerland, Lenin wrote the always essential revolutionary pamphlet. *Imperialism: the Highest Stage of Capitalism* was widely discussed in Switzerland but published only after Lenin's return to Russia in 1917. The parallels to Hobson are clear. Capitalism, according to Lenin, had advanced to its highest stage as colonialism, extending its powers imperialistically. Whereas the Marxian orthodoxy saw colonies such as British India as markets for capitalism's surpluses, Lenin saw the colonies as outlets for investment and economic development. Monopolies now had hands across their borders: In this regard, Lenin is closer to Hobson than to Marx.

Lenin noted, accurately, but contrary to Marx, that workers, inconveniently, had become less revolutionary as capitalism had grown stronger through imperialism. With European and American capitalists gaining more power, they could bribe workers with higher wages. Money was a splash of cold water in the face of worker militancy. Worse, imperialism was too successful for its own good. There was little land left to colonize. The Great War was a desperate last land grab by the capitalistic countries, a war patriotically supported by co-opted labor.

The capitalists had always blamed the poor countries for their own backwardness. Lenin now placed the blame for the impoverished countries squarely on the shoulders of the capitalists and their workers. To escape poverty, the poor countries would have to revolt against their colonial masters. Whereas Marx and Engels expected a spontaneous communist revolution only in the industrially advanced nations, Lenin made necessity the mother of all revolutions in Latin America, in Asia, in Africa but, first of all, in Russia.

As noted, in March 1917 there was some kind of "revolution" or at least a revolt in Russia. Lenin learned of it while in Zurich. Since he was supposed to be the revolutionary, Lenin had to go to Russia. But how? If he tried to go through France, they would arrest him, for the French could see no good coming from Lenin back in Russia. If he tried to go through Germany, the Russians would think him a German agent. In one of the great serendipitous events in history, the Germans aided Lenin's flight to Russia because they believed his meddling would serve their aims well.

Lenin, his mistress (the beautiful frenchwoman Inessa Armand), and twenty fellow Bolsheviks sped through Germany in a non-German (or extraterritorial) train! Both Lenin and the Germans were protected because he made his passage in a sealed train, albeit over German railroads. He arrived at the Finland Station in St. Petersburg on April 3, 1917: In November Lenin and the Bolsheviks filled the vacuum formed of Kerensky's Provisional Government. Not denying the force of Lenin's demonic will to revolution, his rise to power depended on the weakness in Russia inflicted by the Great War, Kerensky's vacuousness, and, ironically, a sealed train trip provided by Russia's enemy. Lenin succeeded in great part because others failed.

Thereafter, Lenin's luck was to run out. Although the Bolsheviks occupied the most important cities, the broader outreaches of Russia were brought under control only after three years of brutal civil war. Ultimately to worse effect, Joseph Stalin was assigned the role of hammering out solutions to the remaining tough economic and political power issues. He became general secretary of the Central Committee of the Communist party in 1922. Lenin died in January, 1924, and, his bodily remains carefully preserved, still rests in a tomb in Red Square. Stalin became the undisputed master of Russia by the late 1920s.

Ayn Rand and the Antecedents of the Cold War

Alice Rosenbaum, later to become the novelist Ayn Rand, was a 12-year-old witness to the first shots fired during the Bolshevik Revolution. She and her family lived near the edge of starvation during the civil war and the continuing repression. The experience shaped her hatred of the Bolshevik theme that man must live for the State. This, and the absence of individualism, was the horror at the root of all the other horrors taking place about her—the bloodshed, the arrests in the night, the fear gripping a city she loved. These experiences are retraced in Ayn Rand's first novel, *We the Living*; they inspired an antithetical view of the State. Alice reached New York just as Stalin was taking over.

Stalin's totalitarian regime, completely at odds with the original goals of Marx, emerged in the 1930s. The coercive apparatus of police and courts was used to collectivize agriculture for the surpluses required for forced industrialization. Stalin's paranoia showed in the Great Purges of 1934 to 1938 in which millions of people, both communists and non-Communists, experienced a nightmare of arrest, torture, slave labor camp, and execution. Stalin, it is claimed, killed more communists than any fascist dictator ever had. Later, the breakup of the Big Three Alliance (Soviet Union, United States, and Great Britain) marked the onset of the Cold War. It was not until the early 1990s that Russia could face—however precariously—the prospect of democracy, something it had never experienced. Although the Soviet brand of communism appears doomed, the Eastern version of Cowboy capitalism may not prevail. By the mid-1990s, the Russian people only began to appreciate socialism after having had a taste of unregulated capitalism.

Whether attributed to economic forces alone or more complex motives, including the hubris of empire and nationalism, what happened in Europe spread as American isolationism came to an end. In turn, the Great War of 1914 to 1918 set in motion social, political, and economic forces that changed America forever. But these changes were for years seen as temporary dislocations that would in time yield naturally to a restoration of the old order. On the whole, as we shall see, the neoclassicals proved to be no more discerning of the future than anyone else.

The Great War brought death and destruction not only to Europe's peoples, but also to Europe's colonial empires and traditions. At the war's end, President Woodrow Wilson and Comrade Lenin (a.k.a. Vladimir Ilich Ulyanov) faced each other at opposite ends of a devastated continent and began to shape the next 70 years of world history. Wilson would dominate the peace conference in Paris, and his 14 points would be the foundation of the Versailles Treaty and the seeds of World War II. Lenin would lead the Bolshevik revolution in Russia and then die, leaving Stalin and set the stage for the Cold War.

JOHN MAYNARD KEYNES AT VERSAILLES

The Great War disrupted even Bloomsbury, and Keynes was called to the Treasury. At war's end, he went to Paris as the senior Treasury official on the British delegation to the Peace Conference at Versailles and the official representative of the British Empire on the Supreme Economic Council. Still, while he had a wonderful view, he had no power to interfere with the course of the game. He watched in great frustration as President Woodrow Wilson was outfoxed by Clemanceau of France.

Keynes resigned in anguish in June 1919, disillusioned and disheartened by the terms of the treaty that officially ended the Great War. The Versailles Treaty created, he said, a "Carthaginian peace": The sums that Germany and its allies were forced to concede in reparations to the Allies were both excessive and impossible to collect. Versailles would bring nothing but trouble. Keynes retreated to Vanessa Bell's residence and hurriedly wrote a polemic attacking the treaty, *The Economic Consequences of the Peace* (1919), which combined the skill of a novelist with the unsparing insight of the Bloomsbury critic. The instant success of his devastating, brilliant book thrust Keynes before the public eye and established his reputation as a pundit. It remains a literary classic.

Strachey's biographical essays of *Eminent Victorians* (1918) had ridiculed the Great Men of the Age ending. Keynes's polemic is something of a bold sequel in which he attacks his contemporaries, the conference's Great Men. Of Clemenceau he wrote, "He felt of France what Pericles felt of Athens—unique value in her, nothing else mattering; but his theory of politics was Bismarck's." Clemenceau, said Keynes, "had one illusion—France; and one disillusion—mankind, including Frenchmen, and his colleagues not least."[4] Of Woodrow Wilson he wrote, "...like Odysseus, he looked wiser when seated."[5]

The conferees of the major powers, wrote Keynes, looked at everything but the problem at hand: "A Europe starving and disintegrating before their eyes, was the one question in which it was impossible to arouse the interest of the Four." As to reparations, "they settled it as a problem of theology, of politics, of electoral chicane, from every point of view except that of the economic future of the States whose destiny they were handling."[6]

Keynes foresaw a bleak and perhaps bloody future. He warned of "rapid depression of the standard of life of the European populations to a point which will mean actual starvation for some (a point already reached in Russia and approximately reached in Austria). Men will not always die quietly."[7]

The degree of responsibility of the peacemakers for later events remains open to debate. Some call the conference the first act of World War II. Many see the rise of Stalinism in Russia linked to economic depression there. Certainly, the printing of money by Germany to make cash reparations payments and its depressed economy led to its incredible hyperinflation in 1919 to 1922.

The Economic Consequences of the Peace, reinforced by Keynes's public pronouncements, had an import on public opinion and through it contributed to the scaling down of reparations, beginning with the Dawes Plan in 1924. But the relief came too late for Germany, which had already suffered great social and economic damage. Hitler's rise to power was already set in motion by the terrible economic conditions in Germany.

Keynes's book was prophetic in another way too. It showed him to be ahead of his fellow economists in recognizing the sea change in public attitudes toward wealth and work. He cast doubt on the durability of the supposed national economic virtues of frugality and accumulation. The Great War, said Keynes, "disclosed the possibility of consumption to all and the vanity of abstinence to many."[8] Whereas most people in capitalistic societies had formerly accepted great disparities in wealth as essential to capital accumulation and thus to material progress, now they wanted their share.

The early capitalism of the Industrial Revolution had stressed labor and thrift, a dedication to work, and a rejection of consumption for its own sake. Leisure was equated with idleness. Keynes saw, however, that as early as the turn of the century, ordinary people had begun to look at work as a secular activity leading to the enjoyment of the money it brought. The commitment to work and thrift were watered down by devotion to consumer pleasures.

THE VIEW FROM AMERICA

In the United States, factory whistles and church bells announced the news of the Armistice on November 11, 1918, scarcely a year and a half after America entered the war. The toll on Europe had been great—more than ten million dead in battle and an equal number of slaughtered civilians. The total cost of the devastation has been estimated at $350 billion in 1918 dollars.

America had suffered far less (the flu epidemic of 1918 killed four times as many Americans as did German bombs and bullets), but in its 18 months of war the country had become more like Europe. Under pressure from the Allies to produce, the government had begun to intervene in the national economy—allocating resources, regulating prices, supervising the giant cartels, running the railroads, and even commandeering factories. The war forced on producers the necessity of mass production on a scale greater than ever before.

This grand economic and political alliance was victorious but with mixed results. Europe was saved, but the political upheavals that followed the Armistice toppled the old regimes and spread the fear of the "Red Menace." As a million doughboys returned from France, American industry was struggling to retool for peace.

For many, peace meant a withdrawal not only from bloody foreign lands but from insidious foreign notions and influences as well. The mood of the country again was isolationist, and about 250 alien radicals were deported just in time for Christmas 1918. In the Red Scare of 1919, some 2,700 communists, anarchists, and assorted union radicals were arrested. When the Boston police went on strike, the National Guard was summoned to deal with them. Many Americans saw no difference between unionism and Russian communism.

John Dos Passos' sweeping novel, *U.S.A.*, illustrates this attitude in dialogue between a reporter and her publisher, as he is assigning her to expose the "labor movement conspiracy" in the Pittsburgh steel mills:

> "Mr. Healy, aren't conditions pretty bad in the mills?"
> "I've got all the dope on that. We have absolute proof that they're paid by Russian reds with money and jewels they've stole over there; and they're not content with that, they go around shaking down those poor ignorant guineas... Well, all I can say is shooting's too good for 'em."[9]

In fact, many union organizers *were* shot, stabbed, clubbed, or tarred and feathered.

America ratified its return to conservatism and isolationism in 1920 by elevating the notably middling Senator Warren G. Harding (R-Ohio) to the presidency. The country, said Harding, needed "an era of normalcy" rather than revolution, agitation, experiment, or internationalism. But what happened to the American economy was anything but normal. Beginning in late 1920, the U.S. economy contracted, and a short but severe depression filled 1921.[10] Real gross national product (GNP) plunged six percent, while the unemployment rate soared to 12 percent.

The mobilization of national economies during the Great War had made some political leaders realize that governmental actions could have wide-ranging economic consequences. Thus, during the ensuing periods of economic depression and crisis, governments began to call on renowned economists to give advice on economic policies affecting the entire population, a practice continued to this day.

The Advice of Economists: Recovery from Depressions is Automatic

Most economists were not really prepared for this role. Since neoclassical economics dealt with individual industries and firms and the relative prices of specific commodities, economists began to explore new ground. At first, they combined the various strands of microeconomic theory to explain general economic conditions such as levels of national income and employment.

The neoclassicals were, for the most part, content to embellish the theories of the French economist and popularizer of Adam Smith, J.B. Say (Chapter 3), who had argued that price adjustments would prevent an economy-wide oversupply of goods (in excess of demand). The economy continually refurbishes itself as competitive markets wave aside uncertainty about the future and wash away any need to stuff wages into mattresses or to keep profits in the company safe. Income received is immediately respent one way or another, making both chronic shortages and gluts impossible.

This theory does not mean that no one ever saves any money. It means that the amount of money saved is always precisely equal to the funds demanded by business firms for investment purposes, and therefore the money is never idle. The interest rate that savers get for postponing consumption is equal to the rate that investors pay for use of the money. The interest rate is a self-regulating mechanism—a clocklike pendulum—maintaining a "correct" balance and always guaranteeing an equality between saving and investment.

Marshall's version of the competitive labor market was used to further explain how full employment is guaranteed, except for temporary lapses. First, a high wage rate will attract more workers. Second, a lower wage rate will make producers willing to hire more workers. In neoclassical economics, the wage is expressed in money of constant purchasing power: A *real* wage rate. Quick adjustments in supply and demand will presumably equalize the workers' need for more income and the producers' need for more revenue. The "right" wage will be the equilibrium real wage rate arrived at when the quantity of labor demanded is precisely equal to the quantity of labor supplied.

Suppose the number of workers offering their services to be greater than the number demanded. Then, says the theory, some of these workers must be *unwilling* to work at a wage equal to their market worth. If the wage rate is temporarily above the equilibrium rate and workers are unemployed, they can obtain work simply by going to an employer and offering their sweat at a lower rate. Workers unwilling to accept these conditions of equilibrium are *voluntarily* unemploying themselves. Thus, in theory, full employment is always attainable.

Alfred Marshall's View of Money Prevails

Though Alfred Marshall initially embraced Say's law without much qualification, his view of money loosened the law quite a bit. Marshall seldom took strong stands, but near the end of his life, his writings barely say what Say said.

In Marshall's view, individuals demand cash primarily in order to engage in commercial transactions. The demand for cash holdings or cash *balances*, however, derives from liquidity needs. That is, people prefer to hold some cash balances to bridge the time gap between the receipt of money income and its expenditure.

If this preference is such that the stock of money turns over at, say, an average rate of four times a year, a money supply equal to a quarter of the money national income will be held in cash balances at any time. Thus, the demand for cash for each dollar of national income (which Marshall denoted as k) equals the reciprocal of the rate that money is turned over, or its velocity of circulation. If V is velocity, k equals $1/V$. In our example in which V equals 4, then k equals 0.25. That is, at a particular moment, the average household will want to hold a quarter for each dollar of current income.

Nevertheless, Marshall viewed people with "excess" cash balances as borderline psychotic. For example, holding a half dollar of each dollar income might be deemed "excessive." After all, money earned no interest, unlike bonds. In nonclinical terms, money was not an *asset* to be held solely for its own sake. Thus, Marshall's k becomes a fixed value because the turnover rate of money (V) would be constant. Then, if $V = 4$, each dollar of the money supply would be spent a remarkably stable four times a year.

A particular commodity price, such as the price of unmentionables (relative to mentionables) from Victoria's Secret, is not related to the money supply or to the overall price level. That is because cash or checking account holdings are not substitutes for the *real* things (such as lacy, flimsy underwear). Money—lacking the attribute of an asset—serves only as a medium of exchange. There are no cash balances beyond those required for day-to-day household needs and business trade so that money received from the sale of products is always used (ultimately) to purchase other commodities.

After all this is said (and done) and despite Marshall's fussy qualms, the requirements of Say's law are more or less met in Marshall, as in most of neoclassical economics. That is, cash is held only temporarily in order to buy either consumer or producer goods, so that a particular output calls forth an equal value in expenditures. A slippage in Say's enforcement occurs only if V varies. Even the pre-1914 youthfully exuberant Keynes claimed that adherence to the quantity theory of money was a test of scientific competence.

It would be a mistake, however, to conclude that all the neoclassical economists were unified in their fealty to the quantity theory of money and the exactitude of Say's law. For example, an important exception was John Gustav Knut Wicksell (1851–1926), a Swedish economist, who repudiated the reliability of market flexibilities, and sketched very tersely a theory about—of all things—a business cycle. Already by 1921, John Maynard Keynes was urging the use of interest rates—raising them during booms and lowering them during depressions—to moderate booms and busts.

Still, for the majority of economists, the theory of automatic employment adjustment was gospel, and it allowed them to reassure governments in 1921 that whatever the state of demand for commodities in the economy, wage changes would always create a tendency toward full employment. Not to worry. Throughout the Great Depression (which began during the 1920s in Britain), Arthur Pigou, Marshall's favorite student, repeated the soothing message. In explaining temporary unemployment, he suggested "that such unemployment as exists at any time is due wholly to the fact that changes in demand conditions are continually taking place and that frictional resistances prevent the appropriate wage adjustment from being made instantaneously."[11]

THE ROARING TWENTIES

Even though the real-world view of money was that it should be accumulated in great amounts by any means necessary, the Jazz Age in the United States spared the neoclassicals total embarrassment. Sure enough, the economy bounced right back from the 1920 to 1921 depression, seemingly of its own accord, and what followed was a decade of unprecedented economic growth for the United States and prosperity for many of its citizens. The explosion in mass marketing was led by productivity gains translated into lower prices, and the expansion of credit translated into electric lights, inside flush toilets, and automobiles. Mortgage debt grew to $19.2 billion during the 1920s, compared with a meager $3.6 billion during 1910 to 1919, and installment debt roared by $4.5 billion during the twenties, compared with only $1.3 billion during the first decade of the century.[12]

The Roaring Twenties introduced a majority of American households not only to Zelda Fitzgerald and the Flapper but also to the automobile, starting a love affair that has yet to end. Scott Fitzgerald, the Prophet of the Jazz Age, sent the final draft of *This Side of Paradise* (1920) to his publisher in August 1919, a month after Keynes had fled Versailles. In 1920, the now ubiquitous Model T was priced at $850 and about 25 percent of households owned cars; by 1930, despite economic hard times, the share had soared to

60 percent. Industrialist Henry Ford and his assembly line were largely responsible. Determined to produce a car for the masses, Ford revolutionized the manufacturing process, then cut prices. Lower prices stimulated the number of cars demanded, increasing sales and facilitating long production runs, which allowed Ford to cut prices even further. In the 20 years ending in 1929, the sticker price of a typical Ford fell 80 percent.

To compete with Ford, other producers had to follow. In this way, in the 1920s the auto industry played the leading sector role that railroad construction had played from 1865 to 1893—both pulling along new demands for materials (backward linkages) and creating new industries (forward linkages). Productivity in the industry had increased fivefold between 1909 and 1929.[13] Unhappily for Henry Ford who stuck with the Model T, consumers preferred to move up to something with more style, comfort, and exotic engineering features. With the rise of nonprice competition, leadership of the automobile industry shifted to General Motors.

The multiplying of gasoline service stations and the growth of road building combined to transform the oil industry, and automobile manufacturing became the prime source of demand for steel, plate glass, and rubber. The magical American invention of installment credit made cars affordable to those of modest income: By the mid-1920s, three of every four car purchases were financed.

In addition to giving new privacy to the young, the automobile lured Americans into the suburbs and the commuting life. Building the new suburbias caused housing construction to boom, further encouraged by the extension of the traditional five-year mortgage to a 20-year term. More houses meant a bigger market for other durable goods—radios, refrigerators, washing machines, and other electrical appliances. Rising demand for electricity required new and expanded electrical power facilities. The greater use of radios invited the creation of more radio stations. Productivity gain for the decade was 72 percent in manufacturing compared with eight percent in the prior decade. Per capita GNP grew 19 percent (although the growth had been 26 percent during the 1890s), and earnings of nonfarm employees expanded 26 percent compared with 11 percent the prior decade. And on and on, and up and up.

During the giddy decade of the 1920s, the share of households with electricity almost doubled and the percentage with washing machines tripled. Households with inside flush toilets more than doubled. By 1929, it seemed as if everything was flush except bank accounts, as consumer credit rose to about 15 percent of all nonfood purchases. Agriculture was the great exception: It was in a decade-long depression in which its prices fell by more than automobiles. Agriculture worldwide had emerged from the Great War with excess capacity. The coming of the tractor (a by-product of automobiles) not only freed acreage once devoted to horses and mules but also increased the surpluses failing to create their own demands. The failure of Say's law was a failure for farmers.

Not surprisingly, the banking House of Morgan reigned supreme during the 1920s. The values and institutions of capitalism had changed: The American Dream had shifted away from thrift, work effort, and luck as ends and toward consumption and the making and use of financial instruments as the new means. Even Nick Caraway, Fitzgerald's narrator in *The Great Gatsby* [1925] was a bond salesman. Meanwhile, orthodox economic theory remained stuck firmly in Victorian values.

Perhaps we can learn something about the new values from the Bloomsbury circle and still more from contemporary fiction and biography than from Alfred Marshall. Like F. Scott Fitzgerald's fictional Jay Gatsby and the real-life Joseph Kennedy, the new rich of the Jazz Age had huge fortunes but lacked the traditions associated with inherited wealth. They were therefore deemed vulgar by those with old money. Still, as Kennedy no doubt realized, it was better to be *nouveau* than not to be *riche* at all! Others, like Fitzgerald's Buchanans or the real world's Jack Morgan, son of Pierpont, had establishment wealth and thus possessed inherited traditions. They were more likely to be corrupted by the purposelessness and ease their money provided.

Edward Stettinius, a Morgan partner during the 1920s, had six cars and several houses. It cost him $250,000 a year just to cover basic living expenses. Even during Prohibition (perhaps the last political victory of rural and small-town America over the rising tide of urbanites), the cellar of Stettinius' Park Avenue mansion held enough liquor to refloat the Titanic. By his own count, Stettinius had over a thousand bottles of fine liquor, including 40 bottles of Haig and Haig Scotch, possibly smuggled into the country by that vulgar Joe Kennedy.

In *The Great Gatsby,* both new and old wealth lead to human failings, though the failings are manifested differently. Early in the novel, Jay Gatsby is observed in the attitude of a worshipper, alone, stretching his arms toward a single, faraway green light at the end of the Buchanans' dock across the water—the visible symbol of his aspirations. Green is the color of promise, of hope and renewal, and, of course, of money. For Gatsby, ideals are wrapped up with wealth, and so the means corrupt the ends. But it turns out that Daisy Buchanan is unworthy of his vision of her, and her "vulgar, meretricious beauty," her pretentiousness, is a snare. Having confused Daisy with the American Dream, Gatsby dies disillusioned, while Daisy lives on, oblivious. So much for Gatsby-like hope and the shallowness of this new version of the American Dream.

Fitzgerald was more complex than he was given credit for during this lifetime. He had fun with Horatio Alger, often writing parodies of his stories or their characters. Not only had Fitzgerald read Marx, he has Nick Carraway and Gatsby looking vacantly at Clay's textbook on economics. Clay made clear his dislike of Social Darwinism and his affection for Veblen's ideas, notions that especially instructed Fitzgerald as he began to write *The Great Gatsby*. The novel, initially set during the age of the robber barons and, later shifted to the 1920s, satirizes the rich in much the same way as Veblen's *Theory of the Leisure Class.*[14]

Even so, the economic expansion from 1922 to 1929 was more than a spending spree by Gatsby and the new leisure class. It was supported not only by demand for housing and consumer goods (especially durables), but also by private investment, business construction, and government road building. Moreover, as noted, productivity grew. Electric motors replaced steam and water power;

assembly-line and mass production techniques burgeoned; advances in chemistry were applied to production processes (e.g. rayon, high-octane gas); and management techniques were improved. The Jazz Age was not all booze and Buicks.

THE FIRST MRS. ROBINSON, MR. CHAMBERLIN, AND NONPRICE COMPETITION

Like Benjamin Braddock (Dustin Hoffman) in the 1967 movie, the automotive industry had graduated. Buicks came not only in many colors but in different sizes and appointments. The Buick and Jay Gatsby's cream-colored Rolls Royce were differentiated from Ford's generic black model T. Whereas neoclassical economics could explain the supply and demand for generic goods, it failed to explain goods different only in appearances and the "market *imperfections*" that they created. The pink-suited Gatsby would have been insulted.

As the world of economics looked again toward Cambridge in England, theories of *imperfect* competition came into view.

During the 1920s Piero Sraffa, a Cambridge economics teacher and a former student of Marshall's, showed economists how to study the business firm as an imperfect competitor. In a description that could have come from Henry Ford's pen, the unit cost of production of a commodity may decline, wrote Sraffa, as the output of the firm climbs.

With such decreasing costs, Sraffa concluded, demand rather than competition may be the force limiting the size of a firm. Ford was wise to pay his workers $5 a day. Automakers, however, can manipulate demand to some extent by making functionally identical products appear to be different. The Buick and the Ford were both providing passenger transportation, but the Buick offered different amenities, including even different model names. By the Jazz Age, few realists could view the world through the monochrome glasses of perfect competition in which *all* commodities are generics. Besides, advertising had become sufficiently important that Daisy could be attracted to Gatsby because he reminded her of "an advertisement."

Manufacturing and marketing devices could influence not only Daisy's preferences but consumer preferences generally and infringe somewhat on the consumer's sovereignty.

A widely acclaimed reexamination of competition came from another Cambridge economist and another "Mrs. Robinson," Joan Robinson, who published her *Economics of Imperfect Competition* in 1933. Robinson was affiliated with Cambridge as both a student of Keynes's and a teacher. Following the lead offered by Sraffa's work on decreasing costs, she dragged fellow economists kicking and screaming into the new conceptual world of monopolistic competition.

Meanwhile, at Harvard University in another Cambridge (Massachusetts), the economist Edward H. Chamberlin (1898–1987) published in fateful 1933 a book on the same subject. A large joint-stock firm, not subject to the ravages of Smithian competition, could engage in nonprice competition by attracting buyers through special features and services rather than through the normal method of competition, which is to reduce prices. The producer could then advertise the product as being "unique," attracting new consumers with new designs without reducing its price.

Chamberlin and Robinson did not totally agree. He saw the "advantages" of imperfect competition, whereas she, like Scott Fitzgerald, saw "the wastes." Economists still do a lot of wishful thinking about the analytical grayness between the pure monopolist and the pure competitor: It remains a land of ambiguities, much like Fitzgerald's "wasteland" between New York City and West Egg. As it turned out, the uncertainties in the theories of imperfect competition were no match for the balanced forces achievable in theory by the Newtonesque clockwork of perfect competition. Its absence in reality bothered few economists at the time.

As to Bloomsbury, its members gave themselves the license to behave as the Victorian upper class always had. By modern standards Bloomsbury was restrained in its language, and romantic passion drove sexual relationships. They did reject sexual taboos, and women were on an equal footing with men. Their feminism—unlike the puritanical feminism of the nineteenth century—was libertarian.

Mostly, they shared discussion in "pursuit of truth" and with a contempt for conventional ways of thinking and feeling. Some say that they were the last of the utopians; others, that they were the last of the Victorians.

NOTES

1. Apart from schoolboy experiences, Arthur Lee Hobhouse, a handsome young Trinity (Cambridge) freshman, was Keynes's first great love. According to a biographer, "over the next seventeen years he [Keynes] had several love affairs with men, one of them [Duncan Grant] of central importance, as well as a certain amount of casual sex." Robert Skidelsky, *John Maynard Keynes: Hopes Betrayed, 1883–1920* (New York: Penguin Books, 1994), p. 128. Keynes's sexual preference for males lasted about twenty years.
2. There are many books on Bloomsbury. For a sprightly, brief introduction to the group that nonetheless brings it alive, there is Quentin Bell, *Bloomsbury* (New York: Basic Books, 1968). If you want to know virtually everything about the members and their works, there is S.P. Rosenbaum, *Victorian Bloomsbury* (London: The Macmillan Press, 1987), which begins with the "father" of Bloomsbury, Leslie Stephen, father of Virginia Stephen (Woolf), and ends with a huge bibliography.
3. John Maynard Keynes, "My Early Beliefs," in his *Essays and Sketches in Biography* (New York: Meridian Books, 1956), p. 253. [1938].
4. John Maynard Keynes, *The Economic Consequences of the Peace* (London: Macmillan & Co., 1919), p. 32.
5. *Ibid.*, p. 40.
6. *Ibid.*, pp. 226–227.
7. *Ibid.*, p. 228.
8. *Ibid.*, p. 22.
9. John Dos Passos, *U.S.A.: The Big Money* (Boston: Houghton Mifflin, Boston, 1946), pp. 150–151.
10. Until the 1930s and the Great Depression, all economic downturns were termed either **panics** or **depressions**. The need for a name for more modest downturns gave birth to the euphemism, **recession**, now used to describe downturns measurable in months rather than many years or a decade. American presidents remain apprehensive even regarding the use of this less frightening word.

11. Arthur Pigou, *Theory of Unemployment* (London: Macmillan & Co., 1933), p. 252.

12. U.S. Department of Commerce, *Historical Statistics of the United States*, X-551.

13. See Stanley Lebergott, *The Americans: An Economic Record* (New York & London: W.W. Norton & Co., 1984), p. 440.

14. The discovery of the Veblen-Fitzgerald connection was made in E. Ray Canterbery, "Thorstein Veblen and *The Great Gatsby*," *Journal of Economic Issues* 33, No. 2 (1999): 297–304.

10

John Maynard Keynes and the Great Depression

Though he already was a famous economist by the time of the Jazz Age, John Maynard Keynes (1883–1946), some would say, suffered one glaring defect; he had read Marshall's *Principles,* attended Marshall's lectures, and hence was a conventional, though brilliant neoclassical. Keynes's neoclassicalism was doomed by his genius, which eventually made him a scientific maverick and an earthshaker. Because of him, two generations of economists saw a different world. We have to go back to Karl Marx, who died the year Keynes was born (1883), to find an economist of comparable influence.

Keynes already was far more than an economics scholar. Besides being the principal representative of the Treasury at the Paris Peace Conference, deputy for the Chancellor of the Exchequer, and editor of the most renowned economics journal of the time, he became a director of the Bank of England, trustee of the National Gallery, chairman of the Council for the Encouragement of Music and the Arts, bursar of King's College, Cambridge, chairman of the *Nation* and later the *New Statesman* magazines, and chairman of the National Mutual Life Assurance Society.

Besides his contributions to the arts (his wife, Lydia Lopokova, was a renowned star of the Russian Imperial Ballet), he ran an investment company on the side and still found time to play an important role in the development of the economics faculty at Cambridge. Every waking hour was put to some use: At one point, speculating in foreign exchange, Keynes would call in orders by phone while still in bed each morning for half an hour, amassing a fortune then worth $2 million.

Shortly after completing his revolutionary General Theory, in 1937 Keynes had a heart attack, which slowed him to only a manic's pace. The government gave him a room in the Treasury during World War II to pick his brain. He wrote a book on *How to Pay for the War*, was the dominant figure in the establishment of the World Bank and the International Monetary Fund at Bretton Woods, chaired a new government committee concerned with music and the arts, and accomplished many other things. He was by now Lord Keynes, Baron of Tilton. After negotiating England's first postwar loan, Keynes prepared to resume teaching at Cambridge. But, after a fit of coughing, and with Lydia at his side, he died.

Keynesianism, if not the original Keynes, dominated national macroeconomic policy in the United States from the end of World War II until about 1968. Keynes' ideas dominated British economic policy from the mid-1930s until Margaret Thatcher became prime minister in 1979. The Keynesian policy revolution was forged in the fires of the Great Depression that began during the 1920s in England and dominated the 1930s in the United States.

THE PRELUDE TO DISASTER

The Great Depression cannot be separated from the upheavals of the Great War and the excesses of the Jazz Age. The postwar prosperity was always mixed and uneven. Farmers, in particular, did not share in it for long. Partly because of rising exports during the Great War, agricultural production had soared, and farmers had taken on debt to put more land under cultivation. But after the war, this wartime capacity began to come up against European competition, and prices began to fall, leading, in turn to declining farm incomes.

The depression of 1921 accelerated the price slide, and farmers had to produce even more to meet mortgage payments, turning to tractors and more efficient combines and away from workers. But the agricultural cornucopia combined with sated domestic demand pushed prices still lower. With many farms no longer profitable, the bankruptcy rate soared from 1.7 percent of all farms in 1920 to almost 18 percent in 1924 to 1926.

Structural change also beset coal mining, another highly competitive industry. Coal prices were low and falling, and competition from electricity and oil was beginning to tell. The textile industry, too, failed to share in the prosperity. Like agriculture and coal-mining, the textile industry was an old, established industry faced with "too much" competition. A picture of the Flapper, patterned after Zelda Fitzgerald, reveals how little cloth was required for dresses. As skirts came up short, so did textile profits.

And, as early as 1916, the relative position of the railways had begun to slip. Again, capital investment and increased productivity reduced employment. Competition with the railways came from the automotive revolution and the increase in road building, highways subsidized by the government in the same way that railbeds had been subsidized before. An economy once dependent on railways for its growth now had shifted into high gear with the automobile.

THE SPECULATIVE BUBBLE

What is remembered with greatest nostalgia is the phenomenal speculative bubble. While some workers were already experiencing hard times, other folks never had it so good. According to one estimate, the five percent of the population with the highest incomes in 1929 was receiving about a third of all personal income. The personal income accountable to the well-to-do such as interest, dividends, and rent was about twice as great as in the years immediately following World War II. While a mere 24,000 families enjoyed yearly incomes in excess of $100,000, fully 71 percent of families had incomes below $2,500. In the race against deprivation, the poor were getting less poor but the rich were beating them 40 to one.

Wealth inequalities in 1929 were even greater. Whereas four-fifths of the nation's families had no savings, those same 24,000 families at the tip of the top held a third of all savings. Fully two-thirds of all savings were controlled by the 2.3 percent of families with incomes above $10,000 yearly. Stock Ownership was even more concentrated.[1]

Questions of fairness aside, this financial imbalance presented problems of its own. Except for what is purchased as necessities, the large discretionary income of the rich is not dependably spent. It must go for mansions, yachts, Rolls-Royces, and Caribbean travel or else be saved and thus be subject to the even less predictable behavior of producers. It is one thing for producers to issue new equities and bonds to expand their facilities, it is quite another for rich people to buy and sell existing securities among themselves, changing only the prices and ownership of the pieces of engraved paper. The amount of unanchored cash chasing other pieces of paper probably had never been so high.

When such great volumes of savings are held in so few hands, they must be parked somewhere or moved from lot to lot. Despite the obvious trouble that can be caused by cash on the loose, the average citizen threw caution to the restless winds: He wanted nothing so much as getting rich quickly with a minimum of exertion. These excesses began to bubble to the top well before 1929.

By the mid-1920s, a classic speculative bubble inflated over balmy Florida. Miami, Miami Beach, Coral Gables—in fact the whole southeast coast as far north as Palm Beach—basked in the warmth of the great real estate boom. "Ocean view" lots often required telescopes, and Charles Ponzi's subdivision "near Jacksonville" was actually 65 miles west, closer to the Okefenokee than to the Atlantic. Still, nearly everybody acted as if prices of Florida real estate would go forever skyward, and it took not one but two hurricanes out of the autumn skies of 1926 to blow away the bubble. The bigger one showed "what a Soothing Tropic Wind could do when it got a running start from the West Indies."[2] It killed 400 people and launched yachts into the streets of Miami.

The collapse of the Florida land boom did not end speculation; it merely ended Florida's prosperity. The rise in stock prices had been rather steady beginning in the second half of 1924. When the hurricanes blew away the Florida land bubble that October, stock prices dipped a bit, but a recovery soon began. The true stock market boom got underway in 1927, by the end of which the *Times* industrials, predecessor to the Dow, had gained 69 points to end at 245.

What happened next is neatly summed up in a classic book by John Kenneth Galbraith:

> Early in 1928, the nature of the boom changed. The mass escape into make-believe, so much a part of the true speculative orgy, started in earnest ... the time had come, as in all periods of speculation, when men sought not to be persuaded of the reality of things but to find excuses for escaping into the new world of fantasy.[3]

During 1928, the *Times* industrials gained a remarkable 35 percent, climbing from 245 to 331. Radio had gone from 85 to 420 and Wright Aeronautic from 69 to 289. Radio had never paid a dividend! Trading on the margin—on borrowed money—soared like Wright Aero. The speculator could buy $1,000 of stock with but $100 down.

Investment trust companies had made their first appearance in America earlier in the decade, their numbers growing by leaps and bounds through 1929. Their sole purpose was to buy the securities of other companies and make sponsors richer. J.P. Morgan and Company, for example, co-sponsored United Corporation in January 1929. J.P. Morgan offered a package of one share of common stock and one of preferred to friends, some Morgan partners, for $75. When trading in United began, the stock quickly reached $99 and was resold at a tidy profit.

Even ignoring fraud and larceny, the great surge in holding companies and investment trusts leveraged businesses in the same way that stock buyers were leveraged. Dividends from the firms actually producing goods paid the interest on the bonds of the holding companies. A slump in earnings from production meant a cut in dividends and possibly default on the bonds. Such inverted corporate pyramids invite toppling from the bottom up.

Meantime, the American economy had peaked during the summer, and "the most expensive orgy in history," as F. Scott Fitzgerald's epitaph[4] for the Jazz Age reads, soon had to end.

THE GREAT CRASH

The panic of 1929 began on Black Thursday, October 24th. Shortly after a normal opening of the Exchange, prices began to fall on a rapidly rising volume. The stampede of selling by 11 o'clock was so wild, it would have scared even the Merrill-Lynch bull. The collapse of prices being so complete by eleven-thirty, fear became genuine panic. A crowd gathered outside the Exchange on Broad Street, New York City.

The first wave of panic subsided at noon, when word spread of a meeting at 23 Wall Street, the offices of J.P. Morgan and Company. The gathering of bankers pledged to pool their resources and turn the market around. But they could only lean—with their great bulk—into the wind. By Monday afternoon the effort had clearly failed. The *Times* industrials were down 49 points for the day, with General Electric alone down 48. Since the ticker tape could not keep abreast of trading, no one knew how bad it was by the end of the day. The bankers reassembled at Morgan's at four-thirty. Now they would try to save themselves, minimizing their losses by selling short. The next day, Tuesday, October 29, was the most devastating, with no buyers at all on many issues. As the *Times* industrials closed down 43 points on enormous volume, alarm gripped Wall Street.

The stock market would continue its relentlessly downward slide. The *Times* industrials, which had reached 331 at the start of 1929, closed at 58 on July 8, 1932. Its stocks had lost 82.5 percent of their value. General Motors had plummeted from 73 to 8. But the low was barely noticed in the press or in the market: Attention by now had shifted to an economy in free fall.

When the crash is viewed in the economist's rearview mirror, it is clear that early warning signs were abundant: The stock market collapse was a part of the already developing slump. But few were willing to believe this to be the end of the good times, and so the signs were ignored and the trauma made worse.

THE AFTERMATH

Since the market had become imbedded in American culture and the symbol of prosperity, consumer and producer confidence was crushed by its collapse. Moreover, the decline in stock prices made the (mostly rich) stockholders "poorer," and this slowed consumption spending on luxuries. Finally, the crash broke the circular flow of international financial capital.

United States financial capital flowing to defeated Germany had been funding the circular flow of reparations payments (demanded by the Allies at the Paris peace conference) from Germany to the former Allies, that in due course flowed back to the United States as war debt repayments. As Keynes had anticipated, an economically troubled Germany ceased reparations payments. Not only was the international exchange system weakened, but international trade slumped, further dampening global demand and thus output and employment.

The banking system was problematical even before the crash. The banks held call loans on stock purchases of about $4 billion. As stock prices fell, some banks could not cover their loans by sales of securities and suffered significant losses. In the agricultural states of Missouri, Indiana, Iowa, Arkansas, and North Carolina, bank failures greatly increased in November and December 1930. The Bank of the United States of New York failed. In the absence of deposit insurance, these bank failures led people to increase their holdings of cash and to reduce their bank deposits. Runs led to still more failures.

American banking is based on fractional cash reserves in which, for example, only $10 of cash in hand may support $100 in checking account liabilities, $90 dollars of which can be bank *loans*. The system is so interdependent that a failure of one bank can bring down several more. That is, deposit liabilities too are heavily leveraged. Leveraging works both ways: When things are going up *and* when they spiral downward. A window with a view from the top of the credit pyramid reveals why the failure of banks holding $600 million, or only three percent of the U.S. money supply, could cause the panic in the winter of 1930.

What had begun as a banking rumble reached a crescendo in the spring of 1933. Bank loans that had been good during the 1920s went sour as the prices of the goods they marketed and the value of real estate collateral plunged. President Franklin Roosevelt came into office on March 4, 1933, and closed all private banks that week by declaring a "bank holiday," an action that prevented the complete collapse of the American banking system.

THE DEPRESSION OF THE 1930s

Most economists consider the length of the Great Depression to have been over ten years in the United States—from 1929 until U.S. mobilization for World War II in the waning months of 1940—granting that within that span there were ups and downs. The fall in gross national product (GNP) from a cyclical peak of $104.4 billion in mid-1929 to a low of $55.6 billion in the cyclical trough in the spring of 1933 comprised the worst part of the Great Depression. By 1933, almost 25 percent of the civilian labor force in the United States was unemployed.

The Federal Reserve had not helped: It's policy at the time was only to increase credit according to the "needs of trade," meaning if business was not interested in borrowing, the Fed did not increase the money supply. It is difficult to imagine a more inept policy, for it caused bank credit and the money supply to fall during bad times. Amidst a collapsing banking industry and a manufacturing industry too frightened to borrow anyway, the money supply slumped by a third over the cycle ending in spring 1933.

Only the U.S. Congress could rise to this level of incompetence. Under pressure from the farm lobby, Congress passed (and President Herbert Hoover signed) the notorious Smoot-Hawley Tariff in mid-1930, leading to retaliatory tariffs around the world and a trade war in which world trade spiraled ever faster downward. Figure 10.1 pictures this downward spiral more dramatically than could a thousand words.

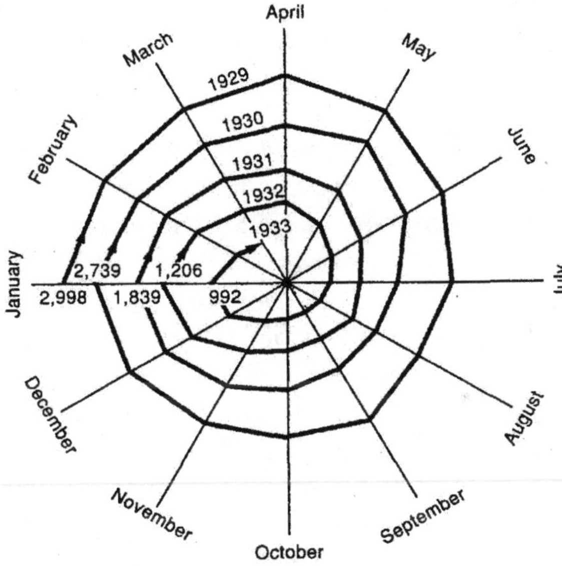

Figure 10.1

CONTRACTING SPIRAL OF WORLD TRADE, JANUARY 1929 TO MARCH 1933: TOTAL IMPORTS OF 75 COUNTRIES

NOTE: Monthly values in terms of old U.S. gold dollars, millions.

SOURCE: Charles Kindleberger, *The World in Depression* (Berkeley: University of California Press, 1973), p. 172. Reprinted by permission.

Not surprisingly, then, some historians and economists use the term "Great Depression" to describe only 1929 to 1933, because the real GNP (in 1929 prices) began recovering thereafter. The establishment of the deposit insurance system in 1933 helped to restore confidence and credit, and the money supply rose sharply in 1934 to 1936. The economy expanded slowly under the stimulus of government job-creation projects and from the gathering business and consumer confidence to $109.1 billion in spring 1937, slightly higher than in 1929. Then, the 1937 to 1938 recession brought real GNP down to $103.2 billion in 1938.

Whether one calls it a separate recession or the last great crisis of the Depression, the downturn lasted from the spring of 1937 to the summer of 1938. During that year, industrial output dropped by about a third and unemployment rose by about a fifth, according to the official data, leaving about 6.5 million people unemployed in 1937 and about ten million in 1938. After six years of crisis, the unemployment rate was higher in 1938 than it had been in 1931 (see Table 10.1).

The relapse of 1937 to 1938 was partly a result of a sharp reduction in the federal budgetary deficit (see Table 10.2) plus a sharp contraction in the money supply. That is, at a time the government was reducing its spending, businesses were not investing despite a call loan rate in New York City that fell below one percent in 1938. And yet—contrary to the neoclassical view—business did not invest, apparently having regained its pessimism about returns on investments in machines, people, and plants. For example, machines more than ten years old, which made up about 44 percent of the total in use in industry in 1925, had risen to about 70 percent by 1940. Thus the recession of 1937 to 1938 came in the wake of confidence in the economy insufficient to bolster business investment.

THE NEOCLASSICALS ADDRESS THE ISSUES

Amidst this cataclysm, only reassurances emanated from some of the world's most prominent economists. Arthur Pigou explained how

Table 10.1

GREAT DEPRESSION UNEMPLOYMENT RATES (PERCENT OF CIVILIAN LABOR FORCE)

	Official (%)	Darby (%)
Peacetime prosperity		
1919	3.2	–
The Great Depression		
1930	8.7	–
1931	15.9	–
1932	23.6	–
1933	25.2	20.9
1934	22.0	16.2
1935	20.3	14.4
1936	17.0	10.0
1937	14.3	9.2
1938	19.1	12.5
World War II begins		
1939	17.2	11.3
1940	14.6	–
1941	9.9	–
1942	4.7	–

Sources: U.S. Department of Commerce, Bureau of the Census, *Historical Statistics of the United States: 1960 Series* (Washington, D.C.: U.S. Government Printing Office, 1975), p. D46; and Michael Darby, "Three and a Half Million U.S. Employees Have Been Mislaid: Or an Explanation of Unemployment, 1934–1941," *Journal of Political Economy,* 84 (February 1976).

"with perfectly free competition ... there will always be at work a strong tendency for wage rates to be so related to demand that everyone is employed."[5] Yet Pigou's own England was in its second decade of debilitating depression.

Lionel Robbins, a professor of economics at Bentham's University of London, wrote in 1934 that "... in general it is true to say that a greater flexibility of wage rates would considerably reduce unemployment. If it had not been for the prevalence of the view that wage rates must at all costs be maintained in order to maintain the purchasing power of the consumer," he added, "the violence of the present depression and the magnitude of the unemployment which has accompanied it would have been considerably less."[6] The return to full employment only awaited the unleashing of free market forces.

The statistical appendix to Robbins's otherwise timely *The Great Depression* contradicts his recommendations even as it describes the ruin. Prices, as expected, followed wages in a downward spiral but (in Robbins's own data) the cost of living in the United States is dropping nearly 25 percent between the end of 1929 and the end of 1933, while the index of industrial production is dropping by almost the same share. Wages in the United States are dropping by about one-fifth from the end of 1929 through the end of 1933, while the number unemployed is increasing from nearly zero to over 13 million in 1933—a quarter of the U.S. labor force.[7] The neoclassicals persisted in the myth about falling wages bringing with them, full employment.

The devastation, however, did not escape contemporary literature. John Steinbeck's novel *The Grapes of Wrath*, published in 1939 as the United States struggled to escape the Great Depression, is an intensely dramatic story of the suffering and privation experienced by poor farmers during the 1930s:

> The decay spreads over the State, and the sweet smell is a great sorrow on the land. Men who can graft the trees and make the seed fertile and big can find no way to let the hungry people eat their produce. Men who have created new fruits in the world cannot create a system whereby their fruits may be eaten. And the future hangs over the State like a great sorrow.[8]

Steinbeck's pessimism was widely shared.

KEYNES'S ACADEMIC PRECURSORS

Not every British economist was in agreement with Pigou and Robbins. In addition to Keynes himself, others were nibbling away at the edges of conventional economics, among them, Keynes's student, friend, and colleague at Cambridge, Dennis Robertson (1890–1963). When, in 1930, Keynes published his self-described *magnum opus, A Treatise on Money*, it met immediate criticism, notably from Robertson, Joan Robinson (1903–1983) and Sir Richard K. Kahn (1905–1989) at Cambridge,[9] and their dissents aided Keynes, who soon began rethinking his ideas.

In a 1933 article, Joan Robinson succinctly explained how measured savings and measured investment can be equal without equalizing the savings desired by households and the investment spending planned by producers. It is the failure of the two sets of intentions—those of the households and those of the businesses—to mesh that creates downturns. By intending to save more and buying fewer Fords, households will leave unsold cars at the dealers. Such cars would be inventoried, and an increase in inventories is one form of business investment (albeit *un*intended). A pile-up of inventories leads to production and employment cutbacks at the factory. Measured savings being equal to measured investment is scant comfort to the dealer when unsold cars, a part of the measured investment, is contrary to his intentions. And unemployment is cold comfort for the automobile worker.

Kahn began with the notion that public employment can have a multiplier effect in the economy. Building on an idea that Keynes had put forth two years earlier, Kahn showed in 1931 that government expenditure on public works will be distributed to workers in the form of wages, a large part of which will be spent on consumer goods and services. Store merchants will then spend a large fraction of their receipts from the consumers on wages, inventory, and so on and on and on. If the government hires 200,000 workers to rake leaves and, as a result, employment in consumer-goods industries (secondary employment) is increased by 400,000, then total employment is increased by 600,000. There is thus an **employment multiplier** of three. It seemed a matter of simple arithmetic.

Meanwhile, the official view could be found in the cheerful oratory of President Herbert Hoover during the first three years of the Great

Depression. In January 1930, Hoover said, "business and industry have turned the corner," a phrase repeated sufficiently during those years that "turning the corner" became a proverbial cul-de-sac. Hoover viewed government relief programs to aid the jobless, homeless, and starving as socialist and communist. Nonetheless, even he belatedly set up a public-works program, though wholly inadequate.

In truth, American capitalism was dying, despite bedside affirmations from the neoclassicals and the President of the patient's early recovery. The occasion is reminiscent of the reassurances given to Alexander Pope while he was on his deathbed. The doctor assured him his breathing was easier, his pulse steadier, and so on. "Here am I," commented Pope to a friend, "dying of a hundred good symptoms."

KEYNES'S POLICY SUGGESTIONS

Keynes's new ideas steadily evolved from 1931 to 1934, as capitalism was devolving. In the earliest months of the 1930s, Keynes expressed his belief that the fundamental cause of the slump was a lack of new plants and equipment, a result of the "poor outlook" for capital investment. To improve the outlook, profits needed to rise; that would stimulate investment. But greater profits must not be achieved by cutting costs; that would be deflationary. Keynes decided that profits could be raised either by inducing the public to spend a larger share of their income or by inducing business to convert a larger portion of its revenue into investment, but not by both.

At this point, Keynes was still relying in part on neoclassical thinking: An increase in consumption required sacrificing savings otherwise available for business investment. He did not yet envision the pleasurable possibility of both total consumption spending and total investment spending growing simultaneously.

Even so, Keynes told his British radio audience in 1931 that heightened spending was necessary to counteract the Depression, an intuition that proved to be more useful than the advice of the neoclassicals. Keynes attacked thrift, a Victorian virtue, because he saw the fallacy of expecting large savings to be offset by investment when there were virtually no investment opportunities in sight. By 1932, for example, American industry was selling less than half of its 1929 output.

Keynes urged families to spend more (as did President George Bush during a recession in December 1991, by his purchase of socks in J.C. Penney's) and the government to increase its public works expenditures (much as President Bush did in his visit to a Texas highway project the same month). He rejected Arthur Pigou's suggested wage reductions; that would, Keynes felt, only make matters worse.

In 1931, Keynes also served on the Macmillan Committee to investigate and make recommendations about economic conditions in Britain. Anticipating his later theory of the multiplier, Keynes and other dissenting (from the neoclassicals) members of the committee argued that with private unemployment already high, public spending by government would not divert resources away from private investment but would rather have a compounding effect.

Although Keynes admitted that public-works programs might dampen business confidence for a short time, he thought that, on balance, increased government spending would be helpful, even desirable. Keynes was beginning to suggest that, if free markets did not produce working people and humming factories, then it would be necessary for the government to intervene to restore higher levels of economic activity.[10]

Until Keynes, critics of the neoclassicals were easily dismissed; they simply did not understand. But Keynes obviously did, and he had to be taken seriously when he condemned laissez-faire governmental policies. This he did in an essay in 1926 called "The End of Laissez Faire," in which he denied the Smithian principle of natural liberty and the close relationship of private and social interest with enlightened self-interest. Keynes doubted that there would always be enough expenditure to stabilize the economy—that is, he questioned Say's law. But at this point he lacked a counter theory to Marshallian economics: He had only a fuzzy vision.

PRIMAL KEYNESIANISM AND THE EARLY NEW DEAL

Keynes had sensed a lack of confidence by consumers that blighted the business community. Confidence is precisely what Franklin D. Roosevelt (1882–1945) undertook to restore first when he took office as president in March 1933 and began what became known as the New Deal. Although decried then (and often since) as outright socialism, the program was aimed at saving American capitalism. Those economic policies, though not socialist, were certainly radical by peacetime standards, that is, they attempted to uproot the laissez-faire system and make government an active partner in the conscious steering of the economy. In retrospect, it is best described as "primal Keynesian."

Beginning in March 1933, Franklin Roosevelt began implementing primal Keynesian before Keynes had fully developed his revolutionary theory. Roosevelt noted in his first address the corrosiveness of lack of consumer confidence: "So first of all let me assert my firm belief that the only thing we have to fear is fear itself—nameless, unreasoning, unjustified terror which paralyzes needed efforts to convert retreat into advance." By May 1933, the Federal Emergency Relief Administration (FERA) was given $500 million to provide relief funds for the destitute, marking the beginning of the federal welfare program.

Relief kept people from starving, but Roosevelt's basic New Deal strategy was to create jobs even while removing people from the charity rolls and restoring their self-respect. It gave Americans dozens of new federal government agencies. Some, like the Civilian Conservation Corps (CCC), which provided jobs for young males ages 18 to 25 years in conservation work, were successful. Others, like the Agricultural Adjustment Administration (AAA), which raised farm prices by paying farmers not to produce, were not. Pigs were slaughtered and corn plowed under (by government decree), even though people were near starvation and black sharecroppers and tenant farmers were thrown off the uncultivated land.

The government also funded new infrastructure. The Tennessee Valley Authority (TVA) was a socialized hydroelectric power program producing not only electric power but dams, fertilizer, reforestation, and recreational lands. TVA also built the Oak Ridge facility, later to provide research and development for the atomic bomb. Private enterprise, faltering during the Depression, was no longer sacred or exclusive.

To shore up a failing banking system, the Federal Deposit Insurance Corporation (FDIC) was created, insuring bank deposits. The Home Owners Loan Corporation also was established to refinance mortgages and to prevent more foreclosures.

The capstone of the New Deal was the National Recovery Administration (NRA), designed to oversee and enforce the National Industrial Recovery Act (NIRA). Deflation had been bankrupting farms and businesses, while plummeting wages were stalling consumer spending. Manufacturers were encouraged to fix prices with impunity from antitrust laws. Wages were fixed at a minimum and hours at a maximum, and collective bargaining rights were extended to workers. Thus the NIRA proceeded to violate the most revered premises of free markets. The NRA did expand labor-union membership (the United Mine Workers grew to half a million), but business abused the price-fixing laws by fixing prices at high rather than low levels.

The Depression ground on through the mid-1930s, even as the Supreme Court unanimously declared the NRA unconstitutional. Undeterred, Roosevelt set up the Works Progress Administration (WPA) in 1935 (in 1939 its middle name was changed to Projects). The WPA hired workers to build ten percent of new U.S. roads, alongside new hospitals, city halls, courthouses, and schools. It built, for example, the bridges and roads connecting the Florida Keys with Miami. It built Boulder Dam (now Hoover Dam), the Lincoln Tunnel connecting New York and New Jersey, the Triborough Bridge system linking Manhattan and Long Island, the East River Drive in Manhattan, and a warehouse for official gold holdings called Fort Knox. In addition to its construction activities, the WPA employed thousands of down-and-out artists, writers, and musicians in its artistic projects.

The deficit spending was hardly radical in magnitude: Federal government expenditures had risen to 10.2 percent of gross domestic product by 1934, hardly an imposing number by the standards of the more prosperous 1990s when government expenditures averaged about a fifth of gross domestic product. However, as about a fifth of the New Deal federal outlays was budgeted for employment creation and these outlays (and an expanding money supply) had contributed to the recovery in real GNP to 1929 levels sometime in 1937 makes the official unemployment data suspect. Economist Michael Darby has corrected the official unemployment data to include this public employment (see Table 10.1).

Darby's numbers on public employment erase an annual average of six percentage points from the "official" unemployment rate in the years 1934 through 1939. Still, Roosevelt's make-work alphabet of programs did not elevate the economy to full employment, even

Table 10.2

U.S. FEDERAL GOVERNMENT EXPENDITURES AND DEFICITS AS PERCENTAGES OF CURRENT GROSS DOMESTIC PRODUCT, 1931–1939

	Expenditures (%)	Deficit (%)
1931	4.7	0.6
1932	8.0	4.7
1933	8.3	4.7
1934	10.2	5.6
1935	9.0	3.9
1936	10.2	5.4
1937	8.6	3.1
1938	8.0	1.4
1939	9.8	4.3

Source: Based on data from U.S. Department of Commerce, *Historical Statistics of the United States, Colonial Times to 1970* (Washington, D.C.: Government Printing Office, 1975); and U.S. Department of Commerce, NIPA, 1929–1976 Statistical Tables, September 1981.

in the "best" year of 1937. The economy had to wait for World War II and war-related employment to achieve full employment.

THE FAMOUS KEYNESIAN MULTIPLIER

Meanwhile, Keynes had found the missing link required to complete his new theory. In the neoclassical parable, saving and investment in the loanable funds market set the interest rate. At the same time, the equilibrium interest rate ensures an equality between saving and investment. If saving temporarily exceeds investment, the interest rate will fall (and the amount of investment will increase) until they are equal again and full employment is ensured. As the gloomy months of depression unremittingly rolled on, however, Keynes watched businesses refuse to invest even though interest rates were very low, and he concluded that the level of income and employment must depend on more than simply the equality of saving and investment as set by the interest rate. Once this fundamental flaw was understood, a revolution occurred in economic theory.

Keynes adapted to his own purposes his colleague Richard Kahn's idea of the employment multiplier. It was far from new: Many economists had speculated on the multiplicative effects of government spending coming from successive rounds of consumer spending. But none had been able to make it part of an acceptable new theory.

Keynes appropriated Kahn's mathematics as the key link. He used the term **investment multiplier**: If government or industry invests an initial $1 billion and national income thereby rises by $2 billion, the investment multiplier is two. (Without the data or the statistical tools, Keynes had correctly guessed that the multiplier in England indeed was 2.)

At the risk of some oversimplification, the multiplier relation can be shown in a schematized example (see Table 10.3). The example has every consumer planning to spend three-quarters of every new dollar of after-tax income (Keynes's marginal propensity to consume) and intending to save one-quarter of every new dollar (the marginal propensity to save). To start the process, we presume that business investment rises by $5 billion as a result of improved profit expectations.

Table 10.3 shows what happens. In this process, the $5 billion is multiplied by four to become, in the end, $20 billion of new national income. The multiplier of four derives from only one-fourth of all income increments going unspent.[11] After all rounds are played, the change in saving caused by the change in investment will be equal to the original investment increment. Higher investment spending, either private or public, multiplies itself in terms of national income changes, and out of higher wage disbursements workers are able to save more. Therefore, the initial investment ends up raising enough savings to finance itself.

Table 10.3

THE MULTIPLIER PROCESS

	Change, Income		Change, Consumption		Change, Saving	Initial Change, Investment
Initial increase, investment						$5.00
First round	$ 5.00	=	$ 3.75	+	$1.25	
Second round	3.75		2.81		0.94	
Third round	2.81		2.11		0.70	
Fourth round	2.11		1.58		0.53	
Fifth round	1.58		1.19		0.39	
All other rounds	4.75		3.56		1.19	
Totals	$20.00		$15.00		$5.00	$5.00

In neoclassical economics, not only does saving depend mostly on the rate of interest, but any saving increment comes at the expense of consumption. The Keynesian multiplier ends this zero-sum game. Consumption depends not on saving but on income. There is a stable psychological propensity in the modern community such that consumers reliably spend more when their income rises and less when it falls. Unlike the Victorians, consumers of this new breed see virtue in buying lavishly and avoiding the pain of abstinence. Scott and Zelda Fitzgerald had glamorized this shift in attitudes during the Jazz Age.

If income is important to consumption, it must also be important to saving, because saving is simply "not consuming." To warrant any particular level of employment, there must be an amount of business investment spending equal to the difference by which total output (at the particular employment target) exceeds consumption. That is, investment must jibe with the employment (and output) desired by society.

Surviving fragments of early drafts of Keynes's *The General Theory of Employment, Interest, and Money* (1936), show that as early as 1932 he was using the multiplier concept in his theoretical system. Yet during these writing and advising years, Keynes was considered by most other economists to be only a thorn in an otherwise flawless rose garden of neoclassical economics.

ILLUSIONS AND THE NATIONAL INCOME

In the neoclassical parable, freely moving wages and interest rates led to full employment. Keynes circled the neoclassicals like an attorney in cross-examination. Argued Keynes, the free movement of wages and interest rates presumed inevitable in the neoclassical world either (1) will not occur or, *if* it does occur, (2) will not bring about full employment.

Keynes understood massive wage cuts to be an impractical policy notion. Furthermore, even *if* it could be accomplished, a decline in money wages alone would not elevate employment. Even though it would enable producers to reduce costs and thus prices, the money wage decline would also reduce the income that is the wellspring of consumer demand. The boost to total demand in the economy would then have to come from some other source.

What the neoclassicals saw as virtuous thrift rewarded, Keynes saw as employment denied. Higher *intended* saving means lower *desired* consumption, a decline in demand for goods and services resulting in lower production levels, less income from which to save, and therefore less saving than originally intended. This lower than expected saving will match investment at a lower national income level. This equality can be achieved at levels of total demand (and spending) insufficient to employ everyone in the labor force. There was a paradox in thrift.

Total demand is the sum of what is spent by consumers, business investors, and the government. When total planned expenditure exceeds total output, then output rises to meet the demand. Conversely, if total planned expenditure is less than total potential output, then output tends to fall. The tendency, then, is toward a national income equilibrium.

Here is a rare point of agreement between Keynes and the neoclassicals. But they said that this equilibrium is *always* at an output sufficient to maintain full employment, an outcome Keynes denied, contending that the simultaneous occurrence of such natural equilibria in all markets—labor, money, and commodities—at *exactly* full employment was improbable. Furthermore, he said, the failure of the equilibrium process could have dire social consequences.

When total expenditure matched potential output or total supply, say at $490 billion, the neoclassicals cried "Equilibrium!" and went home early. It had to be equilibrium because at any other level of output demand would either be "too low" or "too high." But, Keynes argued, a national income equilibrium does not necessarily coincide with full employment.

Private business investment, dependent as it is on uncertain expectations, cannot be counted on to guarantee jobs for all. At this point government spending comes in. Only the government, contended Keynes, can be expected to take a hand in stabilization policy and increase its net spending (i.e., minus taxes) by the necessary amount.

Suppose current government spending and private spending generates an equilibrium income level no higher than $490 billion and employ no more than 75 million workers, leaving five million out of a total labor force of 80 million unemployed.[12] A level of $510 billion would be sufficient to employ the entire labor force of

80 million workers. Suppose the investment multiplier equals four. Keynes would have argued that somehow we need to generate $20 billion in additional output and income to raise output to that $510 billion necessary to employ everyone. With an investment (and other spending) multiplier of four, we need generate an extra increment of only $5 billion (20/4) in spending.

The gap can be filled by a sustained net government spending boost (i.c., minus taxes) of $5 billion. (A spending increase not accompanied by an equal tax increase causes a government deficit.) At the *new* $510 billion national income equilibrium level, the entire labor force of 80 million would be employed.

However, said Keynes, even this contrived "equilibrium" was unstable—at the mercy of such things as fluxes in profit expectations. The real economy oscillated unsteadily between equilibria, like the billowing and wafting of the Wright brothers' first airplane. Sometimes it would even crash!

MONEY AND UNCERTAINTY

Once the individual has decided how much of his income he will consume and how much he will save, there is a further decision that awaits him. In *what form* will he hold this command over future consumption? Rational people do not hold savings in the form of cash or checking accounts, so said Marshall and most other neoclassicals. But holding cash balances for their own sake, countered Keynes, is perfectly rational when the future is cloudy, dark and foreboding. Uncertain economic conditions can make cash a more attractive asset than bonds, even if stuffed in a mattress and earning no interest. Cash as an asset can be like Linus's security blanket in "Peanuts." As Keynes put it, to hold cash "lulls our disquietude."

The rate of interest required for our parting with cash in exchange for earning assets measures the "degree of our disquietude." Certainty is the illusion. Rather than as a neoclassical reward for Victorian abstinence, Keynes saw the interest rate as a reward for illiquidity, the payment needed to overcome the individual's **liquidity**

preference. Thus the amount of money people want to hold decreases only with a rise in the interest rate (the liquidity preference schedule is downward sloping).

This essential difference between Keynes and the neoclassicals is linked intrinsically to the market for bonds. The price of bonds varies with supply and demand, both of which can be unpredictable. However, the dollar amount of interest paid for holding a bond is fixed. For example, take a bond, any bond (except James Bond), that sells for $1,000 and for which the holder receives $100 in interest income per year. The annual interest rate on such a bond is $100/ $1,000, or ten percent. If the supply of bonds at that rate and maturity greatly (and often unexpectedly) diminishes, the price of the bond in question—already in the market—will rise. For example, if the bond price doubles to $2,000, the interest rate falls to five percent ($100/$2,000)

Thus a bondholder who buys the bond because the interest return is greater than the zero percent that cash yields can prosper if the interest rate is stable or if the price of the bond rises, providing a handsome capital gain. But if the bond price falls, and if the bond was bought at a relatively high price (low interest rate), a subsequent small drop in its price will cause a loss in the value of the bondholder's capital sufficient to wipe out the small amount of interest income earned from illiquidity. Suddenly, cash is a more attractive asset than a bond.

In Keynes's mind, this point is where the trouble really begins. If bond prices are so high that individuals do not expect them to soar more (i.e., interest rates have bottomed out), the preference for liquidity or hoarding cash and keeping it idle then may be almost unlimited. If virtually everyone holds onto cash instead of bonds, interest rates in the bond market will not decline further. The economy is in what Keynes's friend and colleague Dennis Robertson was to christen a **liquidity trap**.

If holders of cash and bonds sense doom amidst the gloom, imagine how a firm's CEO might feel about putting funds into a new plant based on sales forecasts over the next 30 uncertain years!

Even an exceedingly low interest rate may not incite business firms to borrow money and invest in new plants and equipment. Indeed, if business prospects are sufficiently dismal, a negative nominal interest rate, an impossibility, may be required to stimulate investment.

Inside and Outside Money Supplies

Where does this money, hoarded or spent, originate? Keynes saw it as coming into existence with debts, which are contracts for deferred payment. Money comes into being because there is a lag between the production of commodities and the receipt of cash. Henry Ford turned out hundreds of Model A's weekly, but they had to go to the dealers and the sales staff had to convince customers to buy them—all of which took time. The time gap is filled by the banking system or by new bond issues, which finances goods in process. Such money is created *inside* the private enterprise system. This is Adam Smith's circulating capital, channeled through the modern banking system.

In the modern economy, most money is held in the form of checking deposits, a liquid asset for the individual and a liability for First National Bank. Since modern banking is a fractional reserve system, a certain portion of a bank's deposits can be loaned out to business firms. Loans by one bank become new checking deposits for a second bank, which in turn can loan out a large share of these deposits, and so on throughout the banks in the system. In this way, the money supply is enlarged with a mathematical regularity similar to Keynes's multiplier. The money supply grows as long as more loans are being made to businesses for expansion, the financing of inventories, or the financing of production processes.

Other money originates *outside* the banking system. If it so chooses, the government may also create debt through its deficit spending. The U.S. government did so, for example, with remarkable regularity during the 1980s and the early 1990s. Governmental expenditures greater than tax revenue can be financed by selling bonds to the central bank, which uses them as backing for loans to commercial banks and for the issuing of currency, thereby increasing the money supply.

The total supply of money therefore depends chiefly on the actions of private commercial banks and those of the monetary authority as both respond to the demands of individuals, businesses, and government. In this way, money is created out of thin air from both inside and outside the private banking system.

Interest Rates and Uncertainty Upends the Quantity Theory of Money

The supply of money and the demand for money set the level of interest rates. Unlike their role in the crude version of the classical quantity theory of money, money supply changes can influence income and the price level only *indirectly,* through the money rate of interest. Then, if expected business sales revenues are sufficiently high and interest rates sufficiently low, firms will borrow from private banks and engage in active investment activity.

If the filament supplier to General Electric sees its sales prospects brightening, it may borrow to buy more modern production equipment to meet its client's needs. Again, however, the interest rate may not fall low enough because of the liquidity desires of the public (a liquidity trap), or else the uncertainty regarding investment prospects may be too great to entice business to invest at *any* rate of interest.

Recall Alfred Marshall's favoritism toward both the quantity theory of money and Say's law and you can see the severe damage done to Marshall's theory by Keynes's view of money. First, the turnover rate of money (*V*) is no longer stable, much less constant. If the demand for money or liquidity preference is sensitive to interest rate changes (bond price movements) or to mood shifts regarding economic prospects, *V* might as well stand for volatility. The rate of turnover of money will vary with the swings in the public's desire for cash (liquidity). Indeed, in the liquidity trap the public's desire for liquidity will be infinite. Money balances no longer will stay precisely equal to those funds required for day-to-day household needs and business trade. The desire by individuals and businesses to hold money balances when they expect bond prices to stall in mid-air is one of the broken links in Say's chain of events.

Money and the Great Depression

Keynes did not say that money is irrelevant. Rather, he wanted to show how money is an active ingredient in producing income, output, and employment. Nonetheless, his message eluded some of Keynes's interpreters. They were driven by the overwhelming need to move the economy out of the Great Depression, whose conditions coupled a liquidity trap with gloomy business expectations.

In such a double trap—where interest rates cannot be pushed any lower and business investors are wary—monetary policy is of no avail. The central bank cannot increase the money supply if private bankers are unwilling to make loans. Private bankers will not make loans if they have no takers. Then, the velocity of money (V) sinks beneath a tide of bankruptcies. The central bank ends up pushing on a wet noodle. The interest rate will not fall to zero because individuals do not expect to see bond prices go any higher (or interest rates any lower). Some economists today, such as Paul Krugman at MIT, contend that Japan of the 1990s has been in a liquidity trap.

During such a monstrous slump, the only recourse is for the government to spend more than its tax receipts, creating a deficit, and sell its debt (bonds) to the central bank. Not only would the government have to create *outside* money, but it also would have to ensure its use—its velocity—by spending it. The consequent government outlay raises aggregate demand, which leads to a renewed flow of output and increased employment and income, which further has a multiplier effect. The emphasis placed on deficit financing by an important group of Keynes's interpreters, the *fiscal Keynesians*, is better understood in the dimness of what seemed to be the twilight of capitalism.

KEYNES, HARVARD AND THE LATER NEW DEAL YEARS

The connections between the later architects of the New Deal and John Maynard Keynes were indirect. Although President Roosevelt welcomed Keynes himself to the White House in 1934, the President was quite unimpressed with this "fancified mathematician." As John Kenneth Galbraith has said, the Keynesian Revolution went to Washington by way of Harvard,[13] where Keynes's ideas had blown in like a gale force wind. Washington officials regularly attended Harvard seminars on Keynesian economics. We will return to those seminars in the next chapter.

In some ways, the Keynesians were preaching to the choir. In Washington, Marriner S. Eccles, head of the Federal Reserve Board, had anticipated the ideas of Keynes. The remarkable Lauchlin Currie, once Eccles's assistant director of research and statistics and later the first professional economist at the White House, also was "Keynesian" before the *General Theory*. They and Galbraith were able to place reliable Keynesian economists in various government posts.[14]

The later New Deal also brought the "welfare state," already in place in Europe, to the United States, to the bastion of capitalism where Henry Ford in 1931 could blame the laziness of workers for the calamity shortly before closing a plant and firing 75,000 workers. Ford saw a silver lining in the ragged coats of these men on the road again: "Why, it's the best education in the world for those boys, that traveling around! They get more experience in a few months than they could in years at school."

For all its radical solutions, the New Deal was profoundly conservative. It worked within capitalism—then in critical condition—to preserve that system. What it was failing to do, had to be done—however imperfectly—by the federal government. And it was. Jobs were created and the hungry fed. In the process, the federal government was transformed from a negligible influence on the typical household into a widely felt presence, becoming massive in scale by the end of World War II. So necessary was much of this to the survival of the American political system, it probably would have happened even if John Maynard Keynes had never been born.

In the end, Keynesian economics was to justify policies already in vogue.

THE KEYNESIAN REVOLUTION: WHY?

What was revolutionary is clear. Whereas the English neoclassicals saw full employment as automatic, Keynes said it was not and advocated government action to get it. During slumps, private spending would have to be supplemented by public expenditure, a recommendation flying in the face of the virtue of Victorian frugality—or so it seemed.

The broader question is why did Keynes's ideas sweep the field of academic economics and set the standard for the next 40 years. The answer lies not so much in Keynes's creation of an elegant and impregnable theory (it was not) as in the thoroughness—some would say savagery—with which he demolished the orthodox position.

In his literary attack on Say's law, Keynes was also attacking Alfred Marshall—the man who had begged Keynes to shift from mathematics and philosophy into economics—because Marshall was once a staunch defender of the law. In finding examples of Marshall's defense of Say, Keynes had to turn to Marshall's early work, because, as he grew older, Marshall had become more skeptical about the French economist's "law." As Keynes admitted, "It would not be easy to quote comparable passages from Marshall's later work."

Keynes—of ascetic countenance, intent, flashing eyes, and unsuppressed impatience—also assailed the work of Arthur Pigou, who had invited the student Keynes to breakfast once a week. Again his choice of targets was dictated by its size: Pigou's *Theory of Unemployment* was the only available detailed account of the neoclassical theory of employment. Keynes's focus on it is a compliment of sorts, although the critique is no less devastating for that.

Joan Robinson offers an explanation for Keynes's motives:

> [He] went out of his way to pick out the interpretation of Marshall most adverse to his own views, to pulverize it, mock it and dance upon the mangled remains, just because he thought it a matter of great importance—of real, urgent, political importance—that people should know that he was saying something fresh. If he had been polite and smooth, if he had used proper scholarly caution and academic reserve, his book would have slipped down unnoticed and millions of families rotting in unemployment would be so much the further from relief. He wanted the book to stick in the gizzards of the orthodox, so that they would be forced either to spew it out or chew it properly.[15]

The theory was there, but Keynes's rhetorical devices carried the day.

Keynes no doubt was blessed with extraordinary luck that he parlayed to his advantage. Marshall's influence had given all Cambridge economists superb reputations. And the *General Theory* was greatly strengthened by the help of the bright young economists who surrounded Keynes. Some of its pieces were worked out by others, and over time its vitality increasingly depended on amendments.

To be sure, Keynes guaranteed a large audience for the book by his vigorous attack on Marshall, Pigou, and the British Treasury's view of economic policy. And, of course, the conditions during the Depression provided an instant display for Keynes's dire conclusions. Only the technical competence of the neoclassicals at Cambridge could have kept that tradition alive long after it had the power to solve the crucial problem of unemployment. Ironically, the neoclassicals now could not extinguish the revolutionary fires lit by economic realities when the flames were being fanned at Cambridge, England, itself.

POSTSCRIPT AND PRELUDE

There is no agreement today among economists about what is most important in Keynes's theory. Keynes himself, immodest as usual, wrote the famous playwright George Bernard Shaw (a friend and a Fabian Socialist) in 1935, "You have to know that I believe myself to be writing a book on economic theory which will largely revolutionize—not, I suppose at once, but in the course of the next ten years—the way the world thinks about economic problems...."[16] Robert Heilbroner emphasizes the policy consequences of the revolution: "There was no automatic safety mechanism after all!.... A depression ... might not cure itself at all; the economy could lie prostrate indefinitely, like a ship becalmed."[17]

Keynes's adherents were themselves divided from the outset, strongly disagreeing on what Keynes *really* meant. The initially dominant Keynesian view was favored by the conditions of the time; the revolutionary antidepression policy carried the day. However, Keynes's failure to replace Marshall's price theory at the *microeconomics* level (Keynes thought it unimportant to his main arguments) opened the door to an interpretation that led to a counterrevolution. *Theory*, not the killing field, is the battleground of economists.

That Keynes had an enormous impact on antidepression policy in England is not in doubt, and his ideas had a great effect on post-World War II stabilization policies throughout Europe, in Canada, and in the United States. National governments now had an obligation to their constituencies to guarantee sufficient levels of total demand in order to fully employ the nations' labor forces. In Great Britain, this new ethic meant the end of frugality and laissez-faire in government economic policy until the rise of Margaret Thatcher.

The consequence of Maynard Keynes combined with other forces has been a very low level of British unemployment during the post-World War II years up to Thatcherism. In the United States, this new ethic led to the Employment Act of 1946, which committed the federal government to follow policies that would provide employment opportunities for those able, willing, and seeking work. Keynesian economic policies were vigorously pursued by the Truman Administration, and a modified Keynesian program was perhaps most successfully followed by the Kennedy and Johnson Administrations prior to the escalation of the Vietnam War in 1968.[18]

Keynes did not write the *General Theory* in order to solve puzzles about hypothetical conditions but out of an urgent concern that governments would fail to end the massive unemployment and deprivation of the 1920s and 1930s in Britain and of the 1930s in the United States. In the 1980s and 1990s, we lost or forgot much of Keynes's message on social injustice, namely, the growth of wealth is not dependent on the abstinence of the rich, and therefore one of the chief justifications for great inequality is removed.

After the Vietnam War, U.S. economists focused on the "equilibrium" tendencies used by Keynes as academic argument, thus obscuring his stress on the uncertainty of the future on economic fluctuations. If we rush unthinkingly into the arms of equilibria every chance we get, we are simply substituting a mechanical analogy for history. At equilibrium nothing can be done—because we are already there.

CONCLUSIONS

Even though conditions during the Depression in the United States directly conflicted with neoclassical thought, this reality simply remained invisible to most economists. Economic science was changing more slowly than the values and institutions of capitalism.

Even the ideas of imperfect competition from Joan Robinson and Edward H. Chamberlin were lost in the debacle. The Great Depression sidetracked this theory, much as it had derailed the new consumerism of the Jazz Age, relegating imperfect competition to a mere advance in the technique of economic analysis and not a revolutionary idea or ideology. The differentiation of goods was of little concern to those who were unemployed or on welfare; they were more interested in whether or not there would be anything to eat tomorrow.

Nonetheless, Joan Robinson's presence and the Depression were the introductory elements to the first widely acknowledged revolution in economic thought since Alfred Marshall: The Keynesian Revolution instigated by yet another student of Marshall's at Cambridge, the neoclassical heretic John Maynard Keynes.

NOTES

1. These data are gleaned from Maurice Leven, Harold G. Moulton, and Clark Warburton, *America's Capacity to Consume* (Washington: Brookings Institution, 1934), pp. 54–56, 93–94, 103–104, 123; Selma Goldsmith, George Jaszi, Hyman Kaitz, and Maurice Liebenber, "Size Distribution of Income Since the Mid-Thirties," *The Review of Economics and Statistics* (February 1954): 16, 18; Robert J. Lampman; *The Share of Top Wealth-Holders in National Wealth, 1922–1956* (New York: National Bureau of Economic Research, 1962); James D. Smith and Steven D. Franklin, "The Concentration of Personal Wealth, 1922–1969," *American Economic Review*, 64 (May 1974): 162–167 and; John Kenneth Galbraith, *The Great Crash 1929* (Boston: Houghton Mifflin, 1954), pp. 177, 180, 182, 191.
2. Frederick Lewis Allen, *Only Yesterday* (New York: Harper, 1932), p. 280.
3. Galbraith, *op. cit.*, pp. 11–12. I have drawn shamelessly on bits and pieces of this book in this and the next section. There is no other source on 1929 that blends so magically, information and entertainment. I direct the reader to *The Great Crash 1929* for the more extensive and detailed history of its subject.
4. F. Scott Fitzgerald, "Echoes of the Jazz Age," *Crack-Up*, p. 21.
5. Arthur Pigou, *Theory of Unemployment* (London: Macmillan & Co., 1933), p. 252.
6. Lionel Robbins, *The Great Depression* (London: Macmillan & Co., 1934), p. 186.
7. Among the various wages and conditions reported in 1932 are: In Pennsylvania, wages in saw mills were five cents an hour, in brick and tile manufacturing six cents, and in general contracting 7.5 cents; in Tennessee, some workers were paid as little as $2.40 for a 50-hour week [reported in Arthur Schlesinger, Jr., *The Crisis of the Old Order* (Boston: Houghton Mifflin, 1957), pp. 249–250].
8. John Steinbeck, *The Grapes of Wrath* (New York: Viking Penguin, 1939), p. 448.
9. Others include James Meade, Austin Robinson, and the late Piero Sraffa (1893–1983).
10. My private correspondence with the late Joan Robinson over several years greatly improved my understanding of the evolution of Keynes's pre-*General Theory* thinking as well as directing me away from some errors in interpretation of the subtler aspects of Keynesian thought. My late colleague and friend, Abba P. Lerner, provided similar guidance even though he and Joan were not always in agreement. In the end, I became the referee where their ideas or opinions collided. Not everyone will agree with my arbitration.

11. A simple mathematical relationship between the marginal propensity to consume (or the marginal propensity to save) and investment expenditures gives the value of the multiplier. It is Investment Multiplier = 1/(1 – MPC) = 1/MPS. From the numbers in my example, the Investment Multiplier = 1/(1/4) = 4.

12. Keynes actually followed neoclassical tradition so that total output increased (with employment), but at a decreasing rate because of diminishing returns. This complication is not necessary to establish the national income equilibrium, and, for simplicity, constant returns are displayed.

13. See John Kenneth Galbraith, "How Keynes Came to America," in *Economics, Peace and Laughter* (Boston: Houghton Mifflin, 1971).

14. See John Kenneth Galbraith, *A Life in Our Times: Memoirs* (Boston: Houghton Mifflin, 1981), pp. 68–70.

15. Joan Robinson, *Economic Philosophy* (Chicago: Aldine Publishing Co., 1962), p. 79. Robinson's view is supported by a passage in Keynes's correspondence with the late Roy Harrod, in which Keynes says he wanted to be "sufficiently strong in [his] criticism to force the classicals to make rejoinders." See letter to R.F. Harrod, August 27, 1935. In *The Collected Writings of John Maynard Keynes*, ed. Donald Moggridge (New York: St. Martin's Press, 1973), Vol. 8, p. 548.

16. Roy Harrod, *The Life of John Maynard Keynes* (New York: Augustus Kelley, 1969), p. 462.

17. Robert L. Heilbroner, *The Worldly Philosophers*, 6th ed. (New York: Simon & Schuster, 1986), p. 271.

18. The details of policy as applied theory during these years are provided in E. Ray Canterbery, *Economics on a New Frontier* (Belmont, California: Wadsworth Publishing Co., 1968).

11

The Many Modern Keynesians

Keynes, writes John Kenneth Galbraith, was long held suspect by his colleagues because of the clarity of his writing. But "in *The General Theory* ... [he] redeemed his academic reputation. It is a work of profound obscurity, badly written and prematurely published."[1] Perhaps fog is to be expected when one sails into uncharted waters. Keynes struggled to avoid comparison of the *General Theory* with his earlier literary efforts such as *The Economic Consequences of the Peace*. In the struggle, Keynes succeeded all too well, and Keynes's classic beget a host of interpretations.

Several loosely chartered schools of "Keynesians" can be discerned in the mists. This chapter treats the neo-Keynesians and the more diverse Post Keynesians, in the order of modernerity.

"Neo-Keynesian" is itself a neo-term, but the position defining the school is not. It belongs to the new generation of economists growing up during the Great Depression and, then, emerging from the fire and smoke of World War II. According to James Tobin, 1981 Nobel prize winner and a neo-Keynesian, the basic issue is whether there are "market failures of a macroeconomic nature in a market economy. Neo-Keynesians think there are and that the government can do something about them. They think that demand management policy can assist the economy to stay close to its equilibrium track."[2] Broadly, two branches of neo-Keynesians have emerged—fiscal Keynesians and neoclassical Keynesians. One school that may or may not be truly new, the New Keynesians, will be discussed later.

First, however, we consider the transformations confronting the post-Great Depression, post-World War II American economists.

WORLD WAR II TRANSFORMS THE ECONOMY

Depression and war not only transform economies, they change minds. John Maynard Keynes was not the only writer to anticipate a second world war. The novelist Thomas Mann, born in Germany in 1875, published *Mario and the Magician* in 1929. In this tale, a German family is marooned in late summer in a quintessentially European hotel. Staying longer than it had intended, the family goes to a performance by a famous magician. The magician, apparently a fraud, nonetheless holds his audience with a strong power that they cannot resist. The family wants to leave, but cannot; something holds them in their chairs. Mario, who is humiliated by the magician, obtains his revenge, but it gives neither he nor those who respect him any satisfaction. There is no remedy: There is only the hope that the performance will end sometime, although it may go on forever.

Mann's story is about Fascism, which had already overtaken Italy and had influenced many Germans. He had seen the "masters of deceit" and believed that people would have difficulty distinguishing between reality and illusion. In 1933, Hitler's government forced Mann into exile; in 1944 he became an American citizen.

Ernest Hemingway (1899–1961), the American novelist, experienced warfare up close, being seriously wounded at age 18 during World War I. Thereafter, living in Paris, F. Scott Fitzgerald already was famous, but Hemingway was about to emerge from his shadow. Hemingway's novel, *The Sun Also Rises,* was about that "lost generation" of Americans living in Paris after World War I. In *A Farewell to Arms,* he mixed romance with heroic male exploits and, in still other works, captivated a male generation that saw World

War II as a "good, just and necessary" battle. His war-time experiences eventually led Hemingway to see virtue in collective action. In his 1937 *To Have and Have Not*, its dying hero gasps, "One man alone ain't got ... no chance." Later, in *For Whom the Bell Tolls*, Hemingway makes a plea for human brotherhood.

Certainly, the children of the Great Depression and the veterans of World War II did not compose a lost generation. They learned from life what Hemingway's hero had learned from death. They learned new skills and they gratefully went to college on the G.I. Bill. Some of these men learned about Keynes at Harvard University and became the leading economists of their generation. James Tobin, among the others, had left Harvard to go off to war for four and a half years, and then returned to graduate. A very young Paul Samuelson and a slightly older John Kenneth Galbraith were already teaching there, as well as the much older Alvin Hansen, Edward Chamberlin and Joseph Schumpeter. Robert Solow, who had remembered from his childhood the unpleasantness of the Great Depression for his family and others, came to Harvard in 1940. When the war came, it seemed more important than studying and he joined the army, only to return in 1945 to study economics. Alvin Hansen and these younger personalities, who believed that "one man alone" didn't have a chance, will play major roles in the story of American Keynesian economics.

Much as World War II had moulded a new generation of economists, it also greatly altered the American economy. This time—unlike World War I—a postwar depression was avoided. Rather, after postponing consumption for 16 years, through depression and war, Americans put their accumulated liquid assets into houses, automobiles, and other durables. The G.I Bill also helped to feed the expansion, and the country rediscovered consumer credit. Finally, the Marshall Plan to rebuild European factories guaranteed that the Allies would buy American products in the meantime.

During the war, an immense arsenal of federal programs had emerged. Besides the military services within the War Department, there were the War Manpower Commission, the War Production

Board's Controlled Materials Plan, the War Labor Board, the Office of Price Administration, and many more. Directives were issued and resources moved around. The New Deal already had enlarged the federal government's role in the economy: World War II confirmed its lasting presence.

The Employment Act of 1946, which established the President's Council of Economic Advisers, proclaimed "the continuing policy and responsibility of the Federal Government to use all practical means ... to promote maximum employment, production, and purchasing power." It was a Keynesian document, written by New Deal Democrats, but it had bipartisan support. President Dwight D. Eisenhower, the first Republican president since Hoover, initiated public works spending to fight the recession of 1953 to 1954. The recession of 1957 to 1958 witnessed still greater reliance on public spending and social insurance.

Keynes had come to the White House in 1934, only to be not understood. But Keynesians were to dominate economic policy during the two postwar decades. Like other Americans of their generation, they had come of age during years of economic hardship, had had their lives disrupted by the war, and had matured in national service. And they were tied together by friendship.

THE FISCAL KEYNESIANS

When Keynes came to America, his most important recruit in the later 1930s was Alvin H. Hansen, a Harvard professor initially critical of the *General Theory*. Since Hansen was a prestigious figure in American academia, the economic establishment could ignore neither his tardy endorsement of Keynes nor the views of his students, among whom was Paul Anthony Samuelson.

Samuelson's textbook, *Economics: An Introductory Analysis,* first published in 1948, aroused a storm of dissent for its devotion of so many pages to Keynesian theory. Ultimately, however, it was to instruct millions around the world in fiscal and then neoclassical Keynesianism. Above all, Samuelson's text made Keynes an accepted part of American economic thought. And it did so just as Keynesian approaches were becoming more operational with the appearance of national income statistics.

Paul Anthony Samuelson: Enfant Terrible Emeritus

Paul Samuelson went on to become the 1970 Nobel Memorial Laureate of Economic Science and one of America's most esteemed liberal economists. Born in 1915 in Gary, Indiana, a company town created by U.S. Steel, Samuelson got an early practical lesson in the Keynesian multiplier: As the steel mills flourished, his father's drugstore business also grew. His family later moved to Chicago, and Samuelson attended the University of Chicago, even then the fountainhead of laissez-faire economics.

In 1940, Samuelson, a mere instructor in the economics department at Harvard, sailed down the Charles River to a full professorship at the Massachusetts Institute of Technology. The short, curly red-haired young man became a very popular teacher, noted for his wit and erudition. At the end of World War II, Samuelson began teaching basic economic principles, and out of this course his textbook evolved.

Samuelson's *Economics* popularized the idea, despite its then radical nature, that unemployment could be ended by the intentional creation of governmental deficits. *Economics* dominated postwar undergraduate teaching in the field, much like Alfred Marshall's text during the early twentieth century. An adviser to President John F. Kennedy during the early 1960s, Samuelson thereafter wrote a column for *Newsweek*. He was considered sufficiently radical during the Nixon Administration to win a place on the infamous "enemies list."

By most accounts, the Kennedy Administration was the high tide of U.S. Keynesianism.[3] President Kennedy had appointed a gifted Council of Economic Advisers (CEA) headed by the bright, personable, and persuasive Walter Heller. A second member of the CEA was James Tobin. In turn, a star-studded Council put together perhaps the best supporting cast of economists in history, including 1987 Nobel Prize winner Robert Solow of MIT; Charles Schultz from the University of Maryland, and Lester Thurow, later dean of the MIT business school.

After Kennedy's death in 1963, his fiscal program, centering on tax cuts and credits, was shoved through a willing Congress by President Lyndon B. Johnson. The powerful economic performance that followed was textbook fiscal Keynesianism.

So much for Samuelson's influence on the fiscal Keynesians. Not only later editions of his *Economics* but also an abstruse mathematical treatise by Samuelson was to influence neoclassical Keynesianism, but we are getting ahead of our story.

The Keynesian Cross

Samuelson's 1948 version of Keynes's thought became associated with the "Keynesian cross," the intersection of Keynes's aggregate demand function and a 45-degree line, a line from Samuelson's *Economics.* Aggregate demand and aggregate output are equal only at points along the 45-degree line. Samuelson viewed the Keynesian cross as having a significance as great as the Marshallian cross for demand and supply curves, because it provided the basic orientation for postwar fiscal policy.

The Keynesian cross is drawn "as if" production technology and the size of the labor force were unchanging givens. All values are expressed in current money terms. On the vertical axis is the total dollar value of expenditures for consumption and investment goods. On the horizontal axis is the dollar value of national income or product.

The Keynesian cross or the "45-degree model" shows that as national income rises, the dollar value of goods and services potentially supplied rises by the same amount. That is, every time incomes received rise by one dollar, the total available goods and services also rise by a dollar along the 45-degree line. This is virtually a "Keynes law" wherein "demand creates its own supply."

Consider an economy in which full employment (everyone who wants a job at prevailing wages has one) requires a national income of $2,200 billion. But, alas, the national income cannot reach that high. In national income equilibrium, expenditures must exactly equal the dollar value of goods and services, a condition met at an income level of $1,600 billion. With the national income at $2,200 billion, the dollar value of goods and services supplied would be $200 billion in excess of the total demanded at that national income level. Samuelson referred to this condition as a *deflationary gap*.

True to Keynes, government expenditures could close the deflationary gap and induce full employment if they reached a net level of $200 billion. That would raise total demand to $2,200 billion. The seemingly magical multiplier (of three) would increase national income by an even greater amount, from $1,600 to $2,200 billion. Then the equilibrium level of national income *and* full employment would be simultaneously achieved at $2,200 billion. So, having suffered the despair of the Great Depression, policymakers clung to the old Keynesian cross, for it promised an end to the suffering from unemployment and to massive uncertainty.

However, an acutely depressed economy is something of a special case. In "normal" times, when national income is stimulated by fiscal policy, part of the increase comes from rising prices and part from increased goods and services—more tons of steel, more hours of lawyering. The Keynesian cross cannot distinguish these two sources; it cannot tell real increases in national income (higher productivity) from nominal increases (higher prices). Samuelson and the fiscal Keynesians initially ignored this limitation and proceeded to use the cross to explain purely inflationary conditions.

The level of national income required for full employment may be $2,200 billion but national income equilibrium may now happen at $2,800 billion. Samuelson referred to this difference as an *inflationary gap*. Here, the dollar value of national income at equilibrium is obviously inflated, because if there is no surplus of workers, the goods and services on hand must be rationed by the raising of prices. The total dollar demand of $2,400 billion at $2,200 billion national income is $200 billion *greater* than the total dollar value of supply.

In this portrayal of Keynesianism, the only cause of inflation is too much demand relative to supply—too much air pumped into the industrial balloon. (Other writers, with other metaphors, have called this variety of inflation *demand pull.*) Faced with ballooning prices, the Keynesian policymaker simply reverses the stimulative, antidepression policy of Keynes. If total demand can be reduced (to $2,200 billion in this example), prices will descend to their previous level.

The prescribed policy then would be to partially deflate the balloon with cutbacks in government spending, increases in tax rates, and upward movements in interest rates—all ways to diminish spending on durable goods. In the parlance of the times, a "tight federal budget" and "tight money" deflate the economy.

As we move from theory to policy, this balloon theory of prices is shown to be full of hot air. For the model to work neatly, the entire amount between the stable-price national income ($2,200 billion) and the actual national income ($2,800 billion) has to be price inflation—pure hot air. Otherwise, when restrictive monetary and fiscal policies caused national income to fall, production would also be reduced, and so would the employment associated with that production. The balloon would not descend gently.

The Phillips Curve

In fiscal Keynesianism, there is not supposed to be a trade-off between inflation and unemployment. But there is. A.W. Phillips, an economist from down under, looked up, saw the anomaly, and drew the Phillips curve. It relates the percentage of change in the money wage rate and the associated cost-of-living inflation, on the vertical axis, with the unemployment rate on the horizontal axis. Wage inflation translates into price inflation when it exceeds the long-run rate of productivity growth (about two percent per year in recent years).

The shape of the Phillips curve presumably reflects competitive labor markets. During booms the enhanced demand for labor accelerates wages, which translates into higher production costs and higher product inflation rates. (Wages comprise the largest share of production costs.) At such times the unemployment rate falls. The opposite sequence follows during slumps.

Applied to the U.S. economy of the 1950s and 1960s by Samuelson and Solow, the Phillips curve showed the trade-off for lower unemployment rates to be indeed inflation. Furthermore, the relationship was stable. This was not good news for voter-conscious presidents, who hoped to have both low inflation *and* low rates of unemployment. In the real world, a policy reducing inflation from six to three percent might raise the unemployment rate from five to seven percent. For the incumbent, that could mean "Goodbye, Washington," even if Washington is not the real world.

THE NEOCLASSICAL KEYNESIANS

Samuelson's Foundations: The Micro-foundations of Macroeconomics

As noted, Paul Samuelson's stature and style in economics also were to influence the neoclassical branch of Keynesian.

American economists, hypersensitive about their economics being a "science," seldom win praise within their own profession for contributions to public policy, public debate, or education. Among economists, Samuelson's stature is derived from his arcane *Foundations of Economic Analysis* (1947), the book most responsible for making mathematical economics part of mainstream economics scholarship. *Foundations* is mostly MICROeconomics, but its mathematics and focus on equilibrium mesmerized the neoclassical Keynesians. *Foundations* takes Marshall's crude mathematics from the footnotes of his *Principles*, brings the mathematics up to date, and then converts it to main text.

Foundations expresses Marshall's economic essentials in pristine, resolute, unassailable mathematical form. Samuelson connects with Marshall across the years via the physicist James Clerk Maxwell, a Marshall contemporary and mentor. In his 1970 Nobel Prize acceptance speech, Samuelson credited one of his important ideas on consumer demand theory to Maxwell's "charming" *Introduction to Thermodynamics*.

In that same speech, Samuelson laid another economic discovery at the feet of his revered physics teacher at Harvard, Edwin Bidwell Wilson: Raising any input's prices while holding all remaining input prices constant will reduce the amount demanded of that input. (Proofs of even the simplest propositions often require intricate mathematics.)

Though surely not his intention, Samuelson's stylistic choice of mathematics eventually undermined Marshall's and Keynes's economics, rich with real-world possibilities, and replaced it with an abstract "choice-theoretic" economics. Each and every part of microeconomics could be reduced to a simple maximization problem. An equation would be written telling what was to be maximized or minimized—profits, wages, or prices—depending on one's status as buyer or seller. These ideas became the microfoundations of neoclassical Keynesianism.

The choices required to maximize/minimize were always subject to constraints. Indeed, choice was viewed as the singular economic act of selecting among quite limited options. The choices of the family shopper are limited by the household budget. The choices of the business decision maker are limited by competition from other firms, the cost of productive resources, and technology. Most important for interest rates and macroeconomics, the choice of the financial asset holder (given their net worth) could be between money and bonds. However, since all the limitations are "givens," they quickly became invisible barriers.

Perfect competition emerged from choice-theoretics as the "ideal." We have Samuelson's word for it from his preface: "At least from the time of the physiocrats and Adam Smith, there has never been absent from the main body of economic literature the feeling that in some sense perfect competition represented an optimal situation." Even Milton Friedman has called Smith's idea no more than "the maximization-of-returns hypothesis." From here, the surgical implant of perfect competition into Keynesianism was a quick and easy operation.

Once out of the surgeon's bag, choice-theoretic economics was out of control; it dominated the articles published during the 1970s in the leading U.S. economics journals. At Chicago the maximization scheme was personalized to decisions involving marriage, extramarital affairs, homosexuality, divorce, and choice of religion. The economists held nothing was sacred.[4]

Towards The Hicks-Hansen Synthesis

Paul Samuelson was not to embrace neoclassical Keynesianism at its conception. As is so often the case, a long time lapsed between the sowing of the seeds of neoclassical Keynesianism and the growth of the new branch.

The *General Theory* was barely in the hands of the public when Professor John R. Hicks, an English economist (and 1972 Nobel Prize winner), recast its message in neoclassical terms. Hicks followed the neoclassicals' time-honored tradition of seeing all variables as *real*. Thus, in the Hicksian version the current national income would be adjusted by a price index. For policymakers confronted with inflation, this permutation compounds the difficulty: They must describe the causes of price inflation where no prices are present!

In Marshallian economics, Keynes had noted, investment and savings alone were inadequate to account for the interest rate, but they could join with the interest rate to predict the level of income, or with the level of income to predict the interest rate.[5] As Keynes's explanation of the interest rate was incomplete, Hicks merged Marshall with Keynes, devising what became, in the textbooks, the IS-LM framework. The entire economy was reduced to only two curves crossing at a single point, telling the world the value of the interest rate *and* the national income.

Most wonderful of all, equilibria are found simultaneously in the money *and* the goods markets. Almost magically, a single interest rate equates the money demanded with its supply and, at the same time, the goods demanded with those supplied. Hicks demonstrated the *possibility* of simultaneous equilibrium in the money market between the demand and supply of money and in the goods market between investment and savings.

Still, for economists, the greatest excitement is naturally reserved for equilibrium. Where the IS *and* LM curves cross, general equilibrium exists. The equilibrium interest rate allows not only the demand for money to equal the supply of money but for investment to be equal to saving. Hence the national income also is in equilibrium.

This little apparatus is important for monetary and fiscal policy; even today, IS-LM is relied on by policymakers. It shows how an increase in the money supply produces a lower equilibrium interest rate and, predictably, more national income. A larger Federal budget deficit increases national income but not without a rise in the interest rate. There is a classical-style "crowding out" of some investment at higher debt-inspired interest rates. This latter effect—a dampening in the Keynesian multiplier as interest rates rise—is the most important new feature for Keynesianism.

At the time Keynes disagreed; notably, in a letter to Hicks dated March 31, 1937.[6] For one thing, argued Keynes, Federal budget deficits would not necessarily raise the interest rate; it all depended upon all the underlying conditions in an economy. For another thing, the use of current national income in the IS-LM model disguised the critical importance of expectations in determining business investment. Moreover, the model makes no judgment regarding labor market conditions.

When attempting to put income, investment, and the demand for money all together in explaining interest rates, Keynes was remarkably unclear. Nonetheless, Hicks at the time missed Keynes's main point—namely, how expectations and uncertainty outweighed the interest rate in the investment decision and in individuals' preferences for liquidity—for cash.

As we have said, Hicks's impact was delayed—on this side of the Atlantic, by the success of the American Keynesians in carrying the Keynesian cross to Washington during the late 1930s as well as to the millions of students reading Samuelsonian economics after World War II.[7]

In fact, it seemed for a time that the American Keynesians would be spared Hicks's reinterpretation altogether, even though Alvin Hansen, the leading American Keynesian at the time, prominently displayed Hicks's smooth curves in a new book in 1953. But Hansen's former student Paul Samuelson apparently read it on the road to Damascus and was converted. Universal equilibrium apparently was irresistible to someone trained in mathematics, with an interest in physics, with an eye for Newtonian metaphor, and writing at a time when economists were struggling to make economics a science in the same sense as natural science. Samuelson incorporated the Hicksian system into his famous textbook, in the 1961 edition jubilantly referring to the rapprochement as the "grand neoclassical synthesis!"

The ensuing debate bore little resemblance to the Epistles, however. Increasingly, the difference between Keynes and the original neoclassicals was described merely as a debate about the exact shape and importance of "various curves." True, national income might decline so much that interest rates would no longer fall. True, in some ranges interest rate gyrations might not stimulate investment spending.

True. But it was judicious fiscal policy, the new gyroscope for the economy, that made simultaneous equilibria in all markets possible. As to the product markets, Keynes's system had left them in whatever state of competition the reader preferred, and the neoclassicals naturally chose perfect competition. Of course, to the extent perfect competition ensures low inflation rates, the belief in equilibrium and economic stability fit reality.

Thirty-seven years after Sir John Hicks unwittingly began the counterreformation, he recanted, admitting to a deeper meaning in Keynes's view of money, investment, and uncertainty.[8] But, just as Hicks' timing was bad initially, it was off once again, for there was little reason for economists to notice. Inflation and high interest rates were not problems during the 1950s and most of the 1960s, and the Hicks-Hansen model was in sync with the data and the times, an era during which Keynesian policies seemed to work well.

SAVING KEYNES'S THEORY

Like the woman in the old country song, economists like to go home with the theory that brung 'em. When inflation became a problem by the 1970s, fiscal Keynesianism and neoclassical Keynesianism seemed less relevant. But naturally those Keynesians who had fathered the new American macroeconomics were ready to fight for their offspring. They wanted to "save" Keynes's theory. But *which* theory?

The Wages of Inflation

It is often said erroneously that Keynes did not worry about inflation. For sure he did not worry about inflation during the Great Depression, nor did the Keynesians. During World War II, he did worry, and he wrote about "How to Pay for the War," in which he recommended that households be required to buy government bonds as a way of "forced savings." Moreover, another model is scattered about in Keynes's classic.

In one place, an uncertainty principle is invoked to account for business fluctuations. In another, Keynes shows how inflation could begin prior to full employment, as pictured by what we now call the Phillips curve. For an industry, writes Keynes, the prices depend on the payments to those who produce the goods, which therefore enter into the cost of production. With a particular production technique and the requisite equipment in place, the general price level depends largely on wage rates. Prior to the achievement of full employment, increases in total effective demand are divided in their effect between swelling output and pumping up prices.

Stagnation, too, was depicted. If wages rise prior to full employment and comprise a cost of production, the total supply line is not the simple 45-degree guide of the fiscal Keynesians. Since wage rates comprise the major component of the unit cost of production, rising wage rates would entice producers to reduce their output. But they would at the same time raise prices to cover the increased cost of production. It is possible for production (and therefore employment) to retrench even while prices are rising. Of course, such an outcome was viewed as an anomaly within either the fiscalist or the neoclassical vision of Keynes, much less the Phillips curve.

This more complete total demand and total supply picture from Keynes was seized on by the self-proclaimed legitimate heirs of Keynes, the Post Keynesians. This, they believed, would save the theory during periods of inflation.

The Case of the Missing Auctioneer

Before we leave Keynes and his many models, we need to mention a second, even brilliant, attempt to resuscitate his theory. Two economists—Robert Clower and the seemingly unpronounceable Axel Leijonhufvud—defended Keynes's notion of disequilibrium. The general equilibrium described by the neoclassical counter-revolutionaries, they claimed, requires instantaneous price and output adjustments in the economy. But such a complete clearing of markets requires a "Walrasian auctioneer" (a reference to Leon Walras, who had everyone "groping" for the correct prices). With the auctioneer calling out prices of everything, including prices of labor (wage rates), every actor in the economy would have sufficient information to make precise adjustments, so all market prices would be true equilibrium ones.

In the real world, said Clower and Leijonhufvud, there is no such auctioneer! Prevailing prices, including the wage rates, are imperfectly established, because individuals do not have complete knowledge. That is, people act on the basis of "wrong" prices, as they are not equilibrium prices.

According to the insightful Leijonhufvud, the responses of individuals are restricted to those their incomes will allow. Unemployed workers provide an unreliable source of spendable funds. Contrary to Samuelson's choice-theoretics, the income constraint *is* critical. Thus, market adjustments to disturbances are made by income reactions and production changes, and only belatedly by price variations. The real world is one of imperfect information, and persons in it will not wait for all these price adjustments to occur. Such price disequilibrium further diminishes the practicality of general equilibrium. From this pioneering work, economists began to develop disequilibrium models. Today, Robert Solow bases his "Keynesianism" on this idea: Output and employment adjust much more slowly than prices and even they are sluggish. For Clower, Leijonhufvud, and Solow, perfect competition does not prevail in the real world.

Keynes himself took an even more drastic view of uncertainty. For example, he compared the stock market to a "game of Snap, of Old Maid, of musical chairs." In his restatement of the *General Theory* a year after its publication, he emphasized almost to the exclusion of anything else the uncertainty of knowledge and foresight as the cause of chronic unemployment of resources.[9] Not only would Keynes then abandon equilibrium in favor of disequilibrium, but he would also question the efficacy of policies based entirely on disequilibrium models. Full employment equilibrium then could only be approximated through governmental actions.

THE POST KEYNESIANS

It often takes adversity to bring diverse strands of economic thought together or, even, to bring diverse people together. In the opening scene of George Bernard Shaw's *Pygmalion* (later a musical, *My Fair Lady*), sundry people are bought together by the common necessity of protecting themselves from a sudden downpour. There, we encounter the impoverished middle-class Clara Eynsford-Hill, with her genteel pretensions and disdain; a wealthy Anglo-Indian gentleman (Colonel Pickering), who seems tolerant enough; an egotistical professor of phonetics (Henry Higgins), who seems exceptionally intolerant; and a pushy, notably rude flower girl (Eliza Doolittle) from the lower class, embodying the essence of vulgarity. These characters never would have been found together except for something like a sudden rain shower.

A number of economists sympathetic to Keynes but not to Keynesianism have long disparaged the vulgarization of the great man's theories and the zealous monetarism that thereby arose. This dissenter movement spent several decades in the economic catacombs. The "sudden rain shower" that brought together diversity extending across oceans and continents was the simultaneous high inflation and high unemployment of the 1970s. This stagflation caused a widespread crisis of faith among "orthodox" neo-Keynesians, those Keynesians classed as "vulgar" by the Post Keynesians.

Post Keynesians have flourished not only in America but also in Cambridge (England) and in Italy.[10] On both sides of the ocean they have returned to the classicals' concern with the income distribution. The Americans, however, have focused more on a monetary economy and the Europeans more on a classical real economy.

By their works ye shall know them. The Post Keynesians have done at least the following things that distinguish them from the hyphenated Keynesians.

- They have extended Keynes's doctrine by demonstrating how income distribution helps determine national income and its growth over time.
- They have combined the notion of imperfect competition with classical pricing theory to explain simultaneous stagnation and inflation (stagflation).
- They have used these two concepts—income distribution theory and price markup theory—to forge a new incomes policy.
- They have conducted a revival of Keynes's ideas on uncertainty, specifically in regard to liquidity preference and business investment, and they have also resurrected Keynes's notion that money is primarily created by the banking system (inside money). As a result, they have defined what monetary policy can and cannot do.

THE INCOME DISTRIBUTION

With regard to income classes, John Maynard Keynes seemed to be of two minds: His General Theory showed how great income and wealth inequalities led to dysfunctional capitalism whereas his personal comfort was found within his own upper class and the ruling elite. This, even though George Bernard Shaw—converted to Fabian socialism by reading Marx—was only down the street, so to speak, from Keynes and the Bloomsbury group. Clara Eynsford-Hill, one of Shaw's characters and superficially without a trace of vulgarity, nonetheless represents aspects of the middle class (bourgeoisie) which Shaw and Eliza Doolittle reject—that is, Clara is disdainful of people whom she considers beneath her. Keynes too disdained the bourgeois world surrounding Queen Victoria, but they were beneath *him*.

In his concluding notes in the *General Theory*, Keynes had the British opposing the further removal of great disparities of wealth and income for the mistaken belief that a great proportion of the growth of capital is "dependent on the savings of the rich out of their superfluity."[11] As his theory shows, "the growth of capital depends not at all on a low propensity to consume but is, on the contrary, held back by it." Indeed, he proceeds to the conclusion that "in contemporary conditions the growth of wealth, so far from being dependent on the abstinence of the rich, as it commonly supposed, is more likely to be impeded by it. One of the chief social justifications of great inequality of wealth is, therefore, removed."[12]

Unemployment is caused by great wealth and income inequalities; this, an economist could easily surmise, is the central idea of the General Theory! After all, investment determines saving, not the other way round. Just when the progressive economist is about to proclaim, "by George, I think he's got it," however, Keynes undoes him; he reopens the closet door to conservatism. "I believe that there is social and psychological justification for significant inequalities of incomes and wealth, but not for such large disparities as exist today."[13] To the conservative, "large disparities" exist only in the dreamworld of the liberal.

It is not then simply a matter of "Why can't the Keynesians be more like Keynes?" There remains the question: Why wasn't Keynes more like a Post Keynesian? Once again, the shorter our answer, the better. Keynes had the Great Depression on his mind; there was precious little time for pursuing every avenue opened by his General Theory. Keynes's ultimately conservative mission was to save capitalism by relying on the intellectual elite in Britain to implement his social program. Besides, class consciousness was one of Keynes's traits. In an attack on *Das Kapital,* Keynes wrote, "How can I adopt a creed [Marxism] which, preferring the mud to the fish, exalts the boorish proletariat above the bourgeoisie and the intelligentsia, who with all their faults, are the quality of life and surely carry the seeds of all human achievement?"[14] There is no contradiction: Keynes relied on the elite—especially the intellectual elite in Britain—to implement his social program.

Eliza Doolittle and the income distribution were left to the Post Keynesians to ponder.

Sraffa's Attempted Purge of Marginalism

The Cambridge, England Post Keynesians for sure have attempted to overthrow the marginalists explanation for income distributions. For this, they begin with a critique of marginalism that reaches back to the ideas of David Ricardo.

The classical system of fixed input proportions was swept away by the marginalists. In classical production in which equal amounts of, say, labor are always combined with a unit of capital, the marginal product of capital is not simply invisible—it is not there! The real wage rate cannot be decided by the marginal physical product of labor or the extra units of output from each additional worker. The theory of value or price of the marginalists vanishes with the margin.

Piero Sraffa (1898–1983), Keynes's pupil, was a brilliant and lovable Italian economist who much preferred leisure to publishing. He managed to edit the many volumes of David Ricardo's works during a few minutes or a few hours of daily effort only because he lived so long. Moreover, he finally published in 1960 a slim volume he had written in the 1920s, an enigmatic book with a curious title, *Production of Commodities: Prelude to a Critique of Economic Theory,* putting Ricardo in modern dress while providing a devastating critique of marginalism.

Capital goods, contends Sraffa, are diverse, and any measure of the "quantities" of capital in terms of a common denominator (such as another good or money) will vary as the prices of the machines themselves vary. And these prices will fluctuate with wage and profit rates. Therefore, the value of capital (its price times its quantity) is not decided by capital's marginal product, nor is the income distribution decided by the markets for land, labor, and capital.

This book was physically produced, for example, using three machines: A computer, a printing press, and a binder. The money values of capital, however, depend on the price times quantity of all these capital goods (and others) combined. The computer, the press, and the binder all sell at varying prices. Profits can no longer be a return on capital for these prices, or the "rentals" for the services from these capital goods, which themselves depend on the distribution of income between workers and capitalists.

This reincarnation of Ricardo is not as remarkable as the interpretation. No economic explanation of the income distribution emerges, and *that* is its central message. Wages and profits are social and political matters. Like John Stuart Mill, Sraffa thus separates issues of production and economic efficiency from income distribution concerns. Sharing of income among classes is determined not by the impersonal forces of the economy but by class struggle, administered wages, and relative bargaining power.

Kalecki's Income Classes: The Workers and the Capitalists

Another contributor to Cambridge Post Keynesianism was the Marxist economist Michal Kalecki (1899–1970). While at Cambridge in 1935 in self-imposed exile from Poland, Kalecki was befriended by John Kenneth Galbraith. "A small, often irritable, independent, intense man," Galbraith relates, "Kalecki was the most innovative figure in economics I have known, not excluding Keynes."[15] Like Sraffa, Kalecki seldom put pen to paper. But when he did, the clarity and depth of his thoughts were powerful.

In 1933, Kalecki had developed a Keynes-style theory of the level of employment, prior to and independent of Keynes's *General Theory*. Kalecki's income distribution views, however, were more in tune with the Ricardian and Marxian chorus about income classes. In fact, Kalecki's theory can be summed up in the adage, "The workers spend what they get; the capitalists get what they spend." It would have made a marvelous line for one of George Bernard Shaw's plays.

The national income or product can be measured from either the income side or the expenditures side, so:

Income

Profits (capitalists' income) + wages (workers' income)
= National Income

Expenditures

Investment + capitalists' consumption + workers' consumption = National Product

In this scheme, all workers' wages are spent entirely on necessary goods, so wages must equal the workers' expenditures on consumption goods—the food, shelter, clothing, and transportation required for life and for work. (In reality, of course, today's workers spend income on some goods and services that are not strictly necessities, but Kalecki is using Marx's and Mill's notion of cultural subsistence.) Sraffa's system reveals the inputs necessary to produce particular outputs; Kalecki's defines the amounts of necessary consumption goods.[16]

If we further simplify by saying that all profits are diligently plowed back into the business to purchase new investment goods, savings as well as investments are equal to profits. The capitalist is the lone saver in this simple economy.

The first surprise? Capitalists can add to their current share of the national income (profits) by having increased their investment spending in a prior period. Investment, Keynes-style, is multiplied in terms of total output. Out of a larger output come greater profits.

More shockingly, even if the capitalists consume their profits in the style of the savings and loan executives of the 1980s—buying yachts, building vacation homes, supporting lovers—they experience no decrease in profits income. Capitalists' income is not vulnerable to *how* it is spent because increases in the purchase of goods lead to higher levels of production. Capitalist profits are like the water of the artesian well: No matter how much water is taken out, the well never empties.

The accumulation of capital is both the rainbow and the pot of gold! If a greater share of national output is devoted to investment goods, the level of employment in the investment sector will be greater and (since investment equals profits) a greater share of the national income will go to the capitalists. Conversely, if a greater share of output is devoted to consumer necessities, the workers snatch a larger piece of the national income pie.

Although the capitalists are masters of their own universe in this sense, Kalecki saw outside elements, such as uncertainties regarding profitable investments, causing unavoidable fluctuations in profits.

THE PRICE MARKUP AND INFLATION

The Imperfection of Competition and Kalecki's "Degree of Monopoly"

The struggle between the working and the capitalist classes shapes not only the income distribution but also classical-style pricing. In turn, the combination of these forces provides one explanation for stagflation—that dreaded combo of stagnation and inflation.

Kalecki was very much into the world of imperfect competition in which production was the business of only a few firms in each industry or oligopoly. A firm can raise its own price right along with its production costs if other firms in the industry do likewise. When General Motors, once the most efficient of only three American producers of automobiles, signs a union contract with the United Auto Workers of America for higher wages, the corporation also raises prices more or less in proportion to the wage hike. Chrysler and Ford then follow suit.

The "degree of monopoly" was the outcome not only of industrial concentration but also of tacit agreements, selling agents, and advertising. In one of his last published papers, Kalecki explained how high markups (of price over costs) would encourage strong trade unions to bargain for higher wages, since oligopolistic firms had the ability to pay them. There is a wee bit of Galbraith (see later) in that paper.

The Price Markup and the Price Level

The introduction of imperfect competition into macroeconomic theory is due not only to Kalecki, John Kenneth Galbraith, and Joan Robinson, but also to Sidney Weintraub (1914–1983) at the University of Pennsylvania. Kalecki's and Weintraub's vision of pricing in the manufacturing sector can be dramatized in Kalecki's cryptic style—markup.[17]

An example will clarify the role of the markup. If the wage cost per personal computer is $700 and the markup is ten percent, the profits flow per unit of production is $70. If one million PCs are sold yearly, industry profits are $70 million. If wage costs rise to $800 per unit, the unchanged markup rate of ten percent over current costs will now generate an earnings flow of $80 million, given the same number of units sold.

If money wages are administered by union-management agreements, the balance of income is provided by the markup over wages, most of which will be retained profits (profits plus depreciation) and dividend payouts. Capacity utilization may move up and down with demand, but the firm usually will stick with the markup that achieves its target level of retained profits. This target depends on its dividend payout ratio to stockholders, its amount of debt relative to its equity, and (according to some Post Keynesians such as the late Alfred Eichner) its perceived investment needs. According to Weintraub, even highly competitive firms price according to a markup rule.[18] Although the margin of prices over current costs already reflects the market power of the firm in a concentrated industry, even a fixed markup allows for a higher price when the unit cost of production goes up.

Income in excess of cultural subsistence leaves a demand wedge and breathing space for producers. The price markup is the breath of fresh air that fills the void. Although the stylized income division between workers and capitalists creates the Marxian drama of a "class struggle," Kalecki understood that such a razor-sharp division cannot fully explain the income distribution and its effects in an "affluent society" (Galbraith's term). The new upper middle-class consumer, once satisfied with a black Model T, must now be motivated to buy a streamlined, racy, colorful machine designed for maximum road comfort and perhaps fulfilling exotic fantasies.

Stagflation

How do we get from firm and industry pricing behavior to the general price level? We begin with the old equation of exchange. If

$$\text{(Price level)} \times \text{(real output)} = \text{(money national income)}$$

or

$$\text{(Price level)} = \frac{\text{(money national income)}}{\text{(real output)}}$$

then stable prices require that money income grow no faster than real output. If the money income per employee rises no faster than output per employee (productivity), the inflation rate is pleasantly zero.

Money wages then become central to the price level. The money wages are inflexible downward, because to reduce money wages violates an implicit contract with the worker or perhaps a written labor contract, which often has been negotiated by an industrial union. If the Teamsters' Union signs a contract for a 30 percent wage increase divided equally over a three-year term, no one would expect the second year increment to be sliced to, say, five percent. In the short run, therefore, product prices must adjust to money wages and the cost of production rather than vice versa. There is a revised sequence in which the price level and inflation are resolved after the money wage rates are determined. Money wages, outside Sraffa's system, are determined by social-political conditions.[19]

This Post Keynesian view exposes the possibility of simultaneous inflation and unemployment (stagflation). The short-run response to any consumer resistance will be not wage or price slowdowns but slower production. Substantial production cutbacks will lead—with a lag—to worker layoffs. This view, too, can explain why recession teamed up with inflation in 1974 to 1975 and again in 1979 to 1980, following soaring world oil prices.

INCOMES POLICY

The Post Keynesian explanation of the income distribution and the price level leads to a third kind of economic policy to supplement Keynesian fiscal and monetary policy. If the tenacious advocacy of deficit spending characterizes the fiscal Keynesians, the relentless pursuit of an incomes policy distinguishes the Post Keynesians.

Some fiscal Keynesians, such as James Tobin, nonetheless have joined hands with the Post Keynesians to endorse an incomes policy. An incomes policy blatantly requires that wages be "controlled" in some sense. The profit margin will be whatever it will be because of the relative consistency of the price markup. However, as time goes by, wages go up and the price level with them.

What to Control? Wages or Profits?

Firms prefer, if anything be controlled, it be wages: Unions favor the control of profits. Equity and political problems quickly emerge with the control of wages alone. A variable markup can be a source of profits-push inflation so that the part of profits not retained by corporations for financing investment also would require regulation. Dividends and corporate salaries might be taxed at a rate that keeps them in line with the growth of wage income. Irrespective of whose ox is goared, all incomes policies have the same theme: Money income changes are to be geared to the pace of productivity.

Real-world incomes policies have ranged all the way from voluntary wage and price guidelines to the mandatory wage and price controls long advocated by John Kenneth Galbraith. Such measures were utilized in different forms and with varying vigor by the Kennedy, Johnson, Nixon, Ford, and Carter Administrations.

The TIP Proposals

An alternative to wage and price guidelines or controls is tax incentives, smart-targeted to modify the behavior of labor unions and concentrated industry. Incentives and deterrents of the price mechanism are used ju-jitsu style against itself. One tax-based incomes policy (TIP) was developed by Weintraub and by the late Henry Wallich, once a governor of the Federal Reserve Board.

TIP works this way. Whenever a corporation grants a pay increase in excess of an established norm—say, six percent—the firm granting the pay raise would be penalized by an increase in its income tax. If a firm increased the average pay of its workers by, say, ten percent rather than by six percent, the firm might be required to pay ten percent more in taxes on its profits. The wage-salary norms would be the average increase of wages and salaries of the firm, so that above-average wage stipends could be awarded to meritorious workers. The goal would be to confine average money wage increases to the gains in average labor productivity in the economy.

What is the premise underlying TIP? Individual businesses will be encouraged to resist unreasonable wage demands only when they are convinced that resistance also will come from other firms and industries. TIP tilts the individual firm in the direction of yielding only noninflationary average wage increases. The laborers would benefit from **real** wage gains as inflation subsides.

A TIP is a very flexible policy: It can provide a penalty for a wage increase above the norm, a reward for a wage below the norm, or both. The late neo-Keynesian Arthur Okun, once economic adviser to President Johnson and later associated with the Brookings Institution, preferred carrots to sticks. If a firm holds its average yearly rate of wage increase below six percent and its average rate of price increase below four percent, Okun's plan would give the employees of the firm a tax rebate (carrot I) and the firm would receive a rebate (carrot II) on its income tax liabilities.

A TIP of the carrot persuasion was proposed by President Jimmy Carter in October 1978. However, the incentive was indirect, a kind of diced carrot. It would have provided tax relief for those workers who stayed below the wage norm if the annual inflation rate ended up above seven percent. Congress rejected the initiative.

Conditions have changed since the original TIP proposal. For one thing, the effective average corporate income tax rate, the original tax penalty base for TIP, has been approaching zero. For another, net interest income as a share of national income increased 14-fold between the end of World War II and 1990. Therefore, it appears essential to obtain a new federal revenue source to exert downward pressure on interest rates as well as a TIP that acknowledges monetary interest as a new, increasingly important source of rising production costs.[20]

MONEY AND THE FINANCING OF INVESTMENT

There is a finance connection between profits and funds for the firm's investment. The markup and investment plans are inextricably linked—in one direction or the other, and perhaps in both. Because of the degree-of-monopoly, prices do not reflect *current* demand conditions; they are more closely tied to *expected* future demand. At times capacity will exceed current needs, but this situation is no problem for an oligopoly.

Kalecki, in particular, sees the oligopoly ensuring its needs for investment funds through its pricing powers. The sensitivity or price elasticity of the demand by workers for necessities is essentially zero. Therefore, producers can raise prices with impunity and raise revenues from consumer necessities in excess of the costs of production as a source of funds for the purchase of investment goods.

Machines and labor have to be combined in order to reproduce machines. Therefore, the sales receipts of the investment or capital-goods industry from the necessities-goods industry will cover the investment-goods industry's labor costs plus the cost of the machine-babies: That is, the capital-goods industry's own machines. Those required investment outlays equal profits of the investment-goods industry.

The combined profits from both industries must equal the value of produced capital goods just as *real wages* (money wages adjusted for the price of necessities) must equal the amount of necessities produced. Likewise, the profits from both industries combine to purchase the output of the investment-goods industry, creating even more profits for the capitalists.

This stylized Kaleckian fable once again has savings = profits = investment. It is instructive, even accurate, as far as it goes. Prior to the 1980s, most fixed capital investment in the United States was financed from retained profits. The giant firm had the power to select a percentage markup over production costs (mostly wages) sufficient to complete its investment plans, much of the time without going hat in hand to a banker or the capital market for funds. That power has diminished somewhat as more country's markets have been opened to U.S. goods and services. In turn, American corporations have gone to the bond market for funds.

"Inside Money"

In Kalecki's and other, more sophisticated explanations of where funds come from for investment, retained earnings or expected profits can be used to obtain bank loans or issue corporate bonds. That part of debt which is bank credit constitutes Post Keynesian "inside money." Moreover, depending on preferences for debt compared with equity financing, the corporation can issue new equities in the stock markets for financing investment needs. Oddly, during the Great

Bull Market of the 1980s and the 1990s, U.S. corporations, in the aggregate, retired more equities than they issued so that negative amounts were "raised" in the equities market.

Post Keynesians Paul Davidson and Basil Moore, like Keynes, Joan Robinson and Kalecki before them, suggest that the supply of money comes into existence, as Keynes and Kalecki describe it, with private debts ("inside" money). Therefore, the money supply is related to debts created by contracts to purchase or produce goods. Because production takes time, the agreements or contracts for the goods are denoted in money units to be paid on delivery. However, the production costs have to be paid during the time of production, so that producer debt may be incurred prior to any sales revenue whatsoever. This process enables producers to operate reasonably well under conditions of uncertainty.

In turn, borrowing from banks and issuance of new corporate bonds add to the money supply unless the increase in loan activity is offset by actions from the monetary authorities—in the United States, the Federal Reserve System. As described in Chapter 10, new loans in a fractional reserve banking system create new checking deposit amounts. In this way, changes in the nation's money supply are in great part decided by business activity itself. That is, in contrast to the monetarists, we have $M \leftrightarrow GNP$.[21]

The largest and most strategic savings reside in the corporation, held as financial assets in the form of bonds or other securities. Altered expectations can cause shifts in these financial asset holdings and worsen an economic downturn. This happens because the price of bonds held by firms tends to be very low immediately preceding the downswing (interest rates being very high). A time of high interest rates also coincides with a sluggish stock market, so that although the price markup can be held constant or even perhaps increased, a slump in consumer demand may culminate in a smaller profits flow and therefore less retained earnings (savings). Even the giant corporation is then reluctant to cash in its bonds at a capital loss or borrow at interest rate peaks in order to expand its facilities or replace aging equipment. This liquidity reluctance can be a monetary source of instability in investment.

The Money Supply and Monetary Policy

Demand deposit creation by the firm and by loans to the firm starts the money-supply train. A contraction in the money supply engineered by the central bank has little direct impact on the private sources of giant firms driven by the real economy. It has an indirect effect insofar as the corporation is reluctant to liquidate bond holdings that are dipping in price. Nonetheless, as long as its sales revenue is growing, the giant firm willingly issues additional stock or borrows from the largest banks.

For competitive firms such as small businesses and the fragmented construction industry, quite a different tale unfolds. Even with MasterCharge, the small firm does not have the markup clout of the giant firm. Small businesses (considered the highest-risk firms and dependent on costly trade credit) are the first to experience difficulty obtaining loans during periods of tight money. Moreover, higher interest rates for housing and construction, as every homebuyer knows, have similar effects. The value of interest payments usually is greater than the face value of the mortgage itself. Rather than reflecting the productivity of capital, the interest rate is a major cost of buying the product. A tight money policy only exacerbates stagflation as it reduces production and creates rising prices simultaneously![22]

The Post Keynesian's effort to reduce the reliance on such a perverse monetary policy has led them to the aforementioned third way, an incomes policy.

Minsky and Financial Fragility

Hyman Minsky (1919–1997), a laconic but persistent American Post Keynesian with Italian connections, connected the dots between Kalecki's mark-up, retained earnings, and inside money to financial volatility. Minsky emphasized how the retained earnings from the markup levered by debt could finance the acquisition of additional capital assets. The capital assets acquired by the nonfinancial firm may be purchased out of the existing plant and equipment (corporate takeovers, etc.) or through the production of new investment goods. Only in the latter case will new increments and industrial capacity be added to the economy's productive potential.

Minsky's theory of investment focuses on how Keynesian uncertainty, speculation, and an increasingly complex financial system lead to business cycles. Any sustained "good times" stagger off into a speculative, inflationary binge and a fragility of financial institutions. Minsky's ideas are no longer orphans; events have overtaken his explanation.

Since business debt has to be serviced (scheduled payments on principal and interest made), Minsky suggests that such cash flows (and debt servicing commitments) determine the course of investment and thus of output and employment. In this manner, Minsky has extended Post Keynesian monetary theory to include not only credit, but the special problems connected with financial speculation in a capitalistic system.

The boom may end because of price resistance by consumers. After all, it is because the price elasticity of demand for products is nonzero that the amount of markup is limited. The boom may end because the central bank begins to contract credit. The hope, eventually, is that wages and thus costs and inflation will slow.

Any slowdown in wage rates, however, does not alter contractual debt commitments so that the burden of debt rises during disinflation or deflation. Debt-financed investment decreases, and purchases of investment goods financed by money supply increments decline. Business firms will begin to pay off debt instead of buying new plant and equipment. As in Keynes, employment falls with the decline in use of the existing capital stock. Once again, business conditions are at the mercy of uncertainty and financial market behavior.

The leveling-off of prices brings financial distress for certain participants and industries. Firms, including farms, have counted on a particular inflation rate for their products in order to service their mounting debt. (The same could be said for middle-class homeowners, who since World War II have counted on the appreciation of houses as a source of net worth.) Yet, those most in the know in the financial markets, the insiders, take their profits and run. This is the start of a race toward liquidity as financial assets are cashed in.

As Keynes had it, the holding of money "lulls their disquietude." Outright financial panic can be avoided only if (1) prices fall so low that people move back into real assets; (2) the government sets limits to price declines (e.g., agricultural price supports), closes banks (e.g., the "bank holiday" of 1933), and shuts the exchanges; or (3) a lender of last resort steps in, as the Federal Reserve did in the financial turbulence following the Penn-Central collapse (1969–1970), the Franklin National Bank bankruptcy (1974–1975), the Hunt–Bache silver speculation (1980), and the stock market crash of 1987, and as the Federal Deposit Insurance Corporation (FDIC) did in nationalizing Illinois Continental Bank (1984) or banks since. Such interventions prevent the complete collapse of the value of assets.

Liabilities such as junk bonds and other financial innovations of the boom are validated as the central bank refinances the holdings of financial institutions. This propping-up of capitalism creates the base for still further expansion of credit during the economic recovery, a process that helps to explain the inflation following the financial crises of 1969 to 1970, 1974 to 1975, and 1980. Goods inflation, but not financial speculation, was tamed by the near-depression of 1981 to 1982.

The International Spectra

Charles P. Kindleberger, late professor of economics at MIT, extends Minsky's theory to the global economy. Kindleberger sees pure speculation spilling over national borders. International links are provided by exports, imports, and foreign securities. Indeed, interest rates in the United States during the 1980s and 1990s would have been much higher in the absence of massive purchases of U.S. Treasury securities by foreigners.

At the same time, however, these foreign purchases add to the credit pyramid that will again tumble should such speculators again lose confidence. Kindleberger points a finger at the enormous external debt of the developing countries, accelerated by rising oil prices (up to at least 1979, we must add), "as multinational banks swollen with dollars tumbled over one another in trying to uncover new foreign borrowers and practically forced money on the less-developed countries (LDCs)."[23] At the international level, however, there is *no* lender of last resort, though the International Monetary Fund has in some recent times tried to be, but with mixed results.

WHITHER ECONOMIC GROWTH?

Economic growth is the long-term trend rate of growth in real gross domestic product (GDP). The business cycle is reflected in movements of GDP above (inflation) and below (recession) this historical trend.

In much of Keynes's theory, the economy appears as a sequence of snapshots rather than as a continuous moving picture and thus is more applicable to the business cycle than to the problem of economic growth. The same might be said, although to a lesser degree of Kaleckian theory. Even a snapshot showing us the way we are today reveals little about what our economic conditions might be over the years.

The dynamic version of Keynes, building his theory to bridge a period of time, originated with Sir Roy Harrod, was extended by Lord Nicholas Kaldor, and was on the grand scale of Malthus, Ricardo, and Marx. Harrod shared the stage with Esvey Domar at MIT. Robert Solow was to build a popular neoclassical growth theory. Since we want to complete the business cycle debates among the many Keynesians and the monetarists, we will postpone the ideas related to the long run until Chapter 13.

CONCLUSIONS

If Keynes were alive today he might not be a Keynesian; instead, he most likely would be a Post Keynesian. Much of his social vision, which began to take form in the 1920s and which was vindicated (in his mind) during the Great Depression, was lost in neoclassical

Keynesianism. Although Keynes's early interpreters made good use of his antidepression nostrums, the Keynesians' version of what Keynes meant was not enduring. It did not work well when turned against inflation, and it displayed fatal weaknesses in its premises of perfect competition in product markets and a general equilibrium as certain as certainty.

The grand neoclassical synthesis was music to economists' ears. The arrangement was always there; it only needed a fine-tuned economy and somebody to write the lyrics. The United States provided the one during the 1960s, and the youthfully indiscreet John Hicks supplied the other. Though the result was a small measure for the neoclassicals, it was turned into a major score for the modern monetarists who next come center stage.

The born-again neoclassicals in the guise of monetarists were not finished with Keynes. Economists would question equilibrium only at the risk of being defrocked. When inflation was too great to be explained by the merely rational economic man, the super-rational economic man was invented. Keynes's theories were taken out of historical time because the past, present, and future are indistinguishable in equilibrium. Keynes had the neoclassicals right where they wanted him!

Although many neo-Keynesians have never been able to understand Post Keynesians because they see no reason for trying, some differences between the two schools are not great. As I noted, some neo-Keynesians, including 1981 Nobel Prize winner James Tobin, have endorsed incomes policies. And Nobelist Robert Solow says, "some of Post Keynesian price theory comes forth from the belief that universal competition is a bad assumption. I have all my life known that." But, he also adds: "I have found it an unrewarding approach and have not paid much attention to it."[24] Paul Davidson has suggested that Solow has since relented and now embraces a larger part of Post Keynesian theory. As we will discover in Chapter 13, however, the two schools' approaches to growth theory remain a fundamental contrast.

Even so, Paul Samuelson came off the bench himself to issue the following epigrammatic verdict:

> A Hamlet-like student, poised in neutral equilibrium between eclectic post-Keynesianism, monetarism, and rational expectationism, would have to be pushed in the direction of post-Keynesianism by the brute factual experiences of America in the 1980s.[25]

Later, we will look at these "brute factual experiences of America in the 1980s."

NOTES

1. J.K. Galbraith, *Money: Whence It Came, Where It Went* (Boston: Houghton Mifflin, 1975), pp. 217–218.

2. Arjo Klamer, *Conversations with Economists* (Totowa, New Jersey: Rowman & Allanheld, 1984), p. 101.

3. For much more detail on the economics of John F. Kennedy, see E. Ray Canterbery, *Economics on a New Frontier* (Belmont, California: Wadsworth Publishing Co., 1968).

4. The gain from marriage by men or women was shown to depend on their income, human capital (lifetime income), and relative wage rate differences. The number of extramarital affairs was found to depend on optimal allocation of leisure hours between spouse and paramour. The individual's religious commitment was also "explained" by the household's optimal allocation of time. Homosexuality was simply another optimal choice: Presumably the author (Gary Becker, the 1992 Nobel Prize winner in economics) had overlooked the advantages of autoeroticism over both homosexuality and heterosexuality since self-stimulation requires fewer inputs and less time. All this analysis was claimed to be "value free," but many economists called these extensions of choice-theoretic economics "economic imperialism."

   For a critique of allegedly "value free" economics, see E. Ray Canterbery and Robert J. Burkhardt, "What Do We Mean by Asking Whether Economics Is a Science?" in *Why Economics Is Not Yet a Science*, ed. Alfred S. Eichner (Armonk, New York: M.E. Sharpe, 1983), pp. 15–40.

5. In prose apparently designed with the torture of economics students in mind, Keynes concluded, "Thus the functions used by the classical theory, namely, the response of investment and the response of the amount saved out of a given income to change in the rate of interest, do not furnish material for a theory of the rate of interest; but they could be used to tell us what the level

of income will be, given (from some other source) the rate of interest; and, alternatively, what the rate of interest will have to be, if the level of income is to be maintained at a given figure (e.g. the level corresponding to full employment)." John Maynard Keynes, *The General Theory of Employment, Interest, and Money* (New York: Harcourt, Brace & World, 1936), pp. 181–182.

6. Elizabeth Johnson and Donald Moggridge (eds.), *The Collected Writings of John Maynard Keynes*, Volume XIV (London: Macmillan & Co., 1971), pp. 79–81.
7. Hicks's dispatch was delivered in "Mr. Keynes and the Classics, a Suggested Interpretation," *Econometrica* 5 (1937): 147–159.
8. Hicks's altered view appears in his *The Crisis in Keynesian Economics* (New York: Basic Books, 1974). It is good reading.
9. John M. Keynes, "The General Theory of Employment," *Quarterly Journal of Economics* 51 (February 1937): 209–223.
10. Two periodicals devoted to Post Keynesian economics, the *Cambridge Journal of Economics* in England and the *Journal of Post Keynesian Economics* in the United States, bear witness to these developments. The founding co-editors of the latter were Paul Davidson (then at Rutgers University, now at the University of Tennessee) and the late Sidney Weintraub of the University of Pennsylvania. John Kenneth Galbraith, one of the founding patrons of the *JPKE*, is chairman of the honorary board of directors. The late Joan Robinson and Lord Nicholas Kaldor were among the founding patrons of the *Cambridge Journal*.
11. John Maynard Keynes, *The General Theory of Employment, Interest, and Money* (New York: Harcourt, Brace & World, 1965), p. 372. [1936]
12. *Ibid.*, p. 373.
13. Keynes, *op. cit.*, p. 374
14. Quoted in Charles Hession, *John Maynard Keynes* (New York: Macmillan, 1984), p. 224.
15. John Kenneth Galbraith, *A Life in Our Times: Memoirs* (Boston: Houghton Mifflin, 1981), p. 75.
16. The author has created this bridge in E. Ray Canterbery, "Galbraith, Sraffa, Kalecki and Supra-Surplus Capitalism," *Journal of Post Keynesian Economics* 7 (Fall 1984): 77–90. This article contains more detail on how the ideas of Galbraith, Sraffa, and Kalecki can be synthesized. See also Canterbery, "A Theory of Supra-Surplus Capitalism," Presidential Address, *Eastern Economic Journal* (Winter 1988).
17. Whereas Kalecki's markup applies only to manufacturing, Weintraub's is more general and applies to all industries, including those that are nearly competitive.

A markup pricing rule is now widely used in orthodox econometric modeling. See *The Econometrics of Price Determination*, ed. Otto Eckstein (Washington, D.C.: Board of Governors of Federal Reserve System, 1974); Arthur Okun, *Prices and Quantities: A Macroeconomics Analysis* (Washington, D.C.: Brookings Institution, 1981); and William D. Nordhaus, "The Falling Rate of Profits," *Brookings Papers of Economic Activity* 74, No. 1 (1974): 169–208.

18. According to Canterbery in "A Theory of Supra-Surplus Capitalism," *op. cit.*, and "An Evolutionary Model of Technical Change with Markup Pricing," in William Milberg, *The Megacorp and Macrodynamics* (Armonk, New York and London, England: M.E. Sharp, 1992), pp. 85–100, the target's highest limit is determined by the current number of firms in the industry and by the firm's perceived price elasticity of demand or consumers' sensitivity to price changes. Generally, the fewer the firms in the industry and the lower the sensitivity of consumers to price increases (the lower the price elasticity of demand), the higher the upper limit to the price markup.

    The motivation for investment "needs" has been variously attributed to market share, growth, and power goals. These explanations have been put forward, respectively, by Alfred S. Eichner, *The Megacorp and Oligopoly: Micro Foundations of Macro Dynamics* (Cambridge: Cambridge University Press, 1976); Robin Marris, *The Economic Theory of "Managerial" Capitalism* (New York: Basic Books, 1964); and John Kenneth Galbraith. To the extent that borrowed funds are used to finance increments to the capital stock, new financial assets are created in the process of business investment. Hyman Minsky takes this position in his *John Maynard Keynes* (New York: Columbia University Press, 1975).

19. Money wages are endogenous in the manner described in Canterbery's vita theory of the labor market: See E. Ray Canterbery, "A Vita Theory of Personal Income Distribution," *Southern Economic Journal* 46 (July 1979): 12–48.

20. In order to deal with these problems, in 1983 I proposed: (1) an equitable value-added tax (VAT) as a new revenue source and as the ideal tax base for the immediate implementation of TIP; and (2) a simplified personal income tax program that would satisfy those critics of VAT who viewed it as inequitable. Several of the features of the simplified personal income tax have been implemented by Congress: VAT remains in limbo. See E. Ray Canterbery, "Tax Reform and Incomes Policy: A VATIP Proposal," *Journal of Post Keynesian Economics* 5 (Spring 1983): 430–439. A later, more detailed version of the proposal appears in E. Ray Canterbery, Eric W. Cook, and Bernard A. Schmitt, "The Flat Tax, Negative Tax, and VAT: Gaining Progressivity and Revenue," *Cato Journal* (Fall 1985): 521–536.

21. This is Keynes's original view of the money-national income interaction. It is also the interpretation of Keynes used by Sidney Weintraub, *Capitalism's Inflation*

and Unemployment Crisis, (Reading, Massachusetts: Addison-Wesley, 1978), pp. 66–77; and by Paul Davidson in "Why Money Matters: Lessons from a Half-Century of Monetary Theory," *Journal of Post-Keynesian Economics* (Fall 1978), pp. 57–65, and in *Money and the Real World* (New York: Wiley, A Halstead Press Book, 1972).

22. For those who wish to take the mystery out of money and interest rates, they can do no better than read George P. Brockway, *The End of Economic Man*, Revised (New York and London: W.W. Norton and Company, 1993), especially Chapters 3, 8, 12 and 13.

23. Charles P. Kindleberger, *Manias, Panics and Crashes: A History of Financial Crises* (New York: Basic Books, 1978), pp. 23–24.

24. Arjo Klamer, *Conversations with Economists* (Totowa, New Jersey: Rowman & Allanheld, 1984), pp. 137–138.

25. Paul Samuelson, "Succumbing to Keynesianism," *Challenge* (November-December 1984), p. 7.

12

THE MONETARISTS AND THE NEW CLASSICALS DEEPEN THE COUNTERREVOLUTION

The neoclassical counterrevolution set the stage for the ascendency of the monetarists, whose roots lay exclusively in the United States in the late 1950s. They nonetheless derive their ideas from the monetary theory of the classical economists and believe in the self-correcting nature of the market system. Once the money supply is growing at a "correct rate," the monetarists rely on Marshallian or Walrasian price outcomes to explain the underbelly of the economy.

We have noted, however, how social problems historically have been intertwined with allegiances to the economic theory, even aged theories. Still the new monetarist counterrevolution's success is found in a combo inflation and unemployment. During the placid 1950s and 1960s, the Keynesians viewed the monetarists as eccentrics. Eccentricity was turned on the "old fashioned" Keynesians during the rocky 1970s.

THE INFLATION-UNEMPLOYMENT CRISIS OF THE 1970s

A dramatic omen of the crisis occurred on August 15, 1971. On that date, President Richard M. Nixon, who had based his political career on the defense of free market laissez-faire capitalism and red-baiting, stunned the nation by adopting extensive wage and price controls. Nixon's policy reversal was an admission of the failure of all neo-Keynesian policy devices to slow inflation without causing a severe depression. A major crisis in economics surfaced: Its failure to explain why price stability apparently can be bought only with very high unemployment levels. There were crisis reruns by 1973 and late 1979, and, again, two new administrations engineered economic recessions in attempts to slow inflation.

There is good reason for juxtaposing social crises with attitudes in economics. Nothing is a social crisis unless society says so. Poverty and racism were not considered social problems prior to Dickens's time, except by a few "strange" intellectuals. Ecology was not a widespread concern in the 1950s. Overemphasis on material values is never deplored unless large numbers of people fail to find satisfaction in "meaningless" work and ostentatious consumption. Having said this, I shall focus on the twin and separate crises of inflation and unemployment, for therein lay the reasons for the counterrevolution.

Consider a typical practicing economist, a male head of household of prime working age, at the end of the 1970s faced with the awesome prospect of personal unemployment and higher prices for his necessities out of a zero current income. Would his policy advice or forecasts have been different?

The economist would have predicted that, in order to resolve the inflation problem, we would have to live with an eight percent unemployment rate. Suppose his employer had told him that his company was willing to live with it, as long as the economist could. The economist might well have considered reversing his forecast and trying to save his job.

Such a personal dilemma paints a human face on the trade-off between inflation and unemployment—for the typical worker *and* the economist. For, no doubt, the greatest embarrassment for many neo-Keynesians was the 1970s' double-digit inflation and high unemployment rates, a coincidence that is not supposed to happen. Nonetheless, and especially after the 1965 escalation of the Vietnam War (and the failure of President Johnson to follow his economists' advice to raise taxes), the momentum of inflation was such that little control was secured from the creation of socially acceptable levels of unemployment.

THE PROBLEMS INFLATION RAISES

Before we consider the policy dilemma created by the twin devils of unemployment *and* inflation, let us consider some of the problems created by inflation, particularly when it is severe. W.C. Fields (1880–1946), an actor during the youth of Hollywood, used a different measure of inflation than humor would allow today's economist. Fields noted, circa 1924, "Inflation has gone up over a dollar a quart." And the twenties roared. Economists dourly define inflation as a sustained increase in the price level, normally calibrated in percentage change in that price level (measured by a price index). Why was inflation a problem during the 1920s and the 1970s?

Inflation is an invisible tax that redistributes income. Rising prices take real purchasing power away from those whose money incomes rise less rapidly than the prices they pay and redistribute it toward those whose money incomes rise faster than the prices they pay. As a rough generalization, those on fixed incomes, such as old-age pensioners and college professors, are heavily taxed by inflation. During this era, highly organized union workers felt less of its sting. For example, between 1967 and 1978 the average steelworker's income (after taxes and effects of inflation) increased 32 percent, whereas that of the average university professor declined 17.5 percent.

Unexpected inflation also redistributes wealth from creditors (those who are lending money) to debtors (those who are borrowing) when debts are stated in fixed dollar terms. Whether you bemoan this redistribution depends greatly on whether you are a creditor or a debtor. Some would argue that creditors are richer than debtors and little worry should be wasted because of cuts in their relative wealth. The relatively lower income debtors are paying back their loans with lower-valued money. Even if you do not "cry for Argentina" from the relative decrease in creditors' wealth, the paying of soaring money interest rates on the loans of the poor and middle-class families might tug at your heartstrings as inflation continues.

Unexpected inflation also redistributes wealth from those whose owned assets rise more slowly in price to those whose assets rise more rapidly. A complete understanding of this issue turns on which prices are rising. For example, homeowners might have experienced a great increase in relative wealth because the price of housing was rising so rapidly during the inflation of the 1970s, whereas those who were holding bonds saw the value of their assets diminish. (This dichotomy is the result of the inverse relation between the price of a bond and its interest rate.) In any case, higher-income families have the financial flexibility to shift their resources from one kind of asset into another that is appreciating more rapidly.

It is difficult to assess precisely the differential effects of inflation on various income groups. Surely, significant inflation creates the greatest social problems when the prices of necessities are rising most rapidly, since the purchasing power of most of the population would be diminished. Much of the inflation of the 1970s was of this uncomfortable variety.

THE SOURCES OF INFLATION

Inflation can be classified by its causes into at least four types: Demand-pull, cost-push, structural, and expectational. (Although useful, this delineation is difficult to identify in practice.) Pure demand-pull inflation has total demand exceeding potential output, the type of inflation found in the Keynesian cross model. Cost-push inflation can be the result of union pressures for higher wages (and management acquiescence) or of higher costs of raw materials and other commodities used in production. Such "seller's inflation" can originate with highly concentrated industries, such as airlines and computer operating systems, that face little competition from products or services that are substitutes for their wares. The price rise for one industry becomes a cost increase for the next, and so on. Seller's inflation from market power can sometimes spread; for instance, from the price of plastic to the price of automobiles.

Structural inflation is the dastardly eclectic consequence of both demand-pull and cost-push forces. Even if total demand is less than potential output, inflation can occur where there is a shift in the pattern of demand. Because of the historical downward rigidity of U.S. prices and wages, an advance in wages and prices in one part of the economy is not offset by comparable declines elsewhere. Hence, the overall average price level continues to rise so long as wages do.

Expectational inflation results from the actions of individuals and institutions reacting to anticipated inflation. In its neo-Keynesian incarnation, we have expectational inflation because we expect inflation, and we expect inflation because we've been experiencing inflation. There are many variants of expectational inflation; however, they all share the same basic labor market explanation. Workers demand higher rates of increases in wages because they anticipate (correctly or incorrectly) higher prices for the products and services they buy.

Expectational inflation can explain a worse trade-off in the short run in an upward-shifting Phillips curve. For any unemployment rate, the higher the anticipated rate of inflation, the higher the actual inflation. If workers expect a rapid inflation, they will demand more generous wage contracts, and firms will then pass these higher wages along as the higher prices that the workers expected. (By the same token, if people expect little or no inflation, then wage inflation will be modest and firms will restrain product-price inflation, a situation descriptive of the 1990s, not the 1970s.) In this view, the long-run Phillips curve is much steeper than the short-run Phillips curve because it would trace out all those points at which the actual and the anticipated inflation rates are equal.

THE MODERN QUANTITY THEORY OF MONEY

Milton Friedman: The Darling of the Neolibertarians

The story of the monetarists begins with the equation of exchange, an idea with more sequels than "Rocky," the classic movie. We should not be surprised: The equation of exchange has been the underdog any time prices have been stable, only to rise from the mat when inflation soars. The newest interest in the quantity theory of money came with the publication of Milton Friedman's *Studies in the Quantity Theory of Money* in 1956. Friedman emerged by the late 1950s as the leader of the Chicago school of economics. Friedman, a contemporary exponent of a libertarian strain of laissez-faire, is also the modern monetarists' guru.

Friedman's fame is such that he became the thinly disguised hero of a novel, *Murder at the Margin,* authored by two economist-admirers.[1] The novel tells of a short, balding, articulate, brilliant professor of economics (an apt description of Friedman) who solves a murder through the use of Chicago-style economics. As the fictional Professor Spearman puts it: "I am interested only in economic laws, laws that cannot be broken." Although the murder violated human-made law, the murderer slipped up because the economic law remained intact.

Like Friedman, Professor Spearman is an unregenerated, rational homoecomicus and libertarian. The good professor decides everything very much like he confronts a glass of tea.

> "I'll have a glass," Spearman said. Pidge joined him.
>
> The ratiocination that had led Spearman to this deceptively simple decision to buy a glass of tea had actually involved the following lightning calculation: The probable satisfaction expected from the glass of iced tea being offered exceeded the pleasure from any alternative purchase at that price.
>
> Until Spearman had noticed the lime accompanying the tea, he had been on the margin....[2]

There is more than a marginal connection between the objectivist philosophy of Ayn Rand (1905–1982) and Milton Friedman's monetarist philosophy. The objectivist philosophy defends the selfishly heroic nature of the economic man, men such as Professor Spearman, or as Ayn Rand has written, "Capitalism and altruism are incompatible; they are philosophical opposites; they cannot co-exist in the same man or in the same society."[3] Rand's novel, *Atlas Shrugged,* is a vindication of the creativity of the industrialist, the author of material production. In it, Hank Rearden, who is on trial for the illegal sale of a metal alloy that he has created and that has been placed under government control, eloquently states the libertarian economics creed:

> I am rich and I am proud of every penny I own. I have made my money by my own effort, and free exchange and through the voluntary consent of every man I dealt with…, the voluntary consent of those who work for me now, the voluntary consent of those who buy my product.… Do I wish to pay my workers more than their services are worth to me? I do not. Do I wish to sell it at a loss or give it away: I do not. If this is evil, do whatever you please about me, according to what ever standards you hold.[4]

Despite the jokes connecting Friedman's New Jersey background with his presumption that everyone is motivated by pure self-interest, the sharp objectivist contrast between the virtue of self-interest and the evils of altruism is not a mere cocktail-time stereotype. In *Atlas Shrugged,* Rand builds a case against altruism which, as she sees it through the eyes of Hank Reardon, requires sacrifice. Rand attacks two views: The mystics of spirit and the mystics of muscle. Reardon is speaking.

> Selfishness—say both—is man's evil. Man's good—say both—is to give up his personal desires, to deny himself, renounce himself, surrender; man's good is to negate the life he lives. Sacrifice—cry both—is the essence of morality, the highest virtue within man's reach.[5]

Though Friedman thinks highly of the late neolibertarian philosopher and novelist, he finds the doctrinaire faith of some of Rand's disciples intolerable. (Sometimes-monetarist Alan Greenspan, the former chairman of the President's Council of Economic Advisers under President Ford and later of the Federal Reserve System under Presidents Reagan, George Walker Bush, Clinton, George W. Bush, was one of Rand's "moderate" disciples.)

Be that as it may, Friedman has been more than simply an unabashed supporter of free markets. Like John Kenneth Galbraith, who calls Friedman "the most influential economist of the twentieth century," Friedman is a political activist. Like Paul Samuelson, he once wrote a column for *Newsweek*. Friedman emerged as Senator Barry Goldwater's major economic adviser in 1964, supporting the presidential hopeful on such vital issues as the volunteer army, law and order, restricted governmental spending, the unlimited virtues of capitalism and individualism, and antibusing. Friedman returned to politics on the coattails of Richard Nixon in 1968; thereafter, he advised Ronald Reagan, often considered a conservative.

Milton Friedman was born in Brooklyn in 1912, the son of poor Jewish immigrants. His father dealt in wholesale dry goods, and his mother worked as a seamstress in a New York sweatshop under the type of working conditions decried by Engels in England. When the family moved the short distance across the Hudson River to Rahway, New Jersey, Friedman's mother ran a retail dry-goods store while his father commuted to his wholesale business in New York. When Milton was 15, his father died, leaving very little money for the education of his son. Although he was raised in a religious environment, the boy had lost all interest in spiritual matters by the age of 13.[6]

Friedman's greatest aptitude was for mathematics and statistics. When he graduated in mathematics and economics from Rutgers University in 1932, Friedman received offers of graduate scholarships from Brown University (in mathematics) and the University of Chicago (in economics). He went to Chicago, but lack of funds forced him to leave after his initial academic year. A job as a waiter, still a low-paying service job, was not sufficient to supplement his tuition scholarship.

Friedman moved to Columbia University, which offered him a much larger fellowship. He completed work on his doctorate in 1941, but the acceptance of his dissertation was delayed until 1946 because his evaluators disliked his attack on physicians, whose organization restricts entry into medicine and therefore tampers with the laws of supply and demand. This episode was for Friedman a personal encounter of the most disturbing kind with the enemies of the free market system.

The Linkage of Money and the Gross National Product

Friedman's fame as an economist rests on his development of modern monetarism. This monetarist doctrine states: (1) Changes in the money supply by the central bank and the government constitute the only predictable element that influences the total level of expenditures and industrial activity in the economy. (2) Government intervention of any kind—regulation of business, taxation, spending, subsidies—interferes with the proper functioning of the substructure, the free markets. (3) With (1) and (2) operating, the only policy required to guarantee long-run full employment and full-time price stability is to direct the central bank to expand the money supply four to five percent annually, a rate about equal to what they believe is the noninflationary growth potential of the economy. Except for some mathematical and statistical details, this sounds like *deja vu* all over again, the classical theory of money.

Friedman's version of the monetarist doctrine was originally inspired by his believing Keynesian economics to be a way of enlarging government, destroying private enterprise capitalism. However, the monetarists' reaction is against the fiscal and neoclassical Keynesians, who opened the door to attack by those who fear inflation. In its later stages, the monetarists' faith has been bolstered by a host of empirical findings showing the money supply and the money value of gross domestic product (GDP) moving in tandem.

One-way causation is inferred from this correlation: The monetarists see money supply changes moving the money value of the GDP, whereas Keynes's General Theory pictures the two totals interacting. If finger-pointing indicates the direction of causation, for the monetarists, $M \rightarrow GDP$; whereas for Keynes, $M \leftrightarrows GDP$. By the late 1950s, monetarism became part of the "counterrevolution" against the Keynesians as Friedman made a wholesale (and perhaps retail) endorsement of a sophisticated version of the old quantity theory of money.

Friedman's version of the equation of exchange is close to Alfred Marshall's approach, or the Cambridge cash-balance approach. To Marshall, money served as an abode—though temporary—for purchasing power between the time of purchase and the time of sale. Friedman's relation is analogous to Marshall's k, based as it was on the transactions' demand for money: As income rises, people tend to hold proportionately more money to exchange for the greater value of goods and services sold. In this view money is at rest rather than in motion. The amount of money people hold depends on institutional arrangements making it easier or more difficult to access their bank deposits.

As we already know, the rate of turnover of money (V) depends on the stability of its demand. Institutional changes affecting the liquidity of assets or even the invention of new financial instruments could alter this stability or even change the definition of what constitutes money. As long as the demand for money to hold is relatively stable, however, only changes in the money supply can cause price changes. We must quickly add that this is so only if the money supply has no effect on *real* national income. In Friedman's exposition, the demand for money, and therefore V, can vary. However, the variation is constant (another definition of money demand "stability"), and thus price changes still can be predicted from money supply movements.[7]

This theory leads to a neat little "predictive" equation for inflation based on percentage changes in prices,

$$\text{Inflation} = (\%\ \text{change, velocity}) + (\%\ \text{change, money supply}) - (\%\ \text{change, real national income})$$

With real output and national income growing at a full-capacity rate and with Hovercraft velocity, price inflation is directly related only to a growth rate of the money supply in excess of the full-capacity growth rate of real output.

Keynes had seen the effect of money on real income in the private economy as indirect, operating through interest rate movements and investment. The monetarists imagine any output effect as direct but fleeting. These transitory output perturbations flow from adjustments in the composition of household assets, including goods and services. Thus the sophisticated theory focuses on the demand for money within a balance sheet or "portfolio" setting. This formulation is somewhat Keynes-like (not Keynesian) in the sense that money is viewed as wealth, that is, as an asset.

The quite stiff monetarist's finger points down a one-way street: From the money supply to GDP. Such changes in the money supply must come from "outside" the economic system. If business borrowing and the private banking system alone were to add to the money supply, producers' activities would be changing the money supply rather than the other way around, the "inside" money supply increments swelling producers' sales revenue. Instead, for "outside" money supply increases, Friedman relies on an imaginary helicopter dropping greenbacks from the sky on palms-up citizens. This corresponds to a government printing and delivery system. Economists call this an exogenous change in the money supply; critics might call it a "helicopout."

After money has fallen on our heads, the new money supply level is higher than the cash balances desired by the public. Therefore, the public must rearrange their portfolios to maximize their returns; the "unwanted" cash is allocated among more goods, more stocks and bonds, and more savings certificates. The demand for goods and services rises, and prices go up as well. If it is expected that prices will continue to rise (an expectation no doubt reinforced by the public's belief in the quantity theory of money), the demand for goods and services rises even faster. Thus, you can see how the aerial drop of the money supply causes the money value of GDP also to give flight.

The bulge in demand for real output is a temporary bubble because individuals—being omnipotent—base spending plans on their "permanent income," the income they expect to receive over their entire lifetimes. The long run—in real terms—is for the most part set. For the price level, it is a different matter.

It is rather easy to envision this extreme version of monetarism, however improbable the vehicular delivery system. When money is created solely by the interplay of producers and private bankers, however, the picture loses its focus. The latter story must run roughly as follows. When private money is used for private purposes, it is always used in "just the right" quantities for "legitimate" purposes. Thus, the privately generated money supply will be just sufficient for production needs and in the monetarists' vision, labor unions and business enterprises are blameless for inflation.

In the same year (1970) in which Friedman published an important summary of his doctrine, government spending accounted for 32 percent of GNP, up from 27 percent in 1960. President Richard M. Nixon, a Friedman favorite, went on television on June 17 to ask that business and labor end inflation by voluntarily resisting wage and profit gains. The President promised to not impose direct wage and price controls, but he did create a new national commission and asked it to suggest ways for increasing worker productivity. The President *did not* mention the money supply. The conditions of the time appear far short of Friedman's program, and the President's policies did not seem at all Friedmanite.

THE FRIEDMANIAN PHILLIPS CURVE

What, we might ask, is the Friedmanian connection between inflation and unemployment? Friedman painlessly ends the policy dilemma of a trade-off between inflation and employment, the Phillips curve, by discarding it.

Recall the omnipotence of every individual. Because of completely anticipated inflation, the monetarists see no trade-off at all in the long run. Their conclusion stems from the natural rate of unemployment, an idea that depends on a classical/neoclassical view of the perfectly adjusting labor market (in real terms). The natural rate is the unemployment rate prevailing in a perfectly competitive labor market. Any rate of unemployment below the natural rate leads to inflation, or so it was said.

If alert workers expect a rapid inflation, they will demand more generous wages. Thus, any increase in anticipated inflation is matched percentage point by percentage point by wage inflation, leaving the real wage rate unchanged. With the real wage rate unaltered, the level of employment and therefore the unemployment rate remain constant (at the natural unemployment rate). Only *un*anticipated inflation can lead to temporary reductions in unemployment below the natural rate. In the long run, inflation is fully anticipated, and there is no trade-off whatsoever between inflation and unemployment.

No doubt the expectation of inflation can be a self-fulfilling prophecy as consumers and retailers stock up on goods to beat the coming price rise. However, when you think about it, this tells us little about how inflation got started in the first place.

FRIEDMANIAN PREDICTION FOR INFLATION

According to Friedman, policy recommendations depend on predictions. In the Newtonian world, for example, the average person identifies cause and effect according to proximity. You are playing golf on a cloudy day threatening rain; your partner has just hit her second shot on a long par four hole to within inches of the pin. She shakes her one iron in the air in exultation, a bolt of lightning strikes the club, and she falls to the ground. As a good Newtonian, you assume that the bolt of lightning caused your golf partner to fall. She may have stumbled or had a heart attack, of course, but whatever actually happened, you *do not* assume that she caused the bolt of lightning to strike. There is no confusion about cause and effect, although in this particular instance there may be error. In Friedman's words:

> There is perhaps no empirical relation in economics that has been observed to recur so uniformly under so wide a variety of circumstances as the relation between substantial changes ... in the stock of money and in prices; the one is invariably linked with the other and in the same direction; this uniformity is, I suspect, of the same order as many of the uniformities that form the basis of the physical sciences.[8]

No one has ever struck a stronger bolt for hard science: Friedman's statement is a bolt of lightening "out of the blue." The elements of the money supply and the GDP, however, *do not* have the simplicity of the lightning bolt and the golfer. GDP and the money supply move together so no one can be quite certain whether the money supply causes the GDP to change or the GDP causes the money supply to change. For *prediction,* Friedman argues, we do not need to know *which* is cause and which is effect. Ignorance, even on the golf course, is bliss!

The golfer "causing" the lightning would be *noooo problem.* Presumably, had the golfer raised a one iron skyward, Friedman's conclusion would be bolstered by senior golf pro Lee Trevino, who claims, "even God cannot hit a one iron." The money supply → GDP prediction leads to a striking policy conclusion: There ought to be a legislative rule prescribing the annual rate of growth of the money supply, thereby removing it from the uncertain, unskilled human hands of central bankers. Of course, the policy suggestion now presumes one-way causation, money supply → GDP. Friedman's test of intelligence for monetary authorities is their acceptance of his ideas.

MONETARISM AND THE GREAT DEPRESSION

An alternative test of the reliability of monetarism as a predictive force is its ability to explain the Great Depression. Irving Fisher, the designer of a precursor monetarist equation to Friedman's, failed not only to predict the Great Depression, but the Great Crash of 1929 as well. Even after the Great Crash of 1929 and as late as May 1930 his optimism was unrestrained, as "the difference between the present comparatively mild business recession and the severe depression of 1920 to 1921 is like that between a thunder-shower and a tornado."[9] He did not mention the causality between a golfer and lightening. Later, with 100 percent hindsight, the modern monetarists see the collapse of the money supply as *the* cause of the Depression.

According to a monumental study by Milton Friedman in collaboration with Anna Schwartz, bank failures caused the Depression.[10] However, as noted, the chain of causation was much longer. Falling agricultural prices and farm bankruptcies led to the bank failures in Missouri, Indiana, Iowa, Arkansas, and North Carolina.[11] If these failures were insufficient, the aforementioned failure of the Bank of the United States of New York stampeded people out of bank deposits and into cash. Other banks began to experience withdrawal pains.

These failures led to a plunge in the money supply by about a third from 1929 to 1933. In anticipation of panic withdrawals of deposits, banks reduced lending, further contracting the money supply. The availability of credit for consumption and investment disappeared, like a desert mirage, before the eyes of would-be borrowers. And, of course, the economic slump made borrowing look about as attractive as a camel on Rodeo Drive. The spiral could only be downward. The free fall in the money supply contributed to the Depression but the Depression contributed to the decline in the money supply.

Besides, if we wish to be theoretically pure in the dispute, most of the contraction in money was of "inside money," not the helicopter money or "outside" money relied on by the monetarists. Even so, the monetarists' criticism of the Federal Reserve's actions during the Great Depression is smart-targeted; whenever the Fed had a choice between doing the best or the worst thing, it invariably chose error.

THE NEW CLASSICALS

Milton Friedman was not the end of monetarism as we know it. While neo-Keynesian economists were struggling with the stagflation of the late 1960s and early 1970s, a handful of other economists were busy building theories from a modern monetarist base potentially devastating to Keynesian thought. Something called "rational expectations" vastly altered the way economists began to think about macroeconomics. First, we look at the players in the newer game.

The Players

Rational expectations became popular once the new classical school began to play ball. John Muth, a modest, unremarkable-looking business school professor at Carnegie-Mellon, introduced rational expectations into the "farm club" or the commodities markets in 1961, only to be ignored for a decade.[12] Then, Robert Lucus, once a colleague of Muth's at Carnegie-Mellon, took the rational expectations from commodities markets and put it into play in the national league or macroeconomics. For macroeconomics it was a whole new ball game.

Lucus, a 1964 graduate of the University of Chicago and Nobel Prize winner in economics in 1995, was strongly influenced by Milton Friedman and the modern monetarists. Indeed, Lucus, a gregarious, impeccably ordered, handsome man, returned to teach at Chicago in 1975, and today teaches at Harvard. Although he and the late Leonard Rapping, later a new left radical, introduced the new classical labor market in 1969, Lucus drew the dramatic implications of rational expectations for macroeconomics three years later.[13]

In a series of articles, Lucus claims irreparable flaws in Keynesian macroeconomics. These criticisms attracted younger, mathematical economists who elaborated on the ideas. Thomas Sargent (Harvard, 1968), an economist as shy and quiet as Lucus is outgoing and articulate, showed, with Neil Wallace, how the "myths" of effective Keynesian fiscal and monetary policies could be exploded with the smart bomb of rational expectations.[14]

Lucus relates the following tale about Sargent at a seminar: "Tom made some point and the speaker didn't seem to understand it. Tom ... didn't say anything for the rest of the seminar. At the end, he just handed the speaker a piece of paper with a bunch of equations on it and said, 'Here's what I was trying to say.' ...The speaker said, 'This is Sargent's idea of a conversation' and laughed."[15]

Other new classical economists contributing to the seemingly unassailable logic of their theory include Bennett McCallum and Robert Barro (Harvard, 1969), jumping the model ship of disequilibrium for new classical equilibrium models, and Robert

Townsend, a student of Sargent and Wallace's at the University of Minnesota, who has added lifeboat-style innovations.

Despite all the fuss generated by these economists, much of the new classical approach is as old as classical economics (hence the name) and as new as modern monetarism (hence the game). The new classicals also are laissez-faire types who presume the relevant model for the economy to be the monetarist's theory. Still, the new classicals are more radically anti-government policy than the monetarists, as unlikely as that may seem.

The stagflation of the 1970s, which derailed the neo-Keynesians and put the monetarists back on the conventional track, also provided the steam behind rational expectations and new classicalism. Predictably, the neo-Keynesians counter new classical equilibrium with business cycles and unemployment, suggesting disequilibrium. In particular, the neo-Keynesians see the new classicals themselves derailed by the high unemployment of 1981 to 1982 and of the Great Depression of the 1930s, for which the new classicals have no explanation.

Those are the players; now, the game is afoot.

THE RATIONAL EXPECTATIONS GAME

Expectations, especially expectations regarding future inflation rates, are critical to the new classical school. The Keynesians and even the neo-Keynesians looked back over their shoulders at past price changes to see if they were gaining on them in order to predict future inflation. The new classicals consider such a view as not only backward but naive and incomplete. A driver who looks only in the rearview mirror may well end up in the ditch.

The world of the new classicals is populated by persons who are remarkably intelligent, looking for the future wherever necessary—be it backward, forward, downward, skyward, under every rock and twig—wherever. Moreover, these wonderfully astute people understand and properly interpret what they see.

When such persons do make errors, they reflect on their mistakes and, if necessary, revise their behavior so as to eliminate *regularities* in their errors. Not only do rational drivers keep their eyes on the road ahead, but their ability to correct the steering after a wrong turn leaves such errors or bad turns of the steering wheel on average uncorrelated with the important, relevant variables in future decisions (such as keeping on the road). The human gyroscope is correct within a margin of error that itself is random.

Of course, it all began with John Muth's vision. Rather than persons looking only at past price behavior to infer the future, Muth showed how persons form their expectations on the basis of *all available relevant information.* Persons use this information intelligently and at little cost. Furthermore, predictions so informed as these will essentially be the same as those derived by the relevant economic theory. For example, workers will use any information they have about the current values of all variables playing a role in setting the price level. So, the rational expectations hypothesis was born.

In an ironical twist, Muth's hypothesis was discovered by Robert Lucus when he bothered to turn, look back, and read his former colleague's article—the way Keynesians form expectations—in order to discover the basis for forward-looking expectations. If economists had been as farsighted as the workers characterized by Lucus, they should have seen rational expectations in their future! Later, Muth argued that his rational expectations applied only to microeconomic phenomena and were being misapplied by the new classicals in the macro arena.[16] (The new classicals refuse to believe that Muth has misspent his youth.)

THE NATURAL RATE OF UNEMPLOYMENT AND OUTPUT

The new classicals presume all persons will optimize—acting out of their self-interest—and markets always clear. The ingredients for the recipe also are clear. The new classicals take Adam Smith's olde market mechanism, add the dash of the maximizing principles from

Paul Samuelson's *Foundations*, stir in the modern monetarist's policy variables, and throw in rational expectations as the new spice.[17]

Since the new classicals begin with Friedman's idea of the natural rate of unemployment, the key clearing market is the labor market. The **natural rate of unemployment** is that rate of unemployment prevailing when the amount of labor demanded and supplied are equal at an equilibrium *real* wage (the nominal wage rate divided by the price level). The workers must have correct expectations regarding the price level so that their real wage rate is also the one they expected.

Since the natural rates of output and employment depend on the supply of factors of production and technology—all supply-side elements—the natural rates of production and employment are unrelated to the level of total demand. The nominal variables can swirl all about the core of real variables at tornado-like wind speeds and leave the foundation of real variables unscathed. Up to this point the labor market looks very much like the classical labor market.

Anticipated Inflation

How do rational expectations alter the classical labor market perspective? The blue collar worker bases his predictions of inflation on the monetarist model. Suppose the Federal Reserve Board has been obsessed in recent weeks about the high level of unemployment. The chairman of the Board, no doubt a neo-Keynesian, envisions an expanding money supply leading to greater production, a lower unemployment rate, and with little inflation.

If the *marginal* blue collar worker reads (on the Monday subway ride to work) about an upcoming Tuesday meeting of the Federal Reserve's Open Market Committee at which, the Chairman of the Fed intimates, the money supply is going to be boosted, the rational worker then expects the price level to rise. A larger money supply pushes up total demand in the economy which—with a particular total supply—will cause the price level to take flight. That is, the worker processes his money supply information in the same way that a good monetarist would.

By the time the train arrives at the station, the marginal worker has done a back-of-the-paycheck-envelope estimate of his future *real* wage rate. Of course, the newly expected real wage will be lower as a consequence of the price level being higher. With the expectation of lower real take-home pay, the worker does an about-face at the factory gate, returns to the station, and rides home. The marginal worker simply reduces his offering of labor services because of the dip in the expected real wage rate.

If enough of the workforce is on the margin of decision, the employer will have to raise wages or face a shrunken work force. The employer therefore raises wages and keeps output up since it is his profit-maximizing choice to maintain output where it was *before* the price rise. Since marginal workers can be found for all levels of jobs, the general wage level rises. The workers' real wage will remain the same. All marginal workers doing the same wonderfully rational thing has national consequences for the effectiveness of the Fed's expansionary monetary policy.

The terminus depends critically on whether the inflation is *anticipated* (as above) or *unanticipated*. In the fully anticipated case, the available information and its optimal use leave little margin for error. With less labor, the total supply of goods declines, putting still more upward pressure on the price level. The demand for labor relentlessly climbs still more. With the prospect of lower real wages from rising prices (from the soaring money supply), the marginal workers will demand and receive nominal or money wage increases of a proportionate amount. Despite all the labor supply and demand curves being in backward and forward motion, after the dust has cleared from the hiring hall, the number of workers employed will end up right back where it all began, at square one. After money wages have risen in proportion to the higher goods prices, the labor market once again clears at the same old equilibrium real wage and employment.

If the same employment prevails as before, so too will the same output. Thus, the initial, heartening advance in total goods demand will be exactly offset by an equal reduction in total supply as the producers react to a higher cost of production stemming from higher money wages. All this happens at roughly the speed of light.

Though they are rare, auction markets sometimes exist. John Steinbeck describes a labor market for migrant workers with auction characteristics during the 1930s in his *The Grapes of Wrath*. A hundred men show up at a farm where only ten jobs are available. The farmer lets the wage fall until ten migrants are willing to work for that wage and ninety men say "the hell with it," and go on down the road.

Rational expectations and an auction-style labor market always clearing have quite dramatic implications for macroeconomic policy. The anticipated aggregate demand policy actions have no effects on real output or employment, even in the *short run*. The real variables such as output, employment, and technology are numb to *systematic* changes in demand management policies. We say systematic because a highly erratic economic policy might fool all the workers—at least for a time—in which case they fail to withhold their labor or to demand higher money wages until they have had time to learn about the new policy game.

The money supply increase could have been anticipated because it was announced in advance by some loud-mouthed official or "leaked" by "high-level but unnamed sources" or because it was a systematic policy action easily predicted.

The shape of the Phillips curve trade-off between inflation and the unemployment rate looks little different from that of the modern monetarists. There, you will recall, the workers eventually (in Friedman's long run, whatever time that may be) end up with nominal wage increases exactly offsetting the increase in inflation. The unemployment rate has gravitated back to its *natural* rate.

The new classical Phillips curve differs from Friedman's in only one respect. In the anticipated inflation case, the workers' behavior and price and wage changes happen all at once. So, for the new classical Phillips curve, there is no difference between the short run and the long run. The movement back to the natural rate of unemployment is lightening fast, and so it prevails both in the short run and the long run. The marathon conflates to the 100-meter dash!

Unanticipated Inflation

The initial effects of an *unanticipated* increase in the money supply (a *monetary surprise*) or any unanticipated increase in total demand from another source are different. Imagine the following sequence of events. For weeks, Fed "insiders" have told *Wall Street Journal* reporters how terrified of inflation is the Chairman of the Federal Reserve Board (chairmen usually are). The morning prior to the change in policy, the Fed's Chairman even visits a large General Motors (GM) factory, complete with cameras and film. As the cameras roll, the Fed Chairman announces, "The Federal Open Market Committee just today advised the New York Federal Reserve Bank to sell more Treasury bills in order to contract the money supply through the banking system. We must halt this inflation, which is destroying the very fabric of our society."

Meanwhile, in a distant enclave of the factory, GM's male management is riveted to a TV set, watching Willow Bay on CNN Moneyline. She announces a flurry of activity in the money market, signifying a massive buying spree of Treasury bills by the Federal Reserve Bank of New York and signaling an *increase* in the money supply. Management, always mindful of the importance of having an informed workforce, announces over loudspeakers: "The Federal Reserve is increasing the money supply!"

Surprise! The workers no doubt believe they have been on uncandid camera. But, the Fed got what it wanted. The Fed's leadership understood the necessity of catching the workers off-balance. If the policy change had been anticipated, the marginal workers immediately would have seen a meltdown in their real wage, grabbed their lunch pails, and headed for the subway station. Then, GM output would have fallen along with employment at the factory. Based on the available Fed information or, more accurately, misinformation, the workers could not have anticipated the money supply increase.

Again, the effects are economy-wide. As before, the increase in the money supply will elevate total demand. As the price level levitates, the demand for labor will also rise. In the short run, output and employment go up. However, the other changes, those related to the fully anticipated case, simply do not happen. The labor supply does not contract nor does the total supply of goods shrink. These consequences comprise the truth of Keynesianism and of short-run monetarism. That is, in the short run, an increase in the money supply can have its intended effects: More workers streaming through the factory gates and more goods spewing out of the factory.

According to the Lincolnesque rhetoric of the new classicals, however, while you can fool all of the workers for a short time (the short run), you cannot fool all of the workers all of the time (in the long run). When the workers begin to rely on Willow Bay instead of the Fed, they will have the correct information. Then, the workers will do what the new classicals expect them to do, and the expansionary monetary policy will fail to move the real variables in the economy.

NEW CLASSICAL ECONOMIC POLICY

From the foregoing, the unwary reader might see the new classical endorsing erratic monetary or fiscal policy as the policy of choice. This would be wrong; the new classicals advance a *policy ineffectiveness postulate.* They see real output and employment as unaffected by systematic, predictable changes in total demand policy. The new classical view that unanticipated total demand changes will affect output and employment in the short run still does not provide a meaningful role for macroeconomic stabilization policy. How so?

Consider the kind of situation unnerving to a John Maynard Keynes. Private investment has sharply declined in the face of the lowest level of consumer confidence since 1946. The drop in investment reduces total demand. Output will decline, and the price level will fall. Then, the demand for labor will fall through the factory floor.

If the workers expected these events from Willow Bay's reports on slumping consumer confidence, they will fully expect their real wages to rise as the price level falls. The amount of their labor supplied will increase, pushing the money wage lower. In the end, the money wage and price level will have fallen sufficiently to restore employment and output to their old levels. When the demand shocks are anticipated, the economy is self-stabilizing and there is no need for an expansionary monetary or fiscal policy.

Suppose the dip in investment had been unanticipated. Without any moves by the workers, the decline in investment demand would lower output and employment. Why not then use an expansionary monetary or fiscal policy to make up for the shortfall in investment spending?

If the blue collar workers failed to anticipate the investment shortfall, so too would the Federal Reserve and White House economists even though their collars are a different color. The policymaker would not have been able to predict the investment drop in advance. The policymaker cannot act to prevent something he does not expect. Once businesses have reduced investment, the policymaker can act to elevate demand if the investment decline is expected to continue. But if investment *is* expected to *continue* to decline, there would be *no need* for an expansionary policy since the workers and producers also would hold the same expectation. Shades of Catch-22!

Although the new classicals arrive by a different route, they nonetheless arrive at the same station as Milton Friedman. They favor a money growth rate rule in order to do away with unanticipated changes in the money supply. Such unexpected changes have no stabilization value and are likely to derail the economy off the natural rate of output and employment track. At the same time a constant growth rate in the money supply would stabilize the inflation rate.

As to fiscal policy, the new classicals oppose excessive or erratic government deficit spending. For example, Thomas Sargent and Neil Wallace were critical of the Reagan Administration's huge budget deficits. Unstable fiscal policy causes uncertainty, making it difficult for otherwise rational workers and producers to anticipate the course of the economy. Sargent and the others also see control of the government budget deficit as necessary for a credible (predictable), noninflationary monetary policy.

RATIONAL EXPECTATIONS AND THE REAL WORLD

Rational expectations, which led to new classical macroeconomics, is not without critics (including Muth himself). The Keynesians and the neo-Keynesians often say (1) it is unrealistic to presume that people or firms process information as intelligently as the hypothesis implies; (2) it also is unrealistic to presume that people use information on all relevant variables in forming expectations because the information collection is difficult and costly (unlike the cheapness of past experience); and (3) everyone armed with the same information may cause a speculative bubble and its subsequent collapse, hardly a rational outcome. John Kenneth Galbraith's spoof of rational expectations in his novel, *A Tenured Professor,* based as it is on the real world of speculation during the 1980s reveals and at the same time illustrates these criticisms.

In the novel the young Harvard economics professor Montgomery Marvin has created a measure of "excessive" optimism and pessimism in the stock market, the amazingly accurate Index of Irrational Expectations (IRAT). His use of IRAT in the stock market makes him rich. "Excessiveness" is contrary to rational expectations in which all market participants have the same information and use it with equal efficiency. The market ends up being efficient in the sense that all profits have been exploited; no one can make any money because it has already been made. In other words, Marvin should not be able to make all these profits.

Marvin invents IRAT from his understanding of the delusions of the crowd—South Sea Bubbles, the manic speculation of the late 1920s, and the financial genius of those men who communicated the errors of euphoria to others. He reads of the glowing reputations of the men who helped produce the stock market boom of the late 1920s. For example, "there was Richard Whitney, the quintessential Harvard clubman, deeply committed to his own economic acuity, a symbol of the highest standards of financial morality as expressed by the New Stock Exchange, who passed quietly into Sing Sing."[18] From this history emerges a principle of finance: "Find out who in any euphoric episode is the greatest hero, who is the most celebrated, and invest in his eventual fall."[19]

While still in graduate school at Berkeley, Marvin realizes that he needs a measure of the euphoria in a company and its stock. Marvin takes measure of a banking legend, the Bank of America. With reality as 100, Marvin sets the measure of euphoria in the bank as twice that figure. With the lights of Berkeley below, those of San Francisco aglow in the distance, he and his wife, Marjie, invent the IRAT. Galbraith, who predicted the 1987 stock market crash in an *Atlantic* article, is toying with the rational expectationists.

Marvin takes a short position in the BankAmerica stock. Marjie understands: Borrow stock, sell it at current prices, and then when the price goes down, replace it, keeping the difference. These profits come at a propitious time, an era when the Reagan Administration is reducing taxes on the top incomes, leaving the Marvins with a great deal more cash than would otherwise have been the case.

By the mid-1980s, "euphoria was becoming endemic and universal."[20] The Marvins discover index trading and begin to use heretofore undreamed-of leveraging. At a time when Ivan Boesky is in descent for using inside information, the Marvins carefully avoid any improprieties; they are honest speculators. The Marvins, going short as usual, become very rich from the stock market crash of October 19, 1987.

The turning point is provided by the Securities and Exchange Commission (SEC). IRAT, it had been determined, was an illegal manipulation of the markets. It was a case of unfair competition with a certain winner. IRAT not only gave Marvin an unfair advantage, but those following his trades had inside information on his purchases and sales. Hence, we have a clear case of insider trading based on inside information on the Marvins' trading—insider trading based on noninsider trading! Market failure is the product of the rational use of irrationality.

Galbraith's send-up of the rational expectationists continues. When the SEC denies Marvin the use of IRAT, he buys stocks in a random walk, informs the SEC, and provides full information of his transaction to the press. Marvin's undiminished reputation is sufficient to bring others onto a bandwagon. Complete information leads to a one-way speculation that *guarantees* Marvin's profits. Even the efficient use of complete information roils the markets!

The rational expectationists answer their critics, including Galbraith, in the following way: (1) All theories or models are "unrealistic" because reality is described in a greatly oversimplified way. The relevant issue is, according to the rational expectationists, which way of forming expectations is the best guide to monetary and fiscal policies. (2) People form expectations optimally so as to equate marginal costs and benefits, which would include the cost of information.

Still, the rational expectationists often point to the stock market as the perfect market in which to test their theory because no one has "inside" information. What is the rational expectationists' explanation for stock market crashes? A market crash is a "monetary shock," and monetary shocks are "transient."

As to reality, the new classicals never said that expectational errors or other shocks to the economy were necessarily small, so that in reality fluctuations in stock prices or unemployment can be large. Monetary and fiscal policy simply cannot perform a positive role in dealing with such massive errors or shocks.

THE NEW CLASSICALS AND DEPRESSIONS

But what about other aspects of the real world? Is the Great Depression a source of embarrassment to the new classicals? Robert Lucus suggests that people made terribly big errors during 1929 to 1933. As he says,

> There were a lot of decisions made that, after the fact, people wished that they had not made. There were a lot of jobs people quit that they wished they had hung onto; there were job offers that people turned down because they thought the wage offer was crappy. Then three months later they wished they had grabbed. Accountants who lost their accounting jobs, passed over a cab

> driver job, and now they're sitting on the street while their pal's driving a cab. So they wish they'd taken the cab driver job. People are making this kind of mistake all the time ... I don't see what's *hard* about this question of people making mistakes in the business cycle".[21]

And so, to Lucus the 1930s was a time when people did not have good information. Lucus would not deny the mistakes, however, only emphasize that people do not make systematic mistakes. In reference to 1929 to 1933, Lucas concludes, "If intelligent actors pursuing their own self-interest are going though the same mistake over and over again which is what seems to happen, we are led to think of informational difficulties."[22] Even so, we could easily get puzzled over a theory beginning with everyone having the intelligence and the information of a professional economist and ending with an explanation of the Great Depression as an information failure. Could it happen again?

As to accountants making mistakes by not taking a cab driver's job or (pushed a bit further) the unemployed cab driver refusing to sell apples for a nickel apiece, surely the job choices available were different in 1933 than in 1928. Moreover, workers surely would have preferred to live in a society in which the decision-making environment had been more upbeat. More fundamentally, when unemployment is massive, not everyone can be a cab driver—be they brain surgeons or college professors—because there will be more drivers than cabs, especially since fewer people can afford to take a taxi. The rational person knew these facts during the 1930s, but that knowledge was not very useful.

Robert Barro gives a monetarist's explanation for the Great Depression. The culprit, the Federal Reserve, wrongly contracted the money supply during 1929 to 1933. Barro also suggests: "The government interventions associated with the New Deal, including the volume of public expenditures and direct price regulations, retarded the recovery of the economy, which was nevertheless rapid after 1933."[23]

The new classicals nonetheless seem collectively puzzled by the high unemployment rates of the 1930s and those of the early 1980s. They perhaps agree with Thomas Sargent that "I do not have a theory, nor do I know somebody else's theory that constitutes a satisfactory explanation of the Great Depression. It's really a very important, unexplained event and process, which I would be very interested in and would like to see explained."[24]

If the rational expectationist cannot explain the past, after all the evidence is in, can we trust the marginal blue collar worker to behave in such a way as to guarantee full employment in our more complex modern economy? Will those workers laid off by GM and IBM be sufficiently wise to drive cabs and sell apples so that economists can keep their day jobs and continue to write about the wonders of full employment?

Thomas Sargent *does* have *an* explanation for the severe 1981 to 1982 downturn. He maintains that the disinflation policy of Reaganomics was not credible to the public. That is, the public expected the monetary tightness to be reversed in order to finance the gigantic budget deficits. Since people predicted a turnaround by the monetary authorities, inflationary expectations were not reversed quickly enough to prevent massive unemployment.[25] The working class was too smart for its own good.

Neo-Keynesian Robert Gordon is less sanguine, concluding that "in the end the 1981 to 1982 recession may prove to have been as fatal to the Lucas-Sargent-Wallace proposition (i.e, the policy ineffectiveness postulate) as the Great Depression was to pre-Keynesian classical macroeconomics."[26]

THE REAL BUSINESS CYCLE

Among the characteristics of macroeconomics that bothered Robert Barro was this: In microeconomics the "agents" always optimize. Since individuals can find out everything to be known about prices and money easily and at little cost, they should be optimizing even when abrupt changes happen in the macroeconomy. It is difficult for Barro to believe that fluctuations in national income is the result of errors made by individuals reacting to policy changes. If so, those economists who oppose government stabilization policies must come up with a new explanation of business cycles, one in which "agents" are optimizing. The real business cycle seemed to do the trick.[27]

In these models, the society is populated with like people so that group behavior can be explained by a representative agent. To humanize the agent, he often is called Robinson Crusoe. Unlike the original fiction, Crusoe is not even allowed to have a Friday. Crusoe optimizes his work hours compared to his leisure hours as well as his future consumption compared with his present consumption. (He apparently does not expect to be rescued any time soon.)

A technology shock changes the ingredients that Crusoe uses to produce things. If the shock is positive, his productivity rises; he can produce dinner quicker than before. If the shock is negative, Crusoe has to work harder to produce the same dinner as before. Either way, Crusoe adjusts to the new conditions by altering his work-leisure trade-off and his future to present consumption trade-off. Thus, no matter what the shock, he returns quickly to an optimal condition.

What is truly shocking about the real business cycle theory is the policy conclusion. Fluctuations in national income and employment simply arise from Robinson Crusoe's reactions to changes in his economic environment. Since his reactions are optimal, any move by policymakers to eliminate the business cycle would be suboptimal to Crusoe even if they could actually do so.

If the government increased tax rates to slow the overheated island economy, Crusoe would choose "too much" leisure—perhaps boating off to some resort a few weeks each year. Any tax change would distort Crusoe's otherwise optimal behavior. Since only real or supply-side variables are considered, money supply reductions or slowdowns can be used to end inflation but would have no effects on Crusoe's production or employment.

In short, the policy recommendations are identical to that of the monetarists and the New Classicals. Often the real business cycle models are included as a twist on the new classical models.

Critics cannot identify any economy-wide "shocks" that could cause a recession. Technological change in one industry that is negative (reduced productivity in textiles) may be offset by positive changes (increased productivity from the use of computers) in another industry.[28] These explanations for the business cycle seem not to be plausible and many economists consider the original story of Robinson Crusoe (and Friday) to be more realistic: Though the shipwreck was shocking, it was not of Titanic proportions.

CONCLUSIONS

The message of the Keynesians is abundantly clear: The suppression of demand by Keynesian economic policy creates unemployment in the short run, whereas doing nothing allows the inflation to continue. The intentional creation of unemployment even for the short run may result in urban riots, voter retaliation, and social hardships and dissatisfaction. Unless policies are implemented that change the structure of the economy so that it behaves as told by neoclassical theory, an even more ingenious solution must be invented.

For the monetarists, no problem exists. The labor market already is perfectly competitive. If the White House and the Congress keep hands off the private economy and the Federal Reserve follows a monetary rule, the natural rate of unemployment (whatever level it may be) will prevail, as well it should.

Contrary to the monetarists and the Keynesians, the new classicals have never expressed a strong interest in the real world. As Lucas puts it, "We're programming robot imitations of people, and there are real limits on what you can get out of that."[29] The higher level of mathematics and statistics required by rational expectations seems very important to Lucas and Sargent: In the words of the latter, "I appreciate the beauty of various arguments.... I tried recently to write a couple of papers in economic history without any equations. It's hard."[30]

For them, they say, modeling is merely a game, just like baseball. If other economists, or worse still policymakers, take the game seriously, that is their problem. But if others confuse a game with the real world and, as a consequence, cause economic difficulties, the victims surely will not like the cards they have been dealt.

There is little doubt about the new classicals' strong belief in free markets quickly correcting all errors in the absence of active monetary and fiscal policies. If so, surely they must on occasion feel frustration when American capitalism fails to work well. I can imagine a new classicalist stirred to taking action of a different sort, of the kind exhibited by Sir William Eden (1849–1915), the father of once British Prime Minister Anthony Eden. On this occasion, when the *weather* had looked promising but then turned to rain, Sir William shook his fist at the clouds beyond the window and yelled, "Just *like* you, God!" He then tore the barometer, which still indicated "fair," off the wall and threw it through that same window with the cry, "There, you damned fool, see for yourself!"[31]

NOTES

1. Marshall Jevons, *Murder at the Margin* (Glen Ridge, New Jersey: Thomas H. Horton & Daughters, 1977). Marshall Jevons is a pseudonym of the economist team of William Breit and Kenneth G. Elzinga.
2. *Ibid.*, p. 11.
3. Ayn Rand, *For the New Intellectual: The Philosophy of Ayn Rand* (New York: Random House, 1961), pp. 62–63.
4. Ayn Rand, *Atlas Shrugged* (New York: Random House, 1957), p. 480.
5. *Ibid.*, p. 1027.
6. Many of the biographical facts about Friedman in these pages were gleaned from the fascinating little book by Leonard Silk, *The Economists* (New York: Basic Books, 1976), pp. 43–85.
7. For details and elaborations, see Milton Friedman, "A Theoretical Framework of Monetary Analysis," *Journal of Political Economy* 78 (1970): 193–238; and "Symposium on Friedman's Theoretical Framework," *Journal of Political Economy* 80 (1972): 837–950.
8. Milton Friedman, *The Optimum Quantity of Money* (Chicago: Aldine Publishing Co., 1969), p. 67.

9. Kathryn M. Dominguez, Ray C. Fair, and Matthew D. Shapiro, "Forecasting the Depression: Harvard versus Yale," *The American Economic Review* 78 (1988): 607. In fairness to Fisher, I should add that Dominguez, Fair, and Shapiro also could not forecast the Depression with either the data available to Harvard and Yale economists at the time or the data available in the 1980s. The behavior of the money supply was not helpful in these forecast attempts. These economists, however, did not use a model incorporating the structure of the economy.

10. Milton Friedman and Anna J. Schwartz, *A Monetary History of the United States, 1867–1960* (Princeton, New Jersey: Princeton University Press, 1963).

11. This view also is developed in the classic by Peter Temin, *Did Monetary Forces Cause the Great Depression*? (New York: Norton, 1976).

12. It all started with John F. Muth, "Rational Expectations and the Theory of Price Movements," *Econometrica* 29 (July 1961): 315–335.

13. See Robert E. Lucas, Jr., and Leonard A. Rapping, "Real Wages, Employment, and Inflation," *Journal of Political Economy* 77 (September 1969): 721–754.

14. See, for example, Thomas J. Sargent and Neil Wallace, "Rational Expectations and the Theory of Economic Policy," *Journal of Monetary Economics* 2 (April 1976): 169–184.

15. This direct quote is from Arjo Klamer, *Conversations with Economists* (Totoway, New Jersey: Rowman & Allanheld, 1983), p. 34.

16. See John Muth, "An Error's in Variables Model," *Eastern Economic Journal* 11 (July–September 1985): 261–279.

17. In praise of Samuelson's *Foundations*, Lucas says, "... I liked Samuelson's book. He'll take these incomprehensible verbal debates that go on and on and never end and just *end* them: Formulate the issue in such a way that the question is answerable, and then get the answer." [Klamer, *Conversations with Economists, op. cit.*, p. 49].

18. John Kenneth Galbraith, *A Tenured Professor* (Boston: Houghton Mifflin, 1990), p. 57.

19. *Ibid.*

20. *Op. cit.*, p. 83.

21. Klamer, *Conversations with Economists, op. cit.*, p. 41.

22. *Ibid.*, p. 40.

23. Klamer, *Conversations with Economists*, p. 57.

24. *Ibid.*, p. 69.

25. Thomas J. Sargent, *Rational Expectations and Inflation* (New York: Harper & Row, 1986), pp. 34–37.

26. Robert J. Gordon, "Using Monetary Control to Dampen the Business Cycle: A New Set of First Principles," National Bureau of Economic Research Working Paper, No. 1210 (October 1983), p. 25.

27. See Robert J. Barro, *Modern Business Cycle Theory* (Cambridge, Massachusetts: Harvard University Press, 1989), p. 2.

28. For a critical review of the new business cycle literature, see N. Gregory Mankiw, "Real Business Cycles: A Keynesian Perspective," *Journal of Economic Perspectives*, 3 (Summer 1989): p. 79.

29. Klamer, *Conversations with Economists, op. cit.*, p. 49.

30. *Ibid.*, pp. 76–77.

31. The story is related by Clifton Fadiman, *Any Number Can Play* (Cleveland: World Publishing, 1957).

13

ECONOMIC GROWTH AND TECHNOLOGY: SCHUMPETER AND CAPITALISM'S MOTION

The atmosphere of industrial revolution—of progress— is the only atmosphere in which capitalism can survive.

—Joseph A. Schumpeter, Konjunkturzyklen II, 1961

Though booms and busts have characterized capitalism, its trajectory has been generally upward. Considerations of the historical path of real output involve the study of economic growth, the rate at which real output grows over historical time.

We open with a discussion of economic growth from those who extended Keynes' General Theory to economic growth. These early followers were soon overtaken by neoclassical theories of growth. The preference of one to the other seemed to depend on the perceived stability of economies over long time periods. Somewhere beyond the horizon of either of these approaches was Joseph Schumpeter's theory of capitalist motion. Living during the same era as John Maynard Keynes, Schumpeter considered himself to be a worthy rival. As we will discover, in many respects, his boasts were not empty.

POST KEYNESIAN ECONOMIC GROWTH THEORY

Roy Harrod, Keynes's friend, originated an economic growth version of Keynes's business cycle theory. Extended by Lord Nicholas Kaldor, this dynamic vision of the longer run was on the grand scale of Malthus, Ricardo, and Marx. Consistent with Kalecki's and Sraffa's constructions, the number of workers per machine in any particular industry remains constant. This glueing of workers to machines is important: The "old-fashioned" neoclassical substitution of capital for labor has gone the way of the Model A, but, as it turns out, not for long.

Harrod, sharing the stage with Esvey Domar at MIT, dramatized something underplayed by Keynes. With respect to the investment multiplier, Keynes neglected to mention that continuous investment augments the capacity of firms to produce goods because it adds to machines and plants. In order, therefore, to warrant this extra capacity, it is not enough to experience a one-time increase in investment of a fixed amount.

Investment, as much a reservoir for "supply" in the Harrod-Domar view as it is a source of demand in Keynes's view, must grow at a sufficient rate to generate enough (multiplied) income to buy (given the propensity to consume) enough goods to warrant the available equipment and plant. Otherwise, plants and equipment will not be fully utilized. IBM must not only build and equip a new plant, it (or a firm in another industry) must build a second plant, lest the demand for office equipment be inadequate to justify the first plant, leaving Big Blue simply singing the blues.

As harmless as the Harrod-Domar theme might sound, it raised a perplexing question about the future of capitalism. The dueling banjos of investment, thrumming demand *and* industrial capacity, play a discordant refrain of inherently unstable capitalism. A dynamic yet stable economy depended on an unlikely syncopation—demand and the industrial capacity to satisfy it expanding at the same pace. Following on the dirge of the Great Depression, the Harrod-Domar discordance continues to play the darker side of capitalism, its tendency toward bust and boom.

In Kaldor's version of the Post Keynesian growth model, the stability of capitalism depends on full employment and flexible profit margins. Otherwise, the economy would be, as with Harrod-Domar, on the edge of the abyss. A rise in investment, and thus in total demand, would raise profit margins (and prices), and hence diminish consumption, whereas a fall in investment, and thus in total demand, reduces prices relative to wages and thereby leads to a rise in real consumption. Capitalism is stable at full employment. But, of course, if spasms of unemployment characterize capitalism's contrapuntal theme, any theory (including the neoclassical, *assuming* harmonious full employment as labor markets dutifully clear) is of limited usefulness.

THE NEOCLASSICAL GROWTH THEORY

A combo of American economists in the mid-1950s wrote a new, neoclassical orchestration with themes the opposite of those of Harrod, Domar, and Kaldor. The new virtuoso was Robert Solow.[1] Solow in the front row and Paul Samuelson in the second forsook the chorus about production taking place at fixed proportions of capital and labor. In a return to neoclassical growth rendition, the interest rate and wage rates are flexible and capital and labor easily substitutable, one for the other, depending on whether a low interest rate favors capital investment or a low wage rate favors bringing labor off the back row. These substitutions are sufficiently fine that the economy never really diverges from its stable path. Thus, the knife-edge threat to capitalistic stability is dulled by a new arrangement.

Neoclassical growth theory soothed the nerves of Harrod-Domar-Kaldor readers by showing how changes in labor's wage and capital's price would keep the capitalist economy on a path of steady growth. The economy could be compared to a long-distance jogger who never changes pace and yet runs forever. Neoclassical growth theory still dominated macrodynamics in the late 1970s: The theory, like the economy, had the endurance of the long-distance runner.

Solow, whose Nobel Prize was for his contributions to the theory of economic growth, first followed the echoes left by Harrod and Domar. His discomfort came from their use of the saving rate, the rate of growth of the labor force, and the ratio of capital used to the amount of output as given by nature. Since economies would have an unsteady growth path, the history of capitalism would be one of long periods of worsening unemployment and long periods of worsening labor shortages. Worse, a small departure from steady growth would be magnified perpetually by entrepreneurial behavior.

Solow's main contribution to growth theory was to introduce the theme of technological flexibility. There were a variety of compositions for total production prior to factories and equipment being put into place. Only thereafter do such production techniques become fixed, as indeed they are. The degree of intensity with which capital is utilized in production can vary over time and is a source of great flexibility for capitalist (or socialist) economies. It turns out that the permanent growth of output per unit of labor input (productivity) is independent of the saving and the investment rate. Rather, productivity growth depends solely on technological progress in a broad sense.

As with fiscal Keynesianism, this neoclassical growth model had practical implications. It provided a framework within which macroeconomic policies can be used to sustain full employment. Solow's ideas were written into the 1962 *Economic Report* of the President (Kennedy). Admittedly, however, steady growth depended upon tranquil conditions, the conditions prevailing during the late 1950s and early 1960s. As Solow has written, "the hard part of disequilibrium growth is that we do not have—and it may be impossible to have—a really good theory of asset valuation under turbulent conditions."[2] He made that observation near the end of 1987, shortly after the stock market crash of October.

The quite practical idea of "growth accounting" emanated from Solow's theory of the growth process. Economist Edward Denison used this device to study economic growth in the United States.[3] Real output grew at an annual rate of 2.9 percent in the U.S. during

1929 to 1982. Denison estimated that 32 percent, or about a third of this growth, was due to increases in the amounts of labor.

The other sources of growth are those things that raise labor productivity. Denison estimated that 14 percent of the growth was due to increased education of the labor force. In turn, capital formation accounted for slightly less than a fifth of U.S. growth. Technological change (Solow's focus) accounted for 28 percent of the growth. Denison included new technological knowledge (e.g., ways to employ robots in the production process) as well as new ways to organize businesses (managerial strategies) as technological advances. Since at a given technology, greater amounts of inputs seemed to cause more than a proportional increase in output, Denison estimated that nine percent of U.S. growth came from economies of scale. Finally, other elements such as the effects of weather on farm output and work stoppages had a net negative effect equal to two percent of economic growth. Though Denison had a slightly longer list of sources of growth than did Solow, his results did not conflict with Solow's initial estimates. Technology remains the capitalist engine for growth, with human capital investment following about mid-way in the train. Solow concludes, "we have not learned enough yet about how countries grow."[4]

THE PROBLEM WITH HISTORICAL ECONOMIC GROWTH

The Post Keynesian and the neoclassical growth theories provide an incomplete orchestration of the historical pageant of a capitalistic economy. The mix of output as well as the composition for producing it (technology) do change.[5] Although production techniques and the amount of labor used with machines may remain the same for several years or even for decades during stagnation in an industry, other industries may be switching to different compositions. Steel was slow to go to the oxygen conversion process, but movie studios were quick to adopt animation. It is likely that any new techniques will exhibit different mixes of inputs. For example, the switch by the steel industry reduced the labor required in the production of steel; but animation in movies required more labor.

Solow at once sensed that technology gets "embodied" in new factories, equipment, and tools. Yet Denison did not find any evidence of that effect.[6] In data of growth over very long time periods, a faster growth rate in investment spending does seem to lead to faster technological progress. Common sense would suggest this since laboratory technology produces nothing until it is embodied in a factory process.

In truth, American economic growth between 1850 and 2000 has not been at a steady pace. There have been deep recessions, money panics, the Great Depression, the great stagnation of the 1970s, and the hyper-speculation in securities during the 1980s and 1990s. Still, the growth pace was fairly steady during the 1950s and the 1960s. Explaining different eras may require different models. Moreover, not only Solow but Harrod-Domar cannot make claims to a complete explanation of the dynamics of capitalism.

As we look across the economic landscape, we see some entire industries in decline, some booming, and some simply marking time. New products give rise to new firms and even to new industries. The widespread use of the personal computer was undreamed of less than a decade and a half ago; it has become a growth industry already in sight of modern maturity. In the United States, the textile industry is in decline, but the leisure-time industry is on the upswing; people are having a good time even with fewer clothes. All this is to say that the kinds of technologies will vary drastically as we look at different industries. Moreover, there will be an uneasy coexistence between high-tech firms and the backward and inefficient firms that pay lower wages while earning lower profits. Some older-technology firms will escape lower profits by using the same technologies in emerging nations, paying much lower native wages, and importing the goods at higher prices and profits. The later has become known as the global economy.

How then does technological advance team up with growth in the national income? New technologies remain abstractions—and Solow is generally correct about this—unless they are somehow embodied in new equipment and processes of production. Technology is transformed into factories through doses of investment. The absorption of technological change in this fashion will be more rapid the greater the share of national income devoted to expenditures for real capital formation (investment). If the evidence is sparse on this connection, it may be because economists have been looking under the wrong lamp post.

As we shift focus to the very long run, we see how capitalism's stage of historical development critically alters the amplitude of the business cycle. As an entree, we turn to one of the most neglected of the great economists.

JOSEPH ALOIS SCHUMPETER

Joseph Alois Schumpeter (1883–1950) was born the year of John Maynard Keynes's birth and of Karl Marx's death. We have ignored him until now because only recently has his ideas gained a new appreciation and relevance. The ideas of this second-generation Austrian who considered himself superior to John Maynard Keynes and who had an ego the match of Ayn Rand's will provide a surprise ending to what was, in the beginning, a Keynesian story.

Earlier, other Austrians had defined the psychology that undergirds the theory of capital and entrepreneurship, where entrepreneurs outperform the masses in mental power and energy. Generally, the neo-Austrian's insight into entrepreneurship sees such humans as not only calculating agents but also as keenly alert to opportunities "just around the corner." Still, these agents seem more cunning than productive, more opportunistic than constructive.

Schumpeter's entrepreneur has more substance. Schumpeter elevated the role of capitalism's entrepreneur to the highest plane—to be the central force in capitalistic development. Despite this, he came to the same gloomy conclusion as Marx, namely, that capitalism was doomed. Unlike Marx, Schumpeter decried the self-destructive tendencies inherent in capitalism but nonetheless envisioned it being superseded by a workable socialism.

No doubt Schumpeter's grief was more over the euthanasia of the entrepreneur than that of capitalism itself, even though there was nothing wrong with capitalism that reincarnation would not cure. Various research efforts continue to flow from Schumpeter's theory of capitalism, but the neo-Austrians, who have inherited the Austrians' mantel, have kept Schumpeter at a respectful distance, perhaps because of the volatile mixture of his respect for Marx and his pessimism regarding the future of capitalism.

Born in Triesch, Moravia, now part of Slovakia, Schumpeter was the only child of a cloth manufacturer and a physician's daughter, a bourgeois family of little distinction. A typical Austrian mixture of the many nationalities that lived in the Austro-Hungarian Empire, Schumpeter grew up in the aristocratic milieu of prewar Vienna.

Schumpeter's father died when the lad was only four years old. Thereafter, Schumpeter was left in the care of his adoring mother, who had great ambitions for herself and for Joseph. When six years later she married Lieutenant Field Marshall Sigmund von Keler, some 30 years her senior. His "Excellenz" provided the ticket for Schumpeter's entry into the Theresianum, an exclusive school for the sons of the aristocracy, which he attended from 1893 to 1901. The Theresianum was to Schumpeter what Professor Henry Higgins was to Eliza Doolittle, except Schumpeter adopted the ego and bad temper of Higgins.

Then, from 1901 to 1906, Schumpeter studied law and economics at the University of Vienna. While there, he studied under Friedrich von Wieser (1851–1926) and Eugen von Böhm-Bawerk (1851–1914) (who had ignited the "Austrian tradition"), even while learning from the most brilliant young Marxists of the day. Ludwig von Mises (1881–1973), a diligent student of Wieser's and Böhm-Bawerk's, found his way to Great Britain and, later, to the United States. He charmed Ayn Rand and she recommended him to admirers of her philosophy. Rand's efforts enabled von Mises to reach his potential audience.

Vienna has been described as one of the most pleasant places on Earth during the closing years of the Hapsburg epoch of the Austro-Hungarian Empire, at least for those as properly endowed and trained as Schumpeter. To the end, Schumpeter remained outwardly the cultivated, autocratic, egocentric Austrian gentleman of the old school who found from 1914 onward little evidence of progress in civilization.

After several appointments in continental Europe, in 1932 Schumpeter moved permanently to Harvard University. Although he enjoyed international fame, he was overshadowed by John Maynard Keynes, whose ideas were gaining ascendancy at Harvard during the Great Depression. Schumpeter understandably was hypersensitive to any invidious comparison with Keynes.

Schumpeter's outward gaiety hid his inward depression. He could have spent some time on Sigmund Freud's (1856–1939) couch in Vienna, perhaps to the great benefit of both. Outwardly, Schumpeter was affable but arrogant. He wore horse-riding regalia, complete with riding crop, to his Harvard lectures. At the beginning of the lecture, he would slowly take off his riding gloves, one finger at a time, much as a exotic stripper would, and drape them across the riding crop. Then, although given to ex cathedra pronouncements, he would nonetheless give extraordinarily popular lectures.

Schumpeter was a short, dark, and dramatic-looking man and often said his great ambition was to be the greatest economist, the greatest lover, and the finest horseman in Austria. And, he said, he had accomplished two of the three. Apparently, Schumpeter was not the finest horseman, for he was a libertine who pursued adultery with uncommon passion and claimed himself, not Keynes, to be the *world's* greatest economist. His seeking of adulatory recognition—in and out of bed—apparently was a manifestation of or defense against an inferiority complex. Schumpeter suffered chronic depression, hypochondria, and a sense of inadequacy. He apparently tried to conceal how little he thought of himself while revealing how little he thought of others.

He was, at one time or another, elitist, racist, anti-semitic, eugenicist, and fascist, although never completely so. He took pains with the average Harvard students just as he did with the most gifted. He was outraged when Paul Samuelson was denied an appointment at Harvard because he was Jewish. And, although never having divorced his first wife, the aristocratic poseur fell in love with and married in November 1925 Annie Reisinger, a working-class woman half his age. Tragically, Annie died in childbirth ten months later, and Schumpeter's mother had died the previous June. He was both a scientist and a romantic (not that unusual in Vienna) and thereafter practiced as a psychic a private religion based upon his deceased second wife and his mother.[7]

Belatedly, in 1948, two years before his death and during a period of his blackest moods and worst behavior, Schumpeter became president of the American Economic Association. His contemporary role in economics would have been enhanced had he accepted those Keynesian ideas user-friendly to his business cycle theory. He stubbornly resisted this, however, in deference to himself as the grander economist.

Schumpeter was an unhappy, troubled person, like so many historic figures who have ascended above their emotional difficulties to remarkable achievements. According to Robert Heilbroner, Schumpeter's personal life adds coherence to what is otherwise a puzzling social perspective. His elitist conception of society makes Schumpeter, the visionary, a part of his vision. "It is his self-vindication."[8] Now, fittingly, we turn to the man's titanic genius.

SCHUMPETER'S THEORY OF CAPITALIST MOTION

In Schumpeter's theory of capitalism, the entrepreneur is the agent of economic change—a grander, more dramatic figure than the persona usually described by the Austrians. As an innovator, the entrepreneur does much more than take advantage of price movements; the entrepreneur creates entire industries. This heroic figure seems more like the knight of chivalry. Such a romantic figure comes even closer to the grim, domineering man of action—the Roark, Rearden, and Galt invented by Ayn Rand and stereotyped by actor Gary Cooper.

In *Atlas Shrugged*, Ayn Rand describes the first pouring of Rearden Metal, a new alloy, much harder than steel:

> He stood leaning against a column, watching. The [red] glare cut a moment's wedge across his eyes, which had the color and quality of pale blue ice—then across the black web of the metal column and the ash-blond strands of his hair—then across the belt of his trenchcoat and the pockets where he held his hands. His body was tall and gaunt; he had always been too tall for those around him.... He was Hank Rearden.[9]

Rearden is the entrepreneur, literally the Man of Steel, Schumpeter's Superman. Schumpeter, however, would have described his hero as a man much shorter.

The heroic task of Shumpeter's superhero is to ignite an industry that keeps capitalism on a generally upward path for a half century. Schumpeter did not deny other cycles; there was an inventory cycle of short duration, an investment cycle in which the pendulum swung back and forth for a seven- to 11-year duration, and a long wave sparked by breakthrough inventions like the steamship, locomotive, or automobile. To Schumpeter, the cycles within cycles of capitalism, each unhappily reaching its respective bottom at the same time as the others during the 1929 to 1933 period explained the Great Depression.[10] The three cycles reaching their nadirs could explain much of the debacle of the 1930s. The recession beginning in August 1929 looked like the result of accumulated and unsold inventories; as Keynes discovered, business investment collapsed during the 1930s; and the once innovative automobile industry had become a mature industry, ending a long wave.

In Schumpeter's vista, the long wave is spread over roughly a half century. Schumpeter linked the first long wave—starting in the late 1780s and ending in the 1840s—to the development, in England, of steam power and textile manufacturing. This era emcompassed the Industrial Revolution (see Chapter 3). Schumpeter connected the second wave—continuing to the end of the nineteenth century—to railroads and iron and steel. It included the era of the robber barons. The third long wave—perhaps ending during the 1930s—was charged by electricity and supercharged by the automobile.[11]

Robert Heilbroner, a student in one of Schumpeter's classes at Harvard, suggests, however, that Schumpeter was ambivalent toward the Great Depression. "After removing his long cloak with a flourish, [Schumpeter] told us in heavily accented English: 'Chentlemen, a depression iss for capitalism like a good cold douche'—a statement whose shock value lay not only in the unthinkable sentiment that the Depression had its uses, but in the fact that very few of us knew that a douche was the Europeans' term for a shower."[12] What was happening to industry during a depression was, to Schumpeter, "creative destruction."

In Schumpeter's beginning of the cycle, there is no depression, though there is stagnation. In this stationary condition of "Walrasian equilibrium," there is no extraordinary opportunity for profits; only a circular flow of economic activity takes place, and the system merely reproduces itself. The extraordinary person, the entrepreneur, daringly raids the circular flow and diverts labor and land to investment. Since savings are inadequate for such ventures, the entrepreneur must be provided credit created by the bankers as the capitalists.

Since only the more enterprising and venturesome persons act, innovations appear in "swarms." The innovations include setting up new production functions, techniques, organizational forms, and products. Even though they stand above the reluctant crowd, the heroic entrepreneurs create favorable conditions for other, less venturesome businesspersons to follow. These activities bring growth to the circular flow as well as rents (super-profits) to the temporary monopolists, the entrepreneurial elite. This glowing business prosperity is enhanced by the creation and expenditure of new incomes.

The boom, however, limits itself as, paradoxically, innovations contribute to the downswing. The competition of new products with old ones causes business losses even as rising prices deter investment. Entrepreneurs use the proceeds of the sale of their new products to repay indebtedness and, in this way, bring deflation. The depression results from the slow process of adaptation to innovation and from this secondary deflation. When adaptation to the innovations is complete, deflation ends and Walrasian equilibrium is restored.

In equilibrium, a time when all vital signs are stable, there is little cause for capitalism to suffer cardiac arrest. Left to itself, capitalism even has "trickle-down" benefits—Schumpeter told his students at Harvard how "The capitalist achievement does not typically consist in providing more silk stockings for queens but in bringing them within the reach of factory girls for steadily decreasing amounts of effort." The presence of innovations helps to explain why new industries with these new products for the masses emerge and old ones—with great reluctance and stubborn resistance—die.

It is industrial concentration—the rise of big, stubborn, and bureaucratic business—that weakens capitalism. The early monopoly of the individual, venturesome entrepreneur who makes the breakthrough and corners the market is always acceptable to society. However, the maturing of an industry into a gigantic monopoly generates the political and social attitudes that ultimately destroy it. Andrew Carnegie (like Rearden in *Atlas Shrugged*) was a majestic figure, but the United States Steel Corporation cast a foreboding shadow of death across the face of capitalism. The growth of giant business deprives capitalism of its individual and wonderfully gifted entrepreneurs even as it makes itself vulnerable to political and social assault. The bourgeois eventually would attack private property with as much force as it once used against popes and kings.

In contrast, for the other neo-Austrians private property prevails—as it does for Ayn Rand. In *Atlas Shrugged*, John Galt gives the longest speech (60 pages) ever made in celebration of the victory of private property over collectivism.

But in Schumpeter, even though New Deal nostrums could sustain "capitalism in the oxygen tent" by artificial means—paralyzed in those functions that had guaranteed past glories—inevitably the beneficiary of capitalism's fatal disease was socialism. Socialism would work because it would be run by the same elite that ran capitalism. Whereas most neo-Austrianism wears blinders to giant business, Schumpeter's singular prophecy for capitalism is Marx's denouement; like the Biblical whale that saved Jonah, capitalism is swallowed by the state in order to save it.

THE PRODUCT CYCLE: SCHUMPETER EXTENDED

Although Schumpeter treated demand with nonbenign neglect, he nonetheless saw some branches of industry flourishing while other branches floundered. Schumpeter's "process of creative destruction" is evolutionary, with firms and industries coming into existence, growing, declining, and disappearing. This process is characterized by structural change, not only in the composition of output but throughout economic life. The very long run is one of industrial evolution or even revolution.

Schumpeter's "process of creative destruction" can be extended by introducing the idea of the product cycle.[13] Products have a sales life cycle, and satiation in product markets (contrary to the neoclassicals) takes place. Initially, a product innovation coming from one of Schumpeter's entrepreneurs will be sold to a handful of consumer pioneers, often the richest families. Since a new product is usually very expensive to develop, its introductory price will be very high. However, if a middle-income class exists, the product (like the Apple Computer) is gradually diffused among a larger and larger number of families.

When the product hits Main Street, the sales growth is exponential; the product "takes off." Any market is limited only by its human population and the distribution of income. As Jan Barrett once put it, "Veni, vidi, Visa. (*We came, we saw, we went shopping.*)" When virtually every family of the society has at least one of the "new products," the market is satiated. This product cycle looks like a flattened S and is often called, appropriately enough, the product S-curve. "S" might as well stand for Schumpeter.

Mass production eventually turns the emulator's gold into fool's gold. When products are sufficiently diffused throughout the society, they can be standardized in gigantic factories (as in the steel, automotive, and beer industries) and produced with a large-scale technology that yields low prices. Not only does everyone have at least one of the once-prized possessions, the products all begin to look alike. Surely, clever manufacturers and advertising agencies can postpone mass realization of sameness, although eventually the cause becomes hopeless, especially when all opportunities for real as opposed to imaginary product "improvements" have been made.

The picture reception of the first TV, a black-and-white, was roughly as good as that provided by the window of a front-loading washing machine. Then the quality of the picture and its size were enhanced. Color was added even as the TV set became a carefully crafted, elegant piece of furniture. Eventually the size of the picture could be further increased only with a severe loss in its clarity. TV sets all began to look alike. More important, the U.S. family having fewer than three sets was viewed as impoverished (economically, though perhaps intellectually as well). The market was sated, the price elasticity of demand was low, and the top of the TV product curve was in sight. The middle class awaits hi-definition TV, the latest innovation.

Economic development brings standardized technology even as it increases the complexity of the overall production system. In the agrarian society, generic goods from the land, such as raw potatoes mashed or sliced at home, are the only goods required in consumption. Value added or the difference between the value of sales and the costs of production (and therefore economic surplus) does not exist because goods are not marketed. In contrast, the supra-surplus society, as I have called it,[14] relies on a highly interdependent production system in which a longer and longer chain of suppliers supply each other—adding layer upon layer of value added—until the final product emerges.

A middle class that loses its way in Schumpeter is essential in providing a product market size sufficient to warrant large-scale standardized technology. Thus, income levels and the number of households with those incomes are related to the size of the firms and industries producing goods and services. Household budgets define the overall size of the market for a product, so that the technology is not entirely independent of the size of the market afforded by income levels and populations.

On first commercial introduction (with the initial technology), for example, household personal computers appeared only in the budgets of the very rich. Suppose the introductory average production cost for the personal computer was $10,000, and 1,000 households included the computer in their budgets that year. At a ten percent markup over production costs, a sales revenue of $11 million is forecast for a monopoly corporate producer. After production costs, the producer is left with $1 million profit (more accurately, quasi-rent), which can be used for further investment. After selling the 10,000 household computers during the first year of production, the producer uses a portion of the revenue to conduct market research on the potential for expanding the market. The producer finds that if the price of the computer could be lowered by 50 percent, a slightly lower income class of 4,000 could be enticed into the market. If the producer could devise a way to cut production costs in half, 5,000 computers (4,000 + 1,000) could now be sold at a unit price of $5000, for a total revenue of $27.5 million ($2.5 million in markups).

With diligent basic research, the company's engineers emerge with a new patent on an improved memory chip for a computer that can be produced with less labor and fewer expensive parts. The corporation sells additional common stock, issues more bonds, or borrows funds from its bank to equip its plants for the production of the Model II household computer. With successful Model II sales, the firm can now rely on its profits flow for any new investment.

This example illustrates the general case rather than the exceptional one. Plant size is usually decided by the lowest-cost technology. Given technology, even the smallest plant may be too large for the market. If so, the plant will not be built until incomes, budgets, and population warrant it. In some cases, the smallest plant is gigantic, and its level of production may absorb all the revenue available for the particular product. The telephone companies, regional monopolies, ring those chimes. Nor is it accidental that the American movie industry is dominated by only four to six major studios. With the advent of the giant corporation and corporate planning, according to John Kenneth Galbraith, "there is no clear upper limit to the desirable size."[15]

INNOVATIONS AND THE PRODUCT CYCLE

The idea of a cycle over the cycles or a Schumpeterian long wave of a half century is at once more pessimistic and more optimistic than the gestalt of the American Keynesians. The long wave appears smooth over time. This is an illusion, for, if we look at data points over a sufficiently long historical epoch, they are "stretched out" so much that the appearance is one of continuity. Yet the historical reality is quite different: The world economic crises of 1825, 1873, and 1929 were a bit more like falling off cliffs than gliding through gentle valleys. Moreover, the ups and downs of the 1970s, 1980s, and the 1990s are enough to give continuity a bad name.

Karl Marx depicted the crises of capitalism as cataclysmic. Much more recently, another German economist, Gerhard Mensch, has taken his lead from Schumpeter but favors the pattern of the discontinuous path of capitalism.[16] Mensch's model, which he calls the metamorphosis model, is based upon the product cycle or product S-curve.

In the metamorphosis model, long periods of growth are interrupted by relatively short intervals of turbulence. Despite these breaks and upheavals over time and the variation in tempo of change, there is a regularity that conforms with the S-curves of those industrial complexes that lead the particular expansion. Mensch's view can be modified to show that general economic progress can be extended over several centuries despite the sharp disruptions.

Innovations can be either of the product variety, such as laser disc recordings, or of the production-process kind, such as computer-assisted design (CAD) of automobiles or aircraft. In turn, Mensch has made useful distinctions among various kinds of innovations.[17]

The production of electricity (1800), the first use of the coke blast furnace (1796), the first commercial use of photography (1838), the production of the jet engine (1928), and the production of nylon (1927) were basic technological innovations. These basic technological innovations, of course, do not emerge from thin air. An inventory of scientific discoveries and inventions exists at any time; this inventory is the outcome of an intellectual tradition of idea development, the construction of new scientific theories, and the transfer of knowledge. The time lag between inventions and their commercial application often is very long but variable.

The development of neoprene, a synthetic rubber, provides Mensch with an interesting example of a six-stage innovation process that begins with the development of a new theory (perception).[18] In 1906, Julius A. Nieuwland observed the acetylene reaction in alkali medium and worked for more than ten years to obtain a higher-yielding reaction (invention). In 1921, Nieuwland showed that his material, a polymer, can be manufactured through a catalytic reaction (feasibility). In 1925, Dr. E.K. Bolton of duPont attended a lecture by Nieuwland at the American Chemical Society; duPont took over the further commercial development of the "rubber" material (development). Finally, more than a quarter century after its invention, the synthetic rubber is marketed as a new product by E.I. duPont de Nemours and Company (basic innovation). Today, in the advanced industrialized economies, synthetic rubber is at or past the top of its product S-curve; the product and the industry are now mature.

The remarkable contribution of Mensch is to provide data suggesting that basic innovations do occur in swarms, as Schumpeter claimed; and, importantly for contemporary supra-surplus capitalism, the frequency of the most recent swarm of basic innovations peaked in 1935 (in the middle of the Great Depression!). If the average product lifecycle—from basic innovation to maturity—is a half century, a large share of the 1935-centered swarm would reach maturity, or the top of their S-curves, in 1985. If so, the overall real gross domestic product (GDP) takes on an S-curve configuration that is flat by 1985. Observed satiation in automotive, airline, household appliances, and even housing markets bolsters the idea that stagnation best describes the condition of the advanced industrialized economies—Great Britain, Western Europe, Northern Europe, the United States, and Japan—by 1985.

The innovations from the 1825, 1886, and 1935 swarms epitomize much of what Americans still consider modern today. In 1825, we find the locomotive, Portland cement, insulated wiring, and the puddling furnace; in 1886, the steam turbine, the transformer, resistance welding, the gasoline motor, Thomas steel, aluminum, chemical fertilizer, electrolysis, radar, synthetic detergents, titanium, and—to make rapid change more tolerable—the radio and cocaine; finally, in 1935 appears nylon, perlon, polyethylene, xerography, continuous steelcasting, and—to make recessions more endurable—cinerama.

The effects of such innovations are not always predictable. Computers have led to the Internet. The Internet has led to electronic mass marketing of some products. The World Wide Web has connected global financial markets. New information, good and bad, is instantly available to virtually every person on the planet. This could be the beginning of a new long wave but its fruition might be delayed, just as the markets for innovations from the 1920s were postponed.

STAGNATION AND STAGFLATION: THE LONG VIEW

Stagnation from market saturation and inflation may be two sides of the same coin; at least this is Mensch's claim. Stagnation no doubt describes the condition of the main branches of industry in the advanced industrialized countries since the late 1960s. In automobiles, the leading U.S. industry in the post-World War II era, the Otto-cycle engine still used is more than a century old. The last major innovation related to this engine, the automatic transmission, was widely diffused a generation ago. During much of the post-World War II era, appearance superseded function in the automotive industry.

Basic steel-making technology has not changed greatly since the nineteenth century, despite enormous increases in the scale of steel-making plants and despite the efforts of the fictional Hank Rearden. In the basic chemical industry, the techniques for making nitric acid, sulfuric acid, ammonia, nitrate fertilizer, and other industrial chemicals were being used prior to World War I, even though the scale of plants has greatly expanded.

The "flation" part of stagflation comes from sustained price explosions. Such explosions have occurred three times in the past

700 years: The first in the sixteenth century, a second in the eighteenth, and a third beginning around 1890. The last episode has been the most dramatic by far. The magnitude of the latest inflationary wave may be a result of social innovations such as the giant corporation, the industrial union, modern marketing techniques, and highly flexible financial institutions, plus the various floors placed under incomes and prices by government programs since the Great Depression. This inflationary wave appears to have ended with the widespread phenomena of transnational business firms producing in low-wage developing nations. Deflation characterized much of the global economy by the early 1990s.

One way of summarizing these causes of long wave inflation collapsing into spasms of deflation, is increased complexity in the supra-surplus economies. In other terms, each additional layer adds its own overhead and other costs. As David Warsh has described it, modern marketing (which, of course, did not exist in the sixteenth and eighteenth centuries) had a lot to do with rising costs (prices) from increased complexity.[19] Globalization became the escape route from rising production costs utilized by the supra-surplus economies.

Perhaps if the supra-surplus economies were not suffering the affliction of many product cycles peaking more or less at the same time, the expansion in private and public credit would have fueled a sustainable expansion in real output. As things stand (or stagnate), industrial concentration, complexity, technological stagnation, inflation, recession, and deflation—this collection of terms describes supra-surplus industrial societies between the late 1960s and the early 1990s. Mensch pictures a technological stalemate because of sated markets and the petering out of the last swarm of innovations in the former West Germany. Japan became, along with the United States, a highly speculative "bubble economy" during the 1980s. After the bursting of the bubble, Japan has since suffered a long depression that began in stock and real estate price deflations.

The economy at the end of its long expansion sees the number of industrial branches peaking exceeding those beginning with basic innovations. The rising sunset-to-sunrise ratio of industries means bankruptcies and liquidation of assets; groups whose income and wealth are threatened will circle their wagons at sunset. Producer coalitions demand even more subsidies and protection from foreign imports, and labor groups become even more recalcitrant in their demands for job security.

What Mancur Olson has described as "rent-seeking" coalitions can be viewed as organized efforts to avoid the income-reducing effects of stagnation or competition, be the competition in product or labor markets.[20] When technology is sufficient to create a surplus and inputs are complementary, it is very difficult, perhaps impossible, for even a free market to assign "marginal products" to the appropriate persons, for labor and capital goods are equally necessary.[21] And yet the surplus must be divided by some rule.

If coalitions as "rent-seekers" design the rules, the income distribution is decided by their powers. As long as the growth rates of wages and labor population do not exceed that of "productivity," the rent-seekers divide the surplus without creating much inflation. This could describe the first half of the long-wave expansion. Only when the swarm of innovations has been widely diffused do the rent-seekers contribute to stagflation.

Those who would tell a different story of growth need to explain the complex development of two latter-day American growth industries—photocopying and computers. The Xerox Corporation, dominating the former industry, owes its incredible growth to the improvement of its original Model 914 copier. Xerox went from cumbersome, expensive models to ones that could serve the needs of both the one-person office and the largest corporation.

Xerox's sibling, IBM, has utterly transformed business and government through the use of computers. In the final three decades of the twentieth century, IBM's technology went through four generations; each successive technology increased the capacity, reliability, and speed of information processing. In turn, the cost per calculation was reduced, expanding the market for computers to small businesses and to households.

These two industries no longer rely solely on photocopying and computers for their sales growth. New growth potential must be sought on new frontiers of technology.

Joseph Schumpeter no doubt would be pleased to know of his new-found relevance and of the importance of his ideas in recent economic writings. Or at least his outward gaiety would lead us to think so, even as his posturing would hide his troubled inner world.

NOTES

1. Robert M. Solow's seminal articles are "A Contribution to the Theory of Economic Growth," *Quarterly Journal of Economics* 70 (1956): 65–94, and "Technical Change and the Aggregate Production Function," *Review of Economics and Statistics*, August 1957.
2. Robert M. Solow, "Growth Theory and After," Nobel lecture, December 8, 1987, in *Nobel Lectures, Economic Sciences, 1981–1990*, ed. Karl-Göran Mäler (Singapore/New Jersey/London/Hong Kong: World Scientific, 1992), p. 203.
3. See Edward F. Denison, *Trends in American Economic Growth, 1929–82* (Washington, D.C.: The Brookings Institution, 1985), p. 30.
4. Interview with Robert Solow, *Challenge: The Magazine of Economic Affairs*, January–February 2000, p. 13.
5. See, for example, Joan Robinson, "Keynes and Ricardo," *Journal of Post Keynesian Economics* 1 (Fall 1978): 16–18.
6. Solow soon took such embodiment of technology into account in a model in which capital had different "ages." See Robert M. Solow, "Investment and Technical Progress," in *Mathematical Methods in the Social Sciences*, eds. K. Arrow, S. Karlin, and P. Suppes (Stanford, CA: Stanford University Press, 1960).
7. For in-depth insights into Schumpeter's life of tormented inconsistency, see Robert Loring Allen, *Opening Doors: The Life and Work of Joseph Schumpeter* (New Brunswick and London: Transaction Publishers, 1992), and Richard Swedberg, *Schumpeter: A Biography* (Princeton: Princeton University Press, 1992).
8. Robert Heilbroner, "His Secret Life," *The New York Review of Books*, May 14, 1992, p. 31.
9. Ayn Rand, *Atlas Shrugged* (New York: Random House, 1957), p. 28.
10. See Joseph A. Schumpeter, *Business Cycles* (New York: McGraw-Hill, 1939).
11. Harvard's Simon Kuznets's Nobel Prize in economics is partly related to his collaboration with Schumpeter in identifying in historical detail the three long

waves. See Simon Kuznets, *Economic Change* (New York: W.W. Norton & Co., 1953).

12. Heilbroner, *op. cit.*, p. 27.

13. What follows is a brief version of a more extended discussion first presented in E. Ray Canterbery, *The Making of Economics*, 3rd ed. (Belmont: Wadsworth, 1987) [soon to appear in a 4th ed. (River View, New Jersey/London/Singapore: World Scientific, 2001)], modified by the further development of those ideas as presented in E. Ray Canterbery, "A Theory of Supra-Surplus Capitalism," Presidential Address, *Eastern Economic Journal* 13 (December 1988): 315–332.

14. Canterbery, "A Theory of Supra-Surplus Capitalism," *op. cit.*

15. John Kenneth Galbraith, *The New Industrial State* (Boston: Houghton Mifflin, 1967), p. 76.

16. Gerhard O. Mensch, *Stalemate in Technology* (Cambridge, Massachusetts: Ballinger, 1979).

17. *Ibid.*, pp. 47–50.

18. *Ibid.*, p. 192.

19. David Warsh, *The Idea of Economic Complexity* (New York: Viking Press, 1984), pp. 63–65.

20. See Mancur Olson, *The Rise and Decline of Nations* (New Haven: Yale University Press, 1982), especially pp. 77–98.

21. See Canterbery, "A Theory of Supra-Surplus Capitalism," *op. cit.*

14

THE MANY FACES OF CAPITALISM: GALBRAITH, HEILBRONER, AND THE INSTITUTIONALISTS

It has been the fate of contemporary economists to walk in Isaac Newton's footsteps, reducing economic thought to a machine maximizing Benthamite utility. The calculus is beautiful to behold, the statistics elegant, and the applications confining. In a metaphorical embrace of Newton's universe, economic agents—operating as particles—have displaced the broader social concerns of Adam Smith, Thomas Malthus, Karl Marx, John Stuart Mill, Thorstein Veblen, John Maynard Keynes, Joseph Schumpeter, and even Alfred Marshall. When considering whether narrow-mindedness is wiser than broad-mindedness, we should be thoughtful. Not only are particles devoid of thought, they have no will to organize since, if they are organized, it is by an act of Nature, not of free will.

We cannot ignore free dissent. Dissenters, such as Smith, Malthus, Marx, Mill, Marshall, and Keynes, became the orthodoxy at one time or another. Veblen and the institutionalists missed becoming dominant only by a margin. Of the aforementioned, only Marshall was completely in step with his time, the Victorian Age. We now turn to a handful of the contemporary nay sayers. Though iconoclastic, they all share two characteristics—a passion for explicating the whole economy with a broad social vision, and doing so with masterful prose. In the first respect, they are uniformally critical of those of the orthodoxy, not for their precision or elegance, but for their irrelevance. In the second respect, they, like Veblen, blend art and science by their masterful, inventive use of English prose. The main connection of the contemporary iconoclasts to the past is through Marx and Veblen.

THE INSTITUTIONALIST VISTA

In any storm, as Professor Higgins would attest, it is good to have an umbrella. For iconoclasts, the umbrella best be very large because they are holistic. Since Veblen founded the uniquely American school of institutionalists wherein Galbraith (1976) and Heilbroner (1994) were recipients of their prestigious Veblen-Commons Award, the institutionalist umbrella surely is adequate. Galbraith has long been considered not only a Post Keynesian but an institutionalist. Karl Marx is not without some influence, but generally the institutionalists favor reform movements within an ever-changing capitalism whereas Marx thought capitalism to be a transitory system.

Institutionalists study the society and its economy as part of an entire, organized pattern of social behavior. They are concerned with a culture of customs, social habits, modes of thinking, and ways of living. Such patterns of thought and behavior can be broadly characterized as *institutions;* they need not be housed in building complexes but can include shared beliefs or images, such as chivalry, the Horatio Alger myth, the Puritan ethic, the idea of laissez-faire, and general attitudes toward trade unionism, socialism, or the welfare state.

Veblen's idea of upside-down evolution has provided a theory of social change within economics. From this broader perspective, institutionalists can wonder about the policy implications of attitudinal change. They reject the positive economist's (such as Friedman's) acceptance of "what is" and ask, "How did the economy get to be what it is and where is it leading us?" Their fierce defiance of the orthodoxy is largely rooted in their emphasis on change, which they see to be more basic to economic life than Newtonian equilibria.

Economists sometimes picture Veblen, Galbraith, and Heilbroner as lonely prophets who are little more than minor irritants. Such a picture is out of focus, for they are a part of a uniquely American tradition of social criticism, which rises to the defense of the downtrodden but is restrained in its praise for the privileged. The institutionalists—in the populist tradition—favor liberal, democratic reforms attuned to a more equal distribution of wealth and income. Populism creates controversies that may well reflect clashing value systems such as those between bankers favoring higher interest rates and modest home buyers hoping for lower rates.

The institutionalists have not been so much out-thought as they have been outbred by orthodox PhD-granting universities. The institutionalists—apparently weary of the cold rigor in neoclassical economics—see economic policy evolving within a framework of social, political, legal, historical, and economic perspectives. Ironically, their desire to be relevant makes them sufficiently suspect to be criticized for being irrelevant—to neoclassical theory. In truth, however, the best economists—those secure in their own accomplishments—often come under the spell of the institutionalists. There is a bit of the institutionalist in every good economist.

Five historic figures have dominated the institutionalist school: Veblen, who provided the inspiration and the general framework; Wesley C. Mitchell, who conducted statistical studies of the business cycle, founded the highly regarded National Bureau of Economic Research, and stimulated empirical research in the United States; John R. Commons, who urged the government to legislate economic reforms and greatly influenced the reform-oriented research of the University of Wisconsin's economics department; Clarence Ayres, who wrote of the effect of technological change on the economy and its institutions; and Galbraith.

Today, the institutionalist group calls itself the Association for Evolutionary Economics. It began in 1967 to publish its own journal, the *Journal of Economic Issues,* and has acquired a large following in economics, its articles and authors being among the most generously cited among all academic economics journals.

Since Robert Heilbroner has called attention to the importance not only of defining capitalism but of understanding its transformations, we return to him to find a path back to fundamentals. Thereafter, we turn to John Kenneth Galbraith.

ROBERT HEILBRONER AND THE WORLDLY PHILOSOPHY

Robert Heilbroner was born in New York City into a wealthy German Jewish family. Louis Heilbroner, his father, founded Weber and Heilbroner, a well-known men's clothing retailer between the world wars. A son of privilege, Robert attended Horace Mann School, then an adjunct to Columbia University Teachers' College and a gateway to the Ivy Leagues. How a rich kid developed a great concern for social justice and became one of America's most prominent persons of the left as the author of several classics makes for an interesting story.

After his father died when Robert was only five, his family's chauffeur, Willy Gerkin, became his surrogate father. Heilbroner attributes his social conscience to his feelings of indignation when he realized that his mother could give orders to her chauffeur only because his beloved "Willy" needed the money and she had it. "Willy" was an intimate yet "William" was a servant, distinguished only by the formal driver's uniform that he wore.

From the Ivy League, Robert chose Harvard in the propitious year of 1936, a time when the Harvard Economics Department was debating the meaning of Keynes's *General Theory* even as its members were taking Keynesianism to Washington D.C. In his sophomore year, Robert's tutor was Paul M. Sweezy. Sweezy, founder of the Monthly Review Press, is the most prominent of the "older" American Marxist economists, their main function being to update Marx's and Lenin's ideas about monopoly capitalism. In Heilbroner's instance, his class was learning about the rate of interest as a Victorian reward for abstinence. Sweezy assigned Veblen's *The Theory of the Leisure*

Class as supplemental reading and asked Heilbroner, "What do you think Veblen would have thought of abstinence?"

Though Heilbroner's flowering as an economist was interrupted by service in World War II (like the American Keynesians), a stint in business, and freelance writing, "I still remember a light going on," he says. Veblen's engagement with the social dimensions of economics gave structure to Heilbroner's strong social concerns. In 1946 when Robert walked into Adolph Lowe's course on the history of economic thought at the New School for Social Research, he fell under the professor's spell. Lowe's course became the impetus for the first edition of Heilbroner's classic, *The Worldly Philosophers*, a book that was to draw—like moths to a candle—many college students into economics. It has sold more than a million copies.

Heilbroner is virtually compulsive in his writing habits, but he is a highly effective speaker who has doubtless changed many minds though his friendly persuasion. His kind visage reveals his true nature and his impish smile unmasks a lively wit.

Like the classicals that he animated in *The Worldly Philosophers*, Heilbroner beings a breadth of vision to his writings. The titles of his books suggest as much: *The Nature and Logic of Capitalism*, *Inquiry into the Human Prospect*, *Between Capitalism and Socialism*, *Twenty-First Century Capitalism*, *The Future as History*, *The Crisis of Vision in Modern Economic Thought*, the later co-authored with William Milberg.

CAPITALISM: HEILBRONER'S VISION

In *The Nature and Logic of Capitalism* (1985), Heilbroner examines capitalism not only as an "economic system" but as a "regime," whereby he conjures up political and psychological implications. Heilbroner's view of capital as a social relation is in the same spirit as Marx. The two defining characteristics of this social relation are, (1) the forms in which wealth is held and, (2) the ways that wealth is deployed.

In feudal systems, production surpluses became prestige or luxury goods which gave their consumers social status. The ruling class were those who had the greatest share of prestige goods and who controlled society's surplus. As Veblen had noted, those who amass the surpluses from capitalism engage in conspicuous consumption of prestige goods. Under capitalism, however, unlike feudalism, wealth is mostly held as the means of production. The capitalist ruling classes acquire status though their ownership of the means that generate society's material goods. This ownership confers power because of "the right accorded [the owners of the means of production] to *withhold* their property from the use of society if they wish."[1]

The capacity to withhold capital confers a conclusive bargaining advantage to capitalists over workers, enabling capitalists to command for themselves the lion's share of society's surplus. This inequality in bargaining powers is the source of profits. Heilbroner is siding at once with Adam Smith's admonition about the power of capital over labor as well as Karl Marx's concern with the exploitation of labor by capital. Marx, as Heilbroner writes, sees the commodity "as the carrier and encapsulation of the social history of capitalism, for it contains within itself the disguised elements of the class struggle."[2]

Still, Heilbroner's logic of capitalism deviates from Marxism in important ways. In Marx, the state is the executive committee of the bourgeoisie. In Heilbroner, capitalists emerged out of feudalism as holders of social power that was independent of the state's control over the means of violence (unlike feudalism wherein the political and economic powers of the state were inseparable). Once capitalists had private property rights, capitalists could control the means of production while the state still controlled the means of violence.

Like Marx, Heilbroner sees a strong convergence of interest between these two nodes of power of capitalism. For example, historically the state's violence is almost always deployed against workers to protect the property of capitalists. Unlike Marx, Heilbroner does not consider the distinction between the economy and the state as an illusion. Rather, the power of the owners of the means of production has limited the powers of the state. Such limits on state power allow political dissidents to speak critically of the government while still being able to earn a living out of reach of the state. (Abba

Lerner held a similar view regarding this political advantage of private property rights.)

In the search for what motivates those who wish to accumulate capital, Heilbroner goes beyond Marx to reach out and touch Sigmund Freud. Freud contended that residing in human nature is a universal drive for power and domination. This drive comes from the universal experience of prolonged infantile dependency. Thus, the craving for power and prestige happens in all social arrangements. Since this universal drive manifests itself in hierarchy, it is an obstacle to egalitarianism in socialism as well as in capitalism. If anything, this drive is likely to take more pathological forms such as dictatorship in a socialist than in a capitalist society. Stalinism springs immediately to mind, though capitalism proved to be no barrier to the rise of Hitler in Germany.

The foregoing perhaps explains Heilbroner's placement—like John Stuart Mill's—somewhere between capitalism and socialism. For Heilbroner, human aspiration is best attained in a "slightly imaginary Sweden." The real Sweden embodies a form of liberal democratic capitalism. A "slightly imaginary Sweden," a vision of a cooperative economy, would push liberal capitalism to its limit while allowing democratic politics and egalitarian goals to gain the edge over acquisitiveness. In this way, Heilbroner's analytic pessimism is balanced by his moral optimism. His vision is little removed from his early concern about his mother's wealth being the source of domination of poor Willy Gerkin, his surrogate father.

JOHN KENNETH GALBRAITH: AN INTRODUCTION

Like Veblen and Heilbroner, John Kenneth Galbraith too delights general readers, if not always other economists, with books such as *The Affluent Society* (1958, 1969), *The New Industrial State* (1967), and *Economics and the Public Purpose* (1973). Galbraith (1908-), the best-known contemporary institutionalist and Post Keynesian, has abided Veblen's assault on the neoclassicals. Where the neoclassicals see weakness, Galbraith, like Heilbroner, senses power. Where the neoclassicals advise against intrusion with natural market forces, Galbraith sees economic forces left to themselves often working out in favor of the powerful.

Like Veblen, Galbraith's stature in American letters is ensured, not only by his bestsellers in economics, but also by three widely acclaimed novels and other literary ventures. Galbraith, author of more than two dozen books, competes with Heilbroner as the most widely read modern-day economist, and has served as president of the combined American Institute and Academy of Arts and Letters.

Although he and Veblen share agricultural roots, great sardonic wit, and literary talents, Galbraith, in contrast to Veblen, is a remarkably well-balanced personality and has enjoyed a highly successful lifestyle, not to mention access to the highest level of Democratic Party political power.

Galbraith's nomination to the presidency of the American Economic Association in 1970 was opposed by Milton Friedman on the dubious grounds that Veblen had never been president. "I learned after the election," writes Galbraith, "that this got me by."[3] Later, he wrote an introduction for a new edition of *The Theory of the Leisure Class* and led a drive to save from the ravages of time the Veblen family homestead in Minnesota.

In addition to the major works on economics mentioned earlier, Galbraith has written historical works (*The Great Crash 1929* and *Economics in Perspective*); books on politics (*The Liberal Hour* and *How to Get Out of Vietnam*); memoirs (*The Scotch, Ambassador's Journal,* and *A Life in Our Times*); a satire on politics and measurement (*The McLandress Dimension*); a novel lampooning the U.S. State Department (*The Triumph*); and the aforementioned amusing novel on the corporate raiders and economic policies of the 1980s (*A Tenured Professor*). He also co-authored a book on *Indian Painting* and hosted a TV series on "The Age of Uncertainty."

Galbraith has been a confidant of presidents; a speech writer for Adlai Stevenson, Lyndon Johnson, George McGovern, and the Kennedys; an ambassador to India; and an escort of first ladies. One measure of Galbraith's renown is that in 1968 he was interviewed by *Playboy* magazine, that opulent reminder of the surrogate pleasures open to those with too much money, Veblenian leisure, and limited expectations. (Not to be out-jetsetted, Milton Friedman was later interviewed by the same magazine.)

Galbraith's early life was a prophetic background for his later career as a social critic. He was born in 1908 in a Scotch farming community near Iona Station, Ontario, Canada. His father began as a teacher, turned to farming, and was a leading political liberal in his rather isolated community. When John Kenneth was about six years old, he began to go to political meetings with his father, and perhaps this is when he began to develop his sardonic humor. In *The Scotch,* Galbraith recalls an occasion on which his father made a speech critical of his Tory opponents from atop a huge manure pile, apologizing for having to speak from the Tory platform.

Galbraith attended high school in Dutton, a village split by discord between the rural Scotch and the English townspeople. Most of the Tories were English merchants, whereas the Liberal Party was predominantly Scotch. Their economic disagreements were substantial. In the post-World War I years, the village merchants prospered while (as in the U.S.) the farmers suffered. The Scotch, who thought they were superior in every way to the English (Galbraith agrees), believed that the merchants were better off because they were buying cheap and selling dear. The superior bargaining power of the merchants apparently made a lasting impression on the young man.

Galbraith worked his way through Ontario Agricultural College and took his doctorate in agricultural economics at the University of California at Berkeley in 1936, where he first read Veblen and Marx. Most of his subsequent academic life has been spent at Harvard University as Professor of Economics and, now, as Professor Emeritus.

GALBRAITH'S GENERAL THEORY OF ADVANCED DEVELOPMENT

The object of Galbraith's economic writings is nothing less than the replacement of the neoclassical system. The neoclassical system, he concedes, is useful when applied to the market system, but, he says, modern American capitalism has spawned another system existing side by side with the conventional market system yet far transcending it in massive wealth and power.

The Planning System

Galbraith calls this other system the planning system, by which he means the 1,000 (or so) largest industrial firms. The 1,000 industrial giants in the United States produce a larger share of the gross national product than the remaining 12 million business firms combined. The four largest U.S. corporations have total sales in excess of those of the three million farmers whom Galbraith keeps down in the market system and who produce the food supply. "The size of General Motors is in the service not of monopoly or the economies of scale but of planning," writes Galbraith.[4] The neoclassical system, Galbraith believes, cannot begin to explain the economic reality of the giant corporation.

Galbraith calls his theory the *general theory of advanced development*. It differs from neoclassical theory in two important ways. First, the theory of pricing is not of special importance in planning systems. Second, whereas neoclassical harmony is maintained because no single element in the economy has enough power to control prices, the giant corporation has the power to impose its purposes on others. The only reason that corporate power does not corrupt absolutely is because the power is not quite absolute. Although the corporations do not control all the sources of political power, planning-system power nonetheless is sufficient to impose an "irrational" mode of life on individuals.

According to Galbraith, the monster corporation grew because technology became so complex that a new organizational entity was required to deal with it. "And for this planning—control of supply, control of demand, provision of capital, minimization of risk—there is," according to Galbraith, "no clear upper limit to the desirable size."[5]

The first Model T car was built in a small plant in a short time. But, writes Galbraith, the Ford Motor Company's Mustang, produced in the mid-1960s, required expert knowledge, specialization of labor, a huge outlay of capital, a precise plan for production, and sophisticated organization. From drawing board to the road required years and years of planning. The planning is at the firm level. However, the plan for the firm is often, happily, in the interests of the entire industry.

In the neoclassical textbook world, consumers are kings and queens who can maximize their happiness by freely choosing whatever shirts, skirts, soaps, bath oils, beers, and aperitifs they prefer. In contrast, the Galbraithian planning system perceives serious disadvantages in such freedom of choice. It takes a lot of time and many dollars of capital to "geti-up" the Mustang to the dealer's floor. The corporation wants to do everything it can to make sure that the consumer will buy that Mustang rather than choose a car of a different horse or perhaps even a horse itself.

Therefore, part of the corporate plan becomes the management of what consumers want. By means of advertising, promotion, and salesmanship, the producers create many of the wants they seek to satisfy, an economic phenomenon Galbraith calls the **dependence effect**. Rejecting the neoclassical concept of diminishing marginal utility, Galbraith—going a step beyond even Veblen—envisions something more like *producer sovereignty* in the American economy.

For example, in a discussion of cars, Galbraith observes: "since General Motors produces some half of all the automobiles, its designs do not reflect the current mode, but are the current mode. The proper shape of an automobile, for most people, will be what the automobile majors decree the current shape to be."[6]

Once necessities are satisfied, a whole new world of possible wants is just waiting to be created by billboards showing young women in thongs, TV commercials with giant green men, and magazine ads of liquor in velvet cases. Galbraith notes that "mass communication was not necessary when the wants of the masses were anchored primarily in physical need. The masses could not then be persuaded as to their spending—this went for basic foods and shelter."[7]

In his later *Economics and the Public Purpose,* Galbraith qualifies his want-creation argument somewhat, conceding—though no one may actually need a pink, fully automatic dishwasher—any alleviation of the tiresome job of washing dishes for a large family certainly does satisfy a want. Many giant firms spend part of their resources on research aimed at discovering what these wants—even subliminal ones—are.

Thus, "selling the sizzle" may increase sales and growth for an individual firm, but it also benefits the entire industry. It is a safe form of competition between existing rivals and makes it difficult for new competitors to enter or become entrenched in the field. The combined market research-advertising-promotion expenditure of the three biggest automobile manufacturers increases the allocation of the consumer's budget toward automobile purchases and promotes the growth of the whole industry. Although Galbraith has not extended his analysis to the international economy, the Japanese later were to benefit from the United States "selling" of the automobile to the world.

The Technostructure and Its Purpose

In the planning-system world of giant corporations, groups rather than individuals make the decisions. All the officials who take part in group decision-making are members of the **technostructure**, a collective term that includes not only the most senior officials of the corporation but certain white- and blue-collar workers as well. It embraces only those who bring specialized knowledge, talent, or experience to group decisions. In a very large corporation, it might include the chairman of the board, the president, vice-presidents who have important responsibilities, and people with other major staff positions, such as department or division heads. The technostructure cannot be specifically defined, Galbraith says, but it has taken over corporations in a way supporting Veblen's prediction that all firms would logically be operated by technicians rather than by risk takers.

The technostructure displaces the old entrepreneur and the captain of industry with something more closely resembling a huge committee. Committees have different goals than the steady (or unsteady) hand of the captain at the helm of the company. Whereas neoclassical economics has the individual capitalist aiming (and succeeding) at profit maximization, Galbraith's controlling technostructure has two principal purposes rather than one.

First, there is its *protective* purpose: The technostructure's collectively made decisions attempt to ensure a basic and uninterrupted level of earnings, keeping the stockholders happy and the bankers away from the door as well as providing savings and capital. In this regard, the giant corporation acts as a giant bureaucracy. Second, it has an *affirmative* purpose, which is the growth of the firm. Growth becomes an important purpose of the entire planning system and hence of a society dominated by giant business.

One way to ensure firm growth is by acquisition. Between 1948 and 1965, the 200 largest U.S. manufacturing corporations acquired 2,692 other firms, notes Galbraith, and these acquisitions accounted for about one-seventh of all growth in assets by these firms during this period. In the next three years, the 200 largest corporations acquired some 1,200 more firms.

Unlike Marx and Veblen, who believed industrial concentration to be motivated by a thirst for profit, Galbraith sees the technostructure's motive as one of bureaucratic advantage, a motive also spelled POWER.

Each member of the technostructure sees the logic in growth. A unit of the firm, such as a department, expands its sales. With increased revenue, the department can expand its employment and make new claims on promotion, pay, and perquisites that go with its increased size, the rewards to which members of a non-growing corporation cannot lay claim. And bigness begets bigness, because revenue growth gives the firm more to grow on. When a firm is so large that its production alone can cause price fluctuations, it is far safer for this firm and the few others like it to set prices first and then adjust their production to sell their products at the predetermined price.[8]

The planning system and the technostructure are closely associated with the state because government expenditures are responsible for a large share of corporate revenue. There are still other reasons for an intimate relationship between government bureaucracies and corporations, a bureaucratic symbiosis. Public regulatory agencies, such as the Federal Trade Commission, tend to become captives of the firms they were set up to regulate. The government often supplies capital for technical development, such as for nuclear power, computers, modern air transport, and satellite communication equipment. Sometimes the government can act as a lending agency of last resort, as in the case of the historic bailouts of the Lockheed Corporation, the Chrysler Corporation, and Long-Term Capital Management.

The goal of corporate growth thus becomes inseparable from the goal of national economic growth. What is good for the government is good for General Motors. National economic growth is also an important goal of organized labor, and this goal fits well into the ambitions of the technostructure: Giant firms set prices, so they can usually pass increased wages on to the consumer in the form of higher prices. Everybody wins—except perhaps the consumer.

Galbraith's Principle of Uneven Development

What Galbraith is describing is an uneven power distribution between the planning system and the market system that results from their uneven development. The planning system requires highly skilled workers, and it can afford to pay them very well, often more than they would be worth in the market system for their ability to produce revenue. The market system is thus at a disadvantage in its competition for skilled personnel. Furthermore, the influential planning system can obtain services from the state, which the market system largely does without.

Uneven development favoring the planning system influences considerable social attitudes. For example, consumers have maintained a love affair with private transportation partly because the planning system has convinced them automobiles are essential to their lives. Public transportation is slighted, even though it may be ultimately more beneficial for society.

Galbraith is concerned with social imbalance. The private sector is a glutton and the nonmilitary public sector is starved, a starvation extending into education, the arts, and a variety of public services. General fiscal and monetary policy serves the technostructure's own policy of steady economic growth so that individual consumers can purchase the products of giant business. Inflation may be the result of this marriage, but large corporations are largely immune from restrictive monetary policies because the giants have access to their own immense financial resources. As long as demand in the economy remains high and the public cannot effectively oppose the technostructure, an upward wage-price spiral is the consequence.

The Galbraithian World

Galbraith too has clearly departed from the neoclassicals, his focus being on planning, not on the market. He examines the giant firm, not the small one. He sees prices and outputs decided by the technostructure, not by the market mechanism. He is a believer more in producer sovereignty than in consumer sovereignty. The goal of the firm is growth rather than maximum profit rates.

The relation of the state to the corporation is cooperative. Galbraith sees the quality-of-life concerns in the *composition* of output, not in its magnitude. Because he goes beyond economists to a wider audience, and because he—like Veblen and Heilbroner—views neoclassical economics to be a matter of belief rather than of reality, Galbraith is not universally admired by other professional economists.

CONCLUSIONS

Like John Stuart Mill, Galbraith, Heilbroner, and the other institutionalists have reminded economics of its vast humanistic implications. They have persuasively questioned once again the primacy of pure economic choice over the balance of what is important in life. In particular, they have brought to light in dramatic fashion the unevenness in the development of the American economy in contrast to the presumed smoothness depicted by the neoclassicals. In a sense Galbraith, too—like Adam Smith—is the Scotch moralist urging us to move toward a more fulfilling society. As Heilbroner established in his first book, the economists who are historically most important have tried to break the ruling orthodoxy. That is what Galbraith and Heilbroner are doing, and their terrain is a part of the time-honored country of political economy.

Still, it is the Marshallian or the Walrasian model as a flawless machine of internal consistency claiming the admiration of most economists. Indeed, economists have shown how the neoclassical pricing and resource allocation mechanism can be used under socialism and how the ownership of private property has absolutely no theoretical importance in neoclassical theory, which means, as a tool, the theory exists in its own right, independent of capitalism. Heilbroner complains, "the Harvard economist Greg Mankiw is the author of a popular, well-written textbook, and he is a very bright guy. He talks about the need to use scientific language, but he never uses the word 'capitalism'."[9]

Perhaps this is why Galbraith calls neoclassical economics "a system of belief." It expresses—or at least seems to express—a number of significant Western values, such as freedom and individual initiative. Marxism, on the other hand, is uncongenial to Western ethics in some respects and has had the further disadvantage of a birth in the British Museum, a place outside the gates of Cambridge, England. This lower birth denied it a proper upbringing by academic kingdoms. As to the institutionalists, Veblen never found a secure position in a major American university, whereas Galbraith gained tenure at Harvard as a Keynesian.

The neoclassicals have survived the demise of caricature capitalism because economists have failed to endorse a better machine. Neoclassical economics also survived the brilliant critique of Marx. Still Galbraith and Heilbroner cannot be denied: Their criticisms and challenges have enjoyed a wide public readership because economic and social conditions made them relevant. Orthodox critics do not speak well for their own relevancy.

NOTES

1. Robert Heilbroner, *Behind the Veil of Economics* (New York: W.W. Norton, 1988), p. 38.
2. Robert Heilbroner, *Marxism: For and Against* (New York: W.W. Norton, 1980), p. 103.
3. John Kenneth Galbraith, *A Life in Our Times* (Boston: Houghton Mifflin, 1981), p. 31.
4. John Kenneth Galbraith, *The New Industrial State* (Boston: Houghton Mifflin, 1967), p. 76.
5. *Ibid.*
6. *Ibid.*, p. 30.
7. *Ibid.*, p. 207. This argument can be illustrated with Menger's hierarchy of wants in Table 7.1. Whenever wants I, II and III are met, Galbraith is saying, media persuasion becomes effective with want IV (to be transported) and want V (to enjoy luxury).
8. Those desiring more detail on Galbraith's theory of the corporation would benefit from reading an evaluation by his youngest son: See James K. Galbraith, "Galbraith and the Theory of the Corporation," *Journal of Post Keynesian Economics* 6 (Fall 1984): 43–60. James sees his father's most important contribution to economic *theory* to be his theory of the corporation.
9. "The End of the Worldly Philosophy: Interview with Robert Heilbroner," *Challenge: The Magazine of Economic Affairs* 42, no. 3 (May–June 1999): 56.

15

The Rise of the Casino Economy

As noted, capitalism is Faustian in scope: It has many faces. Another great transformation of American capitalism began during the Reagan Administration; some of the same forces were imported by England during the Thatcher years. It all began with Reaganomics, which required the convergence of three powerful forces. The first was monetarism; as Milton Friedman had told Ronald Reagan, monetarism could bring down inflation with only a temporary slowdown in production and employment. The second force was the rising influence of the neo-Austrians and their desire to free the entrepreneur from the state. The third force was the dream of the supply-siders to free the rich from "excessive" taxation. From these forces came the rise to power of the New Right in the United States during the late 1970s and early 1980s, beginning with Austrian economist Ludwig von Mises in Vienna and coming to rest on the front steps of the White House with Ronald Reagan.

As with monetarism, the rise of the New Right was a reaction to the stagflation crises of the 1970s. Whereas the Keynesians are united in expecting some role for government in the economy, the New Right places its faith in free-market capitalism. The New Right sees the market as the solution to all economic problems, the *only* solution.

The neo-Austrians initial link to political power emanates from the establishment in 1974 of the Charles Koch Foundation; it has since become the Cato Institute in Washington, D.C., a public policy institute. Koch, the head of Koch Industries, established his Foundation to seed the views of laissez-faire economists such as Ludwig von Mises, Ayn Rand's favorite economist. The shared goal of the neo-Austrians and the Cato Institute is to greatly shrink the government. Although they would have preferred an Ayn Rand to a Ronald Reagan as President, his was the only game in town. In part by design, but mostly by error and accident, monetarism and Reaganomics built a bridge to a casino economy.

THE FEDERAL RESERVE'S EXPERIMENT WITH FRIEDMAN'S MONETARISM (1979–1982)

Still, monetarism preceded Reagan's presidency. The inflation beginning in the late 1960s (made much worse by the OPEC cartel during the 1970s) and Milton Friedman's ascension led to a monetarist experiment, which begun in the final months of Jimmy Carter's presidency. Paul Volcker, then head of the Federal Reserve System, made sure that the growth rate in the money supply dropped roughly in half during the first six months of the experiment. The fed funds rate, close to ten percent in mid-summer 1979, by early 1980 had nearly doubled, soaring to 18 percent. Even the highest rated corporations began to pay 14 percent for loans.

Faced with a financial Armageddon, the Carter Administration pressured a reluctant Volcker to invoke a little-used countermeasure, the Credit Control Act of 1969, to regulate the credit of financial institutions. The immediate reduction in borrowing had an equally quick and sickening effect on the economy. In the second quarter of 1980, the real gross national product (GNP) plunged at an annual rate of nearly ten percent. Volcker's monetarism and the Carter

Administration's regulatory error had caused a very sharp business recession, riding on the back of the lengthy, painful recession of 1973 to 1975. Even so, the deep but short recession ended before the monetarist experiment. Volcker began to remove the new controls only two months after he had imposed them. The Fed began pumping money into the economy, only temporarily reversing the experiment.

Carter was defeated in the presidential election of 1980, in great part because of what monetarism had wrought and despite warnings from White House advisers of the consequences of Federal Reserve policy. It was an economy in which only the infectious optimism of Ronald Reagan and supply-side economics, the economics of joy, could turn things around, or so it was thought.

As Reagan came to power, the recovery from the Carter Administration's 1980 recession was incomplete: The unemployment rate still hovered near eight percent. Volcker, now by Reagan's side, faced the continuation of the stagflation malaise, a condition of simultaneous inflation and unemployment afflicting Great Britain and Western Europe as well. Of the twin abominations, Paul Volcker and Ronald Reagan—by then both under the influence of scientific monetarism—considered inflation by far the greater evil.

Reagan fervently believed what Friedman had told him; monetarism could defeat inflation without a noticeable decline in production or rise in unemployment. Reagan believed that Volcker had failed because he had not persevered in his first duel with the inflation demon. In an influential meeting with Volcker, Reagan urged him not only a return to tighter monetary policy but *an even tighter* monetary policy. As a biographer has noted, "Reagan ... *believed* the way a child believes—ardently and absolutely. He believed in Reaganomics; therefore Reaganomics had to be."[1]

Volcker once again cranked up monetarism, slowing money supply growth after mid-1980 and continuing to decelerate its growth in 1981. The cooperation between the self-proclaimed "politically independent" monetary authorities and the Reagan Administration was inspirational, what with the White House and the Fed in unaccustomed agreement: The money supply would grow by no more than a meager 2.5 percent per year. A few blocks from the Fed, the White House staff was singing hosannas about how nominal GNP would be growing at an annual rate of *12 percent* between 1980 and 1984. Any economist failing to believe in the religion of the money supply was turned into salt by the *Wall Street Journal.*

SUPPLY-SIDE ECONOMICS

Like the pamphleteers of mercantilism, the supply-siders relied on dramatic arguments rather than numbers and facts. Supply-side economics was a media event led by Wall Street journalist Jude Wanniski, writer Bruce Bartlett, and pop sociologist George Gilder. All three writers make devoted reference to the neo-Austrians. Still, just as monetarism was a reaction to the perceived failure of Keynesianism to end stagflation, the "supply-side" economics identified with Reaganomics was thought to be a way out of the stagnation.

Monetarism and supply-side incentives, the first scene in the Reaganomics script, would restore the classical utopia. Super-tight money would break inflation while supply-side tax cuts would expand employment and production. Modest personal income tax cuts for workers would cause them to work harder, bolstering productivity. Dramatically large tax cuts for the rich, especially on capital gains, would incite them to save more. The surge in savings would lead to higher levels of business investment.

Lurking behind the supply-side ideas was the classical's old friend Say's law, in its crudest expression; "supply creating its own demand," was the first scene stealer. As Bartlett correctly wrote, "in many respects, supply-side economics is nothing more than ... Say's law of markets rediscovered."[2] Say's law connected Reaganomics to economic growth. Saving races the growth engine because of the guaranteed transmission of saving into investment. The engine always races no matter how chilly the investment climate, since every dollar saved never leaves the race track.

Thus, the higher purpose of the rich lay in their saving. Reaganomics sought out the upper-income class (over $50,000 a year in 1980 dollars) for personal savings because that was where the money was. This incentive provided the moral grounds for lowering marginal tax rates for the well-to-do. As a failsafe, special tax benefits to corporations such as larger tax credits, lower tax rates, and faster depreciation would add still more incentives for investment.

Gilder gave a further boost to the supply-siders even while embracing neo-Austrian entrepreneurship in his *Wealth and Poverty*, required reading for Reagan's 1981 White House staff. The savings to investment connection revealed to Gilder, the author most frequently quoted in Reagan's speeches, the truth: "To help the poor and middle classes, one must cut the tax rates of the rich."[3] The welfare state, Gilder further surmised, motivates the poor to choose leisure over work and is a great disincentive. Moreover, entrepreneurs would play their historically heroic role once they were freed from the shackles of taxation.

The centerpiece of supply-side economics, the Economic Recovery Act of 1981, as promised, cut personal tax rates. Whereas Reaganomics stressed those tax incentives presumably affecting the supply of labor and productive capacity, the full program went further. The federal government's role, expanded by the New Deal programs of the 1930s and by World War II, was to be reduced, except for national defense and the penal system, which were to be enlarged. Finally, Reagan would *balance the federal budget by 1984*, the year that George Orwell had "the clocks striking thirteen."

Judging from the tax cut results, the richest Americans were most in need of motivation. Consider the reductions in the *effective* income tax rate, the true rate paid rather than simply the tax rate from the IRS schedules. The effective income tax rate on the super-rich, the top one percent, had been reduced by 7.8 percentage *points* by 1984. The effective tax rate for the very rich, the top five percent, dropped by 4.2 percentage points and, for the simply rich, the top ten percent, 3.1 percentage points. Moreover, the top tax rate on unearned income from interest payments fell steadily from 70 percent in 1980, to 50 percent in 1982, to 38.5 percent in 1987, and to 28 percent in 1988.

Not only did the rich enjoy much higher incomes—be they from salary, stock options, interest payments, or capital gains—each family now could keep a much larger share of any gains. The *average* tax break for the super-rich, the top one percent, was $52,621 by 1989. The total value of these tax cuts for 1982 through 1990 was nearly *$2 trillion* (in 1985 dollars), a value roughly equal to the *entire* gross domestic product (GDP) for 1960. By 1992, under President Bush, the average tax break for the super-rich had risen to about $78,090 on incomes averaging $676,000.

We now turn our attention to the second scene in the Reaganomics script.

The Laffer Curve and the Mantra of the Balanced Budget

A link was missing: How, with massive tax cuts, would the federal budget be balanced? As "balancing the budget" further fed the media frenzy, the missing link was filled by Arthur Laffer, a former business professor at the University of Southern California. The Laffer curve, the Rosetta Stone of Reaganomics, was drawn for Wanniski on a napkin in a Washington, D.C., "insiders" hotel bar by Arthur Laffer, and was given celebrity status in Wanniski's book, *The Way the World Works*.

The Laffer curve traces the relationship between tax rates and government revenue. At two extremes (zero percent and 100 percent), there will be no revenues for the government. As tax rates rise above zero, the provision of public goods essential for markets to operate (justice, defense, law and order, and primary education) contributes to productivity, output, and, thus, tax revenue. However, as tax rates are raised further, relative price changes cause a decline in the after-tax rewards of saving, investing, and working for taxable income. People begin to shift out of these activities and into leisure, consumption, and tax shelters. The national output and income base on which tax rates apply is eroded, and the tax revenue from higher tax rates falls. Most economists believed otherwise; tax rates were well below this range of perversity.

The opening scenes had been written and the movie set built.

The Angst of Insider David Stockman

David Stockman, the President's first budget director (1981–mid-1985) and once an unabashed supply-sider, quickly saw defects in the program. In the words of a Christmastime 1981 confession, the "Kemp-Roth (the name of the original supply-side tax bill) was always a Trojan horse to bring down the top rate."[4]

A Trojan horse? Supply-side economics was rolled into the enemy camp of labor with a horseload of entrepreneurs. Rather than a Calvinistic response by workers, all the President's men were counting on a literal interpretation of Say's law and on self-styled neo-Austrian entrepreneurship for the stimulation of output, either Puritanical investors or super-alert entrepreneurs. The supply-side theory, in Stockman's view, was really new clothes for the naked doctrine of the old "trickle-down theory"[5] in which benefits to the rich "trickle down" to the workers. After all, the need to cut welfare for the poor and give tax benefits to the rich implied that the working poor had *too much* money and the rich *too little*.

Thus, even through the various tax cuts would increase disposable income, their conjectured effectiveness did not stem from their effects on Keynesian aggregate demand, which were presumed to be nil. Rather, following the neoclassical lead, the effectiveness of tax reductions would come from their changing of relative prices and inducing decision-makers to substitute productive activity (investment, work and exchange) for leisure and idleness, causing output to rise. The Howard Roark's of the world—no thanks to God Almighty—would be free at last to play their role under free-market capitalism. (Reagan never seemed to fathom the atheism of Ayn Rand.) The shift away from leisure and consumption toward productive activity would enhance economic growth.

THE SEQUEL

The Great Recession of 1981 to 1982

Sequels often promise more but deliver less than the original movie. In this regard, the outcome of the supply-siders' proclamation was not unique.

Even Ronald Reagan's optimistic glow could not prevent the calamity. The tight monetary policy of the Federal Reserve combined with rising budget deficits sharply raised interest rates, overwhelming the business tax cuts aimed at encouraging capital formation.[6] Earlier, in 1979 and 1980, the line of "voluntarily" unemployed workers was rapidly growing but apparently not fast enough to keep inflation under control. Still, following the monetarists' prescription to the decimal point, Paul Volcker managed to move the unemployment rate much higher. The nominal GNP growth rate during Reagan's first presidential term was not, of course, at the scripted but wildly improbable yearly rate of 12 percent. In mid-summer 1981, it was the *unemployment rate* that was approaching 12 percent and the highest rate since the Great Depression.

Where were those heroic entrepreneurs when they were most needed?

The National Debt Explodes (1980–1992)

Had the government revenue targets been military ones, though doubtless improved by a handsomely funded Pentagon, the supply-siders would have missed them by roughly a continent. *Budget deficits* began to shatter historical records. A slumping national income meant sluggish tax revenues, especially at the lower tax rates. Reagan's tax cuts combined with the explosion in military spending and the deep recession took the national debt from $908 billion to $3.2 trillion, or *more than treble that accumulated by all of his 39 predecessors, beginning with George Washington.*

Soaring federal budget deficits and debt accumulation did not end with Reagan's second term. President George Bush comforted those habituated to continuity as the federal deficits continued their rise, reaching nearly $400 billion by fiscal year 1992. The national debt weighed in around $4.0 trillion in 1992. Unable or unwilling to reduce the deficits, Bush left it to New Democrat Bill Clinton to cut the deficits by some 60 percent during his first term, move to a balanced budget sometime in 1998, and build his proverbial bridge to the twenty-first century with budget surpluses.

What had gone so horribly wrong?

The Arithmetic of Modern Monetarism in Action

Even if we accept the monetarist's arithmetic, Volcker's monetary policy does not add up. We need look no further than MV = PT, the classical equality for monetarism. In the modern monetarist equation from Friedman, real output or real GNP replaces the T. If we express all values in the equality in percentage changes or growth rates, the growth rate in the money supply plus the growth rate in its velocity equals inflation plus the growth rate in real GNP. That is, the modern monetarist equation becomes

$$\text{Percent Change, } M + \text{Percent Change, } V$$
$$= \text{Percent Change, } P + \text{Percent Change, Real GNP.}$$

The sum on the right side of the equal sign is the growth rate in *nominal* GNP.

In this way, the great promise of monetarism reduces to simple, if wholly embarrassing, arithmetic. Reagan-Volcker's planned pace for the money supply was a meager 2.5 percent for 1980 to 1984.[7] Suppose President Reagan's advisers had asked the obvious question: "How great would the percentage change in the income velocity or turnover rate of money have to be to give their targeted money GNP growth rate (on the right side of the equal sign) of 12.0 percent?" The answer, of course, is 12.0 percent minus 2.5 percent or 9.5 percent. The growth rate in the *velocity of money*, a variable Friedman failed to mention to Reagan, would have to be an astounding 9.5 percent! Yet, the *average growth rate* in velocity was *only three percent* for the entire postwar era, 1946 to 1980. More important, this historical three percent growth rate of velocity added to a 2.5 percent growth rate for money (again, summing the two rates) would allow nominal GNP to grow *only* 5.5 percent a year, not 12 percent. At a White House inflation wish rate of six percent, the real growth in GNP would be –0.5 percent annually (5.5–6.0). *Real GNP declines!* In fact, that's what happened.

In 1981 to 1982, job prospects were appalling, and expected returns from investment dismal and increasingly uncertain, seemingly a Keynesian situation. Households and corporations, however, not only held onto money but placed it in highly liquid financial assets, reducing the income velocity of money. Contrary to the ideas of either Adam Smith *or* Keynes, personal and corporate savings were pouring into financial assets instead of into real business investment. Without rising spending by consumers and business, output falls. Thus, Volcker's tight monetary policy only diminished inflation at the steep cost of a deep recession, just as it had before.

Rabo Karabekian, Kurt Vonnegut's fictional artist-collector in *Bluebeard* (1987), describes well the outcome. Rabo, back in 1933, is looking in the Grand Central Station in New York City for the address of his mentor. Rabo is musing, "the Great Depression was going on, so that the station and the streets teemed with homeless people, just as they do today. The newspapers were full of stories of worker layoffs and farm foreclosures and bank failures, just as they are today."[8] Just as they were in 1981 to 1982

All things considered, the fiscal revolution was stunning, but the President did not get everything he asked for.[9] Although federal income taxes for the "average family" actually rose by one percent, a large number of major corporations such as U.S. Home, Dow Chemical, General Electric, General Dynamics, and Boeing received a negative income tax (refunds or other tax benefits) during 1981 to 1983 even while earning large profits. Not satisfied, President Reagan pushed for still more domestic program reductions in his second term.

Keynes Redux: Reagan's Ersatz Keynesianism

History, as in F. Scott Fitzgerald's novels, is replete with irony. By 1980, Keynesian economics was at a nadir among U.S. economists; the Reaganomics near-depression greatly altered this perception. For one thing, unemployment compensation and other programs from the New Deal placed a floor under disposable income and therefore the decline in consumer spending. Just as Ronald Reagan and his family had been helped by the programs of President Franklin Roosevelt during the thirties, the poor and the unemployed were being served again by the same kinds of assistance. The Reagan Administration looked to gains in consumers' disposable income to stimulate Keynesian effective demand.

Fiscal Keynesianism became the way out of the malaise. Federal Reserve officials, in near panic as the 1930s flashed before their eyes, in the summer of 1982 began to pursue an incredibly expansive monetary policy. Monetarism was scrapped. The tremendous increase in federal military expenditures (about seven percent annually in real terms), although a part of Reagan's original budget plan, provided a sorely needed Keynesian demand yank for the depressed economy. President Reagan and the supply-siders began to defend vigorously Keynesian budget deficits greatly in excess of amounts acceptable to the many modern Keynesians.

CASINO CAPITALISM

A legacy of Reaganomics was the greatly enlarged importance of Wall Street in American society. The central message of Ronald Reagan was that not only were American corporations free to do whatever they wished, so could people with wealth. The perpetuation of these policies by the Clinton Administration, often at the expense of those near the bottom, astonished and angered many Old Democrats.

Little distance separates wealth from Wall Street. Thus, Wall Street became the eye of a hurricane of financial vortices soon to engulf and shape a financially fragile American economy. During 1983 to 1989, the United States imploded into Las Vegas—hence, the term "casino economy."[10] A similar kind of speculative bubble rose over Tokyo.

This unnerving transformation reached an apogee of financial speculation somewhere around the mid-1980s, conflated into a Great Stagnation during the early 1990s, only to reignite into a speculative orgy during the last half of the 1990s. Many seemed to have rediscovered the Veblenesque pleasure in the making of money on money or financial assets rather than depending on profits from goods production. Others, out of greed, rediscovered the Gatsbyesque advantage of stepping beyond the bounds of propriety. The society began to resemble a giant money market fund in which the central function of households and businesses would be speculation.

Private Sector Debt Explodes

The debt epidemic soon spread to the private sector. Business balance sheets shifted from equity financing (issuing new corporate stock) to debt financing (issuing corporate bonds). In 1983, equity and debt issuance were $4.8 billion and $4.0 billion, respectively, a conservative businessperson's dream. In every year of the eighties thereafter, net equity issuance was negative while corporate net bond issues soared (to about $30 billion in 1989).

Although the post-recession 1980s has been Biblically called "the seven fat years," closer inspection makes it look more like simply a rebound from the Great Recession of 1981 to 1982. By mid-1984, the U.S. economy had recovered only to its pre-Reagan level, much like the 1936 to 1937 recovery had reached the pre-Depression GNP level. A contrast can be drawn between two periods highlighted by tax reductions—the decade of the 1960s and that of the 1980s. Real GNP growth during the 1960s amounted to 46 percent, greatly higher than the 28 percent of the 1980s. Industrial production expanded by 67 percent during the 1960s, but only by 29 percent during the 1980s. The unemployment rate never rose above 6.7 percent (1961) during the sixties; it never fell below seven percent during 1980 to

1986, peaking at 9.6 to 10.7 percent in 1982 to 1983. Moreover, financial manipulation and speculation soared.

Since the ownership of interest-bearing debt is highly concentrated, rising interest rates shift the income and wealth distributions toward greater inequality.[11] When only a few have the bulk of the "bullion," they have to become wonderfully imaginative as to where to put it. As providence provided, increasingly deregulated financial institutions became remarkably innovative in creating new financial instruments (CDs, jumbo CDs, junk bonds, options, and so on) in which wealth could be stored momentarily for quick appreciation. Put differently, if the rich are to speculate, they had to have an ample supply of chips. Initially, chips were supplied in the form of new Treasury bond issues; later, additional chips were provided by a new means of corporate acquisition, takeovers by leveraged debt.

Michael Milken Creates the Junk Bond Market

With the path to liberated markets being smoothed by Milton Friedman, the freeing of markets for moneymaking became a moral imperative for Reagan. The sole responsibility of business, wrote Friedman, was to increase its profits, a faith echoed in Reagan's speeches. Word about the "magic of the market" spread quickly from the Reagan White House to the countryside. The key phrases on Wall Street were: (1) The Reagan Administration was against all government regulations affecting *any* market, including bond markets; (2) If money could be made doing something—anything—it was an immoral act not to "just do it" (with needless apologies to Nike). Michael Milken was a natural by-product of this free-market revival.

Milken, an intense business student at the University of California at Berkeley during the mid-1960s, was reading about low-grade and unrated corporate bonds while other students were mellowing out on marijuana. Later, as a securities salesman at Drexel, Milken preached a new gospel. To Milken, the higher yield on low-grade bonds simply reflected a risk well worth taking at such high expected returns. He was convinced that the *only* problem with low-grade debt was its lack of liquidity or quick convertibility into money.

Eventually, Milken dispelled customers initial aversion to high-risk bonds. Milken's sales ability solved the "lack of liquidity" problem; he attracted financiers who saw no stigma attached to low-grade securities. As their returns met or exceeded their expectations, the early buyers became enthusiastic backers of Milken.

By early 1977, Milken already controlled a quarter of the national market in high-yield securities. He had become a *market-maker*. Milken could assure the holder of bonds that he would buy their bonds whenever the holder wanted to cash out or go liquid. In turn, Milken could resell the securities, keeping any difference between the unpublished "buy" and "sell" prices he amassed. Only Milken and a few colleagues knew of the widening spreads between the buy and sell prices, a source of rising richness for Milken.

The Securities and Exchange Commission, the main regulatory agency for the securities markets, did not register the offerings and the Milken Market went unregulated, just as Friedman, Reagan, and the supply-siders fancied. Milken always operated with more knowledge than any buyer or seller because he *was* the low-grade bond market.[12] Those buyers and sellers on the other side of the market might as well have been smoking something; they were no match for Milken's secret information. Thus, much of the "magic" of this market came from Milken's concealment of the key to it.

A half century trend favoring risk aversion and apposing excessive debt ended during the 1980s.

Junk Bonds Lead to LBO Mania

The merger trend in the United States has a long and glorious history, dating all the way back to the era of the robber barons. Concentration is as American as motherhood, apple pie, and John D. Rockefeller. The only things changing were the nameplates on the imploding industries and the methods of acquisition. A new method—leveraged buyouts, or LBOs—was a 1980s' innovation.

The largest American manufacturing corporations, by size of total assets for 1947 to 1983 were oil, automobile, computer, steel, communications, and chemical producers. Those are the industries at or well past their product cycle peaks (as defined in Chapter 13). Exxon (formerly Standard Oil of New Jersey) was still at the top of this heap in 1983, followed by General Motors, Mobil Oil, Texaco, Standard Oil (Indiana), E.I. dupont de Nemours, Standard Oil (California), Ford, and General Electric.

Few giant corporations have been broken up by the antitrust authorities—those initially empowered at the turn of the nineteenth century to do something about the giant trusts of the robber barons—and few mergers have been blocked. For example, Standard Oil was "broken up"; now there were three Standard Oils among the top ten corporations instead of only one.[13] Even among the 500 largest industrial (manufacturing and mining) corporations in 1983, the top 25 garnered 41 percent of their total sales and the top 50, more than half. A similar trend prevailed in the financial industry.

Despite the slippery slope on which the junk bond market was built, it led to a new era of leveraged buyouts (LBOs) during the 1980s and 1990s, and, ultimately, to downsizing the working class. Though *being* the junk bond market was highly lucrative, Michael Milken saw still bigger money in mergers and acquisitions. A corporation, a public company, would be bought out by a group of financiers with money generated by selling junk bonds to insurance companies, banks, brokers, and S&Ls. In this wonderful arrangement, the financiers did not have to use any of their *own* money. Moreover, all those handling the transactions, including the CEOs selling their own companies and Milken, made tens of millions of dollars.

Some new forces would sustain Milken at a time when his business otherwise would have been slowing. During the Reagan years, a conglomerate rush, the merger of unrelated enterprises, was encouraged by both tax policy and by an antitrust policy most notable for its aggressive laxity. By 1983, the arrangement of mergers had become a growth industry led by a legendary Texas tycoon by the misnomer of Slim Pickens. Fortuitously, by 1985 Michael Milken and his Drexel colleagues had more client money than they could place. To increase the supply of junk bonds, they began to finance corporate raiders such as Pickens, Carl Icahn, Ronald Perelman, and, notably, Kohlberg Kravis Roberts & Co. (KKR).

The KKR executives from 1984 to 1989 borrowed more money through Drexel than any other client of the junk-bond firm: KKR became the dominant takeover artist.[14] Insurance companies, banks, and S&Ls virtually stopped financing the buying of capital goods, drilling for oil, or building houses; they instead lent billions to KKR in their purchases of junk bonds from Milken. KKR completed nearly $60 billion in acquisitions during the 1980s, culminating in the purchase of RJR Nabisco for $26.4 billion in late 1988, then the largest takeover in history and sufficiently notorious to become not only a book but a TV movie. These takeovers of large corporations generated billions of dollars' worth of junk bonds, for even the use of leverage diminishes the value of outstanding bonds of former blue-chip corporations to junk. Milken's salary and bonus continued to climb—exceeding $440 million in 1986 alone.

Conglomeration and its consequences are symbolized by the bidding war for Marathon Oil Company. Mobil, which earlier had acquired the Montgomery Ward department store chain (apparently, it was widely speculated, in order to drill for oil in Montgomery Ward's aisles), tried to buy Marathon. Contrary to the claims for the effects of the supply-side tax incentive program, Mobil expressed an interest in buying *existing* oil reserves rather than going to all the time and trouble of actually looking for new reserves. In its boldest gamble since the company was put together by Andrew Carnegie and J.P. Morgan in 1901, U.S. Steel bid against Mobil for Marathon. As a result of its successful acquisition, U.S. Steel, now USX Corporation, became the nation's 12th largest industrial company.

By the spring of 1990, RJR Nabisco nearly sank into bankruptcy from the cost of keeping its junk-bond debt afloat. KKR, too, was close to sinking. These savings, including those from seniors' social security checks, went, not into new software development or factories, but into junk bonds with values eroding in the high tide of debt. However, unlike many senior citizens and the S&L's, not only did

KKR survive the storms, but by the mid-1990s it was again listing shares of companies it owns on the New York Stock Exchange and expanding its operations.

If net new industrial capacity came out of these acquisitions during the 1980s, it does not show up in the data. Net fixed investment as a share of net national product fell from 6.7 percent in 1970 to 1979 to 4.8 percent in 1980 to 1988. More important, the growth rate in capital services in private business dropped from 4.2 percent in 1960 to 1969, to 4.0 percent in 1970 to 1979, to 3.2 percent in 1980 to 1988, and to 1.3 percent in 1985 to 1988. Productivity also slowed.

This massive consolidation and restructuring was financed by a new breed of financiers. It is a breed well-described by Tom Wolfe in his novel, *The Bonfire of the Vanities*, published in November 1987 just as the bubble was beginning to burst. Sherman McCoy, Wall Street's top bond salesman and the "Master of the Universe," lives in a sumptuous 14-room duplex apartment

> on Park Avenue, the street of dreams! He worked on Wall Street, 50 floors up, for the legendary Pierce & Pierce, overlooking the world! He was at the wheel of a $48,000 roadster with one of the most beautiful women in New York—no Comp. Lit. scholar, perhaps, but gorgeous—beside him! A frisky young animal! He was of that breed whose natural destiny it was ... to have what they wanted![15]

This unreal McCoy was going broke earning a million dollars a year. As one of those "serious bond dealers representing Wall Street," the Master of the Universe

> wore a blue-gray nailhead worsted suit, custom-tailored in England for $1,800, two-button, single-breasted, with ordinary notched lapels. On Wall Street double-breasted suits and peaked lapels were considered a bit sharp, a bit too Garment District. His thick brown hair was combed straight back. He squared his shoulders and carried his long nose and wonderful chin up high.[16]

During the first half of the 1980s, much of the power of commercial bankers and S&Ls had shifted to Wall Street arbitrageurs such as the Master of the Universe, Ivan Boesky, Robert Rubin, investment bankers such as Milken at Drexel as well as the old reliable J.P. Morgan and Company, and stock brokers. In this fast-moving decade, Wall Street nonetheless was scandal-ridden by 1985 and closer to its Trinity Church graveyard by 1987. The Street suffered a fate similar to that of the Master of the Universe; once again, life was imitating art. The great stock market crash of 1987 and the mini-crash two years later, however, did not end the speculative fever nor the new importance of Wall Street in the economy. It simply provided a buying opportunity for those already made richer by tax cuts, interest payments, and capital gains.

The Bursting of Bubbles

For nearly four decades beginning in the mid-1950s, new credit was added to the debt pyramid at a faster and faster pace. Speculative bubbles in real estate and in financial markets during the 1980s were driven by an acceleration in new credit. But toward the end of the Reagan era, the pace of growth slowed dramatically as Chairman Alan Greenspan of the Federal Reserve shifted toward a zero-inflation goal. This reversal of a 40-year trend meant lower real estate values and a slowdown in earnings growth for both financial and nonfinancial corporations.

Weaknesses in real estate were visible by the mid-1980s, but the great stock market crash of October 1987 was the most dramatic omen that the first phase of speculation was about to end. By this time, the S&L industry already had virtually collapsed. By mid-1990, the U.S. Treasury predicted that more than 1,000 S&Ls—more than 40 percent of all thrifts—would have to be taken over by the government. Private sources put the figure closer to 2,000, virtually the entire industry! The final cost to taxpayers could be over $1 trillion, or $4,000 per person. The total number of properties to be sold by federal regulators could eventually rise to one million (a figure excluding the tens of thousands of homes repossessed by commercial banks).

There were close ties between the junk bond dealers and the bonfire of the S&Ls, between Michael Milken and, as examples, Tom Spiegel of Columbia Savings & Loan and Charles Keating at Lincoln.[17] By the end of the 1970s, the S&Ls were paying interest rates of 12 or 13 percent to attract deposits and receiving a pittance from their residential mortgages. By 1982 they were effectively wiped out. In order to "save" them, the White House and the Congress agreed to let thrifts lend money for just about anything. Moreover, *anyone* now could open an S&L. Rogues and outright criminals saw the possibilities. When Willie Sutton was asked why he robbed banks, he answered "because that's where the money is." That's why Charles Keating formed the notorious Lincoln Savings and Loan. Columbia, Lincoln, Vernon, and many of the others inflated their assets with junk bonds.

As the leveraged companies such as Integrated and Campeau began to fail in 1989, the junk bond market began a monumental collapse. Led by the plunge in takeover stocks, there was a "mini crash" of the stock market on October 13. Defaults were the order of the day, and the junk bond assets in the S&Ls approached worthlessness. In the end, nearly every savings and loan that was a major purchaser of Milken's junk was declared insolvent and taken over by the government.

Meantime, commercial banks got caught in the squeeze. A nationwide glut of excess commercial and residential properties was pushing rents down, depressing the value of bank assets. Banks foreclosed on $26 billion worth of commercial properties in 1991, or 32 percent more than in 1990. Although fewer than ten banks per year had failed in the United States from 1943 to 1981, the tide had turned.

What happened to key developers suffering foreclosure is revealed by the fate of Charles Croker, the central character in Tom Wolfe's *A Man in Full*. The setting is Atlanta, Georgia, a late-century boomtown full of fresh wealth. Croker, once a college football star, is now a late middle-aged Atlanta conglomerate king whose outsize ego has at last hit up against the reality of over-due bank loans. Charlie has a 29,000-acre quail-shooting plantation, a young and demanding second wife, but also a gigantic, half-empty office complex built with a huge unpaid debt.[18]

Because of banks lending to developers like Charlie Croker, the FDIC, which has insured bank deposits since 1933, went broke for the first time in 1991. Bank failures drained the fund as 882 banks with assets totaling $151 billion failed between 1987 and 1991. Unlike the failures of many small banks during the Great Depression, these were tumbling giants. Only 11 percent of commercial banks actually posted losses in 1991, but those banks held more than *a fifth* of the $3.4 billion in total system-wide assets. Banks were once considered by the Federal Reserve to be "too large to fail"; now they may be too large to save.

When nonfinancial corporations can no longer service their soaring debts, they too fail. These failures had risen to nearly 1,400 a week in 1987, retreated to a level of about 900 a week by 1989, and then soared to over 1,700 in 1991, rising still higher to 1,800 in early 1992. The same principal and service apply to households. Total personal bankruptcies skyrocketed more than 150 percent during the 1980s to a record 720,000 in 1990.

The further consolation of industry and of financial institutions was turned over to the federal government and to the Federal Reserve System, including taxpayer bailouts of S&Ls, commercial banks, and giant insurance companies. Much of the financial industry was being liquidated by the time that Michael Milken was being sentenced to ten years in prison on November 21, 1990 (only to be released in 1993 on a greatly reduced sentence). In 1996, Michael and his brother, each still among the Forbes 400 richest Americans, invested $250 million to create Knowledge Universe (KU), an educational-services company. Within two years, KU acquired 30 companies and has more deals pending. Some things never seem to change. Who, people were beginning to ask, would bail out the typical wage earner?

Reaganomics was the impetus for the takeovers by the financial wealth holders, and the end of its fallout is not yet in sight. It is difficult to know where all those federal funds and tax breaks went.

In a sense the funds were gone with barely a trace, reminiscent of the experience of Rabo Karabekian, Kurt Vonnegut's aforementioned fictional artist-collector in *Bluebeard*. All of Rabo's own paintings had destroyed themselves because of unforeseen chemical reactions between the sizing of his canvases and the acrylic wallpaint and colored tapes he had applied to them. Yet, people had paid handsome amounts for his paintings.

As Rabo remembers, "...people who had paid fifteen- or twenty- or even thirty thousand dollars for a picture of mine found themselves gazing at a blank canvas, all ready for a new picture, and riglets of colored tapes and what looked like moldy Rice Krispies on the floor." Yet, Rabo had been assured by advertisements that the Sateen Dura-Luxe paint would "...outlive the smile on the 'Mona Lisa.'"[19] People had paid handsomely for Rabo's paintings; now they were gone with barely a trace, and so was the money. Yet, Rabo continued to amass a fortune from his collections and resales. Rabo was like a junk bond dealer and the holders of his paintings, owners of deposits in the S&L's.

THE GROWING INEQUALITY DURING THE 1980s

The Reaganauts' Trojan horse tactic was as successful as it had been for the Greeks in their Trojan War victory of 1200 B.C. Affluent Americans made robust real-income gains, while poorer Americans actually experienced income losses during 1980 to 1984. With about half of American families enduring real-income losses over Reagan's first term, some liberal Democrats were diminished to jokes about the Reaganomics tide "raising all yachts." As family income grew more slowly during the 1980s than in the 1970s or between World War II and 1973, the rich got richer while the poor were getting poorer throughout the Reagan years. The abrupt shift to greater inequality provided $11,317 per family more in 1988 than in 1979 for the top five percent and a loss of $1,200 per family in the bottom three-fifths. The share of income received by the upper one percent soon would be greater than that of the bottom 40 percent!

Any "trickle-down" benefits were illusive. The U.S. official poverty rate had declined to 11.7 percent and 26.1 million persons in 1979, but had rebounded to 13.1 percent and 31.9 million in 1988. In that same year, one of every five children lived in poverty. The poor also were getting poorer, as the gap between actual incomes and the poverty line rose from 8.9 percent in 1973 to 1979 to 15.5 percent in 1979 to 1988.[20]

What happened to wealth inequality was even more dramatic. When we look at those racing to finish the 1980s with the most toys, some were already near the finish line. At the starting line the Federal Reserve Board's survey of consumer finances shows that families in the top two percent—nearly or actually the super-rich—already owned some 39 percent of corporate and government bonds and 71 percent of tax-exempt municipals. The wealthiest ten percent, the simply rich, then owned 70 percent of the bonds and 86 percent of tax-exempts.[21] Most of the values of the holdings of corporate stock and other financial assets also was held in a few hands.

Incredibly, as Reagan's two-term national debt or the value of Treasury bonds outstanding soared to $3.2 *trillion,* his tax cuts had given rich Americans a $2 trillion windfall for their purchase. Tax breaks for the very wealthy enabled them to buy something like $700 billion of Reagan's new bond debt. Even the distribution of these holdings was tilted toward the upper one percent or super-rich, and still more to the upper 0.5 percent or supra-rich. Most, if not all, of these extra dollars went into securities portfolios. Not only were the bonds—in massive quantities—initially created during the Reagan years, but so were the means to buy them. The tax breaks continued through the end of the twentieth century.[22]

Among households, the massive interest payments by the U.S. Treasury blessed the few holding bonds, while crowding out federal expenditures. Since only three percent of all families then directly held any bonds (public or corporate), the top one percent of wealth holders, the super rich, got half of all interest payments going to households, while the top five percent divided up the residual fifth. Compound interest alone was creating new millionaires and billionaires. By the late 1990s, still only four percent of all families directly held any bonds. The 1980s decade's entire increment of disposable income is more than accounted for by the rise in the share of interest income.

Meantime, the entrepreneur's share of national income declined drastically, hardly a Golden Age for entrepreneurship. Productive capitalism builds factories, but the casino economy redistributes and concentrates income and financial wealth.

The interest income trend outlived the Reagan-Bush years. In 1998, Americans paid as much in taxes as interest payments to the bond holders as they paid to run the navy, air force, army, marine corps, intelligence agencies, and the defense administrators and staff. That's about 14 cents of every federal government dollar spent! Largely because of the growth of the bond markets, 13 cents of each dollar of personal disposable income (personal income after income taxes and social security deductions) was coming from interest payments by 1996. In bold contrast, only four cents of each dollar of income came from stock dividends.

A NET WORTH PERSPECTIVE: WHERE THE MONEY WENT

Economists generally do not like to look at net worth or wealth. If we are to understand the effects of the shift to a casino economy, however, we will find the answers in balance sheets.

Inflation in the prices of ordinary goods and services during the 1980s and 1990s declined, while the prices of financial assets boomed. Moreover, the values of tangible asset values were declining or stagnant, even as debt burdens soared. When we consider the distribution of assets by type—financial or tangible—we can further understand why wealth inequalities widened so rapidly.

The super-rich (top 0.5 percent of families) held 46.5 percent of corporate stock and 43.6 percent of outstanding bonds in 1983, whereas the lower 90 percent of American families held only 10.7 and 9.7 percent, respectively. For real estate, the source of a typical family's net worth, the shares are nearly flipped, about half of all real estate being held by the lower 90 percent.

The great disparity between financial asset inflation and tangible asset deflation or stagnation had adverse effects on the lower 90 percent during the 1980s. In the 1983 to 1989 period, the average wealth of the top one percent, the super-rich, rose from $7.1 million per household to $9.0 million. This is the *average*. Meanwhile, wealth fell for the bottom fifth (from –$3,200 to –$18,100 per household and for the next fifth (from $12,300 to $10,100).[23] Michael Milken had made $3 billion in his junk-bond deals during a few years ending in 1989, and was one of the ten richest persons in the United States. It would be easy to conclude that—since the rich were getting richer—business firms must be too. This would be easy, but like so many easy things, would be wrong. Drexel Burnham Lambert Inc., Milken's own firm, filed for bankruptcy protection on February 13, 1990.

As to other firms, if the change in net worth of businesses is combined with that of households, the annual growth of net worth per adult is a flatliner during the 1980s. Moreover, from 1982 to 1992, the net worth of the nonfinancial business sector grew at the feeble pace of 0.62 percent yearly. The growth of net worth in the economy apparently had switched from business firms to selected families. The United States was getting poorer even as its elite was getting richer.

By the time of the presidential elections of 1992, the country seemed to be mired in a dark, foreboding malaise. A troublesome recession, beginning July 1990, ending officially in 1991, and followed by several years of snail-paced growth gave character to the Great Stagnation even as the greatest American bull market in stocks began to roar.

CLINTONOMICS: CONTINUITY WITH THE FEDERAL RESERVE

Historically, a frequent complaint has emanated from New York and Washington: "Those politicians inside the beltway do not understand Wall Street's needs." Unlike so many disputes, the quarrels between The Street and Washington have ended. The head of the Federal

Reserve System, two successive Treasury secretaries, and the bondholding class, itself a joint product of Washington and New York, have moved Wall Street's agenda into the White House. As President-elect, Bill Clinton virtually turned over White House economic policy to Alan Greenspan and to the Treasury heads, all choices of Wall Street. By mid-April 1993, the administration had embraced the preferences of the financial market players for budget deficit reduction and free trade, a dream program for Eisenhower Republicans.

Greenspan and Clinton: An Unholy Alliance

The initial alignment of Clinton and Greenspan seemed as unlikely as that of Venus and Mars. In the 1950s, Alan Greenspan, well to the political right of the Eisenhower Republicans, was drawn into the tight little New York circle led by Ayn Rand. Greenspan had been one of the first students at the Nathaniel Branden Institute, the "think tank" founded to further the ideas of Ayn Rand. Rand's other followers called Greenspan "the undertaker" because he always dressed in a black suit, much like the one he wore to her funeral. Greenspan later took to wearing only blue, perhaps so he would seem less the villain to blue collar workers.[24]

Greenspan was a member of a radical right group known to themselves as The Collective and, to Rand, as the Class of '43, named for the year of her novel, *The Fountainhead*. The Collective converted Greenspan into a lover of free markets, a man not only suspicious of do-gooders but having a righteous hatred of government. Greenspan told the *New York Times* in 1974, "What she [Rand] did—through long discussions and lots of arguments into the night—was to make me think why capitalism is not only efficient and practical, but also moral."[25] Whatever irony attends a free-marketeer becoming the world's most powerful bureaucrat is exculpated by the revelation that Greenspan, the Howard Roark of central banking, has been the lonely hero freeing Wall Street from the chains of government.

Greenspan never strayed from his radical ideology, though as head of the Federal Reserve he stated it with less clarity.

In sharp, dramatic contrast to Greenspan's pedigree, Clinton was a Southern populist who had governed the poor, backward state of Arkansas. He was one of the New Democrats; they were more centrist than the old Democrats, but they nonetheless wished to retain the social programs from Franklin Roosevelt's New Deal. They still believed that the federal government had an important role in maintaining full employment. It was, they believed, the responsibility of the federal government to increase opportunities for the poor, because the rich had the resources to care for themselves. Moreover, Clinton had run for president on a platform of public investment in the infrastructure such as roads, airports, bridges, and schools. By his run for a second term, nonetheless, these issues had long since been abandoned unless "building a bridge to the twenty-first century" is considered a new infrastructure.

Greenspan's Financial Market Strategy

A new psychology came forth: Slow economic growth was *good* because it led to higher bond prices and hence a bullish stock market. Interest rates were to be kept low not by an easy money policy but by managing to keep the economy soft. Even the hint of a speed up in economic growth created a chill on Wall Street. If necessary, the Fed would raise short-term interest rates so that longer-term or bond interest rates might fall.

Greenspan pictured bond holders and traders as "highly sophisticated," by which, he meant that they expected the federal budget deficit to continue "to explode."[26] With such vast federal expenditures, inflation would inevitably soar. In Greenspan's view, the budget deficits from government spending, not soaring oil prices, had induced the double-digit inflation of the late 1970s. Wary investors in long-term U.S. Treasury bonds then demanded higher returns because of the expectations on deficits. This unfavorable spin on federal deficits was the new twist in the post-Reagan policy strategy.

With deficits under control, Greenspan said, market expectations would change, and long-term rates would drop. Since homeowners had increasingly used refinancing as a source of consumer credit, they would buy more automobiles, appliances, home furnishings, and other consumer goods. This borrowing and spending would wonderfully expand the economy. Moreover, as the bond holders got lower yields on bonds, they would shift money into the stock market, and stock prices would take off like a flock of geese. Finally, in this congenial environment, economic growth from deficit reduction would increase employment. Clinton, as president-elect, signed onto Greenspan's post-Reagan policy strategy.

Public Infrastructure is Sacrificed to Reduce the Federal Budget Deficit

Clinton's economic team came to conclude that without Greenspan's cooperation, they were doomed. With visions of stock market crashes, depression, and collapsing banks dancing in his head, Clinton assured everyone that a major deficit reduction plan was already in the works. Clinton, the extraordinary mix of true Democrat, populist, Southern pulse-taker, man-of-the-people, and brainy policy student was out: The Washington-Wall Street establishment had swooped down and stolen Clinton's economic policy.

Gradually the 30-year bond rate did come down, and the capital gains of bond holders went up. There followed an undramatic but steady expansion of GDP. In the interest rate-sensitive sectors of the economy, real GDP rose by 11 percent, while the noninterest-sensitive sectors showed virtually *no growth*. Greenspan and Lloyd Bentsen, the Secretary of Treasury, credited the growth to "the financial markets strategy."

The Greenspan-Clinton alliance nonetheless had the life span of a butterfly. In January 1994, Greenspan told Clinton and his economic advisers that inflation expectations were mounting. Two weeks later the Fed raised short-term rates, with the Fed raising rates a third time on April 18, 1994. The long-term benchmark rate moved higher than any time in Clinton's first term. Greenspan had broken his promise to the president to bring interest rates down if Clinton narrowed the deficit. By the end of this process, Greenspan had raised the fed funds rate seven times.

The same parts of the economy very sensitive to interest rate reductions are equally or even more sensitive to interest rate increases. By early 1995, signs of an economic slowdown appeared. Moreover, a Republican-dominated Congress was pushing for deficit reduction though spending cuts and greatly reduced tax rates for the rich, using Reaganautic rhetoric. Meanwhile, President Clinton was taking a beating in the polls, despite the only significant deficit reductions since the Nixon Administration.

During most of the decade, Greenspan relied on the relationship between the actual unemployment rate and the natural rate (recall the Non-Accelerating-Inflation Rate of Unemployment or NAIRU). Generally, Greenspan used pre-emptive strikes, raising interest rates before even the natural rate flashed the accelerating signal. Though the Federal Reserve had estimated the natural rate at 6.3 percent for 1994 to 2000, the actual unemployment rate, at 4.3 percent in May 1998, had reached a 28-year low and inflation was near zero. Despite the deflationary reality, the Fed continued to fret during 1996 to 2000 about impending inflation. Certainly, this natural bias against inflation and full employment pleased the wealth holders.

Despite the *financial markets strategy* being in disarray, job improvements during the campaign, Clinton's adoption of the Republican agenda, and a lackluster campaign from Bob Dole was sufficient to reelect Clinton in 1996. Meanwhile, Greenspan's strategy had created the greatest bull market in stocks in American history. Though it was his creation, he began to worry that the bubble might burst, a concern echoed in an address in December 1996 about the possible "irrational exuberance" of the market. Thereafter, unable to talk the stock market down, the Federal Reserve generally conducted itself in a manner least likely to precipitate the greatest stock market crash in American history.

In early September 1998, when Greenspan merely hinted that he was as likely to *lower* as to raise interest rates, the Dow made its then-largest point rise ever, a 380-point leap in one day.[27] The Dow swung wildly—hundreds of points from week to week, sometimes from day to day, sometimes *within* the day. The extreme volatility visiting the financial markets during the final years of the twentieth century was unprecedented. In an apparent effort to contain financial market hyper-volatility, President Clinton reappointed Greenspan to head the Federal Reserve for a fourth term a full half year before his third term was to end.

As before, those whose net worth or wealth improved the greatest with booming financial markets were the rich. Projections have the largest increases (in percentage) going to the top one percent. Wealth for the super-rich in the 1989 to 1997 period will grow an estimated 11.3 percent (a $1 million average gain). Meanwhile, the bottom fifth will move closer to breaking-even with a net wealth gain of –$18,100 to –$5,900 while the second fifth will at least see a gain in average household wealth (from $10,100 to $12,300). Still, even with bull market gains, households in the middle fifth of the wealth distribution had a lower level of wealth in 1997 than they had in 1989![28]

THE CLINTON LEGACY: ENDING THE PROGRESSIVE AGENDA

In his second term, President Clinton abandoned domestic economic policy concerns and was looking to foreign policy achievements as a way to elevate his historical place among American presidents. He had fought Greenspan and Wall Street and had lost: Progressives were deeply disappointed with his capitulation to Wall Street.

The Clinton Administration presided over the final phase of a historical shift to monetary policy at the exclusion of fiscal policy. The Reagan Revolution had created so much federal debt (intentional or not) that it left no room to use intentional deficits to stimulate or slow the economy. Besides, political rhetoric had shifted from using the federal budget as a stabilizing force and toward a mantra of balancing the federal budget. Then, budget surpluses were touted and, *finally*, the elimination of the national debt altogether. Since the Federal Reserve buys and sells government securities in the conduct of monetary policy, a national debt of zero would make the conduct of monetary policy virtually impossible. If monetary policy is condemned to the same trash heap as fiscal policy, there will be no need for macroeconomics.

These forces have created and sustained a class rich beyond common imagination. Soon, euphoria combined with price volatility would engulf the sale of bonds, public and private, providing new profit opportunities for daily traders. After huge capital gains had given the bond market long-denied respectability, playing the bond market—joined at the hip by a gyrating but bullish stock market—required the agility of a racquetball champion. The bondholding class, as I call it, carved out of soaring inequality and now operating in a newly deregulated financial environment, would contribute not only to the reversal of fortunes of the lower 95 percent of families, but to the creation of a financial casino.

The completion of the "Reagan Revolution" continued to be promoted by the GOP majority and the editorial page of *The Wall Street Journal*. In 1997, Clinton signed onto a "trickle-down" package of capital gains and inheritance tax cuts. The richest one percent of households once again benefitted by far the most, with each paying $16,000 less in taxes. The bottom 20 percent of U.S. households saw their taxes *rise* by an average of $40 a year. The second 20 percent saw no change, and the middle 20 percent gained only $150 a year. New Democrats, it has been said, are the pragmatists who are able to compromise with the GOP. By that standard, if by no other, Bill Clinton was the most compromised Democrat president in history. In winter 1998 while Greenspan's words still were moving financial markets, the president was impeached by the GOP he had emulated. *That* is the way the world *really* works.

CONCLUSIONS

Like the advertisements for "Sateen Dura-Luxe paint," Reaganomics did not yield the benefits it had promised and Clintonomics kept

Reagan's fiscal revolution alive. Only the smile of "Mona Lisa" seems authentic.

The failures of Reaganomics revived Keynesianism—originally designed by Keynes to save capitalism from itself—at a time when neoclassical Keynesianism appeared comatose. Still, casino capitalism seemed unstoppable at the start of the twenty-first century. Financial deregulation during the 1980s and 1990s opened the door for heretofore unheralded abuse. The initial euphoria of intense competition among suppliers of credit has floundered on the shoals of massive bankruptcies, mergers, and even greater financial concentration.

NOTES

1. Edmund Morris, *Dutch: A Memoir of Ronald Reagan* (New York: Random House, 1999), p. 447.
2. Bartlett, *op. cit.*, p. 1.
3. Gilder, *op. cit.*, p. 188.
4. Quoted by William Greider, "The Education of David Stockman," *Atlantic Monthly*, (December 1981), p. 46. Stockman's confessions had been made to journalist-friend Greider.
5. *Ibid.*, p. 47.
6. In reaction to the massive tax revenue losses, in 1982 Congress repealed a scheduled further increase in accelerated depreciation allowances and eliminated safe-harbor leasing, a 1981 provision that allowed unprofitable companies to sell their tax credits and depreciation write-offs to profitable ones. These 1982 tax changes left the expected return from plant and equipment investment about 17 percentage points (rather than 28) above the pre-Reagan tax treatment return. In the deep economic slump, however, sales were not sufficient to warrant investment in new capacity and the tax cuts could provide no stimulus.
7. An alternative measure of the money supply, M2, was relatively stable during this time. The Federal Reserve, however, was using only M1 as its guide. Later, the Fed would look at a variety of measures of the money supply. M2 includes not only currency, checkable accounts and traveler's checks (M1) but also small-denomination time deposits, savings deposits and money market deposit accounts,

money market mutual funds shares (non-institutional), overnight and term repurchase agreements, overnight Eurodollars, and a consolidation adjustment. Obviously, as Wall Street invents more instruments in which liquid assets can be held, whatever comprises the money supply changes. The other measures, M3 and L, include larger denomination deposits plus financial instruments of long maturities. The search for the "correct" measure of the money supply goes on.

8. Kurt Vonnegut, *Bluebeard: The Autobiography of Rabo Karabekian (1916–1988)* (New York: Delacorte Press, 1987), p. 85.

9. The U.S. Congress rejected Reagan proposals that would have; greatly reduced social security benefits for workers taking early retirement, disability benefits for veterans, federal aid to low-income families for home-heating expenses, spending on the Food Stamp program; eliminated school-lunch programs for middle- and upper-income children; increased payments by Medicare patients for most hospital stays; greatly reduced spending on primary and secondary education programs for the disadvantaged and handicapped; greatly reduced the student-loan program; cut spending for highway and bridge construction; raised interest rates on farm disaster and Small Business Administration loans; sharply reduced general welfare payments; eliminated the Legal Services Corporation and Juvenile Justice programs; drastically cut the budget for maternal and child healthcare, including programs for low-income women who are pregnant; and cut deeper than Congress would allow numerous other domestic programs, including energy conservation, the Environmental Protection Agency, federal mortgage insurance commitments, economic development grants, American Indian assistance, job training, Medicaid, and community services grants.

10. I first introduced the term "casino economy" in *The Making of* Economics, 3rd ed. (Belmont, California: Wadsworth, 1987), pp. 342–343.

11. In 1995, ten percent of families owned 89.8 percent of bonds, and 88.4 percent of corporate stock and mutual funds, with the top one percent alone owning half of all stocks and mutual funds. Finally, the richest ten percent held 71.6 percent of household net worth (value of assets minus value of liabilities).

12. Many more details about Michael Milken and many other Wall Street characters can be gleaned from Pulitzer Prize-winning reporter James B. Stewart's *Den of Thieves* (Simon & Schuster: New York, 1991).

13. The Rockefeller Standard Oil trust was "dissolved" by the U.S. Supreme Court in 1911. The "old" Standard Oil was divided into separate companies whose

operations were allocated to different areas of the United States. Generally, each of these same Standard companies remains the dominant factor in each of the original marketing areas. Among the dominant stockholders of each company are the Rockefeller family, Rockefeller "interests," and the Rockefeller Foundation.

14. The complete story of KKR is told in George Anders, *Merchants of Debt: KKR and the Mortgaging of American Business* (New York: Basic Books, 1992).

15. Tom Wolfe, *The Bonfire of the Vanities* (New York: Farrar, Straus & Giroux, 1987), p. 80.

16. *Ibid.*, p. 50.

17. This connection is established in a wonderfully entertaining way by Michael Lewis, *Liar's Poker* (New York: W.W. Norton, 1989), pp. 206–228. Lewis, now a journalist, was a bond salesman at Salomon Brothers during much of the 1980s. A lively, detailed account of Michael Milken's lucrative life of crime at Drexel Burnham Lambert Inc. is provided by James B. Stewart, *op. cit.*

18. For the "full" story, see Tom Wolfe, *A Man in Full* (New York: Farrar Straus Giroux, 1998).

19. Vonnegut, *op. cit.*, pp. 19–20.

20. See Lawrence Mishel and David M. Frankel, *The State of Working America, 1990-1991* (Armonk: M.E. Sharpe, 1991), p. 168. Additional, related historical data are developed and presented in this important book and its later editions.

21. The categories of richness are defined in E. Ray Canterbery, *Wall Street Capitalism: The Theory of the Bondholding Class* (Singapore/New Jersey/London/Hong Kong: World Scientific, 2000).

22. The massive tax cuts for the rich combined with the torrent of new Treasury bonds was the impetus for what I have called the rise of the bondholding class in *Wall Street Capitalism, ibid.* Much of what follows is a summary of facts and ideas developed in that book; for the details and other ideas, see the original.

23. See Lawrence Mishel, Jared Bernstein, and John Schmitt, *The State of Working America, 1998–1999* (Ithaca and London: Cornell University Press, 1999), pp. 258–275.

24. A much more detailed account of the Clinton-Greenspan years appears in Canterbery, *op. cit.*

25. Quoted by Steven K. Beckner, *Back From the Brink: The Greenspan Years* (New York: John Wiley and Sons, 1996), p. 12. Beckner first became acquainted with Greenspan through his writings on the virtues of laissez-faire economics and

the gold standard in Ayn Rand's journal. Later, Beckner covered Greenspan as a financial journalist in Washington. For the most part, Beckner's book is laudatory, though what Beckner praises Greenspan for, others might condemn him.

26. Bob Woodward, *The Agenda: Inside the Clinton White House* (New York: Simon & Schuster, 1994), p. 69.

27. The day was Tuesday, September 8, 1998. The percentage gain of 4.98 percent, however, was only the 58th largest ever in percentage terms.

28. See Mishel, Bernstein, and Schmitt, *The State of Working America 1998–1999, op. cit.*

16

THE GLOBAL ECONOMY

In its dramatic shift toward freer trade and deregulation of international financial markets, the Clinton Administration actively promoted the further integration of the United States into the world economy. The "global economy," contrary to contemporary pundits, is nothing new. The Roman Empire was virtually global and international trade experienced a rebirth with the early Crusades. What is new is the nature of who trades what and the increase in the volume and speed of movement of financial capital and information around the world.

The great reduction in the cost of transportation and communications have facilitated these movements. The cost of covering distances by sea and air have fallen about one fifth since the 1920s and 1930s, respectively. A three-minute telephone call from New York to London in 1930 cost $250 dollars (in 1990 prices), falling to $50 in 1950, and to just $3.32 in 1990. Meanwhile, the price of processing information fell from $1 per instruction per second in 1975 to one cent in 1994. The costs of using satellites have also fallen in dramatic fashion. These greatly lower costs have come from revolutionary changes in technology and our abilities to spread it.[1]

GLOBALIZATION AND THE GROWTH OF MULTINATIONAL CORPORATIONS

Globalization means different things to different economists. Peter Gray prefers to call it "international economic involvement" (IEI) which itself involves multilateral trade negotiations under the General Agreement on Tariffs and Trade (GATT), now under the World Trade Organization (WTO), bolstered by new free trade areas (European Union), the growth of multinational corporations (MNCs), and the integration of financial markets globally. The consequences of IEI are that nearly all countries are much more deeply integrated into the global economy, domestic markets are much more easily supplied from abroad, and more domestic production is exposed to foreign competition (even the almighty USA).

More than trade is involved: The elements of production such as labor, capital, technology, finance or hot money flows, and direct investment in foreign nations are more mobile. Much of this mobility, such as the movement of managers from country to another and the building of plants in other countries (foreign direct investment), happens through MNCs.[2] Since the 1980s, foreign direct investment—though volatile—has grown 13 percent per year while world trade has expanded only six percent per year, and world industrial production, a mere two percent per year.

Economist Horst Siebert defines globalization as a reduction in market segmentations and an increasing interdependence of national markets. His expressed reasons and consequences of globalization are similar to Gray's. As reasons, he adds the reduction in the political tensions from the ending of the Cold War and Apartheid in South Africa. He cites too the radical changes in the former Soviet Union and Eastern Europe, as well as the opening of China and some movements toward growth in India.[3]

According to Gray, proprietary knowledge or "created assets" is an important, even critical, element of production in the multinational firm. These firms often produce technology-reliant goods or what Gray calls S-goods (the "S" being a nod to Schumpeter). In the detail, two kinds of S-goods dominate: (1) Those requiring industry- or firm-specific inputs (proprietary knowledge, advanced technology), and (2) those that can be differentiated by styling, advertising, salesmanship, promotion, and so on. The hi-tech S-goods include products such as space shuttles, super-trains, microchips, biogenetics, and supersonic aircraft. Differentiated S-goods includes products such as automobiles, motion pictures, and designer clothing. As S-goods become more important, so do multinationals and imperfect competition.

Trade in natural-resource products such as bananas and generic manufactured goods such as cloth dominated the more mundane world of David Ricardo. His idea of comparative advantage did not require the use of created assets nor advertising budgets. Items in trade were plain enough to see. By assumption, no factors of production such as manufacturing plants moved; the movement of the factors would preclude the movement of finished goods and services, or so he thought. In bright contrast, S-goods are the colorful by-product of the supra-surplus economies such as the United States. They require not only technology, but great salesmanship.

The multinationals and S-goods dominate the supra-surplus countries, but are rare in the developing nations. As a result, global manufacturing today is concentrated in the developed countries. Still, the manufacturing that had 30.4 percent of the gross domestic product (GDP) of the developed market economies (members of the Organization for Economic Cooperation and Development) in 1960 had only 23.1 percent by 1987. Manufacturers as a share of world trade increased from only 24 percent in 1965 to 45 percent in 1986 in the developing countries. Much of this export expansion came in the newly industrializing economies of South and East Asia and involved what might be called competitive advantage rather than comparative advantage. How this happened can be explained by returning to the idea of long-term economic growth.

THE INTERNATIONAL PRODUCT S-CURVE

Since Schumpeter's S-goods have come into being, it is not surprising to find that Schumpeter's ideas have relevance for the global economy.

We have entered the era not only of interdependencies of economies, but also of the world product, multinationals, international labor standards, and global ecological concerns.

It is useful to think of the (predominantly) market economics of the OECD and of Eastern Europe as the "North" and the developing countries as the "South." The dream of the low-income countries, dominated by agricultural and other raw materials exports, is to increase the size of their manufacturing sector—to industrialize. Ironically, Northern consumers are nearly satiated with manufactured products and, because of high labor costs, the unit cost of production is substantially higher in the North than in the newly industrializing countries, such as Mexico, the Republic of Korea, Turkey, and Venezuela. For example, Dario Sanchez Delgado's pay was $1.75 an hour in an auto plant in Mexico in 1992; Michael Schultz, a welder at Chrysler's Sterling Heights, Michigan, plant was being paid $16 an hour. Even so, in the supra-surplus economies, there remains the need to market the hyper-surpluses.

The developing countries' sales are nowhere near the flattening-out and turning-down range of their S-curves. The global patterns of the S-curves, have been neatly portrayed by economist Raymond Vernon. The dynamic product cycle is divided among three developmental stages: New product, maturing (growth) product, and standardized product. These patterns are displayed in Figure 16.1.

In the early stage, an entrepreneurial near-monopoly guarantees a small number of firms and high prices. When the production plant becomes large enough and the product price low enough to satiate the domestic market of the supra-surplus economy, production levels off. Long before that happens, however, the marketeers of that product begin to look for sales possibilities abroad (Adam Smith's "vent for surpluses"). In this regard, U.S. corporations established multinational empires on foreign soil; West German and Japanese firms initially established mostly distribution branches abroad and kept production on domestic soil. More recently, Japan and a newly unified Germany have been building factories in the United States and in other countries.

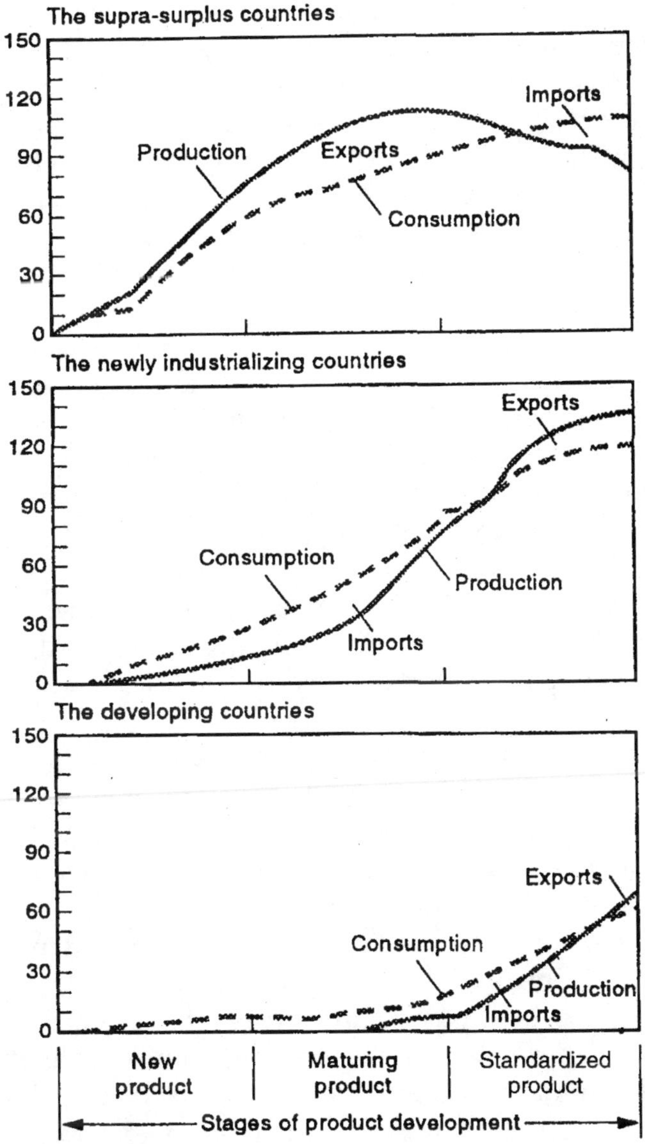

The supra-surplus countries
150
120
90
60
30
0
Imports
Production
Exports
Consumption
The newly industrializing countries
150
120
90
60
30
0
Exports
Consumption
Production
Imports
The developing countries
150
120
90
60
30
0
Exports
Consumption
Production
Imports
New product
Maturing product
Standardized product
Stages of product development

Figure 16.1

In the mature (standardized) stage, the markets in developing countries became a vent for surpluses because the supra-surplus economy encounters competition from other affluent economies as the monopoly positions are eroded. (This happened as the OECD countries became more alike in their postwar recoveries and sated each other.) The newly industrializing countries (NICs) became effective competitors because their adoption of the now-standardized technology is coupled with cheap labor. State-of-the-art steel plants are found in Brazil, Mexico, Taiwan, and the Republic of Korea. These NICs have gone through their "industrial revolutions" and are presently investing large sums in electronics research and development, an act ordinarily assigned to the supra-surplus nations.

In the stagnating developed economies of the 1970s, 1980s, and the early 1990s, charts of the top, flat part of product cycles appeared on U.S. corporate boardroom walls. The giants initially moved toward conglomeration, epitomized by General Motors move into the computer, robot, and robotics vision branches of industry. As noted, the 1980s to 1990s was an era of heated merger and takeover activity, often stoked by junk bonds, and initially epitomized by the R.J. Reynolds-Nabisco drama and later by the activities of Michael Milken and KKR.

Moreover, the close correlation of the business cycles of the OECD countries since the 1950s reflects the overlap of product cycles in nations experiencing similar satiated markets. As a result, the rise in output of products produced through standardized technology but subject to finished product differentiation in the NICs elicited outcries for trade protectionism that became louder and more effective during the 1980s and early 1990s as the need for a vent for surpluses intensified in the beleaguered industries of the North.

The continued dominance of autos, household durables, and steel in many affluent nations is based more on social and political power than on overarching domestic consumer need: The illusion of innovation has masked the reality of stagnation. It is quicker and easier for oligopolists to create the illusion of a product or process improvement than to create a genuinely new and improved product from a new perception. (The neo-Confucian culture does not suffer this defect; it has a much longer time horizon.) Still, Microsoft, the newest monopoly on Atlantic Boulevard, already is well into illusion.

The satiation of a particular or even a collection of product markets is a concern, nonetheless, only for those who take a parochial view. In a global perspective, for example, there is no glut of automobiles. The market for autos in Mexico, being opened by the North American Free Trade Agreement (NAFTA), is new and fresh. Mexico and other developing nations comprise a frontier for products commonplace in the supra-surplus countries. Around the world in 1978, only 300 million autos were available to about 4.25 billion people. We can reasonably expect a global market of about a billion cars at the beginning of the new millennium, and at least a similar tripling (or more) can be expected for other consumer durables.

From the standpoint of global economic development, virtually untapped markets for new product innovations also exist in the supra-surplus countries. The supra-surplus countries have an advantage in those created assets—research-intensive high-technology products. Microchips, biochemistry, genetics research, robots, and exotic manufacturing in outer space can propagate undreamed-of products. At the beginning of the twenty-first century, unskilled workers are being replaced by robots, and semi-skilled calibrators (bookkeepers, typists, and store clerks) already have been replaced by computers in the supra-surplus economies. Manufacturing productivity is reaching perilous heights, and *full-time* human employment could reach perilous depths.

Nonetheless, competitive international advantage, at its core, depends on the progressive (though not necessarily continuous) generation and diffusion of *basic* innovations. The well-known, standardized technologies are, at least in theory, easily transferable from one country to another. The locomotive was invented in 1769, produced in 1824; photography was invented in 1727 and used commercially in 1838; the gasoline motor, invented in 1860, was manufactured in 1886. If the invention and innovation happen in a strategically placed industry and with sufficient diffusion, economic development can follow this *leading* industry.

The lead time between inventions, practical application, and fruition may be getting shorter. (Mensch disputes this.) The fastest-growing industry in the supra-surplus countries is the information industry with its optic cable, microchips, satellites, and laser beams. The only possible barrier to the Chinese knowing about the technology of the supra-surplus nations is lack of Confucian concentration. Even if the time lag between invention and innovation does not shorten, surely the lag between perception and invention will. In any case, the experience of the newly industrializing countries tells us that the diffusion of existing technology happens much faster than in the past, mostly because the cost of information has declined so sharply.

All things considered, in fact, the neo-Confucian culture seems economically more success-oriented than Western culture. The "new Japans" of Taiwan, the Republic of Korea, and Indonesia have already provided some of their own surprises. The American entrepreneur, small and innovative at the start, usually has been willing to "sell out," so that each successive innovation ultimately shares the same fate; namely, virtual monopolization by the giant conglomerate. This process may prevent the United States from leading the global economy out of a stagnation wilderness surrounded by financial fragility.

TRADE DEFICITS AND FULL-TIME JOBS IN THE USA

Perhaps the most important change in the global economy has been in footloose financial capital. Quick money flows and dramatic movements in the prices of currencies (foreign exchange rates) tie many countries to a common fate. This shift has been facilitated by the worldwide proliferation of financial instruments and their unrestrained movements. Financial deregulation at home and abroad during the Clinton-Greenspan years encouraged these developments. In turn, the swiftness with which common national fates can be decided is illustrated by White House international concerns beginning in the mid-1990s.

The U.S. had long been running a trade deficit with its most important trading partner, Japan. Characteristically, when S-goods are traded, the trade is between countries that have similar per capita incomes and similar tastes. Sometime in 1996 White House concerns shifted away from our chronic trade deficit with Japan and toward *its* economic plight. Following the collapse of the speculative bubbles in Japanese stock and real estate markets during the 1980s, its economy went into a depression threatening its banking system. During the twilight of 1996 and the sunrise months of 1997, major White House and Treasury announcements on "balancing the federal budget" were aimed at *strengthening* the dollar to *further expand* Japan's trade surplus with the U.S. and bolster its economy. By then, Japan's collapsing banking system was threatening the world financial markets. Moreover, such a threat could lead to a U.S. stock market crash at a time when Americans considered stock prices to be the best indicator of the economy's health.

A stronger dollar meant a weaker yen, making Japanese S-goods, such as Sony products, cheaper for Americans; greater U.S. imports of Japanese goods and lesser U.S. exports would be a stimulus for Japan's economy. Second, as the great bull market in securities became more and more important to Americans, a new fear arose. Since a weakening dollar reduces the value of U.S. securities held by foreigners, foreign buyers might withdraw en masse from American securities, leading to a crash of the U.S. stock market. By 1997 to 2000, the collapse of many Asian economics and Russia, spreading to Latin America, also made the U.S. a safe haven for rich, foreign bond holders.

America's trade gap with Japan comprised nearly a third of the total deficit and increased 15 percent during 1998. Trade deficits, once a private matter between consumers and firms, now were being sustained to stabilize other financial systems to save our own.

The resultant trade deficit that was a tolerable $20 billion in 1983 set a record at $153.4 billion in 1987. Though the deficit was down to $110 billion ten years later, 1998 witnessed a new record, $168 billion. Much of the more recent deterioration in the trade balance emanated from Asia's plight, with the Brazilian currency crisis threatening to pile still more on the deficit. The falling overseas currencies had made imports cheaper and resulted in a flood of steel, cars and other foreign products into the United States. The U.S. had become the buyer of last resort for a collapsing global economy.

When Americans spend more abroad than foreigners spend in the United States, the net contribution of international trade to the growth of the U.S. GDP is *negative*. While U.S. exports earn national income and contribute to employment, U.S. imports generate income for other nations and greater employment abroad. A U.S. trade deficit of $168 billion means that much less GDP. In short, sales of U.S. securities to foreigners later combined with the Asian and Latin American crises have contributed to the slowdown in U.S. economic growth.

Beginning with the fragile recovery in 1983, the trade deficit was driven not so much by American producers buying foreign machine tools and capital goods, for most were timid, but by aggressively extravagant affluent American consumers. Luxury autos—with nameplates like Lexus, Infiniti Q45, BMW, and Mercedes-Benz—became popular with affluent households. The American preference for foreign luxury goods instead of capital goods continued during the nineties: Even Donald Trump has been buying paintings by Renoir.

American workers have good reason to agonize about the trade trend. For instance, consider a trade deficit on merchandise trade in manufacturers of $168 billion. Since roughly every $54,000 of manufacturing output hires one worker, a $168 billion seepage abroad shrinks the demand for U.S. labor by 3.1 million workers. With the rise of the new leisure class of bond holders and a decline in manufacturing job opportunities attended by downward wage pressures, it is hardly surprising that the economic recoveries from the double-dip downturn of 1979 to 1982 and the recession of 1990 to 1991 were as uneven as brick streets in Boston. In truth, the benefits during the final quarter of the twentieth century were enjoyed only by the upper fifth of families and especially by the richest.

Not all economists agree about the causes of this working class income stagnation. Other elements doubtless have contributed to

American trade deficits. Whatever the other causes of the external deficits, however, the spread of security holdings to trading allies had the same effect, slowing the growth in GDP. Moreover, the rising trade deficits have put further downward pressures on a working class already adrift from union protection. The financial wealth holders, though not the sole cause of growing job insecurity coming from an ill trade wind, nonetheless added a significant dimension to the malaise. Moreover, the downward pressures on wages generally have benefitted the top five percent in the income and wealth distributions—thus far. We next consider the other sources of downward pressures on American full time jobs and wages.

DOWNSIZING AMERICAN LABOR

The Path to Recovery From Junk Bond Debt

As noted, nothing unnerved Alan Greenspan quite as much as a shrinkage in the Reserve's army of the unemployed. Deploying national policy to maintain a large surplus of unemployed workers certainly is an effective way of reducing real wages. However, the adverse effect of this policy strategy on employment has gone well beyond these slow growth policies. These other developments nonetheless help to explain why the *apparent* unemployment rate in the U.S. fell while exerting almost imperceptible pressures on wages and goods prices. At the same time they, too, help to explain why the financially rich got still richer.

Besides their connection to the Federal Reserve's slow growth policies, worker layoffs are directly connected to the financial markets strategy in still another way. The era of mergers by junk-bond leveraging came at a high debt-servicing cost. As noted, U.S. Steel, a.k.a. USX Corporation, became the nation's 12th largest industrial company overnight. The mounting servicing cost of "high-yielding" bonds required cost reductions achieved by laying off workers, including middle management. Initially, at least, getting by with less labor boosts profits and stock prices. The success of the *financial markets strategy* and its encouragement of mergers and layoffs gave bond holders—at home and abroad—capital gains in stocks when not making gains in bonds.

The first wave of downsizing is epitomized by RJR Nabisco. It was able to avoid bankruptcy from its junk-bond financing only by selling off various parts of its business and laying off workers. Of those laid off, 72 percent eventually did find work but at wages about half of what they had been paid. Two subsequent waves of downsizing have eliminated about 2.5 million "good jobs."

The second wave happened, not surprisingly, during the 1990 to 1991 recession. Though workers are always laid off during recessions, this time it was different because the layoffs were *permanent*. Moreover, whereas three blue-collar workers were laid off for each white-collar worker in the 1980 to 1981 near-depression, in the 1990 to 1991 recession the ratio was down to two to one.

The third wave began *after* the 1990 to 1991 recession, during an expansion, albeit a slow and uncertain one. Announced downsizing was in excess of 500,000 workers in each of the three years—1993, 1994, and 1995. By now, corporations were making the highest profits they had made in more than 25 years, helping to fuel the bull markets in bonds and stocks.[4] This wave is epitomized by AT&T's elimination of 40,000 jobs—most in relatively high-paying white collar positions—that welcomed the New Year in 1996.

Thereafter, a *fourth* wave of downsizing began in 1997. Bondholders and shareholders, by now addicted to stunning capital gains, were demanding still more profit improvements. In July, Woolworth and International Paper each euphemistically "shed" at least 9,000 workers, followed by Stanley Works and Fruit of the Loom shedding, not underwear, but nearly 5,000 workers each. The shareholders no longer let companies have very much time to take action. As Whirlpool and Food Lion also announced layoffs, Whirlpool shares immediately spun upward 14 percent, and Food Lion shares, roared four percent.

In 1998, a *fifth* wave of downsizing got underway. In January, the unemployment rate was still fairly low, though rising to 4.7 percent. The rise in unemployment was related to the mass layoffs. This time the alleged villain was the global economy; it had become a jungle out there. The relentless rise in the international value of the dollar and cost-saving restructuring by foreign competitors was forcing U.S. firms to cut their wage bills even more. About a fifth of American workers were exposed to the global tempest. After having cut 142,000 jobs in the last quarter of 1997, the largest since the recession in the early 1990s, toward the end of 1998, major U.S. corporations announced layoffs at a near-record rate of 574,629, the most since 1993. Boeing Co., the aerospace giant, was one of the major U.S. casualties of the Asian currency meltdown, cutting as many as 48,000 jobs by 2000.

An important by-product of downsizing is the temporary worker and the contingent labor force or what might be called "the Wal-Mart labor force." Such workers, often laid off from "permanent" jobs, are compensated less in wages, fringes, and holidays, and are faced with even more insecurity. The male temporary workers earn about half what they would as full-time workers. Most, now among the working poor, were *not poor* when they were working full time, but were middle class. Besides, temporary workers are less likely to have fringes, much less jobs leading to better opportunities. The reduction in employer-provided health insurance and pension coverage (that would otherwise include financial assets) among employed men in the final quarter of the twentieth century has placed still greater stress on families.

Although the Clinton Administration initially was correct to emphasize education and job training that will enable American labor to be competitive in the global marketplace, Greenspan's financial markets strategy undid virtually all that was promised. At the beginning of the twentieth-first century, fear suffuses the employment climate, not simply fear of temporary layoffs, but the fear of layoffs becoming permanent and "permanent" work becoming temporary. Financial holders, of course, are immune to these maladies. Besides, in central bank theory, worker insecurity is good because it keeps a lid on wages and inflation. Alan Greenspan had raised the fed funds rate five times during the new millennium, but prior to April Fool's Day, 2000.

THE GLOBALIZATION OF DEBT AND FINANCIAL FRAGILITY

Chronic U.S. trade deficits had other consequences. Since the U.S. began to run chronic trade deficits, it had to finance ballooning deficits by borrowing from abroad. The multitude of new goods coming in required a tidal wave of money flowing out. The financial aspects of a global economy had arrived at America's banks. For a century beginning in 1870, the United States enjoyed a virtually uninterrupted string of trade surpluses (and positive foreign investment), only to be twanged modestly by the oil crises of the 1970s. Only 40 months into Reaganomics, however, United States foreign investment had become unwound. Within another 24 months, the United States had become the most indebted nation in the world.

With its foreign debt approaching a fifth of its GDP in the year 2000, the United States was beginning to resemble a Latin American country. Since this debt is owed not to ourselves but to others, the nation eventually will have to pay for it by massive productivity increases or by a fall in its standard of living. The United States has become a part of the global debt problem and potentially other problems as well. Any attempt by the United States to quickly reverse its indebtedness would result in a global recession and deflation. At the same time, however, since much of the debt is short-term, a sudden withdrawal of foreigners from American bond and stock markets, would precipitate a stock market crash in the United States.

A comparison of the U.S. situation and the possible global fallout with that of a Latin country is not hyperbole. A global currency contagion brought trouble to the Mexican economy because of the magnitude of Mexico's short-term foreign debt. By 1994, about 40 percent of Mexican treasury notes and about 30 percent of Mexican stocks were held by foreigners. During 1989 to 1993, the Mexican stock market rose by 436 percent in dollar terms. When the rest of world headed north of the border, trying to take their huge profits with them, Mexico was forced to devalue the Peso. By early 1995, this devaluation led to dramatic rises in interest rates—to levels as high as 80 percent. At these rates, Mexican borrowers could not service their debts, and Mexican banks faced insolvency. In turn, the Mexican government not only engaged a $65 billion bank bailout plan, but began to permit foreign ownership of Mexican banks.[5]

The collapse of the peso and the austerity in Mexico spread to the currencies of other emerging market economies. This "Tequila Effect" had spread throughout Latin America and East Asia as early as mid-1995. Although Tequilas do not have the same effect on everyone, the effect in this case led to the "Asian Flu," a sudden and severe collapse of the East Asian developing countries, with Thailand as the first victim. The contagion spread to Hong Kong, Indonesia, Malaysia, the Philippines, and South Korea. Their collapsing currencies threatened the Japanese yen and the Chinese yuan. Worse, as the Flu spread westward, the Russian ruble collapsed, threatening even the bull markets of the United States. The currency crisis circled globally as it hit the backs of Mexico (from whence it had started), Brazil and Argentina. Never in economic history had such a large part of the world fallen so far so fast.

The United States has became dependent on economic growth in Latin America and Asia to avoid a collapse of its banking systems and of global liquidity. The crisis became global because the developing nations owed so much to so few private banks in the supra-surplus countries (especially in the United States). The banks have been gradually "writing off" much of the debt as "bad loans" and its asset value is now only a small percentage of its original dollar value. But these actions, along with other banking problems, have pushed many banks—especially the large New York banks such as Chase Manhattan—close to insolvency. Should a panic and currency contagion begin in the mighty United States, we can only imagine how much faster and how much more devastating the "Dry Martini Effect" might become.[6]

DOWNSIZING THE MIDDLE CLASS AT THE MILLENNIUM

Slower growth, job losses and downward pressures on wages are the most visible adversities from soaring trade deficits in the United

States. This working class blight continued *during an economic expansion, though a slow one,* and was worsened by the Asian and Latin crises. While slow economic growth has contributed to the slow wage earnings growth, slowly rising full-time employment has failed to benefit most families. Those workers retained full-time were working, but not doing better. Moreover, further deterioration of the trade balance from the global crisis slowed growth and kept the unemployment rate higher than it otherwise would have been. The growth rate in real GDP dropped to only 1.4 percent during the second quarter of 1998, well below the speed limit set by Greenspan. Only debt-financed consumer spending leading to a negative personal savings rate could accelerate the American economy thereafter, an expansion increasingly threatened by a tightening of monetary policy during the year 2000.

Thus, as reflected in U.S. Census Bureau data, during most of the nineties the financial condition of the typical worker continued the long deterioration, beginning in the late seventies and accelerating during the eighties and most of the nineties. Over that time, real hourly wages either stagnated or fell for most of the bottom 60 percent of the working population. Still, even the brief episode of substantial economic growth during 1997 to 2000 illustrates the good that growth can do for Americans willing to work long hours. By the end of 1997, median household income had risen to $37,005, bringing the figure to just under the median for 1989, though the gain came from the typical family working four percent longer than at the start of the decade. That is, by working more during an expansion, the typical family had managed to struggle almost back to where it had been a decade earlier.[7]

Americans define the American Dream as achieving middle-class status: It is at least one American middle that is shrinking. This shrinkage is revealed in a different data source that includes both wage and nonwage income. In 1993, 46 million tax returns with incomes between $20,000 and $75,000 were filed, an income range often used to define the American middle class; in that year this "middle" represented only 47 percent of wage and salary earners filing income tax returns. Worse, some 44 million—only two million less than the entire "middle class" or 45 percent of all taxpayers—reported incomes less than $20,000; they are the working poor, an expanding underclass, rapidly approaching half of American taxpayers. The share of American income of the middle fifth of the families declined from 17.5 percent in 1979 to 15.7 percent in 1997.

From 1992 to 1998 while the measured unemployment rate was dropping by more than a third, the real hourly compensation of American workers remained virtually unchanged. Since 1974, the average full-time worker would have to have received $6,000 a year more simply to match the gains in worker productivity. Why, in this environment, would anyone expect that rising wages were threatening to ignite inflation? In truth, the measured unemployment rate counts workers as employed if they hold *any* job—whether it is ten or 40 hours a week; temporary, seasonal, or permanent; paying $7.00 or $70 an hour; or no job, having left the labor force hopelessly discouraged. An unemployment rate reflecting the inability to make a decent living and to gain self-sufficiency would be about three times the official unemployment rate.

CONCLUSIONS

Whatever the other contributions to the reversal of fortunes, some things nonetheless remain clear. Since the weakening of labor unions during the Reagan years, facilitated by the deepest downturn since the Great Depression, intensified by growing trade deficits, and accelerated by the downsizing (which began during the regime of junk bonds and continuing during a period of slow growth engineered by Alan Greenspan), ordinary blue-collar and white-collar workers have greatly diminished wage bargaining powers and live in fear. The only sustained real income growth has come from *unearned* income—mostly from interest on bonds and capital gains on securities. Since most American families have small stakes in financial instruments, the multitudes are dependent upon work for income. Unearned income growing at a historically fast pace during a time of stagnant wages explains the decline of the middle class. The history of the final quarter of the twentieth century has provided a recipe for not only a reversal in the trend toward more income equality since the 1930s, but a shift toward unpardonable wealth inequality.

While the past quarter century has been excellent for the wealthy, its effects have been pernicious for most people. Since richness gained from financial markets does not come directly from exertion, invoking the Calvinistic ethic on its behalf would be presumptuous. Still, the rich would be benign if their gains meant no losses for others. For the financial wealth holders, however, financial success has not depended upon good things happening to the *real* economy in which production takes place. Those working for a living are left to ponder, not the prospect for profits sharing and golden parachutes, but the fate of manufactured products, especially those made for exports in a romanticized global economy.

NOTES

1. These data are found in World Bank, *World Development Report*, 1995, p. 51.
2. See H. Peter Gray, *Global Economic Involvement: A Synthesis of Modern International Economics* (Copenhagen: Copenhagen Business School Press, 1999).
3. See Horst Siebert, *The World Economy* (London and New York: Routledge, 1999).
4. See Lester C. Thurow, *The Future of Capitalism* (New York: Morrow, 1995), pp. 26–29 for a more extended discussion of these experiences. For the data sources, see pp. 334–335.
5. Much of the discussion and data in this and the next paragraph are based on Timothy A. Canova, "Banking and Financial Reform at the Crossroads of the Neoliberal Contagion," *American University International Law Review* 14 (1999): 1571–1645.
6. For suggested modes of regulation, including a tax on foreign exchange speculation, see Canova, *op.cit.* and Canterbery, *Wall Street Capitalism, op. cit.*
7. For a multitude of details on the behavior of wages and benefits, see Lawrence Mishel, Jared Bernstein, and John Schmitt, *The State of Working America, 1998–1999* (Ithaca and London: Cornell University Press, an Economic Policy Institute book, 1999).

17

CLIMBING THE ECONOMIST'S MOUNTAIN TO HIGH THEORY

THE EVOLUTION OF ECONOMICS

We have discovered that economies seem always to be in a state of becoming something else. We might suspect, therefore, to find economic science evolving along with capitalism. We have traced the slow evolution of the market economy out of the failures of feudalism and mercantilism. The international exchange of goods was made possible by the emergence of physical surpluses from the specialization of labor. The value theory of Adam Smith, his attempt to explain the true worth of things, came out of a need to place a "price" on the surplus or net value added.

The Industrial Revolution involved changes in technology so dramatic that theretofore undreamed-of levels of value added were generated. It was the spread of innovations and technology to the United States in the mid-nineteenth century that ushered in the **Gilded Age**. The income of the newly privileged was the household counterpart to surplus production, generating a middle class and extending economic choice beyond the doorsteps of the rich.

Neoclassical economics was directed at the behavior of the upper middle class in England. Still, Alfred Marshall's refinements were in line with Newtonian mechanics. The harmony of markets afforded by the smoothness of the mathematical functions was a major step toward making economics a metaphor of Newtonian natural science; a hardening of the metaphor with Newtonian calculus was completed during the post-World War II era.

A major realignment of the economic stars came from shifting away of Marshall's partial equilibrium approach towards Samuelson's **general equilibrium** approach. Although Samuelson's work comprised much of the beginnings of high theory in the United States, general equilibrium theory was to take theory to elevations of abstraction where even Samuelson's version began to appear concrete by comparison. Since this effort has dominated "higher learning," we should not end without further describing it. In turn, we will learn that climbing to the peak of internal representation is not the same as real-world mountaineering.

HIGH THEORY AND ITS VERSION OF GENERAL EQUILIBRIUM

The trend toward abstraction has its impetus from Walras's **general equilibrium**, continuing with the neoclassical Keynesian model, escalating with the Arrow-Debreu extension of general equilibrium, and culminating in rational expectations and new classical economics. The theory is "general" in the sense that it bridges the gap between micro- and macroeconomics. Where all markets clear at equilibrium prices, all the values of demands, outputs and incomes can be summed into aggregate demand, aggregate supply, and aggregate income. In its preferred mode, Walrasian general equilibrium theory is intended to apply only to completely free markets and free choice.

In contrast to Walras and the contemporary approach, Adam Smith, David Ricardo, J.S. Mill, and Karl Marx had a theory of value driven by the cost of production and zero profit rates under what eventually was to be called perfectly competitive conditions. Generally, however, demand affected only quantities and not prices. Prices essentially were decided by the costs of production. The alternative, the neoclassical theory of value, had demand on a more than equal footing with supply in deciding equilibrium prices. The classicals took markets to be related, but ignored the influence of demand on value. As noted, Marshall understood the idea of general equilibrium but believed that Walras's mathematics was not up to the task. On this, he was correct.[1]

Out of the Walrasian tradition, four main issues confronted the modern theorists. (1) Could the existence of unique equilibria be proven for a Walrasian model? If not, there goes the complete theory of value in interdependent markets. (2) If equilibrium exists, is it stable? If not, multiple equilibria are possible. (3) Will Walrasian equilibria satisfy the criteria of modern welfare economics? If not, how can equilibrium be judged as "good." (4) Will Walrasian equilibria exist under conditions of uncertainty? If not, and if uncertainty exists, the equilibria are irrelevant.

Obviously, since equilibrium in a Newtonian sense is at issue, the questions and the answers are purely mathematical. Algebra and Newtonian calculus, however, were not up to the task. Kenneth Arrow, Gerard Debreu, and those to follow used set theory whereby the values of variables can be "mapped" into abstract spaces.

In 1954, Arrow and Debreu published their proof of the existence of equilibrium for a "competitive economy." They began with a private ownership economy in which tastes (preferences), technology, the initial income and wealth distributions, and the private ownership of firms are "givens." Consumers and firms are price-takers; that is, an individual consumer or firm has such a small, incremental share of incomes and products that no one can influence prices. Put differently, as in Smith, only the market, not any individual or firm, sets the price. Once things are added together, aggregate demand and aggregate supply are equal, their difference being zero. In all markets, this is Walras's law; the value of excess demand is zero.[2]

Though the theory is quite abstract, it can be understood despite the purely technical nature of the achievement. Still, the proof could not have been completed without an earlier publication by John F. Nash, Jr. (1950), showing the existence of equilibrium points for noncooperative games by the use of a fixed-point theorem.[3] The condition quickly became known as a "Nash equilibrium." Game theory, as it is called, comes into play because the actions of each consumer and each firm are restricted by the choices made by all other consumers and firms so that no one has the incentive to choose an alternative action. Put differently, you would have made a different choice if you did not have to take into account the choices that your friends make.[4]

A brief account of John Nash's life and career sheds some light on how he invented his theory of rational behavior.[5] Born in Bluefield, West Virginia, Nash grew up to be a tall, handsome, arrogant, and extremely eccentric man. A genius surrounded at Princeton by the high priests of twentieth-century science—Albert Einstein, John von Neumann, and Norbert Wiener—Nash climbed to his own cadence, one that mostly was in his mind. Instead of ascending a peak along a path on the existing mountain of science, Nash would climb another mountain altogether.

He had one consistency; he was "compulsively rational," the adjective contradicting the noun. He turned life's decisions—whether to say "hello," where to bank, what job to accept, who to marry—into mathematical rules divorced from emotion, convention, or tradition. What he accomplished in mathematics nonetheless was astonishing. While John von Neumann had first analyzed social behavior as zero-sum games, Nash focused on the individual, thereby making game theory relevant to Smithian economics wherein everyone wins. Each of Adam Smith's butchers and bakers would independently choose his best response to the other players' best strategies. Though this young man seemingly was out of touch with other people's emotions, including his own, he could envision a person selecting the purely logical strategy necessary to maximize his own advantages and minimize his disadvantages. It was the proof that Arrow and Debreu used to provide a mathematical solution for Adam Smith's metaphor of the invisible hand. In the end, it was a Nash equilibrium.[6]

By the age of 30, Nash was recognized as one of the great mathematical geniuses of his century. In that year, Nash suffered his first episode of paranoid schizophrenia. For three decades, he had severe delusions, hallucinations, and disordered thought and feeling. Nash, believing himself to be a "messianic figure of great but secret importance," abandoned mathematics for numerology and religious prophecy. Like Zelda Fitzgerald, he had all kinds of drug and shock treatments and experienced brief remissions and signs of hope that lasted only a few months. Finally, he became a sad phantom haunting classrooms at Princeton University and scribbling on blackboards. Meanwhile, his name surfaced everywhere—in mathematics journals, political science books, articles on evolutionary biology, and economics textbooks and articles.

Zelda Fitzgerald wrote self-referentially of her feelings in *Save Me the Waltz*: "Of all things on earth she had never wanted anything quite so much as to possess herself, as it seemed to her, that she could attain a perfected control."[7] Her driving, compulsive interest was in the perfection of her body through ballet dancing. Nash's compulsion was to perfect his mind. The life of the schizophrenic is torn between the desire to reveal himself and his desire to conceal himself. Feeling vulnerable, he becomes adept at self-concealment.

In the end, the story is not as tragic for Nash as it was for Zelda (who never recovered). Nash experienced a rare, spontaneous recovery from schizophrenia. By the early 1990s, he was doing mathematics again. In 1994 John Nash, along with John C. Harsanyi and Reinhard Selten, was awarded the Nobel Prize in economics for "pioneering analysis of equilibria in the theory of noncooperative games." The behind-the-scenes drama behind the award is almost as extraordinary as the fact that a mathematician won the award at all, especially one presumed to be dead.[8] Though Nash was not asked to give the traditional acceptance lecture, he caused no embarrassments at the Nobel ceremonies, simply behaving like the eccentric he had been as a young man.

The Nash equilibrium returns us full circle to the main Arrow-Debreu story. Though existence of some equilibria set was proven, Arrow-Debreu could not prove it to be unique. Any number of equilibria sets might satisfy a particular technology and initial income-wealth distribution. A true understanding of how an economy selects among the many Walrasian equilibria would require a breakthrough greater in magnitude than Walras's original theory *and* Nash equilibrium. Until then, the claim to a new theory of value is vacuous.

A related issue is whether "modern" welfare economics is displaced by Arrow-Debreu. Put differently, are the Walrasian equilibria the same as the optimal conditions in "modern" welfare economics? To this day, welfare economics is based on Pareto optimality. A **Pareto optimum** happens when no further change in the economy (such as a price increase or decrease) would improve the Benthemite utility of one person without reducing the utility of at least one other person. Put simply, a Pareto optimum requires that all the marginal conditions of the **marginalist school** be met. In particular, marginal utilities are equal across all consumers. General equilibrium ideally would extend these marginal optima to all individuals and firms. These criteria of welfare, however, concern only engineering efficiency, not how persons truly feel about their conditions at different *plateaus* of income or wealth.

Maurice Allais, the winner of the 1988 Nobel Prize in economics for his "pioneering contributions to the theory of markets and efficient utilization of resources," demonstrated (1943–1947) that each market equilibrium is socially efficient in the sense that no one can become better off without someone else becoming worse off. Moreover, such a result even follows after a redistribution of initial wealth endowments has taken place. Again, many different sets of equilibria prices and quantities are possible.[9] As it turns out, if competitive conditions prevail, for given technologies and income-wealth distributions, each of the many possible equilibria are Pareto optimal. But, we knew this to be the case as early as Paul Samuelson's *Foundations*.

In 1952, Allais and Arrow independently introduced uncertainty into general equilibrium theory. The same theorems and proofs apply as to Walrasian equilibria. In Arrow, the uncertainty is managed by the introduction of securities and securities trading. Along with the introduction of security markets, Arrow makes use of "perfect foresight" regarding equilibrium price expectations. Each person and firm has a complete catalog that lists all possible sets of future prices and quantities ("states," as it is formally called) in the economy. Think of it as a Sears Catalog; each person and firm has a copy of the same Sears Catalog.

The difficulty is in knowing how everyone could end up with the same catalog, especially since, unlike in Sears, the prices and quantities change every second. Often this is called the "coordination problem." Problem, indeed! Coordination would require, not simply the Walrasian auctioneer, but a supra-Walrasian auctioneer who not only knows tastes, technology and income-wealth distributions, but computes and then somehow announces to all parties all future spot prices for each set of quantities.

The introduction of perfect foresight brings us back to **rational expectations**. The new classicals (See Chapter 12), too, developed a kind of general equilibrium theory because it is grounded in optimization at the level of individual behaviors. The main departure by the new classicals from the Arrow-Depreu-Allais version of general equilibrium is their focus on economic policy failures. All "anticipated" policy changes invariably leave the economy worse off, violating Pareto optimality. Thus, changes beyond those inside of free markets are bad, so that the ideas of the new classicals also fall under the same rubric of high theory.

Still, we would be remiss not to consider other theories besides Walrasian general equilibrium theory that recognize interdependencies in an economy. Moreover, these theories provide a more critical assessment of whether the prevailing high theory will dominate the future of economics. We will address the question of whether the view is better from the top of the mountain or whether perhaps the peak is shrouded in mist, greatly reducing visibility.

INPUT-OUTPUT AND PRICE MARK-UPS: AN ALTERNATIVE VIEW OF INTERDEPENDENT INDUSTRIES

Input-output theory is another way of accounting for interdependencies in an economy. Wasily Leontief (1905–1999), a Russian-born American economist who studied in Leningrad and

Berlin, invented input-output analysis. A short, modest and kind man, Leontief often came to the defense of older and younger radicals of the left when he was at Harvard. He and Arrow were among those who left Harvard in protest when the Harvard economics department purged itself of the brilliant young radicals on its faculty.

Unlike the general equilibrium approach, input-output is driven by technology.[10] The recipe for production decides the type and amounts of inputs required for a unit of a particular output. This technological requirement extends to labor and capital. For example, the *direct* relationship between inputs and output (the technical coefficients) tell us that in 1978 the production of a ton of U.S. carbon steel required 0.95 tons of coal, 8.14 manhours of labor, 1.65 tons of iron ore, 0.10 tons of steel scrap and 11 mbtus of energy. The idea is not just theory, these coefficients were estimated by Leontief. Input-output is empirical and had its beginnings in real-world numbers.

At a particular technology, the technical coefficients are fixed for a time at all levels of output so that constant costs prevail, much as in classical economic theory. With such things temporarily unbending, the difference between total expenditures by industries (the same as the value of total output) and the outlays for materials is equal to the industries' value added or income generated for the economy. In turn, this value added is actually the sum of wages, salaries, interest, rent and profits in the economy. In this way, the value of national output will equal the value of national income. In fact, the national input-output table has been used as a periodic check on the reliability of separately estimated national income accounts.

It is possible to return from the economy's totals to the details in a particular industry. Continuing our earlier example, the 8.14 manhours of labor required to produce a ton of steel multiplied by the wage rate for steelworkers ($11.66 per hour) and, in turn, multiplied by total carbon steel production gives us a total wage bill for the industry. The wage bill divided by total steel produced (in tons) gives the wage bill per ton. If materials costs per ton plus the wage bill per ton is subtracted from the price of carbon steel, we have the residual income or unit "profits" of $29.92 per ton that year.

The entire system, of course, is much more complex than this brief summary can convey. For example, both direct and indirect materials and labor requirements are computed. Continuing our example, the *indirect* requirements in steel production include the tons of coal required to produce the 1.65 tons of iron ore in order to produce directly the ton of steel, as well as the mbtus of energy to produce the 0.95 tons of coal to produce the ton of steel, and the amount of transportation to get the 0.10 tons of steel scrap to the steel plant to produce the ton of steel, and so on.

Consideration of both direct and indirect requirements are important in finding the final prices. The income payments per unit of product that become price include not only the value added of those industries providing direct inputs, but also of those industries providing indirect inputs. Therefore, the prices which must prevail in the long period if each industry is to cover its costs of production will be based on directly and indirectly incurred costs of production and income payments.[11] As I said, the complete system is complex.

Those who read carefully about Piero Sraffa and the Post Keynesians in Chapter 11 will recognize input-output as the technique used in Sraffa's theory of value. In Leontief and in Sraffa, wage rates do not measure the marginal product of labor and the profit rate does not measure the marginal productivity of capital. In Sraffa, the value added in the steel industry will vary as the wage rate and thus the industry's wage bill will move relative to the profit rate. In turn, since the price of steel depends upon value added, the relative price of steel (say, to autos) will change. Technological improvements will also alter prices. In violation of all things held sacred in general equilibrium theory, price changes alter the income distribution even as the income distribution alters prices.

Put differently, general equilibrium prices allocate resources in "an efficient way"; Sraffian prices do not, but rather are the vehicles for redistributing income between workers and capitalists as wage rates move relative to profit rates. Since efficiency depends only on technology—not on relative prices—income is left free to be allocated by the institutions of habit, relative bargaining power, or other institutional forces. Meanwhile, total national output is above the fray and out of harm's way.

Still, a technical issue remains. Can the intermediate output supplied by all industries be reduced to only one type of fundamental input? This central issue in value theory has divided economists, as we have seen, from the beginning. Karl Marx believed labor to be the only source of value. The neoclassicals come closer to the opposite: They would focus on the profit rate as the marginal product of capital. The neoclassical theory is closer to a capital theory of value.

The resolution of this dichotomy is not easy; I will invoke my author's privilege and sketch my answer.[12] Let prices be set on a percentage mark-up placed by each industry on its wage bill, on its direct and indirect materials requirements, and on its direct and indirect profits from all industries. Then, no distinction need be made between the mark-up and the profit margin, even for a growing economy. The percentage mark-up (and the profit rate) is greater, the less sensitive consumers of the product (be they households or other producers) are to price changes, and the stronger the effect of incomes on demands.

Everything said earlier about the effects of advertising and salesmanship on the selling of nonessentials under supra-surplus capitalism apply here. After all, at the risk of seeming mundane, when you buy a new Oldsmobile, the factory has given the Olds' dealership a mark-up on unit production costs (the cost of direct and indirect labor, materials, and capital goods requirements). This difference between the cost of production (factory price) and the final selling price (list or "sticker" price) can be varied depending on how many persons like you have been persuaded that the Olds has the ideal combination of horsepower, handling qualities, comfort, gas mileage, style, and metallic paint of an automobile that you can "afford" at your income level. The factory price, of course, includes all of the factory's direct and indirect costs plus the *factory's* mark-up.

CHOOSING BETWEEN EQUILIBRIA AVENUES: A CRITICAL PATH

These two approaches—general equilibrium and input-output cum mark-up—provide clear choices. Still, as noted, general equilibrium dominated the academic research agenda during the 1990s. Several reasons may be advanced for this. (1) At the outset, input-output was used as a planning device for developing countries, including the Soviet Union. It did not begin as a free-market tool. (2) The collapse of the Soviet economy (and political system) in the 1990s was hailed as a victory of free-market capitalism and the bankruptcy of anything even vaguely based on "a plan." (3) Any theory that does not rely on wages being paid, the value of marginal products and profits being the return to capital, violates the value theory of neoclassical economics and of general equilibrium theory. (4) Set theory is a more elegant form of mathematics than is the matrix algebra used in input-output models. The elegance of set theory nonetheless depends upon an abstractness unenlightened by the real world.

One can only guess as to which of these reasons has been the stronger force keeping Post Keynesian economics at bay. The attempt by Western economists to implant a free-enterprise capitalistic system to replace the old Soviet order has failed. Many economists had claimed that a capitalist utopia would immediately emerge from the Soviet ruins, a vision embedded in general equilibrium theory. In reality, many Russians only began to appreciate socialism after they had tried "capitalism." The Russian experience illustrates how important institutions are in the creation and evolution of a successful market system. Russia was devoid of the capitalist institutions that had evolved over many centuries in Europe and the United States.

The rise of the New Right in the U.S. and Thatcherism in the U.K. has provided a great amount of support—ideological and financial—to those economists supporting the free-market vision. This ideological thrust conveniently ignores the failures of monetarism and supply-side economics. Even in the absence of the ideology, however, many economists are committed to marginalism because the prices generated in the theory are the only "values" in any theory of value that are not contaminated by social or political judgments. Again, however, that is the case in theory only. In particular, the moral defense of capitalism requires that capital be paid no more than what it is worth—the value of its marginal product.

Finally, we cannot ignore the self-interest of economists. The young lions going into the top PhD programs in the U.S. are told that they will need to know the mathematics of general equilibrium to obtain a good position and ultimately tenure in the academy. The graduate student who is not good enough in mathematics to obtain a PhD in that field can be a star in economics. In a survey of 200 economics graduate students in America's top graduate-economics programs, only three percent thought that a thorough knowledge of the economy was "very important"; what mattered far more was "being good at problem-solving" and "excellence in mathematics." Cleverness is in; knowledge of economics is out.[13] No wonder that American economic advisers were telling the Russians that only individual self-interest, not new institutions, would usher in a capitalist utopia.

Thus far, general equilibrium has failed at the empirical level. "Why" is easy to see for a story linked to the creation of the theory of games and to the fixed point theorem. One close and important student of the genre has written, "the 'equilibrium' story is one in which empirical work, ideas of facts and falsification, played no role at all."[14] History, too, we might add, has played no role except to be absent. From this story, nonetheless, we can draw some lessons for the future of economics.

From the beginning, technological change, a "given" in general equilibrium theory, has driven real-world economies. Moreover, history displays three ages—the **Gilded Age**, the **Jazz Age**, and the Age of the **Casino Economy**—in which income and wealth distributions have become highly unequal and in which financial speculation has become more important than production. (Many prefer to call the most recent era "the Information Age"; information, however, should not be confused with knowledge.) Yet in general equilibrium theory, the initial income and wealth distributions are simply "givens." New technologies emerging before a mass market seem to breed financial fragility. A viable economics will have to breeze past general equilibrium theory; the new vision will require an understanding of technological change, income and wealth distributions, and financial instability within capitalism as a moving target.

These thoughts are closely allied with our concluding thoughts regarding the future of economics.

NOTES

1. For an interesting and complete history of the mathematics and the mathematical economists culminating in contemporary general equilibrium theory, read E. Roy Weintraub, "On the Existence of a Competitive Equilibrium: 1930–1954," *Journal of Economic Literature* 21, no. 1 (March 1983): 1–39.

2. There is an excess-demand system of ℓ equations in the ℓ price variables:

$$(1)\ z_i(p_1,\ldots, p_\ell) = 0,\ i = 1,\ 2,\ldots,\ \ell.$$

The forces of supply and demand, which the "givens" (tastes, technology, and income and wealth) define for the economy, will be in balance at prices p^* if and only if p^* solves (1) and, therefore, comprise the set of equilibria prices. In Walrasian theory, value is determined by a solution to (1). A theory of value requires an existence theorem to insure that, for all economies from a broad class, there will be at least one solution to (1) in positive prices. In the aggregate:

$$(2)\ \Sigma_i p_i z_i(p_1, p_2,\ldots, p_\ell) = 0.$$

For a complete but critical survey of Arrow's contributions to general equilibrium theory, read Darrell Duffie and Hugo Sonnenschein, "Arrow and General Equilibrium Theory," *Journal of Economic Literature* 27, no. 2 (June 1989): 565–598.

3. There is little reason for most people to know the definition of the fixed point theorem. But, for the curious, it states that if $x \rightarrow \phi(x)$ is an upper semi-continuous point-to-set-mapping of an r-dimensional closed simplex S into $A(S)$ (the set of closed convex subsets of S), then there exists an $x_o \in S$ such that $\phi(x_o) \in A(S)$. A corollary says that S could be any compact convex subset of a Euclidean space. "Convexity" simply means that factor substitutions, say, capital for labor in the production of a product, gives diminishing marginal products for the factor which is increased.

4. A Nash equilibrium n-tuple of choices has the property that, given the choices of other persons, each person's payoff is maximized. For example, what others

choose influences prices and quantities that determine what a person can afford. Debreu developed the idea of a generalized *n*-person game wherein for each person there is a set of feasible choices that depend on the choices of others. Then, what is feasible depends on the actions of others.

5. For a splendid and moving award-winning biography of John Nash, read Sylvia Nasar, *A Beautiful Mind* (New York: Simon & Schuster, 1998). Some of the biographical data in the next few paragraphs is found in Nasar.
6. *Ibid.*, p. 16.
7. Quoted by Nancy Milford, *Zelda: A Biography* (New York, Evanston, and London: Harper & Row, 1970), p. 242.
8. Read the full story in Nasar, *op. cit.*, Chapter 48.
9. As is the custom, Allais presented a brief biography and an outline of his main contributions at the Nobel Prize awarding ceremony. See Karl-Göran Mäler, *Nobel Lectures: Economic Sciences, 1981–1990* (Singapore/New Jersey/London/Hong Kong: World Scientific, 1992), pp. 215–252.
10. For a non-technical but complete explanation of input-output theory, see E. Ray Canterbery, "Input-Output Analysis," in *The Elgar Companion to Radical Political Economy*, eds. Philip Arestis and Malcolm Sawyer (Hants, England/Brookfield, Vermont: Edward Elgar, 1994), pp. 212–216.
11. These prices, or the "dual price solution" to the Leontief model of production, comprise the value added vector properly multiplied by the Leontief inverse. The Leontief inverse (an inverted matrix) gives not only the direct but also the indirect materials requirements for each industry.
12. See E. Ray Canterbery, "The Mark-up, Growth and Inflation," Paper presented at the Eastern Economic Association Meetings, March, 1979 and E. Ray Canterbery, "A General Theory of International Trade and Domestic Employment Adjustments," Chapter 16 in *International Trade: Regional and Global Management Issues*, ed. Michael Landeck (London: Macmillan, 1994). Eichner, who long before had a fully developed theory to explain mark-ups, employs Leontief, Luigi Pasinetti, Sraffa and Canterbery to build a dynamic or economic growth version of this genre. What enables an economy to grow are the introduction of investment (in capital goods) in excess of what the economy requires simply for its reproduction, as well as the inclusion of business savings as part of industry profits. See Alfred S. Eichner, *The Macrodynamics of Advanced Market Economies* (Armonk, New York: M.E. Sharpe, 1987) and Luigi L. Pasinetti, *Structural Change and Economic Growth* (London: Cambridge University Press, 1981). The Canterbery models (1979, 1994) and those of Pasinetti were developed independently but share some characteristics.

13. Arjo Klamer and David Colander, *The Making of an Economist* (Boulder/San Francisco/London: Westview Press, 1990), p. 18. This entertaining, in-depth look at how economists are being trained and the attitudes of the students reveals much more than can be addressed in this short book.

14. Weintraub, *op. cit.*, p. 37.

18

The Future of Economics

THE QUEST FOR "RADICAL" ALTERNATIVES

The role of "radical economists" has always been to call attention to the gap between reality and the prevailing science, a practice often viewed with bemusement by the orthodoxy. Still, if we are to take a view sometimes at odds with the orthodoxy, a "radical" alternative, by definition, is the only game in town. The radicals have provided alternative visions.

Karl Marx saw instability, monopoly capital, and worker alienation while the classicals idealized the natural self-adjusting characteristic of markets by a force—the invisible hand—that emulated Newton's gravitational constant. Thorstein Veblen observed the reality of the robber barons narrowly focused on money rather than on production and bemoaned the rising importance of product marketing.

More recently, John Kenneth Galbraith has renewed Veblen's attack on the neoclassicals and sees production in the supra-surplus economies requiring a diversion of enormous resources and a special devotion to marketing and advertising so as to ensure spending rather than saving by the more privileged income earners. Robert Heilbroner bemoans the habit of professional economists who theorize about an abstract economy without revealing its attachment to contemporary capitalism. Next, we consider the seriousness of these "radical concerns."

THE KEYNESIAN CHALLENGE

Thus far, the most serious challenge to the orthodoxy is the economics (in one form or another) of John Maynard Keynes. But, Keynesianism fell on its own cutting edge. The General Theory was vulgarized by well-meaning apostles until the theory bore more resemblance to neoclassical economics than Keynes, the neoclassical heretic, could ever have intended. Like Marx who eventually proclaimed that he "was not a Marxist," Keynes doubtless would no longer be a Keynesian.

When science fails, as it did in the nineteenth century, it falters also as faith, and there is that deeper retreat into religion and Spencer's Unknowable. The failure of vulgarized Keynesianism led to the monetarist counterrevolution that became a canon of first-term Reaganomics. Those failures also led to Post Keynesianism, New Right radicalism, and New Classicism.

Modest Keynesianism was deployed during the 1930s and military Keynesianism was fully exploited during World War II. Then, the success of the Keynesian policies of the Kennedy-Johnson Administrations defined the golden age of modern macroeconomics. Since, Reaganomics or supply-side economics has been put into practice. The latter, as noted, required more faith than science.

Policy descended from the lofty perch of high theory to the banality of Reaganomics and Thatcherism: It was at once a giant backward step for economic science and more than a small step backward for humanity. George Gilder, who never won a Nobel Prize in economics, deserves much of the credit for the Reaganomics mis-step; he was able to serve the White House a benign universe, God, and economics on the same platter. "To overcome it is necessary to have faith, to recover the belief in change and providence in the ingenuity of free and God-fearing men. This belief will allow us to see the best way of helping the poor, the way to understand the truths of equality before God...."[1]

Gilder even updates the stories of American clergyman Horatio Alger and the benign universe, wherein wealth was the outcome of chance, appropriate acquaintances, and deservedness. The **Gilded Age** (c. 1870–1910) thrived on these extensions of the Old Testament stories of Noah, Abraham, Joseph, and David. To Gilder, economic innovation requires an ascendancy above narrow rationality and the embrace of religious values, no matter how unconscious the worship of God. Virtue and chance meld as "...the lucky man is seen as somehow blessed. His good chance—and society's redemption—is providence." If the "miraculous prodigality of chance" is replaced by a "closed system of human planning," all is lost because "success is always unpredictable."[2] Essentially the "moral spark" of the **Gilded Age** was being offered to the **Gildered Age**.

The thoughts of Ayn Rand and the neo-Austrians would have been with Gilder on the futility of "planned beehives." However, *their* entrepreneur acts out of rational intelligence and free will, more like a player on the cusp of a Nash equilibrium; luck, providence, and God do not rule in the neo-Austrian cosmic machine. Gilder, along with unrepentant supply-sider Jude Wanniski, were able to rehabilitate Horatio Alger; they became board members of "Working for the American Dream," an organization intent on burnishing Michael Milken's image. This is the same Milken whose prosecutors excoriated for "a pattern of calculated fraud, deceit and corruption of the highest magnitude," whose crimes "were crimes of greed, arrogance and betrayal," part of a "master scheme to acquire power and accumulate wealth."[3] Are these the values inherent in the "American dream"? Were the prosecutors callous in their disregard for the memory of Horatio Alger?

The Post Keynesians, or the more literal interpreters of Keynes, would not fault the neo-Austrian critique of neoclassical method, for they agree on the unrealism of Newtonian equilibria. The Post Keynesians would not even fault Gilder for being even more unabashed than the Austrians in seeing value judgments necessarily embedded in economic reality and therefore in economics. Once we recall that Keynes was responding to the reality of the Great Depression and placed policy before theory, we can appreciate why the Post Keynesians want to have their theory and reality too.

The Post Keynesians' discordance with the Austrians stems from the Austrian view of economic reality. This is so even though Keynes is forever writing of the entrepreneur as the key decision maker. In Keynes, however, the mistakes of the entrepreneur cause depressions; in Austrian economics, the unfettered entrepreneur guarantees prosperity.

As we are in an age in which science is no longer worshipped for its own sake, economists need not be apologetic if they succumb to a new sense of realism, if they detach somewhat from high theory. We do not have to accept a new Social Darwinism in order to allow ethical judgments to enter social science. Rather, if Joan Robinson were alive, she would have economists combating (if they were so persuaded) the new Social Darwinism by elevating social consciousness.

Lives are at stake, and the modern world demands an economics tailored to human needs, one that recognizes that our behavior—especially our social behavior—is both more sophisticated and more unruly than that of particles or bees. And, no doubt, human welfare is closely allied to per capita real income and the distribution of such income, just as it is allied with the distribution of wealth. Thus, the Post Keynesian and the institutionalist stress on the income distribution brings us closer to a human science.

Capitalism—now global capitalism, in which the fading manufacturing sector in the supra-surplus economies depends upon production at low wages and benefits—faces its third crisis since World War II. The Phillips curve trade-off between inflation and unemployment that undid vulgarized Keynesianism remains an anomaly left unresolved by the monetarist experiment. Reaganomics aggravated the problems of poverty, and bequeathed (along with other forces) the Great Stagnation, unsustainable budget deficits, high real rates of interest, financial fragility, and a global debt crisis.

Clintonomics ended the budget deficits, even creating at least fleeting budget surpluses, and bequeathed enhanced financial volatility and nourished the greatest shift toward wealth concentration of the twentieth century. Reaganomics created the Casino Economy but Bill Clinton, by ceding policy to Alan Greenspan and to his Treasury secretaries, celebrated its consequences. By the year 2000, New Democrat presidential candidate Al Gore was betraying Keynesian economics: If a recession occurs, said Gore, we need to maintain a surplus in the federal budget, turning Keynesian policy upside down.

Suppose politicians and economists completely undo the policies that could prevent a depression, retreating to the age of Coolidge and Harding? The euthanasia of the economist class cannot be ruled out; as noted, its youngest members have little faith in the methods they must learn to be employable. Worse, casino capitalism may not survive either. Keynes faced the prospect of a similar outcome, death for old-fashioned capitalism. Then, in the 1930s, as during the final decades of the twentieth century, the most devout defenders of capitalism were among its worst enemies.

FROM THE OLD TO THE NEW ECONOMY: IT'S A LONG WAVE

We have been in what I have described as the Great Stagnation, beginning around 1987. The stagnation is in things that are real—real output, economic growth, and full-time jobs. The other side of the stagnation coin is financial instability. Stagnation and financial instability are not necessarily "forever." Historically, both have had not only a beginning, but also an ending. Their endings are paced differently: Stagnation, by its nature, ends slowly whereas financial bubbles suddenly and unexpectedly burst.

President Bill Clinton entered the White House in 1993 promising to end the Great Stagnation and revitalize the economy with enhanced public infrastructure, including better healthcare and improved education. Most of this program was sacrificed on the altar of zero-inflation and the financial markets strategy of Alan Greenspan. Bill Clinton, the New Democrat, succeeded in doing what his two Republican predecessors had failed to do despite trying mightily: He balanced the federal budget. This act freed the Federal Reserve to do what it has been doing all too well—keeping wages low and unearned income and wealth of the rich high.

The financial casino, now global, cannot remain open for business indefinitely. At some point, real output and secure jobs must enter the picture. Much of the global disease, as I have said, is the maturing of product cycles and the failure to harvest the honey from the latest swarm of innovations. Why does a profits cash flow (the honey from last generation's innovations) often fail to lead to basic innovations? Apparently, it is because giants producing standardized products are not very innovative (think latter-day Microsoft); rather, the market power of such corporations enables them to get by for a long time with mostly imaginary product innovations and with price increases for products whose sales no longer respond significantly to prices. The lone entrepreneur, a David, does not reside generally in the house of Goliath. The true innovations must come from outside the giants.

During the last half of a long-wave economic expansion, a Leontief-styled fixed technical coefficients industrial model takes on an unexpected realism. Once the basic process innovations are widely diffused in the economy, the industrial branch becomes remarkably rigid in its technique. True, the size of plants and of the companies grows large, but the same technique is simply replicated on a larger scale.

In the final throes of decline, ironically, the production technology finally is modified by improvement innovations; in the present wave, automation in the standardized product-manufacturing industries is being used to replace higher-wage labor. Crises begin to break through the rigidities. Purchases of factory automation systems in the United States doubled to $18.1 billion from 1980 to 1985. Computer-integrated manufacturing came into being during the mid-1990s. Still, as noted, there is a great downsizing: Worse, at least for labor, manufacturing has the global option of producing in low-wage countries.

If Mensch's analysis is correct, basic innovations do form Shumpeterian clusters during the technological stalemate. According to his data, about two-thirds of the technological basic innovations to be produced in the second half of the twentieth century happened in the decade around 1989. The greatest surge of innovations occurred in 1984, a year comparable (on the scale of innovations) to 1825, 1886, and 1935.[4] We are in the throes of a rare opportunity.

This narrow window of opportunity for entrepreneurs has happened only every half century or so. However, much like the life of the butterfly, the Age of the Entrepreneur is short and perhaps gets shorter with each wave. The lone entrepreneur often is the one who first commercializes a basic innovation, creating a temporary monopoly in the production of a new product. Eventually an entire new industry is born.

This entrepreneurial activity well describes the historically recent, rapid development of the personal computer industry. Entrepreneurs Steven P. Jobs and Stephen Wozniak got the industry moving with Apple Computer in 1976; as early as 1985 the maturity of the industry was epitomized by Jobs's bitter resignation from the chairmanship of Apple. Bill Gates and Microsoft already were monopolizing the operating system for the personal computer. By the year 2000, Microsoft already was behaving like a sluggish monopolist, and the U.S. Justice Department already had declared it to be a consumer-bashing "monopolist."

The initial monopoly profits attracted (cheaper) imitators who could experience some growth on the exponential part of the computer S-curve. Now, however, there is a major shakeout in the personal computer industry—Hewlett-Packard and IBM were out by the end of the twentieth century—that will leave few survivors. Schumpeter and Keynes's entrepreneurs do come on to the scene roughly each half century. The entrepreneurs' butterfly-like presence helps to explain why small monopolies dominate the early growth of an industry and giant monopoly power characterizes the industry's sunset years. The Age of the Entrepreneur is like Camelot; it is only here for one brief, shining moment each (roughly) half century.

Simple explanations will not suffice. Supra-surplus capitalism, a system of great complexity, deserves an explanation richer than that afforded by Arrow-Debreu. David Warsh, a financial writer for the *Boston Globe,* describes the "idea of complexity" in graphic terms. "The best currently available rough indicator of the complexity of the [U.S.] economy," says Warsh, "is a standard industrial classification (SIC) code, a kind of Yellow Pages for the Nation."[5]

Warsh's idea of complexity encompasses increased specialization *and* interdependencies; the SIC code begins with ten divisions that include agriculture, mining, and manufacturing, moves on to some 800 major classifications, such as mining and quarrying of nonmetallic minerals, and finally ends up with dimension stone, cordage and twine, and so on. In the finest division, there are nearly 10,000 U.S. industries today. The required division of labor is far finer than could ever have been imagined by Adam Smith, for the layers of value added generate a hierarchy of tasks, jobs, and industries that vary in complexity.[6] The contemporary globalization process is extending the U.S.-styled Yellow Pages to the emerging nations.

POLITICAL ECONOMY, AGAIN

Much of the foregoing discussion indicates that a clean line between the political, social, and economic is difficult to draw. Society is a seamless web in which the individual plays several roles: A factor of production (usually labor), a consumer, and a citizen. As a consumer, the person votes with dollars; as a citizen, the person votes (sometimes, again, with dollars) in the political process. The better off citizen is more likely to vote than the poor. Moreover, the rich can buy political access by contribution to PACs. Even so, citizens—sufficiently enraged at a Congress and a president disengaged—could break the link between dollars and votes.

The business firm has enough "dollar votes" to influence public policy by lobbying and political influence. The corporation may have political power disproportionate to the number of people it represents. The most recent support for this hypothesis has come from disclosure regarding how much American tobacco companies knew of the adverse health effects from their products. Although this topography is familiar to today's citizen, the Lockean-Smithian view of liberty tied freedom of the individual to private property. Property, in turn, was an inalienable right. No social obligations accompanied rights to ownership. This conception fit well an economy of large numbers of merchants and small manufacturers. Freedom implied the autonomous person. As the corporation has gone global, however, it has broken its tethers from already lax state regulations.

In our modern complexity, there is a small number of dominant industrial and financial corporations, competition has been largely replaced by administered prices and wages, the government is part of big business, advance planning characterizes industrial manufacturing, and corporate ownership of the giants increasingly is divorced from management. The owner of capital can be described only as a swashbuckling individual innovator in the sunrise industries now falling prey to the giants.

The corporation itself, however, inherited the autonomy without obligation that was once the sole privilege of the individual. By contrast, labor was weak, so it was impelled to organize. Consumer complaints led to governmental regulation—government became responsible for corporations that otherwise had no specific civic duties. Business became less private, more public. It was not so much freedom that was redefined as the conditions under which liberty was otherwise handicapped. Now, however, the countervailing power of government has been undone in a world where factories can be moved to low-wage countries.

Among the newly concentrated industries are the media and the computer, that is, the information industry. Just as land was the source of power during the Middle Ages and capital during the Industrial Revolution, today the source of power is information. As it has been, and perhaps ever shall be, money can buy any new power source. If information too is held in few hands, how will the average citizen gain access to it and perhaps prevent the misuse of information?

THE VOICE OF THE MASTERS

We have not wandered very far from the masters. Adam Smith did not ignore the possibility of economic power corrupting; he simply bred an unfounded optimism. Smith did not deny the love leading to gifts. But, in his time, the concern was with getting the engine of industry started, not with the inability of the engine to provide all of people's needs.

Alfred Marshall did not lack an ethical base, nor did he lack compassion before the age of "compassionate conservatives." His apostles simply removed all the social variables from his engine of analysis. The engine itself is now only a caricature of Newtonian capitalism. Marx and Veblen certainly anticipated the problems of income distribution, excessive corporate power, and worker alienation. Schumpeter described a capitalistic motion that fell well short of perpetual. Yet, the orthodoxy has stripped John Maynard Keynes of his social progressiveness and his moral intent. But Keynes's design still is there, in the *General Theory*, for all to read. In fact, a perusal of the masters would be a good start for anyone interested in economics.

A new vision is critical. There is the ever-present danger that too many failures will be fatal to society. Even if all of contemporary problems are solved, there will be no Golden Age. The real-life complexities of the past, present, and future give us only one certainty: Knowledge will continue to be a series of endless horizons.

NOTES

1. George Gilder, *Wealth and Poverty* (New York: Basic Books, 1981), p. 168.

2. *Ibid.*, p. 267.

3. This is the language used in the prosecutors' sentencing memo. See James B. Stewart, *Den of Thieves* (New York: Simon & Schuster, 1991), p. 441. Milken had entered the federal prison in Pleasanton, California, outside San Francisco, on March 3, 1991, to begin the first of a ten-year sentence. He was able to retain about $500 million of his fortune, and has since been paroled.

4. Gerhard O. Mensch, *Stalemate in Technology* (Cambridge, Massachussetts: Ballinger, 1979), p. 197.

5. David Warsh, *The Idea of Economic Complexity* (New York: Viking Press, 1984), p. 36.

6. In one of Warsh's least elegant examples, the modern pig climbs on the assembly line at birth, lives its entire life indoors, is fed a computer-formulated diet loaded with vitamin and mineral supplements, and goes to the slaughterhouse five months later. Instead of having his throat cut by a man, he is stunned with a hammer and killed by a jolt of electricity, often as not generated by a nuclear power plant.

   Warsh might have added that the pig is fed antibiotics later ingested by humans who may require medical attention from a newly required "specialist." Moreover, meat inspectors now use sophisticated instruments designed and produced by persons as far removed from the Omaha stockyards as most people prefer to be. This more complex division of labor requires a theory of a segmented personal income distribution since some tasks are simple, others ridiculously complex, some overpaid, others underpaid (see E. Ray Canterbery, "A Vita Theory of Personal Income Distribution," *Southern Economic Journal* 46 (July 1979): 12–48.

Glossary of Endurable Terms

Absolute Advantage The ability of one country to produce more of a commodity than another country with the same resources. The idea was advanced by Adam Smith as the basis for mutually beneficial international trade, but it has since been extended to firms and individuals.

Absolute Surplus Value The excess of new production value created in a day over the value of the labor power employed, a value enhanced merely by lengthening the working day. Obviously, the idea comes from Karl Marx. See also **Surplus Value.**

Barter The direct exchange of one commodity or service for another without money as a medium of exchange.

Capital Léon Walras defined capital to include only producers' durable goods—machines, instruments, tools, office buildings, factories, and warehouses. Today, economists also include goods in process or changes in inventories. This definition is narrower than that of the classical economists, who included a wages fund and materials in addition to these other items as a part of capital.

Capitalism An economic system dominated by capital accumulation and the existence of wage labor. The capital is in the hands of private owners, including corporations and joint stock companies, whereas laborers exchange their hours (or, according to Karl Marx, their "labor power") for wages paid by the capital owners.

Casino Economy A society in which the making of money with money instruments is more important than profits from the production of goods and services. Money market funds and highly speculative instruments and behavior cause the economy to resemble nothing so much as an imploded Las Vegas. The term originates with Ray Canterbery.

Communism A form of economic organization in which production is provided according to abilities and consumption is based on needs. It has never existed in a pure economic form.

Comparative Advantage The national capability to produce specific goods or services with a lower resource (input) cost relative to the cost for its trading partners. According to the theory, first advanced with rigor by David Ricardo, a country should specialize in producing and exporting those goods that it can produce at relatively low costs and import those goods for which its production costs are relatively high.

Cooperative Economy A compromise version of the competitive market economy in which specific quantities of products and prices are determined by a free market system but the extremes of distribution of incomes and wealth are influenced by a democratic government.

The Dark Ages A subperiod of the Middle Ages in which social and economic change was gradual. It began at the end of the Western Roman Empire (A.D. 476) and continued through about the 900s. Recent findings suggest that social and economic innovations during the Dark Ages were more frequent than formerly believed.

Dependence Effect By means of advertising, promotion, and salesmanship, producers create many of the wants they seek to satisfy. The term originates with John Kenneth Galbraith.

Depression Until the 1930s, the term (along with the term "panic") was used to describe all economic downturns. Since the Great Depression, the term has been used to describe downturns measurable in years or a decade and during which the unemployment rate has been ten percent or higher. Thus, depression aptly describes present-day conditions in Russia and parts of Eastern Europe.

Differential Theory of Rent The theory, first sketched by Thomas Malthus but refined by David Ricardo, suggests that as population expands and poorer and poorer land is brought under cultivation, the price of grain will be decided by the higher cost of cultivation on the poorest land parcel, with the owners of the better land receiving a differential rent represented by the difference in the two average costs of production.

Doctrine of Increasing Misery The conditions of labor worsen relative to the improved conditions of the capitalist. When the relative conditions become intolerable, the workers revolt. These conditions, according to Marx, help to explain the collapse of capitalism.

Economic Man *(homo economicus)* An abstraction that defines the behavior of humans as an ideal type of rationality and thus of rational choice. The economic man always optimizes through rational choice and is never deflected from his goals by interests other than his own. Although some call the economic man a "rational fool," economic man behavior is at the core of modern neoclassical economics, monetarism, and new classical economics.

Economic Rent As applied to agriculture, it is the price of, say, grain received minus the grain price that would have induced the farmer to keep his land employed in its current use. More generally, economic rent is the "excess return" received from a factor of production that is fixed in supply. In contemporary times, it might be said that Madonna receives rent because she is one of a kind.

Economic Rhetoric The study of economic thought a if it were a form of persuasion through argumentation. The rhetoric relies nonetheless on argumentation within the context of the times.

Economic Table (tableau économique) An illustration of the circular flow of product and income in an economy first developed by Quesnay.

Elasticity In general, the degree of response in amounts being demanded or supplied to a change in price. The price elasticity of demand, for example, is measurable as the ratio of the percentage change in amounts demanded to the percentage change in price. If this ratio is greater than one, the demand for the good is price elastic; if the ratio is less than one, the demand is price inelastic.

The English Industrial Revolution The period between 1780 and 1850 in England, during which production increased markedly in nearly every industry. One of its most significant features was the production of machines through the use of other machines.

The Enlightenment A philosophical movement of the eighteenth century, characterized by much theorizing about politics, a belief in the value of reason as an instrument of progress, and the use of the empirical method in scientific inquiry.

Employment Multiplier The idea that the public employment of one more worker can lead to a total increase in national employment exceeding one. This intuitive idea of John Maynard Keynes's was put into mathematical form by Sir Richard Kahn.

Equilibrium A state of balance among opposing forces or actions at which the variables in question come to rest in a static case and move along a predictable time path in a dynamic case.

Equilibrium Price The price at which the amounts demanded and supplied are equal; the market-clearing price. The price at issue can be related to products, services, labor, or capital.

General Equilibrium An economic theory in which all markets—for finished goods and for factors of production—are simultaneously in equilibrium (see **Equilibrium Price**).

The Gilded Age In the United States, this is the era spanning 1870 to 1910 during which unbridled free-market capitalism led to the accumulation of wealth and capital in a few hands through cutthroat competition, resulting in abusive monopoly power, including the formation of trusts. The name comes from a book authored by Thorstein Veblen.

The Gildered Age The era, beginning in 1981 and continuing, was bequeathed George Gilder's name by Ray Canterbery because Gilder's writings update the stories of American clergyman Horatio Alger and the benign universe popular during the **Gilded Age** as a justification for the behavior of the robber barons.

The Theory of Gluts A general economic surplus (i.e., in many markets for commodities) caused by insufficient overall demand in an economy.

Groping (Tâtonnement) A tendency toward general market equilibrium that eventually is simultaneous. The idea comes from Walras's idea of tâtonnement. In one example, Walras introduced the idea of chits, which entrepreneurs used as provisional contracts in buying and selling goods and services. The chits were made final only if price were actually at equilibrium. Otherwise, they would not be redeemed and a process of recontracting would occur. This groping really is a trial-and-error process whereby markets eventually clear.

Hedonism The view that people never pursue anything except pleasure, or the avoidance of pain. This psychology was a central tenet of Jeremy Bentham's philosophy.

The High Middle Ages A subperiod of **the Middle Ages** that extended from about 1000 to 1300. There was considerable social and economic change during these years, in which many of the characteristics of self-sufficient feudalism gave way to commercial exchange of goods and services among regions and nations.

The Institutionalist (also called **Evolutionist School)** A group of economists who believe that **institutions** broadly defined to include ideas and habits of thought are critical to an explanation of economic behavior and activity.

Institutions As broadly defined, they include formal systems, such as constitutions, laws, taxation, insurance, and market regulations, as well as informal norms of behavior, such as habits, morals, ethics, ideologies, and belief systems. All such things are considered important to the **Institutionalist School** of economists.

Investment Multiplier If government or industry invests an initial $1, the national income will rise by a multiple of $1. This is the employment multiplier expressed in terms of investment requirements. The investment multiplier was advanced by John Maynard Keynes with mathematics borrowed from Sir Richard Kahn's **employment multiplier**.

Iron Law of Wages Wages are presumed to be kept to the minimum required for the subsistence of the wage-laborer. Both Malthus and Ricardo gave arguments for such a "law." Marx accepted the "iron law," but for a different reason.

Jazz Age A term used, mainly with reference to the USA, for the decade between the end of World War I and the Great Crash (1929). The name derives from the white Dixieland version of black jazz which defined the era's dance style and reflected a general atmosphere of excitement and confidence. The flamboyance and economic confidence of the period is portrayed especially well by F. Scott Fitzgerald in his *The Great Gatsby* (1925).

Labor Theory of Value The value of a commodity is determined by the quantity of labor that goes into its production. Although Adam Smith (following John Locke) introduced a labor theory of value, David Ricardo refined it until it became his invention. Although Ricardo used the theory as a theory of price, Marx adopted Ricardo's idea as an explanation of the exploitation of the worker whereby goods are sold for a value in excess of their labor value.

The Law of Demand The proposition that quantity and price of a normal good are inversely related: That the amount of a good an individual is willing and able to purchase will rise as the unit price falls and fall as the unit price rises.

The Law of Diminishing Marginal Utility The idea that the satisfaction derived from an additional unit of consumption is lower than the satisfaction derived from previous units.

The Law of Diminishing Returns The more one input of equal quality is increased in production while the quantities of all other inputs of equal quality remain unchanged, then—at least after some point—the smaller will be the resulting addition to output.

Liquidity Preference The desire to hold a particular quantity of money at a particular interest rate and income level. The idea comes from John Maynard Keynes, who contended that people will prefer to hold more money the lower the rate of interest.

Liquidity Trap A condition in the money market in which the preference for liquidity or money is infinite. No matter how much the money supply is increased, every dollar will be hoarded. Although the idea relates to Keynes's description of conditions during the Great Depression, the name derives from Dennis Robertson. Economist Paul Krugman has suggested that Japan was in liquidity trap during the 1990s.

Macroeconomics The branch of economics that focuses on the aggregate national income, product, employment, and overall price level. This study evolved with the economics of John Maynard Keynes.

The Margin Originally from Bentham, this is the point of change in pleasure or pain. As adopted by the **marginalist school,** it is the point of change in any quantity related to economics and usually has the same meaning as a derivative from the calculus.

The Marginalist School A school of economic thought that began in the 1870s, more or less independently in various countries, and that continues to dominate **microeconomics**. Marginalism gives special place to marginal analysis in which the emphasis is on small increases and decreases or incrementalism.

Mercantilism An economic system in which the government manages the economy for the purpose of increasing national wealth and state power. Generally, the focus is inward so that domestic output is stimulated, domestic consumption limited, and a favorable balance of trade (more exports than imports) encouraged.

Microeconomics The branch of economics that focuses on small "decision units" such as the consumer, the household, and the firm in order to show how their choices determine relative prices and quantities, the allocation of resources, and the functional income distribution.

The Middle Ages A long, diverse period of Western European history that began at the end of the Western Roman Empire in 476 and ended with the fall of Constantinople and the Eastern (Byzantine) Roman Empire (1453) that coincided with the start of the **Renaissance**.

Natural Law Natural law, if it exists, is a system of law binding on persons by virtue of their nature alone and independently *of all* convention or custom. It is presumed that we recognize natural law because we are rational beings.

Natural Order An imaginary social order derived from **natural law**.

Natural Rate of Unemployment The rate of unemployment prevailing when the amount of labor demanded and supplied are equal at an equilibrium **real** wage.

Neoclassical Economics A school of economic thought that emerged after 1870 and that has its roots in both Adam Smith's version of classical economics and in marginalism. Following Alfred Marshall, its emphasis is on competitive markets and equilibrium conditions, and on the principles and operations of a liberal economy (in the eighteenth century English meaning of liberalism).

Newtonian Mechanics The system developed by Newton in which all physical phenomena followed mechanical laws and thus evidenced mathematical regularity. Newton invented the calculus as the new, required mathematics to deal with his laws of motion.

Pareto Optimum An imaginary condition in which no further change in the economy (such as in prices) would improve the Benthamite utility of one person without reducing the utility of at least one other person. The concept is named for Vilfredo Pareto, an Italian economist, who invented it.

Partial Equilibrium An idea introduced by Alfred Marshall whereby prices and quantities in markets other than the one under study were to be held constant or assumed to be small in their effects.

Philosophical Radicalism A reform movement begun by the followers of Jeremy Bentham (1748–1832). Its purpose was to translate liberalism from philosophical premises into practical conclusions of law, economics, and politics. In the early nineteenth century in Britain, these "radicals" formed a kind of intellectual establishment; they included the classical economists James Mill, John Stuart Mill, and David Ricardo.

Physiocracy The law of **natural order** that gave the physiocrats their name.

Rational Expectations Expectations that persons form on the basis of all available relevant information, including that from the future. Not only do persons use this information intelligently and at little cost, but their predictions will essentially be the same as those derived by the relevant economic theory. The relevant theory is usually monetarism.

Real Gains made after nominal values are "deflated" by a price index (as in **real** wages).

Real Balance Effect When effective demand falls as a result of declining incomes, prices also fall and the value of the liquid assets (such as cash) held by households and businesses increases. The increase in real liquid assets reignites consumer and producer spending. This theory was advanced by Arthur Pigou and resurrected by Don Patinkin.

Recession An economic downturn in which, as a rule of thumb, the real gross national product or gross domestic product declines during two successive quarters. The United States relies on the National Bureau of Economic Research to decree what is and what is not a recession. Also, see **depression**.

Relative Surplus Value The **surplus value** arising from improvements in technology that reduce the labor time required to produce a product and lead to a high degree of specialization for the worker. Again, look to Karl Marx as the source.

The Renaissance The period of transition in Europe from the Middle Ages into modern times. Its beginning is usually placed at the fall of Constantinople in 1453; its ending coincided with the end of the seventeenth century. The period was distinguished by the revival of classical arts and literature and early stirrings of modern science.

Robber Baron During the Middle Ages, a feudal lord who preyed on and stole from people passing through his domain. The term was revived in the last quarter of the nineteenth century to describe those relatively few business tycoons who controlled American industry.

Say's Law Production under free market competition will always generate an equivalent amount of demand for the goods produced. In common language, "supply creates its own demand."

Social Rules These are rules made by humans as a way of ordering society. When we speak of law and order, we are speaking of social rules.

Socialism A form of economic organization in which there exists public or common ownership of those branches of the economy decisive for its functioning. In general, socialism is based on the principles of equal opportunity, egalitarianism, administration by the government, and minimization of the accumulation of private property as a form of social control.

Stationary State An economic condition in which the net national product of a country ceases to grow. Ricardo bemoaned it because he considered it to be a condition of stagnation, whereas J.S. Mill and J.M. Keynes welcomed it as a condition achieved at a high level of output per person in an advanced, mature economy.

Supra-Surplus Economy An advanced, industrialized economy in which net production surpluses so greatly exceed the meeting of ordinary consumer needs that private producers and the government have to spend enormous promotional funds and energies to stimulate demand. The term comes from Ray Canterbery.

Surplus Value The amount by which the exchange value of products in the marketplace exceed the labor value required in their production. This value, defined by Marx, is the source of the capital owner's profits.

Technostructure A collective term used to describe all those in a giant corporation who can bring specialized knowledge, talent, or experience to group decisions. It often comprises a committee. The term comes from John Kenneth Galbraith.

Utilitarianism A philosophy of morals, politics, and legislation that finds all practical reasoning in the concept of utility and contends that the right action, the good character, and the right law are those maximizing utility. The test of right action and so on is the Greatest Happiness Principle, which holds that actions should be directed toward promoting the greatest happiness for the greatest number of persons.

Wages Fund As defined by the classical economists, a fund used by producers for buying raw materials and for paying labor.

Walrasian Auctioneer In Walras's **groping** process, an auctioneer processes the bids and offers, decides which will clear all markets, and *only then* allows trading.

World View A widely shared set of beliefs about the individual's relationship to the natural world, to other humans in society, and to the Divine. The medieval world view was summarized in the idea of the Cosmos, a harmony that encompassed all existence, in which God's presence and spirit were embodied in all living things.

Annotated Suggestions for Further Reading

Introduction

Boorstin, Daniel J. *The Discoverers* (New York: Random House, 1983). A brilliant but accessible introduction to the great thinkers who have shaped our world views, from the ancient Babylonians to Einstein. Boorstin sees every discovery as an episode of biography.

Hicks, John. *A Theory of Economic History* (Oxford: Clarendon Press, 1969). Although not an easy read, Hicks uniquely brings pure theory to bear on economic history.

Klamer, Arjo. *Conversations with Economists* (Totoway, New Jersey: Rowman & Allanheld, 1983). The author takes the rhetorical approach literally and recounts interviews with leading economists. The book provides a painless way of getting inside the heads of some of the leading contemporary economists.

McCloskey, Deirdre. *The Rhetoric of Economics* (Madison: University of Wisconsin Press, 1985). This pioneering book, authored by one of the best and cleverest writers in economics, introduced the rhetorical approach to understanding economics.

Swedberg, Richard. *Conversations with Economists and Sociologists* (Princeton: Princeton University Press, 1990). Swedberg brings out both the intellectual and personal qualities of his subjects in "conversations" that are fun to read.

Chapter 1: Feudalism and the Evolution of Economic Society

Braudel, Fernand. *Civilization and Capitalism, 15th–18th Century,* translated from the French by Sian Reynolds, three vols (New York: Harper & Row, 1984). This richly illustrated book chronicles in interesting prose commercial and ordinary life during the centuries leading to the flowering of capitalism.

Cipolla, Carlo M. *Before the Industrial Revolution: European Society and Economy, 1000–1700* (New York: W.W. Norton & Co., 1976). This classic covers a vast amount of history in surprisingly few pages.

Collis, Louise. *Memoirs of a Medieval Woman* (New York: Harper & Row, 1983). A biography based on the memoirs of Margery Kempe, the first autobiography to be written in English. Margery is an extraordinary fifteenth century woman who eventually made a pilgrimage to Jerusalem to expiate a "secret sin" in her early life. The book provides a colorful and detailed picture of everyday medieval life in England and around the rim of the Mediterranean.

Erickson, Carolly. *The Medieval Vision: Essays in History and Perception* (New York: Oxford University Press, 1976). A brilliant and successful effort to explain medieval perception as a different view of reality, a kind of altered reality of an enchantment in which Aquinas could find in angels a level of creation which made the whole of creation comprehensible.

Gilchrist, John T. *The Church and Economic Activity in the Middle Ages* (New York: St. Martin's Press, 1969). Everything anyone would really want to know about the church and the economy.

Hilton, Rodney. *Bond Men Made Free* (London: Temple Smith, 1973). This classic brings feudalism to life.

Keen, Maurice. *Chivalry* (New Haven: Yale University Press, 1985). This—another classic—reveals chivalry both for what naive people imagined it to be and for what it really was.

North, Douglas C. and Robert Paul Thomas. *The Rise of the Western World: A New Economic History* (Cambridge: Cambridge University Press, 1973). Douglas North was awarded the 1993 Nobel Prize in economics in great part because of the insights he (and his co-author) revealed in this classic.

Postan, M.M. *The Medieval Economy and Society* (Berkeley and Los Angeles: University of California Press, 1972). An excellent study of how feudalism shaped the society and how society shaped feudalism.

Tawney, R.H. *Religion and the Rise of Capitalism* (New York: Harcourt, Brace, 1937). Written in fine style, this rare gem by a great historian instructs as well as it entertains. Its title reveals its thesis.

Tuchman, Barbara W. *A Distant Mirror: The Calamitous 14th Century* (New York: Alfred A. Knopf, 1978). A bestselling history of perhaps the worst century of the Middle Ages. It reads like a novel.

Chapter 2: Adam Smith's Great Vision

Heilbroner, Robert. *The Limits of American Capitalism* (New York: Harper & Row, 1966). The author, one of the best and most entertaining writers in economics, shows how capitalism cannot meet everyone's needs.

Heilbroner, Robert. *The Worldly Philosopher,* 7th ed. (New York: Simon & Schuster, 1999). This classic has brought the great economists to life for an entire generation of readers.

Polanyi, Karl. *The Great Transformation* (New York: Farrar & Rinehart, 1944). An absorbing book on the difficulties when the idea of the market mechanism was introduced in the eighteenth century on a nonmarket-directed world. It could provide caution for those today who expect the former Soviet states and Eastern Europe to instantly transform themselves into smoothly operating market economies.

Smith, Adam. *An Inquiry into the Nature and Causes of the Wealth of Nations,* ed. Edwin Cannan, introductions by Edwin Cannan and Max Lerner (New York: Random House, 1937). Smith launched the field of political economy with this volume; filled with diverse passages, there nonetheless are many gems to be mined.

Smith, Adam. *An Inquiry into the Nature and Causes of the Wealth of Nations,* abridged, with commentary and notes by Laurence Dickey (Indianapolis/Cambridge: Hackett Publishing Co., 1993). The unabridged Smith runs some 1000 pages, a daunting read unless you are a devotee. This thoughtful new abridgment has all the right stuff and is enriched by the brilliant commentary by Professor Dickey.

Smith, Adam. "The Principles which Lead and Direct Philosophical Inquiries: Illustrated by the History of Astronomy," in *The Early Writings of Adam Smith,* ed. J. Ralph Lindgren (New York: Augustus M. Kelley, 1967), pp. 30–109. In this essay, we find the origins of Smith's affection for the Newtonian system and natural law.

Smith, Adam. *The Theory of Moral Sentiments,* ed. Ernest Rhys (London: Everyman's Library, 1910). A philosophical treatise in which Smith evokes the critical importance of empathy as the basis of a harmonious society.

Chapter 3: Bentham and Malthus: The Hedonist and the "Pastor"

Bentham, Jeremy. *An Introduction to the Principles of Morals and Legislation,* introduction by Laurence J. Lafleur (Darien, Connecticut: Hafner Publishing Co., 1948). Its originality will appeal to many.

Burtt, Everett, Jr. *Social Perspectives in the History of Economic Theory* (New York: St. Martin's Press, 1972). This is a good source for long quotes culled from the writings of the classical economists. It also has extensive notes for those who want to dig around in the library.

Hartwell, R.M. *The Causes of the Industrial Revolution* (London: Methuen & Co., 1967). This book remains one of the best explanations for the English Industrial Revolution.

Himmelfarb, Gertrude. *The Idea of Poverty: England in the Early Industrial Age* (New York: Alfred A. Knopf, 1984). A classic history of poverty of the age and how it became a social issue.

Malthus, Thomas. "An Essay on the Principle of Population, as it Affects the Future Improvement of Society: With Remarks on the Speculations of Mr. Godwin, M. Condorcet, and Other Writers" in *On Population,* by Thomas Malthus, edited by Gertrude Himmelfarb (New York: Random House, Modern Library, 1960). This is Malthus's classic statement on the causes of the population explosion and the dismal necessity of adversity.

Mokyr, Joel (ed.) *The Economics of the Industrial Revolution* (Rowman & Littlefield, 1985). This anthology includes many of the best articles on the first industrial revolution. The introductory essay by the editor is worth the price of the book.

Chapter 4: Income Distribution: Ricardo versus Malthus

Ricardo, David. *Principles of Political Economy and Taxation* (London: J.M. Dent & Sons, 1937). [1817]. Dry, spare, and condensed, Ricardo is a tough read.

Sraffa, Piero. *Works of David Ricardo* (London: Cambridge University Press, 1951). A multivolume edition containing the whole of Ricardo's writing. The second volume has the unique advantage of reprinting Malthus's *Principles* (greatly more readable than Ricardo), with Ricardo's devastating remarks at every turn.

Chapter 5: The Cold Water of Poverty and the Heat of John Stuart Mill's Passions

Dickens, Charles. *Hard Times* (New York: E.P. Dutton, 1966). [1854]. Though not the most read of Dickens' many novels, this one has the most relevant economics and social commentary for this chapter. As ever, it is greatly entertaining.

Mill, John Stuart. *Principles of Political Economy,* ed. J.M. Robson, two vols (Toronto: University of Toronto Press, 1965). [1848]. It is perhaps the best survey of classical economics for the lay reader; this masterful textbook went through seven editions in Mill's own lifetime. Mill published at his own expense an inexpensive version that was a bestseller among the working class.

Williamson, Jeffrey G. *Did British Capitalism Breed Inequality?* (London: Allen & Unwin, 1985). An eminent economist discusses the causes of inequality.

Chapter 6: Karl Marx

Bowles, Samuel, David M. Gordon and Thomas E. Weisskopf. *After the Waste Land: A Democratic Economics for the Year 2000* (Armonk, New York: M.E. Sharpe, 1990). The authors are leading economists of the New Left or contemporary Marxist thought. The sequel to an earlier book, this is a provocative, well-argued, lively critique of U.S. capitalism and what might be done about its excesses. It can be read by undergraduates.

Dowd, Douglas F. *The Twisted Dream: Capitalist Development in the United States since 1776* (Cambridge, Massachusetts: Winthrop, 1974). A critical view of American capitalism presented by a superb thinker and redoubtable writer.

Marx, Karl. *Capital: A Critique of Political Economy,* ed. Friedrich Engels, Vol. 1, 4th ed., revised (New York: Random House, Modern Library, 1906). The novice could do worse than begin with this volume by the master himself.

Marx, Karl. *Economic and Philosophic Manuscripts of 1844* (Moscow: Progress Publishers, 1959). These writings by the younger, obviously humanistic Marx have had a major influence on the New Left.

Tucker, Robert C. (ed.) *The Marx–Engels Reader*, revised (New York: W.W. Norton & Co., 1978). This edition contains excellent selections from Marx and Engels, including the notorious *Communist Manifesto.*

Wilson, Edmund. *To the Finland Station* (New York: Harcourt, Brace, 1940). This stylish book includes biographies of Marx and Engels and a review of their writings. As odd as it may seem, this is a difficult book to put down.

Chapter 7: Alfred Marshall: The Great Victorian

Eastern Economic Journal 8 (January 1982). The entire issue, mostly in accessible prose, is on Alfred Marshall.

Keynes, John M. *Essays in Biography* (London: Macmillan & Co., 1933). These essays comprise the high literature to which only a Bloomsbury member could rise. They include a nice sketch on Malthus and, of course, the essay on Marshall.

Marshall, Alfred. *Principles of Economics*, 8th ed. (London: Macmillan & Co., 1920). The classic by the greatest economist of his times and a textbook that has instructed more than one generation of economists.

Whitaker, John K. *The Early Writings of Alfred Marshall, 1867–1900* (New York: Free Press, 1975). The author shows how much of Marshall's thought had been completed before the writing of his *Principles.*

Chapter 8: Thorstein Veblen Takes on the American Captains of Industry

Allen, Frederick Lewis. *The Lords of Creation* (New York and London: Harper & Brothers, 1935). Highly entertaining, this is the classic book on the robber barons.

Diggins, John Patrick. *Thorstein Veblen: Theorist of the Leisure Class* (Princeton, New Jersey: Princeton University Press, 1999). This historical biography of Veblen is sufficiently readable to be worthy of Veblen. Diggins shows how Veblen was the only American social scientist of the nineteenth century who was intellectually able to challenge the economic theories of Marx on their own terms.

Dorfman, Joseph. *The Economic Mind in American Civilization, 1606–1865,* 5 vols (New York: Augustus M. Kelley, 1966). In this book of breathtaking scope, the author uniquely reveals how Americans have thought about the organization of American capitalism over the centuries.

Gruchy, Allan G. *Contemporary Economic Thought: The Contribution of the Neoinstitutionalist Economics* (New York: Augustus M. Kelley, 1972). The classic textbook on institutionalist thought.

Hofstadter, Richard. *Social Darwnism in American Thought,* revised ed. (Boston: Beacon Press, 1955). The classic source that has shaped many intellectuals' perspective on Social Darwinism.

Lebergott, Stanley. *The Americans: An Economic Record* (New York and London: W.W. Norton & Co., 1984). A narrative of the economic history of American society with particular emphasis on the process of industrialization. The author is a past president of the Economic History Association.

Tilman, Rick. *Thorstein Veblen and His Critics, 1891–1963* (Princeton: Princeton University Press, 1992). A comprehensive intellectual history as well as a treatise on social and economic philosophy, with its center of focus being the iconoclastic Veblen.

Tilman, Rick. *A Veblen Treasury: From Leisure Class to War, Peace, and Capitalism* (Armonk, New York: M.E. Sharpe, 1993). The only available book that presents, in edited form, the entire spectrum of Veblen's iconoclastic contributions. It focuses on the theory of the leisure class; dispraise of other economic theories, including Marxian; the roots of institutions, but especially business enterprises; American culture; and "pathological" international relations.

Veblen, Thorstein. *The Theory of the Leisure Class* (New York: Viking Press, 1931). Why not go for the gold? This is Veblen at his best, complete with biting and amusing satire.

Chapter 9: The Jazz Age: Aftermath of War and Prelude to Depression

Bell, Quentin. *Bloomsbury* (New York: Basic Books, 1968). This, a brief history of the Bloomsbury Group by a relative of two members, who is himself an artist and writer, captures the intelligence and snobbishness of the membership. It also includes some rare artwork and two rare photographs of John Maynard Keynes.

Dos Passos, John. *U.S.A.* (Boston: Houghton Mifflin, 1946). A sweeping, breathtaking three-volume novel that provides a painless introduction to the history of the United States between the world wars. Dos Passos was inspired to write it by Thorstein Veblen, who is a character in the novel.

Fitzgerald, F. Scott. *The Great Gatsby* (New York: Charles Scribner's Sons, 1925). This classic, along with earlier writings by Fitzgerald, named and defined the Jazz Age. He and his wife, Zelda, as lively participants, became inseparable from that definition.

Keynes, John Maynard. *The Economic Consequences of the Peace* (London: Macmillan & Co., 1919). This masterpiece is worth reading today both for its literary style and for its historical vision.

Skidelsky, Robert. *John Maynard Keynes. Volume One, Hopes Betrayed, 1883–1920* (New York/London: Penguin Books, 1983). One of the best biographies in English of any figure in any period, this volume provides fascinating detail of the formative years of Keynes. It includes insights into Keynes's relationships with his Cambridge and Bloomsbury friends and the writing of *The Economic Consequences of the Peace*.

Sraffa, Piero. "The Laws of Returns Under Competitive Conditions," *Economic Journal* 36 (December 1926): 535–550. The classic theoretical explanation for giant business firms.

Chapter 10: John Maynard Keynes and The Great Depression

Allen, Frederick Lewis. *Only Yesterday* (New York: Harper, 1932). One of the most entertaining and widely read histories of the Great Depression.

Chick, Victoria. *Macroeconomics After Keynes: A Reconstruction of the "General Theory"* (Cambridge, Massachusetts: MIT Press, 1983). A valiant attempt to rescue Keynes from the Keynesians.

Dillard, Dudley. *The Economics of John Maynard Keynes* (Englewood Cliffs, New Jersey: Prentice-Hall, 1948). The first scholarly interpretation of Keynes's "General Theory" and the one most widely read around the world.

Galbraith, John Kenneth. *The Great Crash 1929* (Boston: Houghton Mifflin, 1988). [1954]. The classic history of the great stock market crash of 1929, an extraordinary book written with verve and wit.

Galbraith, John Kenneth. *A Life in Our Times: Memoirs* (Boston: Houghton Mifflin, 1981), pp. 68–70. Galbraith has been close to the great events and great leaders during a large share of the twentieth century. In these memoirs, he combines that proximity with effective, amusing writing. In particular, he sheds light on the New Deal, the coming of Keynes to America, and the Kennedy Administration.

Galbraith, John Kenneth. *Name-Dropping: From F.D.R. On* (Boston: Houghton Mifflin, 1999). For those looking for a brief memoir covering the same topics in a more personal and amusing manner will find much to admire in this little volume.

Keynes, John M. *The Collected Writings of John Maynard Keynes* (London: Macmillan & Co.; New York: St. Martin's Press, 1971), Vols 8, 10, 13–16 and 19. These volumes contain writings pertinent to this chapter.

Keynes, John M. *The General Theory of Employment, Interest and Money* (New York: Harcourt, Brace & World, 1936). It remains the most influential book on economics published in the twentieth century.

McElvaine, Robert S. *The Great Depression*, revised ed. (New York: Times Books, 1993). [1984]. This eminently readable classic, written by a historian, is as much an account of the social and cultural dimensions of the crisis as of the economic dimensions.

Skidelsky, Robert. *John Maynard Keynes. Volume Two, The Economist as Saviour, 1920–1937* (New York/London: Penguin Books, 1994). In this second volume of his biography, Skidelsky traces Keynes's life, his work, and their relationship to world events through the popular reception of the *General Theory* in 1937. Skidelsky again gets personal as he describes the shock of Keynes's Bloomsbury cohorts to his marriage to Russian ballerina Lydia Lopokova.

Steinbeck, John. *The Grapes of Wrath* (New York: Viking Penguin, 1939). A great novelist captures the human anguish of the Great Depression.

Chapter 11: The Many Modern Keynesians

Boland, Lawrence A. *The Foundation of Economic Method* (London: George Allen & Unwin, 1982). If you want to know more about how method controls neoclassical economics, this is a good place to find out.

Davidson, Paul. *Money and the Real World* (New York: Wiley, Halstead Press, 1972). A classic that describes the effects of money in a modern production system. It is one of the books that defines American Post Keynesianism.

Davidson, Paul. *Post Keynesian Macroeconomic Theory* (Cheltenham, United Kingdom: Edward Elgar, 1994). Like the earlier book, this volume encourages students to return to Keynes's focus on real-world economic problems and the design of policies to resolve them. It also discusses the limitations of New Classical and New Keynesian theories.

Eichner, Alfred S. (ed.) *A Guide to Post-Keynesian Economics* (Armonk, New York: M.E. Sharpe, 1979). A very readable introduction to the subject.

Eichner, Alfred S. (ed.) *Why Economics Is Not Yet a Science* (Armonk, New York: M.E. Sharpe, 1983). The essays in this volume are sympathetic to Keynes's original insights. Generally, the authors say that economics cannot be a science in the same sense as physics is.

Hicks, John R. *The Crisis in Keynesian Economics* (New York: Basic Books, 1974). In this readable book Hicks recants: He concludes that he misunderstood Keynes when he (Hicks) developed the IS-LM apparatus. Hicks's mea culpea is engaging.

Johnson, Elizabeth, and Donald Moggridge (eds.) *The Collected Writings of John Maynard Keynes* (London: Macmillan & Co., 1971), Vol 14. This volume includes writings related to the issues explored in this chapter.

Robinson, Joan. *The Accumulation of Capital* (London: Macmillan & Co., 1956). A classic explanation of modern capitalism.

Sraffa, Piero. *Production of Commodities by Means of Commodities* (Cambridge University Press, 1960). This little classic introduced the Italian strain into the bloodstream of Post Keynesianism. Unfortunately for the casual reader, it is terse in the worst Ricardian sense.

Weintraub, Sidney. *A General Theory of the Price Level, Output, Income Distribution and Economic Growth* (Philadelphia: Chilton, 1959). This classic defines the Post Keynesian view of the effect of the income distribution on the macroeconomy.

Chapter 12: The Monetarists and the New Classicals Deepen the Counterrevolution

Friedman, Milton. "The Quantity Theory of Money—A Restatement," in *Studies in the Quantity Theory of Money*, ed. Milton Friedman (Chicago: University of Chicago Press, 1956). This paper is often cited as the impetus for modern monetarism and for the revival of the Chicago School of Economics.

Friedman, Milton and Anna J. Schwartz. *A Monetary History of the United States, 1867–1960* (Princeton, New Jersey: Princeton University Press, 1963). A lengthy empirical study of the behavior of the U.S. money supply since 1867. Monetarists often quote this seminal source as proof that only money matters. It is tough reading.

Galbraith, John Kenneth. *A Tenured Professor* (Boston: Houghton Mifflin, 1990). A satire on the mores of money-getting during the 1980s and the timeless, stuffy manners of academia. Galbraith's deft lampooning of America's hidden agendas in this timely novel is a comic delight. Economists, including the rational expectationists, are not spared.

Lucas, Robert E. Jr. and Leonard A. Rapping. "Price Expectations and the Phillips Curve," *American Economic Review* 59 (June 1970): 342–350. This classic article first integrated the idea of rational expectations into macroeconomics.

Lucas, Robert E. Jr. and Leonard A. Rapping. "Real Wages, Employment and Inflation," *Journal of Political Economy* 77 (September 1969): 721–754. In this seminal article, Lucas and Rapping introduce rational expectations into an analysis of labor markets. This ignited the trend among the New Classicals to view labor markets as auction markets.

Rand, Ayn. *Atlas Shrugged* (New York: Random House, 1957). Rand's principles of objectivism are fully explicated in a 60-page speech by one of the book's heroes, John Galt. At 1168 pages, the book is longer than *The Wealth of Nations;* unfortunately, it was not made into a movie despite several attempts and true fans will have to read to the bitter end.

Sargent, Thomas J. *Rational Expectations and Inflation* (New York: Harper & Row, 1986). This is a good book to read if you are interested in knowing more about rational expectations. The first chapter is very mathematical and tough going; the book becomes more interesting and readable thereafter. It includes an interesting critique of Reaganomics.

Solow, Robert. "The Intelligent Citizen's Guide to Inflation," *Public Interest* 38 (Winter 1975): 30–66. A clever, no-nonsense introduction to the causes and consequences of inflation.

Chapter 13: Economic Growth and Technology: Schumpeter and Capitalistic Motion

Canterbery, E. Ray. "Galbraith, Sraffa, Kalecki and Supra-Surplus Capitalism," *Journal of Post Keynesian Economics* 7 (Fall 1984): 71–89. If you are interested in more about the connections described in its title, this article provides it. As with *Atlas Shrugged,* don't bother waiting for the movie; it probably won't happen.

Landes, David S. *The Wealth and Poverty of Nations: Why Some Are So Rich and Some So Poor* (New York/London: W.W. Norton & Company, 1998). Taking his cue from Adam Smith, economic historian Landes tells a fascinating story of wealth and power whereby—for the last six hundred years—the world's wealthiest economies have been mostly European. He persuasively claims that Europe's key advantage lay in invention and know-how, as applied in war, transportation, generation of power, and skill in metalwork.

Mensch, Gerhard O. *Stalemate in Technology* (Cambridge, Massachusetts: Ballinger, 1979). An important book that quantifies various aspects of Schumpeter's perspective on the long wave.

Olson, Mancur. *The Rise and Decline of Nations* (New Haven: Yale University Press, 1982). The book begins from a narrow base but expands into a grand vision.

Rostow, W.W. The *World Economy* (Austin: University of Texas Press, 1980). This is economics written on the "Gone with the Wind" scale: It provides a panoramic view of the global system.

Schumpeter, Joseph A. *Capitalism, Socialism, and Democracy,* 3rd ed. (New York: Harper & Brothers Publishers, 1950). This is vintage Schumpeter at his best.

Swedberg, Richard. *Schumpeter: A Biography* (Princeton: Princeton University Press, 1991). Swedberg's biography carefully uncovers different layers of this eminent thinker's personality.

Warsh, David. *The Idea of Economic Complexity* (New York: Viking Press, 1984). This stylish book brims with wit and wisdom. Written by a *Boston Globe* financial journalist, it contains an amazingly insightful explanation for secular inflation.

Chapter 14: The Many Faces of Capitalism: Galbraith, Heilbroner, and the Institutionalists

Ayres, Clarence. *The Theory of Economic Progress* (Chapel Hill: University of North Carolina Press, 1944). This classic, by one of the leading American institutionalists, highlights the critical importance of technology in economic change.

Canterbery, E. Ray (ed.) "Galbraith Symposium," *Journal of Post Keynesian Economics* 7 (Fall 1984): 5–102. A series of articles, including one by Arthur Schlesinger, Jr. on the "political Galbraith" and one by your author, that explicate and evaluate Galbraith's contributions.

Galbraith, John Kenneth. *The Affluent Society,* 2nd ed., revised (Boston: Houghton Mifflin, 1969). A classic, entertaining book that introduced several terms now in common use such as "affluent society."

Galbraith, John Kenneth. *The New Industrial State* (Boston: Houghton Mifflin, 1967). In my judgment, this classic is Galbraith's best book on economics. Again, "the technostructure" and the "planning system" of the firm have become part of the English language.

Heilbroner, Robert. *The Nature and Logic of Capitalism* (New York: W.W. Norton, 1985). A master of the subject writing in velvet-like prose.

Chapter 15: The Rise of the Casino Economy

Anders, George. *The Merchants of Debt* (New York: Basic Books, 1992). The compelling story of Kohlberg Kravis Roberts & Co., the leading leveraged-buyout king of Wall Street during the 1980s. The fast-paced narrative takes the reader through the complicated financing of American business during the leveraged-buyout era and shows the tight connection of Kohlberg Kravis Roberts & Co. and Drexel Burnham Lambert's junk-bond chief, Michael Milken.

Bartlett, Bruce. *"Reaganomics": Supply Side Economics in Action,* foreword by Rep. Jack Kemp (Westport, Connecticut: Arlington House Publishers, 1981). One of the early crusading books about how "Reaganomics" would lead to endless prosperity for all.

Canterbery, E. Ray. *Wall Street Capitalism: The Theory of the Bondholding Class* (Singapore/River Edge, New Jersey/London: World Scientific, 2000). This book, largely accessible to the lay reader, provides much more detail regarding the shift to a casino economy and the consequences for the typical family.

Canterbery, E. Ray. "Reaganomics, Saving, and the Casino Effect," in *The Economics of Saving,* ed. James H. Gapinski (Boston/Dordrecht/London: Kluwer Academic Publishers, 1993). This book chapter explains some of the contradictions of Reaganomics and why it contributed to the casino economy.

Chernow, Ron. *The House of Morgan* (New York: Atlantic Monthly Press, 1990). As fascinating as it is lengthy, this book recounts the rise, fall, and resurrection of an American banking empire. As fast-paced as a good novel, the book ends with the leveraged buyouts involving RJR Nabisco during the 1980s.

Dolan, Edwin G. (ed.) *The Foundations of Modern Austrian Economics* (Kansas City, Kansas: Sheed & Ward, 1976). A good, highly readable introduction to its subject.

Feldstein, Martin. "The Retreat from Keynesian Economics," *Public Interest* 64 (Summer 1981): 92–105. An article by one of Reagan's chief economic advisers that attacks Keynes and gives three cheers for "Reaganomics."

Minsky, Hyman P. *Can "It" Happen Again? Essays on Instability and Finance* (Armonk, New York: M.E. Sharpe, 1982). "It" is the Great Depression. Minsky concludes that it cannot happen again as long as the central bank stands tall as the lender of last resort.

Minsky, Hyman P. *John Maynard Keynes* (New York: Columbia University Press, 1976). A view of Keynes more in line with what the master had in mind.

Partnoy, Frank. *FIASCO: The Inside Story of a Wall Street Trader* (New York/London: Penguin, 1999). A chilling insider's account of the blood sport of derivatives trading. It is an intelligent yet comical take on the actual fiascos at Orange County, Barings, Procter & Gamble, and many others.

Shand, Alexander H. *The Capitalist Alternative: An Introduction to Neo-Austrian Economics* (New York and London: New York University Press, 1984). A readable coverage of all the main Austrian points of view ranging from methodology through value and on to the business cycle. It also contains a good bibliography if you wish to consult the originals.

Tobin, James. "Reaganomics and Economics," *New York Review of Books*. December 3, 1981. An early, artful attack on Reaganomics by a leading Keynesian and Nobel Prize winner.

Chapter 16: Global Capitalism

Canterbery, E. Ray. *Wall Street Capitalism: The Theory of the Bondholding Class* (Singapore/River Edge, New Jersey/London: World Scientific, 2000). The author finds a dark side for American labor in the integration of economies and expresses concerns regarding the footloose nature of international capital flows, especially those related to financial derivatives.

Gray, H. Peter. *Global Economic Involvement: A Synthesis of Modern International Economics* (Copenhagen: Copenhagen Business School Press, 1999). An up-to-date synthesis of the role of the multinational corporation in the globalization process. It is particularly good in describing the new institutions influencing the global environment.

Siebert, Horst. *The World Economy* (London/New York: Routledge, 1999). Siebert uses more traditional economic analysis than does Gray. Still, if the reader can get beyond the orthodox graphics, he will come away much more informed about historical changes in the global economy.

Chapter 17: Climbing the Economists' Mountain to High Theory

Nasar, Sylvia. *A Beautiful Mind* (New York: Simon & Schuster, 1998). An award-winning biography of John Forbes Nash, Jr., the winner of the Nobel Prize in Economics, it may be the only book having discussions of game theory that will be understandable to the unspecialized. It sensitively depicts Nash's mental illness even as it creates awe of his intellectual powers. In the Hollywood ending, Nash's emotions are finally merged with his intellect for the first time in his life.

Heilbroner, Robert and William Milberg. *The Crisis of Vision in Modern Economic Thought* (Cambridge: Cambridge University Press). An artful, persuasive critique of high theory in macroeconomics.

Chapter 18: The Future of Economics

Brockway, George P. *The End of Economic Man*, revised ed. (New York/London: W.W. Norton, 1991). Brimming with wit and common sense, Brockway's book turns much of conventional economic thought on its head at the expense of the dismal science. This is a good a place as any to start thinking about where economics should go.

INDEX

340 B.C. | 160 | A.D. 200 | 890 | 1100 | 1360 | 1450 | 1500 | 1550 | 1600

Aristotle
384 – 322 B.C.

Caesar defeats Vercingetorix
52 B.C.

Norman Conquest
1066

Gutenberg Bible
1456

Nicolaus Copernicus
1473–1543

Johannes Kepler
1571–1630

Euclid
C. 300 B.C.

Jesus Christ

Charlemagne reigns
768–814

Hipparchus
C. 190 –125 B.C.

Claudius Ptolemy
2d century

Magna Carta
1215

Martin Luther
1483–1546

John Donne
1572–1631

Elizabeth I
1558–1603

Paper Making
1st Century

John Calvin
1509–1564

Galileo Galilei
1564–1642

Watermill
C. 550

Tycho Brahe
1546–1600

Gun/Cannon
1260

Giordano Bruno
1548–1600

Shakespeare
1564–1616

Francis Bacon
1561–1626

Pistol
1540

1830 | 1840 | 1850 | 1860 | 1870 | 1880 | 1890 | 1900 | 1910

John Stuart Mill
1806–1873

Karl Marx
1818–1883

TNT
1863

Telephone
1876

Albert Michelson
1852–1931

Model T
1908

Charles Darwin
1809–1882

Light bulb
1879

J.B. Clark
1847–1938

Airplane
1903

James Clerk Maxwell
1831–1879

The robber barons dominate manufacturing

"Talkies"
1906

Coca-Cola
1886

W.S. Jevons
1835–1882

Alfred Marshall
1842–1924

Max Ludwig Planck
1858–1947

Georg Reimann
1826–1866

J. Willard Gibbs
1839–1903

Thorstein Veblen
1857–1929

Leon Walras
1834–1910

H. Minkowski
1864–1909

Electric motor
1837

Vilfredo Pareto
1848–1923

Ernest Rutherford
1871–1937

1610 | 1630 | 1650 | 1670 | 1690 | 1710 | 1730 | 1750 | 1770 | 1790 | 1810

René Descartes
1596–1650

Cromwell, Lord
Protector of England
1653–1658

Adam Smith
1723–1790

Spinning "jenny" 1770

Battle of Waterloo 1815

Telescope 1608

Isaac Newton
1642–1727

American Revolution begins 1775

Blaise Pascal
1623–1662

Jonathan Swift
1667–1745

James Watt
1736–1819

Christiaan Huygens
1629–1695

Alexander Pope
1688–1744

French Revolution begins 1789

John Locke
1632–1704

David Hume
1711–1776

Jeremy Bentham
1748–1832

Cotton gin 1793

Steam engine 1690

Pierre de Laplace
1749–1827

Steam pistol engine 1712

L. Carnot
1753–1823

David Ricardo
1772–1823

Thomas Malthus
1766–1834

J. B. Say
1767–1832

Mass production 1798

1920 | 1930 | 1940 | 1950 | 1960 | 1970 | 1980 | 1990 | 2000

J. M. Keynes
1883–1946

Great Depression begins 1929

IBM 1944

Laser developed 1960

Synthetic gene 1976

Albert Einstein
1879–1955

E. H. Chamberlin
1899–1967

Atomic bomb 1945

Synthetic DNA 1967

CD player 1984

A. C. Pigou
1877–1959

TV 1926

Werner Heisenberg
1901–1976

Megabit computer chip 1984

Diesel locomotive c. 1920

Joan Robinson
1903–1983

Man lands on moon 1969

Fiberglass 1931

Niels Bohr
1885–1962

Prince Louis de Broglie
1892–1976

CD-ROM 1985

Erwin Schrodinger
1887–1961

Jet engine 1936

Paul A. Samuelson
1915–

J. M. Clark
1884–1963

John Kenneth Galbraith
1908–

Nylon 1937

Jet airliner 1949

Synthetic skin 1986

The Pill 1952